THE NIKONIAN CHRONICLE
From the Year 1425 to the Year 1520
(Volume Five)

Edited, Introduced and Annotated

by

Serge A. Zenkovsky

Translated

by

Serge A. and Betty Jean Zenkovsky

THE DARWIN PRESS, INC.

ISBN 0-940670-04-6

Library of Congress Catalog Card No.: 88-080729

Printed in the United States of America
Published by
The Darwin Press, Inc.
P.O. Box 2202
Princeton, NJ 08543

The paper in this book is acid-free neutral pH stock and meets the
guidelines for permanence and durability of the Committee on
Production Guidelines for Book Longevity of the Council on
Library Resources.

The preparation of this volume and costs associated with its translation and publication were supported by Grants No. RL–25862–78–0526; No. RL–00015–80–1146; No. RL–1146–80; and No. RP–20333–82 from the Translations and Publications Program, Division of Research Programs, of the National Endowment for the Humanities, an independent federal agency.

CONTENTS

PREFACE

This fifth volume of the present English edition of *The Nikonian Chronicle* covers nearly one century—from A.D. 1425 to A.D. 1520. With its publication, we complete the translation of this chronicle as it is preserved in its original and oldest redaction, the so-called *Obolenskii ms.* (further abbreviated, *Obol.*). As with the earlier volumes of this project, this translation is based on the Russian text of *Obol.* published in Volumes IX–XIII of the *Complete Collection of the Russian Chronicles (Polnoe sobranie russkikh letopisei*—further abbreviated herein as *PSRL*—St. Petersburg, 1854–1913). This earliest original version of *The Nikonian Chronicle* (hereinafter abbreviated as *Nik.*) was completed in the 1520s in the offices of the Metropolitan of all Russia, head of the Russian Church, under the supervision and editorialship of Metropolitan Daniel, himself.[1]

In the Russian text of *Nik.* as it appears in *PSRL*, the editor—in the case of these last volumes, the eminent Russian historian, S. F. Platonov—in very many cases provided, together with the original *Obol.* text, additional parallel texts of later redactions of this chronicle. When these parallel passages published in *PSRL* contain important supplementary information or expanded textual material describing events in greater detail than in *Obol.*, the present Editor has included such supplementary information in this English translation, following the material of *Obol.* In each case he has specified from which manuscript of *Nik.*, as found in *PSRL*, this supplementary material is taken. Indeed, in many instances this additional material provides very important historical data. When, however, the parallel texts found in *PSRL* represent just a paraphrasing or merely stylistic embellishment of the original *Obol.* version, then they were not included in the present English translation.

In the preparation and editing of this English translation of *The Nikonian Chronicle*, the translators were constantly confronted with the following problems, some specific to *Nik.*, others of a more general character and encountered in nearly all works of Old Russian literature.

1. *Chronology and the calendar.* Since Russian medieval chronology and the calendar were of quite a different nature than the

1. Kloss, p. 129.

present Western and Russian ones, we had to convert the dating
of events from the Old Russian chronology into the modern one.
In the preceding four volumes, especially in Volumes One and
Two, we extensively discussed this problem. (See Vol. One, pp.
xxxvii–xl; and Vol. Two, pp. xxv–xxvi.) Here, the Editor would
like just to remind the reader that, up to A.D. 1700, in medieval
Russia the new year started not on the first of January but on the
first of September, and in the very early period—the eleventh
through thirteenth centuries—sometimes it commenced on the first
of March. (See Vol. One, p. xxxviii.) This chronology was based
not on the Christian era (B.C. and A.D.), which started with the birth
of Christ, but on the biblical era, in which history began with the
creation of the world—supposedly, some 5508 years prior to the
birth of Christ.

2. *Transliteration of Russian, Western, Greek, Mongol and Tatar
names.* Generally, we used the Library of Congress transliteration.
Yet, since the transliteration of non-Russian names was quite often
altered by the original chroniclewriters themselves, we used the
modern Russian transliteration for Old Russian names, but traditional English transcription for Greek names—particularly for the
names of saints and bishops. Likewise, we used traditional English
spelling for non-Russian names of well-known historical per-
sonalities, as well as for non-Russian geographical names.

A more difficult problem was the transliteration of Tatar-
Moslem names. Indeed, after the Tatars' conversion to Islam in
the late thirteenth and early fourteenth centuries, they used largely
the Arabic Moslem names; but these were frequently distorted,
first, by the Tatars and then by the chroniclewriters. For instance,
the name "Mohammed" is often written by the chroniclewriters as
"Makhmut" or even "Ahmet." We preferred, however, the standard
English transcription, "Mohammed," following the example of *An
Encyclopedia of World History*, edited by William L. Langer (Cambridge, Mass., 1952). Here, it should be added, that in using the
Arabic names the Tatars and other Turkic peoples often pro-
nounced them in their own distinct ways, which were drastically
different from the Arabic way. This was further complicated by
the absence of vowels from the Arabic alphabet.

3. *The complexities and difficulties of the original Old Russian texts
of the chronicles and, specifically, of Nik.* Medieval Russian was not a
very elaborated literary tongue, especially in the early centuries,

i.e., the twelfth and thirteenth. Quite often, being obliged to translate difficult Greek sentences or express complex ideas, the chroniclewriters wrote phrases that were awkwardly organized and not readily comprehensible. This occurred especially frequently when the chroniclewriter had to deal with logical, abstract problems or had to translate the messages of Byzantine patriarchs and emperors. The present translators of this English edition of *Nik.* have tried, however, to produce a meaningful and comprehensible text, and were often obliged to consult the earlier, original sources so as to grasp the meaning of a particular passage. Such was the case, for instance, with the translation of the *Decisions* of the Council of Florence in 1439—which had first been translated from Latin into Greek, and only thereafter into Old Russian, resulting in some passages very difficult to understand. In many cases during work on *Nik.* the present translators were obliged to divide extremely long and complex sentences; or, for the sake of understanding, to interpose some additional word—which was always put into brackets. In most instances this was the only means of rendering a readable and comprehensible text. Withal, the translators endeavored to preserve some peculiarities and style of the original text while nonetheless avoiding changes in the semantic structure of the wording. Working on this fifth volume of *Nik.*, we were fortunate enough to be able to check some unclear sentences and misspelled names against the so-called *Ioasafovskaia Letopis'*, which is the only published part of the prototype of *Obol.* Indeed, as A. A. Zimin and B. M. Kloss have pointed out,[2] the *Ioasaf. Chronicle*[3] is entirely similar for the years 1453–54 to 1520 to the same years in *Obol.*; and for the years 1437 to 1453–54, the two chronicles have many entries in common.

The translation, preparation for publication and actual printing of this very long, complex chronicle—altogether, over 1,500 printed pages *in quarto* in the original Old Russian and in many places so difficult to render into English—was made only possible thanks to the financial support of two institutions and the friendly help of many persons. As this Editor has pointed out in the preceding volumes of this English edition of *The Nikonian Chronicle*, the National Endowment for the Humanities provided generous help, which facilitated the work of over a decade in preparing the

2. Zimin, p. 10; Kloss, pp. 30–32.
3. Published in Moscow in 1957.

present English edition, and the Endowment's grants are gratefully acknowledged by the Editor and his co-translator. Special thanks are due to Dr. Susan Mango of the National Endowment for the Humanities, who, during the entire period of our collaboration, was most generous in giving of her time and counsel.

We also express our thanks to the American Council of Learned Societies, the financial assistance of which permitted the Editor and his co-translator to pursue their research in Russia, where, particularly in Moscow and Leningrad, they were able to visit many libraries and archives and to consult Russian scholars specialized in early Russian history, literature, and particularly, chroniclewriting. Member of the Academy of Sciences of the U.S.S.R., Dr. Dmitrii Likhachev, in Leningrad, on many occasions provided this Editor with advice, indications of sources and libraries, and explanations of the countless problems encountered in Russian chroniclewriting. His *Russkie letopisi* (Moscow-Leningrad, 1947), as well as a large number of his other books on Old Russian literature and culture, were extremely helpful in preparing this English edition of *The Nikonian Chronicle*. The present Editor also remembers with gratitude Dr. Likhachev's colleagues who gave many suggestions and consultations, among whom he would like here to mention L. A. Dmitriev; his wife, R. P. Dmitrieva; O. V. Tvorogov; and G. M. Prokhorov—all of the Sector of Old Russian Literature of the Academy's Institute of Russian Literature. Professors N. S. Demkova and R. G. Skrynnikov of Leningrad University were extremely helpful with their suggestions and explanations. V. P. Budaragin, head of the Section of Old Manuscripts of the Pushkinskii Dom of the Academy of Sciences in Leningrad, permitted the Editor to use these manuscripts and likewise was most friendly in providing advice.

In Moscow, the Editor had the privilege of meeting A. A. Zimin, one of the leading specialists in Russian fifteenth and sixteenth centuries. His publication of the *Ioasafovskaia letopis'* (Moscow, 1957) was particularly useful in preparing the present volume. His sharing of his all-embracing knowledge of Russia's historically transitional period from Ivan III to Ivan IV and his suggestions are most gratefully recalled. This Editor was particularly grateful to him for the fact that despite the very grave state of his health he nevertheless granted many interviews, during which many aspects of Russian chroniclewriting and of Russian history were discussed in depth.

No fewer thanks are due to Dr. Boris Kloss, also of the Institute of History of the Academy of Sciences in Moscow, who spent many hours with this Editor discussing *The Nikonian Chronicle*, and whose *Nikonovskii svod i russkoe letopisanie 16–ogo i 17–ogo vekov* (Moscow, 1980) is essential for any work on this chronicle.

Many American colleagues are remembered with deep gratitude. Among them I would like to mention Professor Valerie Tumins of the University of California at Davis; Professor Ralph Fisher of the University of Illinois; and the late Professor Mark Szeftel of the University of Washington, Seattle, who provided advice and encouragement when this work was undertaken. Several other American colleagues and librarians likewise shared their knowledge and opinions on Russian chroniclewriting with this Editor and his co-translator, and they are all remembered with deep gratitude.

My greatest thanks go to my wife and co-translator, Betty Jean Zenkovsky, for her cooperation, endurance throughout the decade of work devoted to *The Nikonian Chronicle*'s translation, and patient help in preparing it for publication. Without her encouragement and assistance I would never have been able to complete this voluminous undertaking or, probably, to have started it in the first place.

The Editor and his co-translator are aware that in the course of their work on this project some errors and mistranslations have unavoidably been made. They hope, however, that their faults will be excused in view of the magnitude and enormous complexity of *The Nikonian Chronicle*. Regrettably, the first three volumes of the first edition contain errata of a typographical nature, which were brought to the attention of the proofreader and were not the responsibility of the Editor. For these, the Editor extends to the reader his humblest apologies.

Serge A. Zenkovsky
Professor Emeritus
Vanderbilt University

Daytona Beach, Florida 1989

LIST OF TITLES OF ENTRIES
IN VOLUME FIVE OF *THE NIKONIAN CHRONICLE*
A.D. 1425–A.D. 1520

[The titles in brackets were added by the Editor.
The other titles are as they appear in *Nik.*]

Page

The Fifteenth Century

INTRODUCTION

Two entire reigns—that of Vasilii II (1425–62) and of Ivan III (1462–1506], often called "the Great" by his contemporaries and historians—and about half of the reign of the latter's son, Vasilii III (1506–20 in *Nik.*), who died in 1533–are covered in this fifth volume of *The Nikonian Chronicle*. It was, first, a time of tumultuous dynastic struggle in the Muscovite Grand Principality (1431–53), a Russian version of the English Wars of the Roses, which took place in the same century; it was, also, a spectacular transformation of feudal appanage Russia into one unified dynamic Russian state. Suddenly, Russia moved into the ranks of the major powers of Europe. After consolidation of these "Great Russian" (*Velikorusskie*) principalities into one nation, Russia finally resumed contact with Western Europe—a contact which was interrupted for more than two centuries by Tatar domination. Coincidentally, unification of this eastern Russian (*Velikorusskii*) state occurred at about the same time as did the unification and rise to the status of major powers in the West by France and Spain, as well as the strengthening of England under the Tudors. Indeed, during the Wars of the Roses and the first Tudor, Henry VII, England finally became an insular nation whose rulers gave up their ambitions to dominate France. It was quite remarkable that on both the eastern and western belts of Europe there emerged strong, unified monarchies—England, France, Spain, Russia, the Ottoman Empire, and Poland-Lithuania; while in the central belt, in Germany and Italy, the division of national states into a multitude of small, feudal ones continued.

I. VASILII II

Vasilii II (1425–62) became the ruler of Moscow at the age of ten, and almost immediately became involved in a struggle with his uncle, Iurii, and then with the latter's sons, Vasilii the Crosseyed (*Kosoi*), Dmitrii Shemiaka, and Dmitrii the Handsome (*Krasnyi*). While Vasilii II represented a century-long Muscovite tradition of the transfer of the throne from father to son, his uncle and cousins claimed the throne according to the old Kievan system of succession established at the princes' convention in Liubech in 1097, which determined that the throne was to pass from senior brother to the second oldest one. (See *Nik.*, Vol. One, p. 213.) The feud between

Vasilii II and his uncle and cousins lasted for twenty-two years and was characterized by a cruelty reminiscent of Byzantine struggles over the Imperial throne. Vasilii II was blinded by his cousin Shemiaka, while Shemiaka's brother, another Vasilii, was ordered to be blinded by Vasilii II (although he lost only one eye). Thus came about his name, "Crosseyed." Shemiaka, himself, apparently died from poisoning. This fratricidal infighting within the dynasty lasted for more than half of Vasilii II's reign and prevented the Grand Principality of Moscow from further strengthening its position. Despite the fact that the Golden Horde was disintegrating and that Lithuanian-Polish expansion into western Russia abated after the death in 1430 of Grand Prince Vitovt of Lithuania, Grand Prince Vasilii II was barely able to do more than consolidate the borders of his realm. Still, to all practical purposes, he brought an end to the appanage system within the Muscovite Grand Principality.

One of the most important events of the reign of Vasilii II was the emancipation of the Russian church from the Patriarch of Constantinople. Badly pressed by the Turks, the Byzantine Emperor—who, as a matter of fact, at that time was just the Emperor of the city of Constantinople and was looking for the support of the West against the Moslem onslaught—accepted, at the Council of Florence in 1439, the Union with the Roman Catholic church and the subordination of the Patriarchate of Constantinople to the Pope of Rome. Neither the Grand Prince, himself, nor the Russian church were willing, however, to accept the authority of Rome and exchange the Orthodox teachings for the Roman ones. For this reason Vasilii decided upon the separation of the Russian church and broke with Constantinople. In 1443 the Russian church Council—without requesting or expecting a blessing from Constantinople—elected a new head of the Russian church. From that time on the Russian church became completely separate from the so-called Oecumenic Patriarch of Constantinople. Despite all the concessions made by the Greeks in Florence to the Pope, no help was forthcoming from the West and in 1453 the Turks conquered Constantinople. The Byzantine Empire came to its end.

II. IVAN III, THE GREAT

Under Vasilii's son, Ivan III, Russian politics evolved com-

pletely differently from the developments during the reign of Vasilii
II. Probably, it would be quite justified to say that Ivan III was
Russia's most successful and brilliant ruler. In the 1480s he shook
off the remnants of Russian dependence upon the Golden Horde,
which thereafter rapidly disintegrated. Thus Russia became a completely independent and powerful state whose ruler from then on
called himself "Samoderzhets," which meant "Autocrat" in the sense
of "Sovereign" or "Independent ruler." Under him the Grand Principality of Moscow became the Grand Principality of all Russia, or
at least of entire eastern Russia. In 1478 Ivan III annexed Novgorod
and its immense territories, which embraced all northern Russia
from the Baltic Sea to the Ob' River in western Siberia, thus many
times incrementing the size of his state. In 1485 he took over the
land of Tver', which for nearly two centuries had been Moscow's
main competitor for the unification of Russia. Moreover, he added
to his state the lands of Rostov, Iaroslavl', Viatka, and the major
part of Riazan'. In the south and west he took away from Lithuania
the old Russian lands of Chernigov, Briansk, Gomel', and others.
Moving the population from the newly-annexed territories to the
old lands of Moscow, and from Moscow to those new territories,
he greatly increased the cohesion and interdependence of the population of his state.

Ivan's marriage to Sophia Paleologue, the niece of the last
Byzantine Emperor, Constantine XI—who died, losing Constantinople to the Turks—considerably increased the prestige of the
Russian rulers. This marriage also led to the development of the
idea of "Moscow, the Third Rome"—the third and last leader and
defender of true Orthodox Christianity. Since Sophia had grown
up in Italy, this marriage also led to the establishment of closer
relations between Russia and several Italian states, as well as to a
renewal of Russia's connections with many western European countries, which had been practically severed since the Tatar-Mongol
invasion of 1230–40. Ambassadors from the German emperors and
Scandinavian and Italian rulers started visiting Russia frequently,
while Russia sent frequent ambassadors to the West.

During the reign of Ivan III a secretive, anti-Trinitarian sect
of the so-called Judaizers started to spread, first, in Novgorod, and
then in Moscow, endangering Russian religious unity. Toward
the end of his reign, however, Ivan III permitted the Archbishop
of Novgorod and Abbot Joseph of Volok drastically to end the

spreading of this sect. Its leaders were arrested and banned, and
several were, executed after the fashion of the Roman Catholic
Inquisition. It was the first effect of Western spiritual influence on
Russia.

III VASILII III

Grand Prince Vasilii III (r. 1506–33) inherited from his father,
Ivan III, an almost entirely unified Russia. Indeed, after the annex-
ation of Novgorod his father assumed the title, "*Samoderzhets i velikii
kniaz' Moskovskii i Vseia Rusi*" ("Sovereign and Grand Prince of all
Russia"). During his own reign Vasilii III completed his father's
work of Russian unification and annexed the northeastern republic
of Pskov, which was the old rampart against the German Knights
of Livonia; the last part of the southeastern Grand Principality of
Riazan', which controlled the approaches to Moscow from the Don
River and the lower course of the Volga; and the appanage district
(*udel*) of Volok. Thus, all Russian territories located east of Lithuania
came under the aegis of Moscow. Vasilii struggled constantly with
Lithuania for the western Russian lands seized and incorporated
into Lithuania by the Lithuanian princes, Olgerd and Vitovt, in the
fourteenth and fifteenth centuries. He succeeded in reconquering
from Lithuania the important cities of Novgorod-Seversk and
Smolensk. Still, a very large part of the Orthodox western Russian
population from Kiev, Podolia and Galicia in the south, to Vitebsk
and Wilno in the north, remained for nearly another three centuries
under Polish-Lithuanian dominion and strong Roman Catholic,
Polish pressure—which resulted in some cultural differences between the eastern and western regions populated by Russians. Here
it may be recalled that while the original ethnic Lithuanian population inhabited only the extreme north of the grand principality,
roughly within the limit of the present Lithuanian S.S.R., and that
the dynasty was of Lithuanian ethnic background, nearly 90 percent
of the population of Lithuania of that time was Russian, and the
state tongue was likewise Russian.

In his relations with the Tatars, Vasilii III was not very successful. To be sure, the Golden Horde had been defeated by his father
and had even disappeared, but two small khanates, heirs of the
Golden Horde—Kazan' on the Volga in the northeast, and Crimea
in the south—continued the Tatars' traditional raiding of Russian

territories. Under Ivan III Kazan' was to some extent controlled by Moscow and even became a *de facto* Muscovite vassal. Around the 1520s, however, an anti-Russian group of Tatar lords seized power in Kazan', and the Kazan' Tatars resumed raiding Russian territory, especially in the vicinity of Nizhni-Novgorod and the upper Volga. The same occurred in the Crimea. Although the Crimea came under the control of Ottoman Turkey, at the time of Vasilii III the Crimean Khan would join hands with the Polish-Lithuanian kings and raid southern Russian territory along the Oka River. Thus, southern Russia was constantly sacked and its inhabitants often taken captive and sold on the Crimean market to the Near East, to Mediterranean lands and to Western Europe.

IV. CULTURAL EVOLUTION

The Greco-Latin Union of Florence in 1439, which led to Russia's break with Constantinople and the latter's fall in 1453, resulted in a considerable reorientation in Russian culture. Until the mid-fifteenth century, cultural and ideological stimulation, primarily Byzantine, came to Russia from Byzantium and the Balkan Slavs. With the collapse of the Byzantine Empire, the Turkish conquest of the Balkans and Russia's disappointment over Byzantium's betrayal of Orthodoxy at Florence, a new cultural orientation became inevitable for Russia. The Paleologue Renaissance and, with it, Russia's own "pre-Renaissance," in the words of D. S. Likhachev, came to an end.[1] This pre-Renaissance produced Russia's greatest religious painter, Andrei Rublev, who was also one of the world's foremost religious artists.[2] During the Russian pre-Renaissance, literature was dominated by the ideology of the Hesychasts and the style of "Weaving of Words." Now, in place of the Byzantine models, there appear in Russian culture two new, albeit contradictory sources for artistic and literary inspiration. One was the popular original Russian folk art, which penetrates more and more into the arts of the church and of upper society. In architecture, for instance, it could be seen in the "*kokoshnik*" gables of the Cathedral of the Annuniciation built in 1484–89 by masters from Pskov. Later, we can notice the impact of Russian wooden folk architecture which

1. See Likhachev, *Kultura*, p. 20 and ff.
2. Talbot Rice, p. 120; Likhachev, *Poetika*, p. 356.

arises in the *shatrovyi* style, of which the oldest preserved example is the Kolomenskaia Church built in 1532–34.³ In embellishing the Cathedral of the Annunciation, the masters from Pskov also introduced brick ornament under the dome. Inside the church two very talented artists, Theodore and Vladimir, sons of the outstanding artist, Dionysius—himself an indirect follower of Rublev—painted a number of frescoes with instructive group subjects representing religious events such as the Last Judgment, the Eucharist, Christ on the Cross and others. Earlier, the traditional frescoes depicted just single figures—of Christ, of Our Lady, or of a saint. This development of additional detail and ornamentation begins to characterize Russian arts and architecture in the fifteenth and sixteenth centuries.

When Ivan III started rebuilding old Muscovite churches, the local architects—who had not built large buildings since before the Tatar invasion—were unable to cope with the bigger cathedrals envisioned by the Grand Prince. Therefore, in the case of the Cathedral of the Dormition of Our Lady (Uspenskii Sobor), for instance, its construction was entrusted in 1479 to the Italian architect, Ridolfo Fioravanti, whom the Russians called "Aristotle" for his numerous talents and achievements in art and science.⁴ Fioravanti carefully studied the Russian churches in Vladimir, Novgorod, and Rostov, and built the Muscovite Uspenskii Cathedral (of the Dormition) according to the style of the cathedral of the same name in Vladimir. Nonetheless, he used Italian methods of construction and the Italian manner of preparing his construction materials.

In 1505–8 another Italian, Aloisio Novi, built the Cathedral of the Archangel Michael, in which we find a considerable number of Italian embellishments of the church—as, for instance, white stone ornament on the red brick walls. During the reconstruction of the Kremlin—again, by Italian masters—this Muscovite fortress began to resemble the castle of Milano. In the façade of the Granovitaia Palata, also built at that time, many features can be recognized from the façade of the Palazzo Pitti in Florence.⁵

In literature, too, we find more and more folk tales and epics.

3. See Timhomirov, *Istorichiskie Zapiski*, Vol. x, 1941, p. 88.
4. *Nik.*, Vol. Five, year 1479; *Russ. Biogr. Slovar'*, Vol. 21, p. 14.
5. Voyce, pp. 153–64.

It was no accident that in *The Nikonian Chronicle* such stories of the semi-historical, semi-lengendary *bogatyri*, and an ever-increasing number of folk narratives, are encountered.[6] For the first time in Russian letters, too, it is an early sixteenth-century writer, Fedor Karpov, who mentions such non-Christian authors as Ovid, Aristotle, and Homer—all of whom were completely unknown in Russia as long as it remained under the control of the Byzantine church. Thus, new changes and new directions came about in Russian cultural development and, especially, in the Russian arts. The previous Old Russian style, dominated by Byzantine models, was coming to an end. Already as early as the late fifteenth and early sixteenth centuries, these changes became quite obvious and, as mentioned above, found their reflections in *The Nikonian Chronicle*.

6. See *Nik.*, Vol. One, p. 11, year 1001, about *bogatyri*; and see the large number of stories in Vol. Four of *Nik.*

LIST OF BIBLIOGRAPHICAL ABBREVIATIONS

Barsov   Barsov, E., *Drevne-russkie pamiatniki sviashchennogo venchaniia Tsarei na tsarstvo v sviazi s grecheskimi originalami*, Moscow, 1883.

Baumgarten   Baumgarten, N. de, *Genealogie des branches reignantes en Russie*, in Or. Chr., 1934

Bréhier   Bréhier, L., *La vie et la mort de Byzance*, Albin Michel, Paris, 1969.

Dal'   Dal', V., I–IV, *Tolkovyi slovar' zhivogo russkogo iazyka*, M., 1861–67.

Florovsky   Florovskii, G., *Puti russkogo bogosloviia*, 3d ed., YMCA Press, Paris, 1983.

Golubinskii   Golubinskii, F., *Istoriia russkoi tserkvi*, Vols. 1 and 2, in four parts, M. 1900–1917.

Grekov   Grekov, B., and A. Iu. Iakubovskii, *Zolotaia Orda i ee Padenie*, M-L, A.N., 1950.

Hyp.   *Ipatievskaia letopis'*, PSRL, Vol. II. (*Hypatian Chronicle*).

Ioasaf. Chr.   *Ioasafovskaia letopis'*, A. A. Zimin, ed., AN SSSR, Inst. Istorii, Moscow, 1957.

IRL   *Istoriia russkoi literatury*, Vols. I–II, AN, M-L, 1943–48.

IRL X-XVII vv.   *Istoriia russkoi literatury X-XVII vv.*, Ed., Dmitriev, L., and Likhachev, D. S., M. 1980.

Kartashov   Kartashov, A. V., *Ocherki po istorii russkoi tserkvi*, Paris, 1959, Vols. I and II.

Kliuchevskii   Kliuchevskii, V., *Kurs russkoi istorii*, M. 1937, Vols. I and II.

Kloss   Kloss, B., *Nikonovskii svod i russkoe letopisanie XVI–XVII vv.*, Nauka, Moscow, 1980.

Khronograph   *Khronograf 1512*, PSRL, Vol. 22.

Laur.   *Lavrentievskaia letopis'*, PSRL, Vol. 1. (*Laurentian Chronicle*).

Likhachev, *Letopisi*   Likhachev, D. S., *Russkoe letopisanie*, AN, M-L 1957.

Likhachev, *Nasledie*   Likhachev, D. S., *Velikoe nasledie*, Sovremennik, Moscow, 1975.

Likhachev, *Kultura*   Likhachev, D. S., *Kultura Rusi vremeni Andreia Rubleva i Epifaniia Premudrogo*, M-L, 1962.

Lit. Cal.   *Liturgical Calendar and Rubrics*, St. Vladimir's Seminary Press, New York, 1979.

M.	Moscow
M.-L.	Moscow-Leningrad
Meyendorff	Meyendorff, John, *Byzantium and the Rise of Russia*, Cambridge University Press, 1981.
Musc. Late 15th C.	*Moskovskii letopisnyi svod kontsa piatnadtsatogo veka, PSRL*, Vol. 25.
Musc. Late 15th C., Abbr.	*Sokrashchennye moskovskie letopisnye svody kontsa 15-go veka, PSRL*, Vol. 24.
Nasonov	Nasonov, A. N., *Mongoly i Rus'*, M., 1940.
Nik.	*Patriarshaia ili Nikonovskaia letopis', PSRL*, Vols. IX–XIII. (*Obolenskii redaction*).
Or. Chr.	*Orientalia Christiana* (serial), Rome.
PSRL	*Polnoe sobranie russkikh letopisei (Complete Collection of Russian Chronicles)*, AN, Moscow, Vols. 1–34 (and *foll.*, publication continues), 1841—.
Pushkarev	Pushkarev, S. G., *Dictionary of Russian Historical Terms*, Edited by G. Vernadsky and Ralph T. Fisher, Jr., Yale Univ. Press, New Haven and London, 1970.
RIB	*Russkaia istoricheskaia biblioteka*, SPB 1872–1927 (39 vols.)
Rice, Talbot	Rice, Talbot, *A Concise History of Russian Arts*, Praeger, Wash., 1967.
Roty	Roty, Martine, *Dictionnaire Russe-Français des Termes en Usage en Église Russe*, Paris, IES, 1980.
SIE	*Sovietskaia istoricheskaia entsiklopediia*, Vols. 1–16, M., 1961–1976.
Soloviev	Soloviev, S. M., *Istoriia Rossii s drevneishikh vremen*. I–X (in 30 vols.) M., 1959–1966.
TODRL	*Trudy otdela drevnerusskoi literatury*, AN SSSR, Vols. 1–34, Leningrad, 1932.
Tvorogov	Tvorogov, O. B., *Drevnerusskie khronografy*, AN, L. 1975.
Vasiliev	Vasiliev, A. A., *History of the Byzantine Empire*, Univ. of Wisconsin Press, 1958, Vols. 1–2.
Vernadsky	Vernadsky, G., *History of Russia*, Vol. 3, Yale Univ. Press, 1953.
Voyce	Voyce, A., *Arts and Architecture of Medieval Russia*, Univ. of Oklahoma Press, Norman, Okla., 1967.

Zenkovsky

Zenkovsky, S., *Medieval Russia's Epics, Chronicles and Tales*, 2d rev. ed. F. P. Dutton & Co., New York, 1969.

Zenkovsky, *Old Bel.*

Zenkovsky, S., *Russkoe staroobriadchestvo* (*The Russian Old Believers*), Fink Verlag, Munich, 1970.

Zimin

Zimin, A. A., Introduction to the *Ioasafovskaia letopis'*, above.

LIST OF ABBREVIATIONS OF LIBRARIES AND MANUSCRIPTS

(For the locations of manuscripts see Introduction in Volume One)

AN	Akademiia Nauk (Academy of Sciences, USSR).
BAN	Biblioteka Akademii Nauk (Library of the Academy of Sciences) Leningrad, USSR.
Chron. red. 5 Novg.	*Chronographic redaction of the Fifth Novgorodian Chronicle,* in MS only, in GIM.
GIM	Gosudarstvennyi istoricheskii muzei (State Historical Museum), Moscow.
Ioasaf. Chr.	*Ioasafovskaia letopis',* A. A. Zimin, ed., AN SSSR, Institut Istorii, M. 1957. (*Ioasaf Chronicle*).
Obol.	*Obolenskii ms. redaction of The Nikonian Chronicle.* See Ch. I of Introduction to Volume One of this English translation of *The Nikonian Chronicle,* pp. xxi–xxii.
Patr.	*Patriarshii ms. redaction of The Nikonian Chronicle.* See Ch. I of Introduction to Volume One of this series, p. xxii–xxiii.
SIE	*Sovietskaia istoricheskaia entsiklopediia,* Vols. I–XVI, Moscow, 1961–76.

GLOSSARY OF RUSSIAN, TATAR,
AND BYZANTINE TERMINOLOGY

ACATHISTOS	A long ecclesiastic poetic work, read or sung in praise of the Virgin Mary during Lent; more generally, a praise of Christ or the Virgin Mary.
ARTAG	A Norwegian copper coin of the four teenth—fifteenth centuries.
BASKAK	A Tatar official, primarily a tax collector.
BOGATYR	An extremely powerful warrior, usually the hero of an epic.
BOYAR, BOYARIN	A member of the Russian upper aristocracy from which the members of the prince's council were selected.
CHERNYE LIUDI	("Black people"): the lower class of the population, peasant workers.
DEN'GA	A small copper coin. A rouble consisted of 100 Novgorodian, or 200 Muscovite *den'ga*.
DAROGA, DOROGA, DARUGA	A Tatar official, usually an envoy.
DAY OF THE COUNCIL	The first Sunday of Lent, when the 7th Ecumenical Council of 787, which restored veneration of icons, is remembered.
DESIATINA	A measure of land equal to 2.7 acres. A *desiatina* comprised 2400 square *sazhen'*.
DETI BOYARSKIE	See Junior boyars.
DETINETS	A fortress, a fortified part of a city.
DIAK	The highest official in a department of the central administration.
DRUZHINA	A permanent armed force of the prince; his personal guard.
DVORETSKI	A steward, or manager of a nobleman's household.
DVORIANE	The service nobility.
EMPEROR	In Russian, *Tsar'*, from Lat., *Caesar*. The title used by the rulers of the Byzantine and German "Roman" empires.
END	In Russian, *konets*, the term used for a section of a city, or "neighborhood"; especially in Novgorod, where the city was divided into five *kontsy*.

GERMANS	In Russian, *Nemtsy* (pl.), or *nemets* (s.). In *Nik.*, the term, "Germans," was used to designate all people of Germanic origin, such as Germans, Scandinavians, and English.
GRIVNA	A Russian monetary or weight unit equal to 410 grams, or 96 Russian *zolotniki*.
HETMAN	The supreme military commander in Poland and Lithuania; later, the head of the Zaporozhie and S. Russian Cossacks.
JUNIOR BOYARS	*Mladshie boiare*: "Minor" or "lesser" boyars— the class of lesser service nobility, below the real "boyars." Later, they were usually called "dvoriane" (q.v.). Originally they probably were poorer or younger heirs of boyar families.
INDICTION, INDICT	In the Byzantine system of chronology, a period of fifteen years, beginning on the first of September.
KHAN	In Russian, usually translated as "Tsar'," the ruler of a Mongol or Tatar state, customarily a descendant of Genghis Khan.
KHOLOP	A person who entered a status of bondage, not to be confused with "serf."
KONETS	See "end."
KUNA, KUNITSA	Marten fur—more specifically, a marten pelt, which in Old Russian was used as a monetary unit.
LATINS	Standard Russian expression for Roman Catholics.
MOHAMMED	Originally the name of the founder of Islam; a very common first name among Moslems. In Russian, transliterated variously as "Makhmet," "Makhmud," "Muhammed," "Ahmet," and the like.
METROPOLIA	Denotes the entire territory of the Russian church under the jurisdiction of the Metropolitan.
METROPOLITAN	The Archbishop of the Russian capital and head of the Russian church.
MURZA	Title of a lesser Tatar nobleman.
NEMETS	See "Germans."
NOGATA	A monetary unit equal to 2½ *rezany*, $\frac{1}{20}$ of a *grivna kun*.
OBZHA	Novgorodian land tax unit, usually equal to ten *chetverei*, or fifteen *desiatinas*.

OKOLNICHII	Member of the higher aristocracy, a high official just beneath *boyar*.
OPALA	Term of disgrace, designating disfavor of the Tsar; often connected with banishment; sometimes an economic punishment.
OSMINA, OSMINKA	Unit of dry measure usually equal to half a *chetvert'* (⅛).
PAN	"Lord," master (of serfs). In Poland, a member of the royal Council (*Pany rady*).
PASHA	Very high military or civilian official in Turkey and, later, in Crimea.
PATRIMONY (OTCHINA)	Principality held in hereditary, "patrimonial" succession.
POD'IACHII	Middle, or lower, official.
PODVOISKII	Palace or court official in Lithuania, sometimes in Novgorod and Pskov.
POLÉ	The steppe (prairie), or field; usually inhabited only by nomads.
POPRISHTÉ	Old Russian measure of distance equal to one *versta*.
POSADNIK	In the Kievan era (tenth to thirteenth century), the prince's administrator of a city or region.
PRINCE (SERVICE)	Service Prince: a prince who gave up his appanage and was in the service of the Grand Prince of Moscow.
PUD	Measure of weight equal to forty Russian pounds, or 16.38 kilograms.
REZANA	See "nogata."
ROMANS	Or Latins; Russian appelation for Roman Catholics.
SAZHEN'	Measure of distance equal to 3 *arshiny*, 7 feet, or 2.133 meters.
SCHEMA	Second, highest, monastic tonsure, with very strict rules.
SKHIMNIK	A monk who was tonsured to the *schema*, usually living in isolation.
SERVICE PRINCE	See "prince."
SLOBODA	Originally an independent settlement; later a suburb.
SMERD	Peasant in Old Russia; free in the Kievan period.

SOTSKII

Official elected by 100 households; or head of a military detachment of some one hundred men.

SUNDAY OF ORTHODOXY

See "Day of the Council."

VOEVODA

Administrator of a region or commander of an army.

GENEALOGICAL TABLES

The following genealogical tables are of the most important lines of the princes mentioned in this volume: The House of Moscow, the House of Tver', and the Lithuanian (later Lithuanian-Polish) House of Gediminoviches-Jagellonians. No genealogical table is provided for the Khans of the Golden Horde because in the fifteenth century their succession and lineage through the heirs of Genghis Khan is not always clear. Some of the rulers of the Tatar Golden Horde—for instance, *Temnik* ("Supreme Commander") Mamai or Timur—were not even the heirs of Genghis Khan but upstarts of very unaristocratic origin.

Since not all the dates of birth, rule, and death of these Russians and Lithuanians are available, the following abbreviations have been used: (fl.) "flourished"; (b.) "born"; (d.) "died"; and (r.) "ruled." The data vary slightly (up to one year) in historical works because of the confusion over the March, Ultra March, and September calendars.

1. THE HOUSE OF MOSCOW

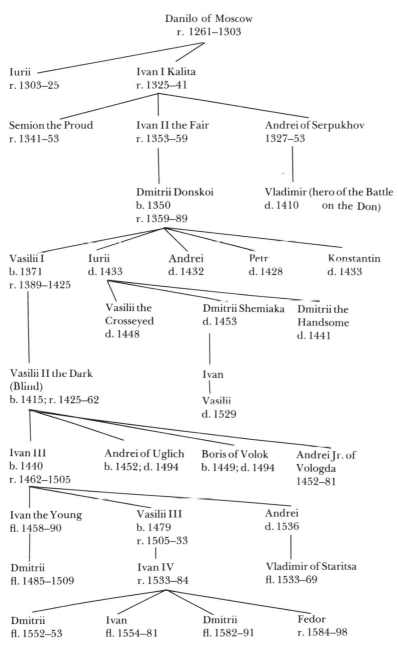

Danilo of Moscow
r. 1261–1303

Iurii
r. 1303–25

Ivan I Kalita
r. 1325–41

Semion the Proud
r. 1341–53

Ivan II the Fair
r. 1353–59

Andrei of Serpukhov
1327–53

Dmitrii Donskoi
b. 1350
r. 1359–89

Vladimir (hero of the Battle
d. 1410   on the Don)

Vasilii I
b. 1371
r. 1389–1425

Iurii
d. 1433

Andrei
d. 1432

Petr
d. 1428

Konstantin
d. 1433

Vasilii the
Crosseyed
d. 1448

Dmitrii Shemiaka
d. 1453

Dmitrii the
Handsome
d. 1441

Vasilii II the Dark
(Blind)
b. 1415; r. 1425–62

Ivan
|
Vasilii
d. 1529

Ivan III
b. 1440
r. 1462–1505

Andrei of Uglich
b. 1452; d. 1494

Boris of Volok
b. 1449; d. 1494

Andrei Jr. of
Vologda
1452–81

Ivan the Young
fl. 1458–90

Vasilii III
b. 1479
r. 1505–33

Andrei
d. 1536

Dmitrii
fl. 1485–1509

Ivan IV
r. 1533–84

Vladimir of Staritsa
fl. 1533–69

Dmitrii
fl. 1552–53

Ivan
fl. 1554–81

Dmitrii
fl. 1582–91

Fedor
r. 1584–98

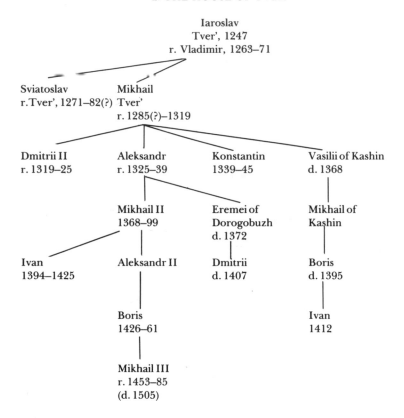

Iaroslav
Tver', 1247
r. Vladimir, 1263–71

Sviatoslav
r.Tver', 1271–82(?)

Mikhail
Tver'
r. 1285(?)–1319

Dmitrii II
r. 1319–25

Aleksandr
r. 1325–39

Konstantin
1339–45

Vasilii of Kashin
d. 1368

Mikhail II
1368–99

Eremei of
Dorogobuzh
d. 1372

Mikhail of
Kashin

Ivan
1394–1425

Aleksandr II

Dmitrii
d. 1407

Boris
d. 1395

Boris
1426–61

Ivan
1412

Mikhail III
r. 1453–85
(d. 1505)

Note: the dates usually indicate the years of rule, "r."; "d."—died.

3. THE HOUSE OF GEDIMINOVICHES-JAGELLONIANS

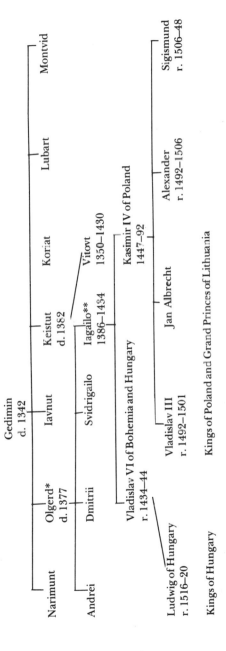

Gedimin
d. 1342

Narimunt

Olgerd*
d. 1377

Andrei

Dmitrii

Iavnut

Keistut
d. 1382

Svidrigailo

Vladislav VI of Bohemia and Hungary
r. 1434–44

Ludwig of Hungary
r. 1516–20

Kings of Hungary

Koriat

Iagailo**
1386–1434

Vitovt
1350–1430

Kasimir IV of Poland
1447–92

Vladislav III
r. 1492–1501

Jan Albrecht

Kings of Poland and Grand Princes of Lithuania

Lubart

Montvid

Alexander
r. 1492–1506

Sigismund
r. 1506–48

*Altogether, had twelve sons.
**Also Jagiello, named Vladislav after marriage to Jadwiga of Poland and after his baptism.

THE NIKONIAN CHRONICLE
(1425-1520)

[THE REIGN OF GRAND PRINCE VASILII VASILIEVICH, GRANDSON
OF THE PIOUS GRAND PRINCE DMITRII IVANOVICH DONSKOI]

In the Year 6933 [1425]. [After the passing of Grand Prince **1425**
Vasilii Dmitrievich, his son, the Grand Prince, ascended to the
throne of the Grand Principality of Vladimir and Moscow.[1]]

Grand Prince Vasilii Dmitrievich, grandson of Ivan, great
grandson of Ivan, gr. gr. grandson of Danilo of Moscow, passed
away on the twenty-seventh of February, on Tuesday of the second
week of Lent, at three o'clock in the morning, having ruled in the
Grand Principality of Vladimir and Moscow for thirty-six years.
The same night Metropolitan Photius of all Russia sent his boyar,
Akinf Aslebiatev, to Zvenigorod for his [late Prince Vasilii Dmitrievich's] brother, Prince Iurii Dmitrievich. Prince Iurii Dmitrievich,
however, was unwilling to go to Moscow and went to Galich. His
brother's son, Prince Vasilii Vasilievich, who at that time was ten
years and sixteen days old, ascended to the Grand Principality of
Moscow. Then Prince Iurii Dmitrievich, his uncle, sent him a warning but accepted an armistice until St. Peter's Day. Having accepted his armistice, the same spring Prince Iurii Dmitrievich sent
throughout all his patrimony for his people to assemble, and when
everyone came to him from all his cities he decided to march to
Moscow against his brother's son, Grand Prince Vasilii Vasilievich.
And [in the meantime] Grand Prince Vasilii Vasilievich brought
together all of his forces; and with him were his uncles, the brothers
of Prince Iurii Dmitrievich. And the Grand Prince went to the city
of Kostroma.

When Prince Iurii Dmitrievich heard about the strong forces
marching with his brother's son, Grand Prince Vasilii, as well as
with his own brothers, the Dmitrieviches, he fled to the city of
Nizhnii Novgorod. Grand Prince Vasilii Vasilievich sent against
him his uncle, Prince Konstantin Dmitrievich, with strong forces;

1. This sentence is in *Litsevoi Svod* only, not in *Ioasaf.* or *Obol.*

1

1425 and Prince Iurii Dmitrievich became frightened, fled beyond the river Sura, and remained there on the shore. His brother, Prince Konstantin Dmitrievich, after standing against him [on the river Sura] for a time, returned to Moscow because it was impossible to cross the [flooded] river. And then Prince Iurii Dmitrievich marched to Nizhnii Novgorod, whence he went to Galich and asked the Grand Prince for a year's armistice. Grand Prince Vasilii Vasilievich took counsel with his [spiritual] father, Metropolitan Photius of all Russia, with his mother, Grand Princess Sofia Vitovtovna,[2] and with his uncles, the Princes Andrei, Petr, and Konstantin Dmitrievich, and he consulted his grandfather, Grand Prince Vitovt Keistutievich of Lithuania.

After a discussion his princes and boyars advised him to send his [spiritual] father, Metropolitan Photius of all Russia, to his uncle, Iurii Dmitrievich. Metropolitan Photius did not refuse and the same year went joyfully to him [to Prince Iurii Dmitrievich] in Galich to discuss the peace. On the day of the Birth of St. John the Precursor he came to the city of Iaroslavl', and forthwith supped with Prince Ivan Vasilievich. The princes of Iaroslavl' asked him to celebrate a mass for them, but he did not heed them and went to Galich.

Learning of this, Prince Iurii Dmitrievich assembled everyone in his patrimony and met him, accompanied by his children, his boyars, and his best people. He [also] brought the common folk from all his cities, countryside, towns and villages, and there were a great many of them; and he placed them on the hill before the city in order to meet the Metropolitan and demonstrate to him how many people he had. The Metropolitan entered the city's suburb and went to the Cathedral Church of the Transfiguration of Our God, Lord and Saviour Jesus Christ. The church was in a field near the lake in the suburb. And he remained in the church, prayed there, walked out, looked at all the people who were standing upon the hill, and addressed to Prince Iurii Dmitrievich the following words: "My son, Prince Iurii! I have never seen so many people in sheepskins," for everyone was dressed in simple sheepskins because Prince Iurii had assembled them in order to demonstrate how many people he had. The Metropolitan considered it a manner of offense. Thereupon he went to his quarters, where he remained, and began

2. Grand Princess Sofia was the daughter of the powerful Lithuanian Grand Prince Vitovt, also called Witold, or Vitold, 1392–1430. His capital was the city of Wilno and his residence was in Troki.

to talk to Prince Iurii Dmitrievich about peace so as to avoid **1425** bloodshed between him and the Grand Prince. Prince Iurii asked for an armistice for a period of time but did not at all want to hear about a permanent peace. Metropolitan Photius became angry, blessed neither him nor his city, and departed from his city.

As soon [as he left] there arose an epidemic among [Prince Iurii's] people throughout his city. Learning of it and seeing it, Prince Iurii Dmitrievich took great fright. Rapidly he mounted a horse and hurried quickly after [the Metropolitan]. And he caught up with him beyond the lake in the town of Pasenkovo, and bowed deeply before him, asking forgiveness of his sins; and only with difficulty and great tears was he able [to attain] pardon [from the Metropolitan]. In this way Metropolitan Photius pardoned him and went back, giving the Prince and the city his blessing. He entered the city and blessed everyone, and from this very moment the wrath of God ceased and the great epidemic came to an end. The Metropolitan preached to the Prince about love and peace, and not only with his brothers but with all Orthodox people. Prince Iurii rendered him great honor and released him, accompanying him with all his people and telling him, "I will send my boyars to the Grand Prince to talk about peace."

After the Metropolitan's departure he sent his boyar, Boris Galichskii, and Danilo Cheshek, and they made peace on these terms—that Prince Iurii should not seek the [Grand] Principality by himself but [only with the intercession] of the Khan [of the Horde]: he who will be granted the Grand Principality by the Khan will become Grand Prince of the city of Vladimir, of Great Novgorod and all Russia.

The same year Grand Prince Ivan Mikhailovich of Tver' passed away. [Before his death] he was tonsured a monk as Job, and the first day of the month of May his son, Prince Aleksandr, ascended to the rule of the Grand Principality of Tver', and the latter's uncle, Vasilii Mikhailovich, became Prince of Kashin.

Beginning with Trinity Day there was a severe epidemic in Moscow. It came from the [Livonian] Germans to Pskov, whence it proceeded to Novgorod the Great and to Tver', and reached Moscow and the entire Russian land. In all places many people died.

The same year in Novgorod the Torgovaia side and the Liudin section burned.

The same year the people of Ustiug fought the Novgorodian land beyond the Volok.

1425   The same year the people of Novgorod fought the people of Ustiug and took a tribute from them of fifty thousand squirrel furs and six times forty sable.

The same year in Novgorod Theodosius, who once had been nominated to be Archbishop, passed away in his Monastery of the Holy Trinity in Sklobsk. Once during an election the lot [to be Archbishop] fell to him, but they [the Novgorodians] did not want him [to be Archbishop].

The same year the Greek Emperor Manuel of Byzantium [1341-1425], son-in-law of Grand Prince Vasilii Dmitrievich of Moscow, passed away.

THE GRAND PRINCIPALITY OF SERBIA [AND DESPOT STEFAN]

After the battle of Ankara[3] when Timur defeated and took prisoner Sultan Bayazid and all his [army], he also imprisoned Bayazid's wife, the sister of Stefan, Grand Prince of Serbia. Grand Prince Stefan[4] sent his envoys to Timur and [they] brought her out of captivity. And he, himself, with his brother Vuk[5] went to the Imperial City [Constantinople] and received the title of "Despot" from the Greek Emperor Manuel, who was still alive. And he was greatly honored and returned home. And Despot Stefan and his brother came to his city of Novobrod, a city which was truly a city of silver and gold. After the assassination of Sultan Bayazid, the Serbian land became free of the Moslem yoke and rule, and from that time Despot Stefan was, by the grace of God, Autocrat and lord of all the Serbian land. And he visited the cities and regions of his patrimony, and he pacified some [regions] and others he submitted to his rule; and those cities and regions which had been taken away from Serbian rule again came under his suzerainty. Likewise, on his way he took Belgrade, which had been earlier captured by Hungarians. The city was taken from the Hungarian land after the peace. This [city of Belgrade] is located within Serbian limits but is still situated in such a way as to be almost in the heart

3. In 1402 the Ottoman Turks under Sultan Bayazid (1389–1402) were defeated by Tamerlane, or Timur, the Khan of the Central Asian Turks.

4. Grand Prince, or "Despot" Stefan, 1389–1427, became ruler of Serbia after the battle of Kossovo, when the Turks defeated the Serbs and where his father, Lazar, was killed.

5. Volk, in *Nik.*

and on the shoulders of Hungarian lands. [Stefan] himself took
back other of his cities which were previously seized by the Turks,
and he began to reside in Belgrade because the city's location is
very attractive and beautified by the sea [*sic!*], rivers, and harbors.
Because ships come to it from everywhere as if winged, and they
would fly [*sic!*] to it with a great abundance of wealth. This [city]
was beautified by Stefan with walls, tsar's palaces, and a cathedral
church. He created an archbishopric there, providing it with all
the necessary supplies and building residences for the monks. The
Archbishop of Belgrade became Exarch of all the Serbian lands.

He built and named a church after Wonderworker Nicholas
and he accommodated it to be a monastery with good buildings
and residences and all other necessary structures; and he gathered
in it a great many sick people and lepers, and planted numerous
gardens there for their comfort. Thereafter he found an uninhabited and beautiful place convenient for silence, and built there a
church of the Life-creating Trinity which he decorated with paint-
ings and other arts. In the vicinity he built a fortress with cells in
the walls. He brought together a great many monks pleasing to
God, settled them there and provided them with all necessities.
From day to day he added treasures there. He built a burial place
for himself there, where he was rather soon buried. And he gave
icons decorated with gold and pearls, and a great many books,
vessels, and vestments decorated with pearls and gold, and golden
lamps, so as to surpass the great Monastery of the Holy Mountain
[Athos]. He invited Patriarch Cyril [of Serbia] with the entire church
council of the Serbian land, and they consecrated the church on
Holy Friday. He started building this monastery in the year 6915
[1407]. And a great many paupers came thither who were given
many alms.

He would always walk, himself, in the streets of the city at
night, distributing raiment and money to the paupers. A certain
person came many times to receive alms there, repeatedly begging.
He [Stefan] gave him [alms], saying "Take it, you, robber and
ravisher," and the other responded, "Not I, but you are the robber
and ravisher, with all your earthly kingdom, because in this way
you plunder and ravage the future kingdom [of God]."

ABOUT THE MOSELM SULTAN [SULEIMAN]

At that time the Moslem Sultan [Suleiman, 1402–11], the first

1425 son of Sultan Bayazid, sent to Despot Stefan in order to conclude a peace treaty.[6] Suleiman, himself, initiated a campaign toward the east to reconquer the realm of his father, and in pursuing he killed his brother, Azbeg, and conquered the eastern countries and the Turkish state. [In the meantime] after concluding a peace treaty with Suleiman, the Serbian land was at peace. The devil, however, could not abide this: he incited [Stefan's] brother Vuk [Volk] to get a multitude of warriors from Sultan Suleiman. He said, "In case my brother, Despot Stefan, gives me half the patrimony, I will serve you with it. If he does not, I will capture him and sack all of [his land]." Despot Stefan, however, did not want the pious flock which had been liberated by God [from Moslems] to be again submitted to the Turks. Vuk, with the sons of Hagar [the Turks], invaded the whole land, taking prisoners, burning and tormenting like a savage beast. When a second [invasion] with more warriors occurred, Stefan did not go against them because he did not want to participate in fratricidal bloodshed. He was also afraid of [the courtiers] who remained with him because they, too, were all receiving invitations from Vuk [to join him] which promised them gifts and pardon. And he would send messages even to those who remained with the Despot.

The Despot, holding [these] messages in his hand, wept before the Saviour's icon in his house in Belgrade. "Behold, Christ," he said, "how unjustly they behave; and even my pages have become traitors, as once occurred to Thy disciple, Judas. Keep with me to the end the small number of those who have remained [faithful] to me." Vuk and the sons of Hagar devastated the entire land. Seeing this, Stefan divided the land. Vuk, who with his nephews served Sultan Suleiman, cooperated with the sons of his sister[7] and in this way he controlled his father's land; Stefan, however, lived in the part which remained to him.

ABOUT SULTAN MUSA [1411–13]

Thereafter the ruler of Hungary-Walachia, who resided in the northeast,[8] invited Suleiman's brother, Musa, giving him an army

6. In *Nik.*, Suleiman is called not "Suleiman" but "Musulman" (Moslem).

7. Vuk's sister used to be Bayazid's wife.

8. This was the Gospodar (Prince) of Walachia, Mirch the Old (1386–1418), who at times also ruled Transylvania or the eastern parts (of Hungary).

to aid him in fighting his brother, Suleiman, and in getting revenge. **1425**
Musa sent to Despot Stefan, to his brother, Vuk, and to the latter's
nephews, [asking them] to campaign with him. Suleiman, however,
made an alliance with the Byzantine Emperor Manuel and with the
Franks.[9] When Musa perceived that Vuk wanted to escape to
Suleiman, he wanted to kill him. Despot [Stefan], however, saved
him and he fled the same night. There was a great battle and
Suleiman routed Musa. Musa encountered Vuk in Philipopolis and
ordered him killed together with his nephew, Lazar. Then he followed his brother like a thief, found him intoxicated with wine in
Adrianople, and ordered him strangled. And Musa came into possession of all the scepters and made peace with Despot Stefan.
Stefan then became the sole Autocrat of the entire Serbian land.
Sultan Musa captured many lands and thereafter undertook a campaign against the Serbian land of Despot Stefan in order finally to
destroy it. He divided the cities among his courtiers and in the year
6921 [1413] he came [to Serbia], occupied many cities and captured
Bolvan, Lipovets, Stalak, and Koprian. Seeing this, Despot Stefan
sent for help to the eastern Sultan, Mohammed,[10] son of Bayazid
and junior brother of Musa, and made an agreement with him.
Sultan Mohammed came from the east, the Despot from the west,
and with him were Hungarian voevodas and Bosnian rulers. Musa
went into the mountains, intending to obstruct the highway so that
none could escape to [join] the warriors of the Sultan and the
Despot. The Despot sent his nephew, Gurg, with warriors, and
there was a battle. Musa was routed and he was drowned in the river.

ABOUT MOHAMMED [1413–21]

Mohammed was Sultan of the East and West and of all the
Turks. He was good and gentle.

[ABOUT DESPOT STEFAN] (*continued*)

Lord Gurg returned and Despot Stefan honored him greatly
with many gifts and thanked God for everything. A great peace
came and he continued, according to his custom, to distribute alms
and to feed travelers and lepers. And he sent liberally to the monks

9. Franks—the Russian and, generally, East European name for
Italians and French. The Italian city-states of Genoa and Venice had vast
possessions in Greece, the Archipelago, and the Crimea.

10. Mohammed I was Sultan of the eastern part of the Ottoman Empire
from 1403 to 1413, and from 1413 to 1421 of the entire Empire.

1425   who lived in *hesychia.*[11] He introduced special ranks for those who served him: [first, for] those who were admitted to his inner sanctum, and with whom [the Despot] discussed the administration of his tsardom and to whom he gave written and oral instructions. He told them to follow the example of those who ruled justly and [who] executed their power conscientiously. He said not to follow a bad example because "Those who follow the way of the Unjust will perish." The second rank he organized in another, exterior, palace—those would receive orders from those admitted to the inner sanctum. The third rank was outside the palace and these were given instructions by the second rank to carry out his orders. He certainly forbade all playing of timpani and all manner of music. He said, "This is good only in war." And he was a generous father to all who served him, but those who did not work properly were chastized by him and removed from the administration. Those who ruined themselves through bad faith or bad service, or in some other way became paupers, were not deprived of their fathers', grandfathers', or great grandfathers' estates. He said, "The Lord does not twice punish those who sin." And in the manner of Solomon he pardoned those who sinned and who became paupers. All those who worked for him and, especially, those who were close to him revered each other, and among them there was no shouting, no calumny, no laughter, and no one was indecently clothed, and they kept their eyes from spying. They behaved themselves in such a way that a powerful one would not be noticed; and the most remarkable was that they would not be conquered by woman's love.

His nephew, Bolsha, ruler of Albania, died and Despot Stefan went [thither] and took the Albanians under his scepter. And to that land, to Belgrade, there came to him from Hungary Constantine, son of Stratsimir, the Tsar of Bulgaria, and he died there in the year 6930 [1422].[12]

ABOUT SULTAN MOHAMMED

Sultan Mohammed, the last son of Sultan Bayazid, lived in peace with those who were his friends from the beginning. He died

11. *Hesychia* is a particular manner of spiritual exercise of eastern monks. They observe silence and claim that the observation of certain rites, quietude and repetition of the Jesus prayer reveal divine light.

12. Ivan Stratsimir was Tsar of northwestern Bulgaria, with his capital at Vilin. In 1396 the Turks conquered this last Bulgarian state.

in Adrianople [1421]. Several [lords] from Despot Stefan's land **1426** suggested that he [Stefan] take his army and seize his [Mohammed's] land. He said, "I swore to the Sultan that I would do only good to his children." Murad was [the senior] son of Sultan Mohammed, the junior son being Mustafa.[13] The Byzantine Emperor supported him [Mustafa], and he was accepted in the eastern part of the country. Murad sent armies against him [Mustafa]. Mustafa came out of Nicea to the battle and was killed there,[14] and Murad became Sultan of the eastern and western Turks.

Because Byzantium supported his brother, he started warring with it, but he had great friendship for Despot Stefan. Thereafter the Despot developed infirm legs and he called his nephew, Gurg, and appointed him Despot of all the Serbian land.[15] Soon thereafter, on the nineteenth of June, 6935 [1427], he passed away and the same day there was in Belgrade awful thunder such as never was before. And darkness came like night over our land, and only at sunset did it become a little clearer. [The people of Serbia], weeping greatly, buried Despot Stefan in the grave which he had built, himself, in the Monastery of the Lifegiving Trinity in Belgrade.

THE BYZANTINE EMPIRE

In the Year 6933 [1425]. After [the death of the Byzantine] Emperor Manuel, his Orthodox son, *Kyr* John, began to reign in Constantinople.[16] During his reign Sultan Murad, son of Mohammed, remembering that his brother had received military support [from Byzantium], undertook a campaign against the Imperial City [Constantinople]. Thereafter, however, he concluded a peace treaty with them.

In the Year 6934 [1426]. In September the plague ceased in Great Novgorod but then developed very strongly again in Pskov, in Great Novgorod, in Torzhok, in Tver', in Volok, in Dmitrov, in Moscow, and in all Russian cities and provinces and towns of the entire land. And there were sadness and great grief among the people. And in Moscow the same fall Prince Andrei Volodimirovich died; he was the grandson of Andrei, great grandson of Ivan, gr.

13. Murad was the Ottoman Sultan, 1421–51.
14. In 1422.
15. Gurg (George) Brankovich was the last important ruler of medieval Serbia, 1427–56.
16. John VIII, Byzantine Emperor, 1425–48. "*Kyr*" means "lord."

1426   gr. grandson of Daniil Aleksandrovich of Moscow.[17] He [died] being tonsured and named Savva in place of Andrei, and was buried in the Monastery of the Holy Trinity and St. Sergius.

The same fall the Tatars came to the Riazan' *ukraina* [prairie, frontier] and returned with captives to the *polé* [prairie]. The people of Riazan' followed them, caught them, defeated them, and took back the captives.

This same fall the Turks started fighting against the Byzantine land.

The same fall Prince Iaroslav Volodimirovich, grandson of Andrei, great grandson of Ivan, gr. gr. grandson of Daniil Aleksandrovich of Moscow, passed away.

The same year Prince Ivan Vasilievich of Iaroslavl' passed away.

The same year the Grand Prince of Lithuania, Vitovt Keistutevich, campaigned against Pskov with a vast army. With him were [warriors] from the lands of Lithuania, Poland, Bohemia, Walachia, and his own Tatars,[18] and he asked Khan Mohammed to send him his guard. And first he came to the Pskovian town of Opochka. But the people [of Opochka] locked themselves in and hid so the invaders would think the city was deserted. The Tatars rode their horses onto the bridge. The citizens [of Opochka] had put the bridge on ropes and had put sharp poles under it. When the bridge was filled with the [Tatar] troops the citizens cut the ropes, the bridge fell down on the poles, and all of them were killed. Many Tatars, Poles, and Lithuanians were taken captive while they were streaming into the city. They cut off the Tatar's penes and put the penes in their mouths to humiliate them so that Vitovt, himself, and those with him could see them. And they skinned the Poles, Czechs, and Walachs. Vitovt saw it and was filled with shame, and departed the city, not having succeeded at all. He came to the other fortified city, Voronoch, and remained there with his many troops. At night there came a horrifying and very awesome cloud with great thunder and with burning lightning. Those who were with Vitovt became desperate. Such thunder struck, and lightning, so that the earth trembled. Vitovt seized the pole of his tent and

17. He was Grand Prince Vasilii Vasilievich's uncle. His grandfather, also Andrei, was the ruling prince of Serpukhov.

18. Some Tatars lived in Northern Lithuania near Troki (close to Wilno). They settled there after the battle of Vorskla (see *Nik.*, Vol. IV, year 1399).

started shouting, "Lord, have mercy," wailing and trembling, believ-   **1428**
ing that he would be swallowed up by the earth and would descend
into hell. And when this horrifying cloud passed, there approached
the city, [coming] from Moscow, Aleksandr Volodimirovich Lykov,
envoy of Grand Prince Vasilii Vasilievich, reporting that Grand
Prince Vasilii Vasilievich [asked], "Why do you do this despite the
armistice? You are supposed to be together with me but you campaign in my patrimony and turn it into a desert." And the people
of Pskov came thither at the same time, greeting Vitovt with three
thousand rubles [as ransom]. Vitovt Keistutevich followed [the ad-
vice] of his grandson, Grand Prince Vasilii Vasilievich,[19] retreated
from the town, took from the Pskovians only one thousand rubles,
and returned to them two thousand. And so he returned home
with all his armies after he had remained at Voronoch for three
weeks.

In the Year 6935 [1427]. There was a great plague in all the
Russian cities and in all lands, and [people] died from boils. Those
who were to die had blue boils and they died on the third day;
those who were to survive had red boils, and they remained lying
till the boils healed. After this plague, just as after the flood, the
people could not resume living [as usual] for many years for they
were still short-lived, emaciated, and weak.

The same year during the same plague Prince Vasilii Volodimirovich died. [He was] the grandson of Andrei, great grandson
of Ivan, gr. gr. grandson of Danilo Aleksandrovich of Moscow, and
he was buried in the Cathedral of the Archangel in Moscow.

The same year Blessed Hegumen Cyril of the Beloozero
[Monastery] passed away, the ninth day of June, and he was buried
in the Monastery in Beloozero.

The same year the construction of the Church of the Holy
Saviour, built by Euthymius, Bishop of Novgorod, was completed
in Novgorod.

In the Year 6936 [1428]. Prince Petr Dmitrievich, grandson of
Ivan, great grandson of Ivan and gr. gr. grandson of Danilo Aleksandrovich of Moscow, passed away.

The same year Grand Prince Vitovt Keistutevich of Lithuania,
with strong forces, started a campaign against Novgorod the Great,
and with him were artillery guns and mortars and cannons. One

19. Vitovt's daughter was the mother of Grand Prince Vasilii
Vasilievich.

1429 of the cannons, named Galka, was so large that it was transported by forty horses between morning and lunch; by another forty horses between lunch and midday; and by another forty horses till evening. And they arrived at the city of Porkhov, and master Mikolai [who built] this gun boasted to Vitovt, saying, "Prince, this gun will not only raze the tower but also will destroy the stone Church of St. Nicholas in the city." The tower and church were built with very strong stones. He was permitted to fire from this cannon and this cannon razed the tower to its foundation and pierced the front and back walls of the sanctuary of the Church of St. Nicholas and cut the stone merlons of the battlements. And then [this] cannonball passed through the city and hit Vitovt's regiments, killing Vitovt's voevoda of Polotsk, slaughtering many of Vitovt's warriors, and frightening a great number of horses. This happened during the liturgy itself, and the priest who was celebrating in the Church of St. Nicholas was not hurt at all. And the German master who built the cannon and boasted that he would ruin and destroy the Church of the Holy Wonderworker Nicholas was so smitten asunder that it was impossible to find either his body or his bones anywhere, and there remained only half of his coat. But Vitovt commanded that the city be besieged and ordered that it be bombarded. The *posadnik*,[20] Isaak Boretskii, as well as Grigorii Kirillovich Posakhno, and others departed the city and petitioned Vitovt, weeping, promising him a ransom. At that time there came from Novgorod Bishop Emelian, who was nominated by Metropolitan Photius to be Archbishop [of Novgorod, under the clerical name] Euthymius, and with him the *posadnik* and *tysiatskiis* of Novgorod. They petitioned Vitovt and gave a tribute of ten thousand Novgorodian rubles, and Archbishop Euthymius of Novgorod paid Vitovt three thousand Novgorodian rubles for the captives, and silver was taken from all Novgorodian volosts [regions] and from the Trans-Volok volosts, and every ten people gave a ruble. And Vitovt told them, "This has happened to you because you used to call me 'traitor' and 'drunkard,'" and went home with all his forces.

In the Year 6937 [1429]. The [Kazan'] Tatars came unexpectedly to Galich against Prince Iurii Dmitrievich, and they remained in Galich for one month. On Epiphany they reached Kostroma and occupied Kostroma, Pleso, and Lug. And then they retreated to

20. *Posadnik*: elected senior commissioner of the city.

the lower Volga. Grand Prince Vasilii Vasilievich sent after them   **1430**
his uncles, Princes Andrei and Konstantin Dmitrievich, and with
them Ivan Dmitrievich, with their regiments. They went as far as
Nizhnii Novgorod but were unable to catch [the Tatars] and returned. Prince Fedor Starodubskii-Pestroi and Fedor Konstantinovich Dobrynskii, however, without permission of the princes
and voevodas, rushed with troops after the Tatars and caught their
rear guard. And some were dispersed and some were killed, but
neither the sons of the Khan nor the princes were caught.

The same year in Great Novgorod the stone Church of the
Holy Fathers,[21] in the court of the Prince, collapsed.

In the Year 6938 [1430]. In Smolensk there appeared a naked
wolf, without fur, which ate many people. In Lithuania in the city
of Troki [the water in the] Lake Zhidovskoe remained red as blood
for three days. The same fall on the first of November Archbishop
Euthymius of Novgorod passed away. He was Bishop for five years,
and when he was nominated he remained in the Bishop's palace
for one year and two weeks. The same month of November the
monk-priest Euthymius from Lisiia Gorka was nominated by lot to
be Archbisop of Holy Sophia [Novgorod].

The same year Photius, Metropolitan of Kiev and all Russia,
was in Troki [visiting] Vitovt. And at that time people came to
Vitovt from all lands: his grandson, Grand Prince Vasilii Vasilievich
of Moscow, King Iagailo Olgerdovich of Poland, as well as Grand
Prince Boris Aleksandrovich of Tver', and the Grand Prince of
Mazovia, as well as a cardinal of the Pope of Rome, and the Grand
Prince of Vatm [?], the King of Bohemia, voevoda Iliash of Walachia, the German voevoda Kunshter, the [grand] master of the Prus-
sian and German knights [of the Teutonic Order], and many other
princes and voevodas. And Vitovt went with all of them from Troki
to Wilno, where he honored them very much and gave them many
gifts and released them. From thence they all returned to their
lands. He, however, left with him Photius, Metropolitan of all Russia, and kept him after these eleven days. After rendering him
many honors, he let him go to Moscow. Metropolitan Photius arrived in Novogrudok in Lithuania and there received tidings that
the Grand Prince of Lithuania, Vitovt Keistutevich, had died on

21. Usually the three early teachers of the church are meant by "Holy
Fathers": St. John Chrysostom, St. Gregory the Great, and St. Basil the
Theologian.

1431   the twenty-fourth of October, exactly three days after the Metropolitan had left. And he had ruled for thirty-eight years. After him his cousin, Svidrigailo Olgerdovich, became the Grand Prince of Lithuania, and he came with his brother, King Iagailo Olgerdovich of Poland, to Novogrudok of Lithuania and he honored Photius, Metropolitan of all Russia, and with affection and honor he permitted him to go to Moscow.

This very year there was a severe drought and there was very little good water. The land, the woods, and the forests burned and there was such great smoke that sometimes people could not see each other. And from this smoke the animals and birds and the fish in the water died, and the people were in great need and perished.

The same year in Novgorod there was erected in the prince's court a stone Church of the Holy Fathers, in the same place where the old one had collapsed. The same year the Novgorodians built a second, stone wall in the city of Porkhov. The same year there was an assembly in Novgorod to build a fortress. Every five people designated one of themselves to work.

In the Year 6939 [1431]. In the month of October, Aidar, a prince of the Horde, campaigned against the Lithuanian land and came to the city of Mtsensk, and stayed there three weeks but was unable to take the city because Grigorii Protasiev was there. And Aidar pledged to Grigorii according to his faith [not to harm him], and he [Grigorii] believed this pledge and came out of the city; but Aidar took him with him to the Horde, to Khan Mohammed. Khan Mohammed, however, did not praise Aidar but scolded him, and he honored Grigorii and released him to Russia with honor and gifts.[22]

The same winter Prince Iurii Dmitrievich broke the peace with his nephew, Grand Prince Vasilii Vasilievich.

The same spring Grand Prince Vasilii Vasilievich sent troops under Prince Fedor Davydovich Pestroi against the Bulgars of the Volga and Kama, and he went thither, campaigned against them, and occupied their whole land.

The same summer there was an omen. In the sky there appeared three fiery columns and [later] there was a great drought, and the earth, forest and marshes burned. There was great starvation in the entire Russian land.

22. Ulug-, or Ulu-Mohammed; or Makhmet.

STORY ABOUT PHOTIUS, METROPOLITAN OF KIEV AND ALL RUSSIA,   **1431**
WHO HAD A VISION OF AN ANGEL OF THE LORD
WHICH TOLD HIM ABOUT THE END OF HIS LIFE

Photius, Metropolitan of Kiev and all Russia, had a vision in Moscow. After matins he was in his bedchamber and prayed according to the rules. It was on Friday of Holy Week in the year 6938 [1430], when the memory of Blessed Theodore the Hairy was celebrated. And he was lying on his bed, sleeping, when suddenly in his chamber a miraculous light appeared from all directions, and a radiant man, who looked like a distinguished northerner, approached him. His hair was as gold and he had a tsar's crown on his head; his vestment was ornamented with all manner of beautiful design beyond the imagination of man. He had a golden staff in his hand and he stood before Metropolitan Photius in silence. Photius was frightened. After a certain time, however, he recovered and asked him, "Who are you, man, who has astonished me? How have you managed to come to me while my doors were locked? It is written [in the Bible], 'One who comes not through the door is a thief and robber.' " And he who had appeared to him answered, "You have the wrong idea about me. I am neither a thief nor robber nor earthly mortal. Nothing can stop me, neither stone walls nor the iron gate of a fortress when I wish to enter, because I am the angel of God, sent to you from Lord God Almighty of Sabaoth. The Lord God commanded me to tell you how your life is to be. Be attentive to yourself and to your flock and Christ-God gives you seven [terms] for re-examining your life and for the administration of your flock."

The Metropolitan, hearing this from the angel, was in awe and trepidation, and he fell in tears at the angel's feet. He could no longer see the angel of God, who became invisible to him. Thereafter Photius' mind became excited from this vision and he became gravely ill, and lay for many hours until the monks from the cells near him entered, took him up with their hands, and put him on his bed; and he was as if dead, unable either to speak with his mouth or to see with his eyes. Thereafter, the spirit returned to him. With difficulty he told of his vision, relating everything to those present. After the apparition of the angel of God, Metropolitan Photius lived for one year, three months and twenty days, and so passed seven terms according to the word of the angel of God. There were seven terms of seventy days each, and Photius, Metropolitan of Kiev and all Russia, passed away the second day of the

1431   month of July of the year 6939 [1431], and was buried in the Cathedral Church of the Most Pure Mother of God, which was the Metropolitan's church in Moscow.

[He was buried] on the right side [of the church] where is located the sepulchre of Cyprian, Metropolitan of all Russia. Before his passing he wrote his epistle about his life, forgiving and blessing everyone and asking forgiveness of all. And he instructed [them] to live [their lives] according to Scripture, in the following words:

THE LIFE AND WILL OF METROPOLITAN PHOTIUS

"In the Name of the One Indivisible and Lifegiving Trinity, I, the servant of God, humble Photius, by the grace of God Metropolitan of Kiev and all Russia—Thou alone, knowest why—I was appointed to the great rank of Metropolitan, which I never desired. It is a great work of shepherd and teacher because one must care for oneself and even more for the flock. One is supposed to be aware at all times of humility and exaltation and blessed quietude and just wrath and salvation and many other things which are the keys to the work of a shepherd.

"Since I have seen my weakness and did not want anything like this position, but still [desired] at least a partially righteous life, therefore I did not engage myself in marriage and did not involve myself in the dreams of this vain and rapidly-passing world. Most of all, it was pleasing and important for me, humble one, to save my soul and to be able to appear before the Lord God, My Saviour, and Creator of all pure creatures of the world.

"And so I gave up life in this tempting and vain world which is poor and passes quickly. And I was taught and instructed by the blessed and most holy Acacius, who was my elder and instructor and who was respected by all patriarchs, bishops, and emperors, who was sought by everyone as a sweet ray of sunshine. From my youth I followed him and worked for him and was taught the divine scriptures and spiritual wisdom and all ways of the spiritual life. And I submitted myself to my instructor and always obeyed him without anger or hesitation, and followed him and worked for him. I learned and understood primarily how to mortify myself, encountering [the temptations of] the world, and how to separate myself from the tempting life and to be with Christ.

"My destiny, however, was decided by divine will. I did not want it and have never had it in mind. From Morea[23] I was sent

23. Morea: the medieval name of Peloponnesus, Greece.

by Acacius, my blessed elder, remarkable among the prelates, to   **1431**
the Imperial City of Constantinople, to His Holiness, Patriarch and
Lord Matthew, and to pious Emperor and Lord Manuel. There,
unexpectedly, they imposed upon me the title and duties of Bishop,
which I could hardly bear; I could not escape God's way and could
only be sad. And Patriarch and Lord Matthew consecrated me in
the Council to be Bishop of the Kievan Metropolitan Diocese and
of all Russia. And they sent me [thither] and I went with great
sadness and sorrow, weeping, crying, lamenting, remembering my
quiet and peaceful existence. And so, weeping, I journeyed and
came to the Most Holy Metropolitan Diocese of Russia, and from
that time only God knows how often I wept and cried either because
of my weakness and for not having sufficient spiritual strength or
because I heard about the misfortunes of my human flock which,
before my arrival there, was captured by the sons of Hagar[24] and
was therefore embittered; and later [I wept] because of our frequent
sins, and especially because I witnessed incessant plagues, starvation
and fratricidal feuds.

"And I have been exhausted with all these griefs and pitiful
occurrences, and I was afflicted by them and wept greatly, and my
soul was scorched and I shed many years because I was plunged
into all these cruel disasters. And in addition to that I was tormented
with strife and division in the Kievan Metropolitan Diocese and all
Russia. Therefore, however, God permitted and granted grace to
unite the Church in all its beauty, as it used to be of yore. And
thereafter I relapsed into sorrow because of the passing to the Holy
Spirit of my [spiritual] son, Grand Prince Vasilii Dmitrievich, and
I was overwhelmed by illnesses and misfortunes and by my own
rejection of too many actions. And more than anyone else I, humble
one, saw spitefulness, calumny and despair, weeping and shedding
of tears. And there were rebellions and fratricidal feuds, and I had
grief upon grief and sorrow upon sorrow, and there were more
famines and deaths. All this distress and sorrow have completely
destroyed and annihilated me, and my eyes were ruined from tears
for the flock of Christ and because of the innumerable pestilences
and droughts.

"And since I became embittered at these many sorrows and
griefs and misfortunes, and because of my sins I was often punished
by the Manloving God, my various diseases and illnesses multiplied,

24. Sons of Hagar: here are meant the nomadic Mongols and Tatars.

1431   which do not presage anything but death and the last and awesome judgment of My Lord Christ, God.

"For these reasons and despite your love, I have to leave you! The first thing in which I believe, and beseech you to maintain, is the faith of the Apostles and Holy Fathers given by God, the real piety of true Orthodoxy of the Holy Trinity; and since I accept and respect with love from the whole depth of my heart and with all faith the Holy Church and the Sacred Scripture which were received from God, from the Holy Apostles and the Holy Fathers, and from holy oecumenic and local councils, and from truly saintly persons, I also beseech and order you likewise to observe them. And also [I ask you] to observe entirely and without changes all other rules of the divine church as they are established by the Holy Apostles and Holy Fathers. And do this in the same way as I confessed them in the divine church when I was ordained bishop by the Most Holy Patriarch Matthew of Constantinople and the entire Oecumenic, Holy, and Sanctified Synod.

"In view of the fact that I am departing this life but am still alive, I give all of you remission in the Name of Christ and ask the same of all of you; and I give peace and love and apologies to all holy patriarchs, those who have passed away and those still alive, and implore the same of them. Likewise, I give my blessing and forgiveness to all Orthodox emperors, as well as to all pious and Christ-loving grand princes of Russia and to their grand princesses who have passed away already, as well as to those who passed away during my years; I give them my blessing and forgiveness and ask the same of them. Also, I give my blessing and forgiveness to all God-loving bishops of Russia who are within the limits of our conciliar Metropolitan Church, as well as the other [bishops], to those who passed away before or during our years, and I ask the same of them. Also, I give my blessing and forgiveness to all pious princes and princesses of Russia who passed away before and during our years and ask the same of them. Also, I give my blessings and forgiveness to all clergy and monks who passed away before and during my years, and I ask the same of them. Also, to all Orthodox Christians who passed away before or in our years during droughts and epidemics, in water, and in fire, war or captivity, and who died from all inevitable deaths during our years I give my blessing and forgiveness and pray to receive the same, myself, from them.

"To the pious, honorable and Christ-loving Grand Prince **1431** Vasilii Vasilievich, who, in the Holy Spirit, is my son, and to his mother, Grand Princess Sofia, I bestow peace and love and blessing and my last embrace and forgiveness. To my pious and honorable sons in the Holy Spirit, Prince Georgii [Iurii] Dmitrievich and his brother, Prince Andrei Dmitrievich, with their princesses and their children, I give my blessing and forgiveness. Also, to all grand princes of Russia who are [ruling] within the limits of their grand principalities, and to all feudal and local princes with their princesses and children I leave my blessing in Christ and forgiveness. In the same way to all governing bishops within the limits of our Russian Metropolia, and all Orthodox bishops of the entire earth and to all clergy and monks I bestow peace and blessing and forgiveness and ask the same of them. Also, to all boyars, lords and merchants, and all Orthodox Christians with their wives and children I bestow peace and my blessings and forgiveness and a last embrace, and ask the same of all of them.

"And all those who, following the Gospel words of Christ, served and worked for us as He said, 'He who obeys you, obeys Me, and he who accepts you, accepts Me. And he who accepts the prophet in the name of the prophet, accepts the prophet's reward. And one who accepts the just in the name of the just accepts the reward of the just.' And since all those who worked, served, loved and honored us did so for the sake of God and of the Gospel, and did so in the cities, in the towns, in the empty lands and in different lands, the grace of God and of the Most Pious Mother of God and all saints must remain with them, as well as our blessing, and God, as He promised, should reward them in this age and in the future one.

"And the grace of God and of the Most Pure Mother of God and all saints, as well as our blessing, should be on those princes and boyars, men and women who, together with us, care for well-being with purpose of amendment, and the Most Merciful Christ-God should recompense them in this age and the future one. And those who, since my consecration of the holy rank of bishop in the year 6917 [1409], the first day of September, the second interdiction, and to the interdiction nine of the year 6939 [1431], were interdicted by me with or without cause and who did not ask from me the release of this interdiction because they forgot it or were

1431   simple of mind or for some other reason, as well as those who did
not follow my punishment or instruction—all those I pardon in the
name of the Holy Spirit and bless; and I bestow on all of them
peace, my blessing and forgiveness. And all those, whether they be
bishop, prince or great lord and boyar, clergyman or monk, simple
layman, men or women, who, during all of these past years[25] envied
me or condemned me openly or secretly, and who confess it and
ask for forgiveness, will be forgiven in this age and in the future.
And all those who were ashamed or careless to do so or forgot it
or did not consider it important or feared me and, fearing, did not
confess to me, be they dead or still alive—all those should be blessed
and forgiven because it is in my power to forgive them; and I ask
them to do the same. And I remove the interdiction and bless and
forgive everyone except those priests whom I forbade to officiate
so as to help them to understand [their sins] and for their own
spiritual benefit and salvation. I cannot remove such interdiction
because it is not in my power.

"And I remit my soul unto the Man-loving God and I leave
everything [I possess] to the house of the Purest Mother of God
and my son in the Holy Spirit, pious Grand Prince Vasilii Vasilievich.
It is well known to you, my son, as well as it was known to your
father, the [spiritual] son of our humility, Grand Prince Vasilii
Dmitrievich, and your mother, the [spiritual] daughter of our
humility, Grand Princess Sofia, and your uncles, boyars and lords,
and all Orthodox Christians, that when, after [the death of] my
brother [in Christ] Cyprian, Metropolitan of Kiev and all Russia, I
came to this holy Metropolia, I did not find anything in the household of the Metropolitan Church. Everything was devastated and
spent and had disappeared, no one knew whither. And I, humble
one, labored diligently for the sake [of the church]. And I order
you, my son, Grand Prince Vasilii Vasilievich, as well as your children and your grandchildren and all [future] generations and generations, and so to the end of the ages, that everything which came
to me for the household of the church of Christ and His Purest
Mother, either from the dominion of your great realm or from
other realms and states of other grand princes, or from the Lithuanian land or from honorable and pious princes, boyars, lords, merchants, Orthodox Christians, men and women, or from all those

25. Metropolitan Photius ruled in 1409–31.

who gave for the salvation of their souls to the house of Christ and   **1431**
the Purest Mother of God, whether it was gold or silver or pearls
or gems or silver chalices, lands and water—all these should be
kept and never taken by anyone because all this was given to God
for the household of the Purest Mother of God and for the remission
of the sins of Christians.

"As far as my soul is concerned, I command you, my son,
Grand Prince Vasilii Vasilievich, and your children, to care for it
and hold memorial services. Remember, my son, that nothing
should be forgotten which happened since baptism in the font,
whereunto I witness to God for you, and that I cared for you and
stood with you in many events at all times.

"I also give you my blessing and I order that you care for and
protect your boyars, monks, and servants, from the youngest to
the oldest, so that in the Name of the Purest Mother of God they
be protected from evil and not be exposed to any kind of harm
from anyone. It is well known to you, my son, Grand Prince, and
to all pious princes, boyars, lords, and merchants, that because of
our sins all church charters burned; but, despite this, no harm
should come to the household of Christ and the Purest Mother of
God, and nothing should be misused by anyone forever and ever.[26]

"It is no small sin to take what belongs to the church, what was
given to God and to the Purest Mother of God. It is well known to
all that when I came to this holy Metropolia of Kiev and all Russia,
all houses of Christ and of the Purest Mother of God of the Metropolitan Church, as well as all towns [belonging to the church]
were empty, exhausted, and wasted. As far as Lord God gave
strength to my humility, I built and filled them all and I protected
them from plague, drought, and Tatar invasions; and what was
lost was lost because of God's will. And what remains, and what I
bought for the house of Christ and the Purest Mother of God, the
inhabited lands and the towns and the uninhabited land and the
water—all this must remain inalienably and forever and ever in the
possession of the Church of God and Purest Mother of God, and
nothing should be wasted. I beseech and bequest that you, my son,
Grand Prince Vasilii Vasilievich, as well as your children and grandchildren and all pious princes, boyars, and lords, heed all this which

26. Here Metropolitan Photius was speaking, primarily, about the
church's landholdings which were taken by the boyars or princes.

1431   I have written and willed. And if these written [behests] are un-
heeded, there will ensue chastisement from God and the Purest
Mother of God. Therefore I beseech all Orthodox people and ask
them to heed what was written by my humility because I wrote it
according to the will of the Holy Spirit.

"And may the mercy and grace of the Lord God and Purest
Mother of God remain with you, my son, Grand Prince Vasilii
Vasilievich, with your children and grandchildren, with all their
great realm, and with all pious princes, boyars, lords, merchants,
and all Christian people; and may they be with you, as well as peace
and salvation and our blessing, now and ever and ever and unto
the endless ages. Amen."

And in this way His Holiness, Photius, Metropolitan of all
Russia, after having written this will and fulfilled the seven terms
of seventy days which were announced to him by God's angel,
passed away to God on the second day of the month of July in the
year 6939 [1431] and he was buried in the Metropolitan Cathedral
Church of the Purest Mother of God in Moscow in its right side,
where lies the tomb of Cyprian, Metropolitan of Russia. And he
was shepherd of the church of God for twenty-two years and ten
months.

THE RIVALRY BETWEEN GRAND PRINCE VASILII VASILIEVICH AND HIS UNCLE, PRINCE IURII DMITRIEVICH, OVER THE GRAND PRINCIPALITY AND THEIR JOURNEY TO THE HORDE

The same year, 6939 [1431], Grand Prince Vasilii Vasilievich
had a contest with his uncle, Iurii Dmitrievich, about the Grand
Principality of Moscow, and they decided to go to the [Golden]
Horde, to Khan Mohammed: he who should receive the Grand
Principality from Khan Mohammed would become the Grand
Prince. And so Grand Prince Vasilii Vasilievich in the month of
August began preparing [his journey] to the Horde. On the holiday
of the Assumption of the Most Pure Theotokos, after the liturgy,
he commanded that a service be held in honor of the Most Pure
Mother of God and the great Wonderworker Peter, and he wept
and commanded that many alms be distributed to all paupers in
all churches and monasteries of the city of Moscow; and he commanded that the same be done in all his cities; and the same day
he went to the Horde. He dined under a tent in his meadow across
from St. Simeon [Monastery] and started his journey.

In the Year 6940 [1432]. On the eighth day of the month of   **1432**
September, the holiday of the Nativity of the Most Pure Mother
of God, Prince Iurii Dmitrievich went to the liturgy in the Church
of the Most Pure [Virgin] in Storozhi and also set out for the Horde
after Grand Prince Vasilii Vasilievich. When they arrived at the
Horde they were received in the residence of Min-Bulat, the *doroga*[27]
of Moscow, and Grand Prince Vasilii Vasilievich was greatly honored by him, while Prince Iurii Dmitrieivich had dishonor and was
obliged to wait.

Shirin Tiagin, who was an important lord in the Horde, however, was on good terms with Prince Iurii and he went and, applying
force, took him away from Min-Bulat and promised to give him
the Grand Principality. Shirin Tiagin and Prince Iurii went to pass
the winter in Crimea but the Grand Prince remained with Min-Bulat
in the Horde. With Grand Prince Vasilii Vasilievich there was the
boyar, Ivan Dmitrievich [Vsevolozhskii], who worked on behalf of
Grand Prince Vasilii Vasilievich and petitioned important princes
of the Horde—such as Lord Aidar, Min-Bulat, and other Tatar
lords—to help his sovereign Grand Prince Vasilii Vasilievich; and
he told them the following: "My lords, how can you, verily, be
devoted to the Khan and how can your words be trusted about our
sovereign Grand Prince if the Khan can do nothing contrary to
Tiagin's advice and pays no heed to any of you? Heeding Tiagin's
counsel, he would rather give the Grand Principality to Prince Iurii!
Should the Khan follow his counsel, Iurii will be Grand Prince in
Moscow and Svidrigailo, whom he called his brother, will be Grand
Prince in Lithuania. Then Tiagin, in the Horde, will manipulate
the Khan without consulting you."

These words struck their hearts like an arrow and therefore
all the lords of the Horde started petitioning the Khan on behalf
of Grand Prince Vasilii Vasilievich and thereupon consulted with
him. They persuaded the Khan, who said, "Should Tiagin speak
on behalf of Prince Iurii for the Grand Principality, I will command
him to be killed."

When spring came Tiagin returned to the Horde from the
Crimea and wanted the Grand Principality to be granted [by the
Khan] to Prince Iurii. A chamberlain to the Khan's, a certain Tatar
named Husein, who was Shirin Tiagin's cousin, informed him of

27. *Doroga* is a Tatar term for a high fiscal officer or envoy.

1432   the Khan's and lords' decision: "If someone speaks on behalf of Prince Iurii, he will be killed." When Shirin Tiagin heard this he did not dare dispute with them [the Tatar lords] or oppose them.

The Khan ordered his lords to come to some decision about the Russian princes, and there was great argument among them: Grand Prince Vasilii Vasilievich sought his throne because his father and grandfather [had been grand princes], while Prince Iurii Dmitrievich, his uncle, based his case upon the chronicles, the old charters and the Will of his father, Grand Prince Dmitrii.

Then Ivan Dmitrievich, the boyar of Grand Prince Vasilii Vasilievich, addressed the Khan and the Tatar lords: "Sovereign and voevodas! Permit me, servant of the Grand Prince, to speak. Our sovereign Grand Prince, Vasilii Vasilievich, is seeking for himself the Grand Principality, which is a part of your state; and he seeks it [on the basis] of your [Khan's] own decrees and charters; and this right of bestowal is before you. Our lord Prince Iurii Dmitrievich, his uncle, however, wishes to have the Grand Principality not on the basis of Your Autocrat's bestowal but on the basis of the charter of his dead father. You are free in your realm, however, to bestow [The Grand Principality] according to your will to whomsoever you wish. Already our [late] lord Grand Prince Vasilii Dmitrievich gave the Grand Principality to his son, Grand Prince Vasilievich, and he did so in agreement with your bestowal. And my lord has already been on his throne for several years on the basis of Your bestowal, ruling according [to the will] of You, his Sovereign and Autocrat, and this is known to You." And then Khan Mohammed gave the Grand Principality to Prince Vasilii Vasilievich and commanded his uncle, Prince Iurii Dmitrievich, to lead his horse. Grand Prince Vasilii Vasilievich [however] did not wish this or to dishonor his uncle.

Shirin Tiagin opposed the Khan and wanted to leave him because at that time Khan Kichik Ahmet set out against Khan Mohammed.[28] The latter took fright at doing this[29] and, heeding Shirin Tiagin's counsel, added the city of Dmitrov with the adjacent *volosts*[30] to the principality of Prince Iurii Dmitrievich, and the Khan let them go to their patrimonies.

Grand Prince Vasilii Vasilievich came to Moscow on St. Peter's

28. Ulug Mohammed, Grekov, p. 42.
29. That is, at dishonoring Prince Iurii Dmitrievich.
30. *Volost* is a territory which includes several towns.

Day and with him was the Khan's envoy, Lord Mansur Ulan. The **1433** latter let him ascend the throne of the Grand Principality, near [the Church of] the Most Holy [Mother of God] at the Golden Gates. And Prince Iurii Dmitrievich, his uncle, went to his patrimony, to Zvenigorod, and from thence to Dmitrov.

The same year in the month of June Prince Andrei Dmitrievich of Mozhaisk, uncle of Grand Prince Vasilii Vasilievich, passed away in his patrimony of Mozhaisk and his body was brought to Moscow and was buried in the Cathedral of the Archangel [Michael].

The same year Prince Iurii Dmitrievich, fearing his nephew, Grand Prince Vasilii Vasilievich, went from Dmitrov to Galich, and the Grand Prince took Dmitrov for himself and either deported or arrested his uncle's officials.

In the Year 6941 [1433]. Ivan Dmitrievich [Vsevolozhskii], the boyar of Grand Prince Vasilii Vasilievich—who, with his counsel and loyal heart had gained in the Horde the Grand Principality for him from Khan Mohammed—wanted Grand Prince Vasilii Vasilievich to marry his daughter. He talked of this with the Grand Prince. But Grand Prince Vasilii Vasilievich and his mother, Sofia Vitovtovna, who were in Moscow, did not want this but wished for him the daughter of Iaroslav [as wife]. And so Grand Prince Vasilii Vasilievich became engaged to Princess Maria, daughter of Iaroslav, granddaughter of Vladimir [hero of Kulikova], great granddaughter of Andrei Ivanovich and the granddaughter of Maria Goltiaeva. And because of this offense Ivan Dmitrievich left Moscow and went to Prince Konstantin Dmitrievich of Uglich, who was the uncle of Grand Prince Vasilii Vasilievich, and from thence to Tver', and from Tver' to Galich to Prince Iurii Dmitrievich, uncle of Grand Prince Vasilii Vasilievich.

The same winter on the eighth day of February Grand Prince Vasilii Vasilievich married Princess Maria, daughter of Iaroslav Vladimirovich and granddaughter of Maria Goltiaeva.

The same winter Ivan Dmitrievich moved from Tver' to Galich to Prince Iurii Dmitrievich, and advised him to seize the Grand Principality. Heeding his suggestions, Prince Iurii sent for his children, Prince Vasilii and Prince Dmitrii Shemiaka, who were then in Moscow at the wedding of Grand Prince Vasilii Vasilievich. There [at the wedding] Petr Konstantinovich[31] noticed that Prince Vasilii

31. Petr Konstantinovich was namestnik of Grand Prince Vasilii Vasilievich in Rostov.

1433   Iurievich [son of Iurii Dmitrievich] had a golden belt with chains and gems, one which once had been given [as dowry] by Prince Dmitrii Konstantinovich of Suzdal' to Grand Prince Dmitrii Ivanovich [Donskoi]. We write of this because it was the beginning of the great evil. During that wedding of Grand Prince Dmitrii Ivanovich the tysiatskii, Vasilii, substituted it [the belt], giving a smaller one to the Grand Prince, and the [original] belt he gave to his son, Mikula, who was married to Maria, [another] daughter of the same Prince Dmitrii Konstantinovich of Suzdal'; and [later] Mikula gave this belt as a gift to [boyar] Ivan Dmitrievich [Vsevolozhskii]. Ivan Dmitrievich, however, gave it to Prince Andrei Vladimirovich, who married his daughter. After the death of Prince Andrei and after the journey to the Horde, Ivan Dmitrievich arranged the engagement of his granddaughter, the daughter of Prince Andrei, to Prince Vasilii Iurievich, and gave him that belt. And at the wedding of Grand Prince Vasilii Vasilievich it was on him [Prince Vasilii Iurievich].

[Noticing it] Grand Princess Sofia at once took his belt away from him and therefore Prince Vasilii Iurievich and Prince Dmitrii Iurievich hurried from Moscow to their father in Galich, sacked the city of Iaroslavl', and robbed the treasuries of all the princes [there].

PRINCE IURII DMITRIEVICH WAGES WAR AGAINST HIS NEPHEW, GRAND PRINCE VASILII VASILIEVICH

When they [Princes Vasilii Iurievich and Dmitrii Iurievich] went to their father in Galich, he was already prepared with his people to march against the Grand Prince. Upon their arrival [Prince Iurii Dmitrievich] went with them and with strong forces against Grand Prince Vasilievich, and Ivan Dmitrievich [Vsevolozhskii] was with them; but the Grand Prince did not know of this. At that time Petr Konstantinovich rushed from Rostov, where he was namestnik, to Grand Prince Vasilii Vasilievich and told him that his uncle, Prince Iurii Dmitrievich, was marching against him with his children and with vast forces, and that he was already in Pereiaslavl'. The Grand Prince could not manage to do anything, but he sent to them his envoys, Fedor Andreevich Lozh and Fedor Tovarkov, to talk [of peace] and they met him at the Trinity [and St. Sergius] Monastery. He did not want peace, however, and marched forward because [boyar] Ivan Dmitrievich did not provide

any opportunity to speak even one word about peace. Between the **1433**
two boyars [Fedor Lozh and Vsevolozhskii] there was a great argument and indecent words, and the envoys of the Grand Prince
returned, having achieved nothing.

Grand Prince Vasilii Vasilievich, also, mobilized his people who
were around him, as well as the merchants of Moscow and others,
and went against Prince Iurii, meeting him on the river Kliazma,
twenty versts from Moscow. There were many warriors with Prince
Iurii but very few with the Grand Prince. He fought with them,
however, and from the people of Moscow there was little help
because many of them were drunk, having brought mead along so
as to have something to drink. Grand Prince Vasilii Vasilievich,
realizing that help was not forthcoming from anywhere, retreated
rapidly to Moscow. Frightened, he took his mother, Sofia, and his
[wife] Princess Maria, and hurried forthwith to Tver', and from
Tver' to Kostroma. This battle occurred on the twenty-fifth day of
the month of April, on Saturday, on the eve of the holiday of the
Myrrh-Bearing Women.

ABOUT PRINCE IURII DMITRIEVICH AND HIS SONS

Prince Iurii Dmitrievich came to Moscow, seized suzerainty
over the Grand Principality and sent his children to get his nephew,
Grand Prince Vasilii Vasilievich. They were told that the Grand
Prince was in the city of Kostroma and Prince Iurii Dmitrievich,
himself, and his children went thither to Kostroma with vast forces.
When he arrived at Kostroma he captured him and he [Prince
Vasilii Vasilievich], shedding tears and weeping, petitioned boyar
Semion Morozov, who was in great favor with his uncle [Prince
Iurii Dmitrievich]. Prince Iurii Dmitrievich honored and loved this
Semion very much. [Boyar] Ivan Dmitrievich became wroth at this
because he did not like it at all that [Prince Iurii Dmitrievich] had
pardoned him [Prince Vasilii Vasilievich] and even wanted to give
him an appanage. In this respect he was not alone because other
boyars and servants [of Prince Iurii] became very angry at this
because they did not like it at all.

ABOUT SEMION MOROZOV

[Boyar] Semion Morozov, however, was very influential with
his lord, Prince Iurii Dmitrievich, and he interceded on behalf of
Grand Prince Vasilii Vasilievich and attained for him the peace

1433   and love [of Prince Iurii Dmitrievich] and the appanage of Kolomna. Prince Iurii Dmitrievich offered a banquet in honor of his nephew, Grand Prince Vasilii Vasilievich, to whom he gave many presents, and let him go with all his boyars to his appanage of Kolomna. This peace, love and appanage were the work of Semion Morozov, the favorite of Prince Iurii.

Arriving in Kolomna, Grand Prince Vasilii Vasilievich summoned all his people from everywhere and very many gathered around him. Also, the princes, boyars, voevodas, the gentry, and the servicemen began to break away from Prince Iurii Dmitrievich on behalf of Grand Prince Vasilii Vasilievich, and they were going uninterruptedly from Moscow to Kolomna, and there were both the small and the great because none of them liked Semion Morozov, the favorite of Prince Iurii. The children of Prince Iurii— Prince Vasilii the One-Eyed[32] and Prince Dmitrii Shemiaka, as well as Prince Dmitrii the Handsome—realizing that no one among the Muscovites remained for their father, felt offended and embarrassed; and there Prince Vasilii the One-Eyed and Prince Dmitrii Shemiaka, sons of Iurii, on the porch of the shore side [of the palace] killed boyar Semion Morozov, their father's favorite, saying, "You, malefactor, intriguer, you arranged all this misfortune for our father and us. For a long time you have been an intriguer and evil-doer." And so, killing him, they left him dead and themselves went to Kostroma. Prince Iurii, realizing how uncertain was his rule of the Grand Principality, that his children had run away from him and that all the people were joining the Grand Prince, sent to the Grand Prince, saying, "Return to the Grand Principality, to Moscow, and I will go to Zvenigorod." And so he went to Zvenigorod, and from thence to Galich.

ABOUT GRAND PRINCE VASILII VASILIEVICH

And Grand Prince Vasilii Vasilievich came to Moscow, assumed the Grand Principality, made peace with his uncle, Prince Iurii, on condition that the latter not receive his children or help them.

ABOUT THE SONS OF PRINCE IURII

The same year Grand Prince Vasilii Vasilievich sent his voe-

---

32. Or "Crosseyed"; it was later that Prince Vasilii was blinded, although only one eye was actually destroyed.

voda, Prince Iurii Patrikeevich,[33] with his retinue and many people   **1434**
in arms, toward the city of Kostroma, against Prince Vasilii and
Prince Dmitrii Shemiaka, the sons of Iurii. And with the latter there
marched the levies of Viatka and the levies of Galich. They came
to the river Kus so as to fight. They routed the army of the Grand
Prince and captured Prince Iurii Patrikeevich, voevoda of the Grand
Prince. They went again to Kostroma, and when the Volga froze
they moved to Turdei's ravines.

The same summer Prince Iurii Semionovich came with his
princess from Lithuania to Great Novgorod. The same summer
there was a conflagration in Novgorod and the Zagorodskii and
Liudin sections burned, up to Luke Street. The same year was
completed the building of the stone Church of St. George in Bor-
kovets. The same summer in Novgorod Monk Euthymius, who was
nominated Bishop, built in his lord bishop's court a stone palace
which had thirty doors, and it was built by German masters from
beyond the sea and by Novgorodian masters.

HOW THE GRAND PRINCE CAMPAIGNED AGAINST PRINCE IURII

In the Year 6942 [1434]. Grand Prince Vasilii Vasilievich heard
of the treason of his uncle, Prince Iurii Dmitrievich, because in the
battle [on the river Kus in 1433] his voevodas with many troops
were with his—Iurii's—children. Therefore the Grand Prince
started campaigning against him with a great army and went toward
Galich. He [Prince Iurii Dmitrievich] escaped to Beloozero, and
the Grand Prince took the city of Galich and burned it and captured
people and did much evil to this land; and returned to Moscow.
But Prince Iurii Dmitrievich returned to Galich, sent for his children, and began gathering [troops] against the Grand Prince; and
he assembled great forces and brought along the people of Viatka.

PRINCE IURII DMITRIEVICH WITH HIS CHILDREN CAMPAIGNS AGAINST GRAND PRINCE VASILII VASILIEVICH

And he went the same spring against the Grand Prince, and
with him were his children—Prince Vasilii the Crosseyed, and two
other [sons], the Princes Dmitrii Shemiaka and Dmitrii the Handsome—with strong forces. Hearing of this, Grand Prince Vasilii

33. Prince Iurii Patrikeevich was the son of the Lithuanian Prince
Patrikei Narimantovich, but joined the Grand Prince of Moscow as a service
prince.

1434   Vasilievich moved against him, together with Prince Ivan of
Mozhaisk. And they met near the [Monastery of] St. Nicholas on
a mountain in the Rostov region, and on St. Lazarus' Saturday
there was a battle between them. Prince Iurii Dmitrievich won and
the Grand Prince escaped to Novgorod the Great, while Ivan of
Mozhaisk [fled] to Tver' because his mother also had fled thither,
to her daughter. And the Grand Prince sent to Prince Ivan of
Mozhaisk [his boyar], Andrei Fedorovich Goltiaev, asking him not
to abandon him but to stand together with him. Prince Ivan
answered Andrei, telling the Grand Prince, "My Sovereign Lord,
wheresoever I shall be, I will be your man, provided only that I
not lose now my patrimony and that my mother not be obliged to
roam in foreign lands; but otherwise, I am always yours."

But Prince Iurii [also] sent him Iakov Shestov, asking him to
come, and Prince Ivan of Mozhaisk went from Tver' to meet Prince
Iurii at the Holy Trinity [and St. Sergius Monastery]; and [then]
went with him to Moscow. On Wednesday of Holy Week Prince
Iurii Dmitrievich approached the city of Moscow and remained
near the city for a week, and on Wednesday of Easter Week he
took Moscow and captured the Grand Princesses [Sofia and Maria],
sent them to Zvenigorod, and began to rule the Grand Principality.
[In the meantime] the Grand Prince went from Novgorod to
Mologa, then to Kostroma, and from thence to Nizhnii Novgorod;
Prince Iurii Dmitrievich sent after him his sons, Dmitrii Shemiaka
and Dmitrii the Handsome, who came to the city of Vladimir with
great strength. The Grand Prince could not expect help from anywhere and wanted to go to the Horde. When the Princes Dmitrii
were in the city of Vladimir they received the tidings that their
father, Prince Iurii, had passed away and that their senior brother,
Prince Vasilii [the Crosseyed] had started ruling in the Grand Principality, in Moscow. Thereupon he sent to them to announce their
father's death, his [own good] health, and his rule; but they responded, "God did not want our father to rule; but we, ourselves,
do not want you."

ABOUT GRAND PRINCE VASILII VASILIEVICH

And they sent to Nizhnii Novgorod for Grand Prince Vasilii
Vasilievich. And the Grand Prince came, they made peace, and he
marched to Moscow while Prince Vasilii Iurievich the Crosseyed
fled from Moscow to the Horde after ruling the Grand Principality

for one month. Grand Prince Vasilii Vasilievich came and took over **1435**
his patrimony and began to rule in the Grand Principality of Moscow. He gave the [appanage of] Uglich and Rzhev to Prince Dmitrii
Shemiaka; and to the junior Prince, Dmitrii the Handsome, he gave
Bezhetskii Verkh. Prince Vasilii Iurievich the Crosseyed [mean-
while] went to Kostroma and began to gather warriors against
Grand Prince Vasilii Vasilievich.

The same year the nominated Archbishop, Euthymius of Novgorod the Great, journeyed on the twenty-sixth day of May to
Metropolitan Gerasimus in Smolensk so as to receive consecration
because, since the passing of Photius, Metropolitan of Kiev and all
Russia, there was no Metropolitan in Moscow.

The same year Prince Vasilii Iurievich the Crosseyed came to
Novgorod the Great.

The same year the Lithuanians fought against the Germans.

The same year Prince Vasilii Iurievich the Crosseyed went to
the river Msta, to Bezhetskii Verkh, and to the Zavolochié, and
sacked there.

The same year in Novgorod posadnik Grigorii Kirillovich and
Osif Andrianovich Goroshkov built a stone Church of St. John
Chrysostom on the old basement in Kolotok.

PRINCE VASILII IURIEVICH CAMPAIGNED AGAINST THE GRAND PRINCE

In the Year 6943 [1435]. Grand Prince Vasilii Iurievich the
Crosseyed marched with strong forces from Kostroma to Moscow,
and Grand Prince Vasilii Vasilievich, hearing of this, assembled
[his forces] and went against him. On the sixth of January, they
met at [the Monastery of] Cosma and Damian of Kotorosl' in the
Iaroslavl' region and there was a battle between them. God helped
Grand Prince Vasilii Vasilievich, and Prince Vasilii Iurievich the
Crosseyed escaped to Kashin. Gathering [forces] in Kashin, he
moved out to Vologda against the vanguard of the Grand Prince.
When he arrived there he captured the Grand Prince's voevodas,
Fedor Mikhailovich Chelednia, Andrei Fedorovich Goltiaev, Vladimir Andreevich Zvorykin, Mikhail Chepetskin, and many others.
He went to Kostroma and sent for the levies of Viatka, and the
levies of Viatka joined him. Grand Prince Vasilii Vasilievich, learning of this, marched against him to Kostroma, and coming thither
he camped on the cape at the [Monastery of] Hypatius the Wonder-

1436   worker, which is between the Volga River and the Kostroma [River].
They could not fight because the river Kostroma was between them.
They made peace and Grand Prince Vasilii Vasilievich gave to
Prince Vasilii Iurievich the Crosseyed the city of Dmitrov as his
domain. That spring was very cold. Prince Vasilii Iurievich the
Crosseyed went to Dmitrov and sojourned there one month.

The same year the posadniks of Novgorod—Ivan Vasilievich
and Grigorii Kirillovich—and the Novgorodian tysiatskii, Fedor
Eliseevich, and many other voevodas with strong forces campaigned
against Rzhev, the Popovskii limit, and Borodov. They occupied
many districts and towns, and burned them, captured a multitude
of people of Rzhev, and took them back to Novgorod. The same
year Grand Prince Vasilii Vasilievich of Moscow and the Novgorodians pledged on the cross that the Grand Prince would not claim
the Novgorodian lands of Bezhetskii Verkh, Lamskii Volok and
Vologda, and that the Novgorodian boyars would not claim [lands]
of the Prince, wheresoever they might be; and that exchange of
the land would occur on St. Peter's Day; and that the boyars of the
Grand Prince and the Novgorodian boyars would be at the exchange.

The same year the Archbishop of Novgorod, Euthymius,
started building at his court over the gate a foundation of a stone
Church of St. John Chrysostom. It was completed the same year
and hardly did the people step away from the church than it completely collapsed to its foundation. This was a portent that the
power of the Novgorodian posadniks, tysiatskiis, all the boyars, and
the entire Novgorodian land would perish.

In the Year 6944 [1436]. Prince Vasilii Iurievich the Crosseyed
marched again from Dmitrov to Kostroma, sent his scouts to Grand
Prince Vasilii Vasilievich, and sojourned in Kostroma till the winter
roads were prepared. Then he journeyed to Galich, from thence
to Ustiug, and the levies of Viatka were with him. He sojourned
in Ustiug for nine weeks and captured the city of Ustiug, killing
Prince Gleb Ivanovich Obolenskii, voevoda of Grand Prince Vasilii
Vasilievich. He hanged Ivan Bulatov, *desiatnik* of the bishop of
Rostov. He hacked to pieces and hanged numerous people of Ustiug.

This very winter Prince Dmitrii Iurievich Shemiaka intended
to marry in Uglich the daughter of Prince Dmitrii of Zaozersk. He
journeyed to Moscow to invite Grand Prince Vasilii Vasilievich to

the wedding, but the Grand Prince arrested him and sent him to   **1436**
Kolomna under the supervision of the bailiff, Ivan Starkov.
Kolomna, however, remained his [Shemiaka's] own.

PRINCE VASILII IURIEVICH THE CROSSEYED CAMPAIGNS
FROM USTIUG AGAINST THE GRAND PRINCE

The same spring Prince Vasilii Iurievich, bragging proudly,
went from Ustiug against Grand Prince Vasilii Vasilievich, and with
him went the levies of Viatka and the retinue of his brother, Prince
Dmitrii Shemiaka. The Grand Prince gathered [troops] and met
him near [the Church of] the Intercession of the Holy Virgin in
Skoriatino in the Rostov region; and with Grand Prince Vasilii
Vasilievich were Prince Dmitrii Iurievich the Younger—the Handsome—and Prince Ivan Andreevich of Mozhaisk with his regiment.
At the same time from Lithuania there came, to serve the Grand
Prince, Prince Ivan Baba, who was from the family of the Princes
Drutskii; and he armed his regiment in the Lithuanian manner,
with lances, though all other regiments of the Grand Prince were
armed according to their [Russian] manner. Prince Vasilii Iurievich
the Crosseyed wanted to kidnap the Grand Prince, and sent to him
asking for an armistice till morning. Grand Prince Vasilii Vasilievich
agreed to an armistice and permitted his army to rest, and they
went to divide the provisions.

The same day Prince Vasilii Iurievich went to capture the
Grand Prince. The guard hurried to the Grand Prince, however,
announcing that Prince Vasilii Iurievich was marching rapidly
against him. Forthwith Grand Prince Vasilii Vasilievich sent to all
his camps while he, himself, seized a trumpet and began to trumpet.
At once the regiments of the Grand Prince assembled and marched
against the enemy. Fighting, they chased Prince Vasilii Iurievich
the Crosseyed and his men. Boris Tobolin caught up with Prince
Vasilii Iurievich, recognized him, captured him, and started shouting. Immediately he was joined by Prince Ivan Baba Drutskii and,
having identified Prince Vasilii Iurievich, brought him to Grand
Prince Vasilii Vasilievich. The Grand Prince sent him to Moscow,
[where] Prince Vasilii Iurievich the Crosseyed underwent blind-
ing.[34]

[Before] the Grand Prince marched against Prince Vasilii
Iurievich he commanded that the latter's brother, Prince Dmitrii

34. Apparently only one eye was damaged, which is the reason for
his later sobriquet, "the Crosseyed."

1437 Iurievich Shemiaka, be released from irons and held as a commoner in Kolomna. When, later, the Grand Prince defeated Prince Vasilii Iurievich and came to Moscow, he even sent to Kolomna for Prince Dmitrii Shemiaka and honored him.

The same year the Novgorodians met in *veché* and determined the exchange of land. They sent their posadnik, Grigorii Kirillovich, and Ivan Maksimovich, and the elders, Kozma Tarasievich and Ivan Maksimov, to Bezhetskii Verkh for the exchange of Novgorodian lands; and the others were sent to Volok Lamskii. Yet others were sent to Vologda to exchange the land of the Novgorodian dominion. Grand Prince Vasilii Vasilievich, however, did not send his boyars or return any Novgorodian land to the Novgorodians, or withdraw his troops, or give them any compensation.

The same year Archbishop Euthymius of Novgorod again laid a foundation and completed the building of a stone Church of St. John Chrysostom on the gate of his court in Novgorod. The same year Euthymius, Archbishop of Novgorod, laid a foundation for a stone Church of the Holy Wonderworker Nicholas [in the section of] Vezhishchi.

The same year, God willing, and because of our sins, it was terribly cold and the freeze destroyed all earthly fruit and produce just at the time of the harvest; and this occurred in the entire Russian land, and everything was extremely cold throughout the whole nation. In the city of Novgorod many people migrated to the Germans [of the Livonian Order], so intense became the starvation.

In the Year 6945 [1437]. On the twentieth of September, there was in Novgorod great fratricidal fighting. The same fall there was a great flood in Novgorod, and at night the ice broke seven piers of the main bridge and washed away the Zhilotuchskii bridge and did much evil to the Novgorodians.

The same winter the Novgorodians sent their posadnik, Grigorii Kirillovich, to Grand Prince Sigismund of Lithuania, who was the son of Keistut, cousin of Vitovt and grandson of Gedimin, asking for peace as it used to be of old; and Grand Prince Sigismund Keistutovich gave them his agreement, pledging on the cross before the Novgorodian envoys. He did this according to the Novgorodian charters for all Novgorod; and they established peace and friendship as it was of old from the beginning.

The same winter Prince Iurii Patrikeevich came to Novgorod

from Moscow from Grand Prince Vasilii Vasilievich, asking for the　**1437**
black lumber tax,[35] and the Novgorodians correctly paid the black
lumber tax to Grand Prince Vasilii Vasilievich.

THE COMING OF METROPOLITAN ISIDORE FROM CONSTANTINOPLE TO MOSCOW[36]

The same spring on Tuesday after Easter in Easter Week Metropolitan Isidore came from Patriarch Joseph, from Constantinople

35. *Chernyi bor*, or *chernyi sbor*: a general tax paid in the best timber during the fourteenth and fifteenth centuries by the Novgorodians to the Grand Prince of Moscow.

36. This description of Metropolitan Isidore's arrival in Russia begins the report of the Council of Florence in 1439. This report in *Obol.* is frequently interrupted by reports on other events in Russia in 1437–39. In the Council of Florence of the Orthodox and Catholic churches the Byzantine Emperor John VII and his administration and hierarchy attempted to get the military help of the West and, for this purpose, also, the moral support of the Pope for a crusade against the Ottoman Empire, which had conquered Asia Minor and most of the Balkans and was threatening Constantinople. For this very problematical help the Roman Pope Eugenius IV requested the complete submission of the Eastern Orthodox church to the authority of Rome, and the acceptance of Roman Catholic dogma by the Orthodox church. The Emperor and his hierarchs acquiesced but no help was forthcoming from the West to Byzantium. Fourteen years later—in 1453—Constantinople fell into Turkish hands.

Metropolitan Isidore, a Greek, was strongly inclined toward Union, and for the eastern church's subordination to Rome. Upon his arrival in Russia as head of the Russian church he straightaway left for Italy so as to participate in the Council, where he became the most enthusiastic supporter of Union. On this journey he was accompanied by Bishop Abraham of Suzdal' and by several other Russian and Greek clergymen and envoys. One of them, a Suzdalian priest named Simeon, wrote a strongly anti-Catholic report about the Council of Florence which is to be found in both *Ioasaf.* and *Obol.* These two texts of the "Story about the Eighth Council" are almost identical but in some cases have different wording and provide varying minor details. The text of this report in *Obol.* contains the full text of the decisions of the Council, which is unavailable in *Ioasaf.* According to A. Vasiliev (*History of Byzantium*, Univ. of Wisconsin Press, Vol. II, 1961, pp. 468–69), the Slavonic text of the *Decisions* of the Council (the *Encyclique* of Pope Eugenius) can be found together with Latin and Greek texts in the Laurentian Library in Florence, and was apparently written at the time of the Council. The Slavonic translation as found in *Obol.* is rather poorly done and many passages are hard to understand. In order to render the text more comprehensible, this Editor has used the English translation of the Latin text published by A. Gill in his *The Council of Florence* (Cambridge, 1959). The translation of this text from Latin to English was done by

1437   to Moscow, to rule the Russian Metropolia. He spoke several languages and was erudite. He was met with honor by Grand Prince Vasilii Vasilievich and there was a thanksgiving service in the holy Cathedral Church of the Most Pure Virgin, and Grand Prince Vasilii Vasilievich offered him a joyous banquet and presented him with numerous fair gifts.[37]

The same spring the Tatars approached Riazan' and sacked many frontier towns, then returned home.

The same spring in Novgorod water washed the foundations of the wall in the fortress and the earth eroded from the walls, causing the stone wall and stone belfry on the Volkhov River to collapse. The same spring the stone Church of St. John Chrysostom on the gate of the Archbishop's court was consecrated.—The same spring the Church of St. Nicholas in the Vezhishchi [section of the city] collapsed.—The same year Archbishop Euthymius of Novgorod tore down the old church and laid the foundation at the gate of his court of a stone Church of the Holy Wonderworker Metropolitan Peter of all Russia.—The same year Archbishop Euthymius of Novgorod, during the *veché* and according to tradition, blessed with the cross the posadniks, the tysiatskis, and all of Novgorod the Great, and on Sunday, the seventh day of the month of June, went to Moscow to Metropolitan Isidore of all Russia to receive his blessing and to greet him.

Professor David Redston, to whom this Editor herewith expresses his gratitude. Since, however, the Slavonic text in *Obol.* and the Latin one differ slightly in details, this Editor relied primarily on Slavonic texts, using the English one only to interpret some unclear passages. A. Kartashev (*Ocherki*, Vol. I, pp. 352–54) explains Isidore's attitude by his philosophical humanistic approach to the differences between the Roman Catholic and Orthodox churches.—*Ed.*

37. Isidore (died, 1462) was Greek or a Helenized Bulgarian, and began his career as abbot of a Byzantine Monastery of St. Demetrius. He was an unusually learned man and a decisive supporter of the Union of the eastern and western churches. He was appointed Metropolitan of Moscow because the Byzantine Patriarch and the court apparently expected considerable financial aid from the Russians during the forthcoming Council, at which the problem of Union was to be resolved. Indeed, Isidore collected financial aid from the Russian lands and during the Council in 1438–39 became the most vocal proponent of Union between Rome and Constantinople. Therefore, later, he had to leave Russia, and ended his life as a Cardinal of the Roman Catholic church.

ABOUT METROPOLITAN ISIDORE

The same year Isidore, Metropolitan of all Russia, began talks with Grand Prince Vasilii Vasilievich, telling him that the holy *Kyr*,[38] Patriarch Joseph, and the pious *Kyr*, Byzantine Emperor John, son of Manuel of Constantinople, discussed with the Holy Council, with the princes and with the boyars the need for an Eighth [Oecumenic] Council with the Pope and with all Romans. [This Council should discuss] the dissension and the schism between the Byzantine church and the Roman one, so that there should be no disputation between the lands and realms either about the Transubstantiation of the Most Pure and Most Honorable Body and Blood of Christ which are in the leavened bread and in the wafers, or about [the Procession of] the Holy Spirit; and it was in this way that this earlier supporter [Isidore] of this Council acted. The Grand Prince told him, "Under our forefathers and fathers there was no such union of our [Orthodox] law with the Romans, and I don't want it because we have not received anything from the Greeks concerning this union of law."

Metropolitan Isidore, however, did not heed this and endeavored with all his heart to go to this Eighth Council in the Roman land, to Pope Eugenius, to the Patriarch Joseph, and to the Byzantine *Kyr* and Emperor John. And Grand Prince Vasilii Vasilievich told him, "Father Isidore, we do not advise you to go to the Eighth Council, to the Latin land. You, however, not heeding us, wish to journey thither. You should know, however, that when you return to us you must bring us back our Christian faith of the Greek law which our forefathers received from the Greeks." And he [Isidore] promised to deal thus, and swore that he would not bring anything strange or alien from the Latins or from the Eighth Council to the Russian land but that he would observe true Orthodoxy of the Greek law; he believed that he was wiser than the wise; but, finally, he came to an agreement with those who lost their minds.

In the Year 6946 [1438]. On the fifteenth of September the Princess Eupraksia passed away and she was buried by Isidore, Metropolitan of Kiev and all Russia, and with all the Holy Council, with psalms and with burial chants.

The same fall a son, Iurii the elder, was born to Grand Prince Vasilii Vasilievich.

38. *Kyr*: Greek for "lord."

1438   ABOUT KHAN MAHMET [MOHAMMED]

The same fall Khan Ulug Mohammed[39] of the Great Horde came to the city of Belev and occupied Belev because he [had perforce] to escape from his brother, Kichik Mohammed,[40] Khan of the Great Horde. The same fall in the month of November Grand Prince Vasilii Vasilievich sent against him two princes, Prince Dmitrii Iurievich Shemiaka and the latter's brother, Prince Dmitrii Iurievich the Handsome, and a great many other princes with large armed troops, while the Khan at that time was with small forces. They [the princes and the Russian forces], however, marching toward Belev, sacked their own Orthodox Christians and tormented people so as to get their wealth and their cattle, and they beat them and sent [their booty] back home and did indecent and evil things. When they came to Belev, the Khan took fright, seeing a great many Russian regiments, and said he would do as the Russian princes desired. They did not heed the Khan's speech, however. In the morning, having prepared for battle, the Russian regiments drew near the city. The Tatars made a sortie against them and a great battle ensued. God helped the Christians. They slew many Tatars, killed the Khan's brother-in-law and many Tatars and their princes, and forced them back into the city. On that occasion Prince Peter Kuzminskoi and Semion Volynets were slain in the city. They chased the Tatars into the middle of the city while the other warriors returned from the city. The next morning the Khan sent to the Russian princes and voevodas his brother-in-law, Ali-Berdei, and the *dorogas*,[41] Princes Hussein Saraev and Hussein Khodja. Vasilii Ivanovich Sobakin and Andrei Fedorovich Galtiaev met them to negotiate. The Tatars told them, "Our Khan's word to you is the following: 'I give you as hostage my son, Mamutek, and our princes also give their own. I promise, in the case Allah helps me to be the Khan, as long as I live I will guard the Russian lands and will not ask any tribute or anything else.'"

But they [the Russian envoys] did not agree. Then the Tatar princes told the Grand Prince's voevodas, "You did not agree? Then look behind you." And they looked and saw that their Russian warriors were running away, not pursued by anyone. Because of

39. "Mahmet" in *Nik.*, "Ulug Mohammed," correct name.
40. "Ahmet" in *Nik.*
41. *Dorogas*: financial officials or envoys.

our pride and our many sins, God permitted the infidels to over-   **1438**
come numerous Orthodox Christian troops, because when they
marched they did wrong toward their own; and because of them
many Christians perished. Therefore a small army of infidels overcame [the Russian forces] in such a way that one son of Hagar was
able to overcome and slaughter ten of ours and even more. The
leading princes escaped in good health, and this happened the fifth
day of the month of December. In this battle were killed Andrei
Konstantinovich Shonurov, Prince Fedor Tarusskii, Prince Andrei
Lobanov of Starodub, Nikita Turikov, Semion Gorstkin, Kuzma
Porkhovskoi, Ivan Kuzminskoi, Andrei Khorobrov, Dmitrii Kaka,
and a great many others.

ABOUT METROPOLITAN ISIDORE

The same fall Metropolitan of all Russia, Isidore the Greek,
journeyed from Moscow to Novgorod the Great, and with him was
Euthymius, Archbishop of Novgorod. The other Russian bishops
bade them honorable farewell. Isidore came to Novgorod, blessed
everyone and was honored by the Archbishop and posadniks,
tysiatskis and boyars, and merchants, and all Novgorod the Great.
They gave him, according to tradition, what was due and according
to tradition they gave him all the taxes. Thereafter, in the winter,
Metropolitan Isidore went to Pskov, [then] to the Germans
[Livonia], then to Rome, to the Eighth Council, to Eugenius, Pope
of Rome, to the Greek *Kyr* and Emperor John of Constantinople,
and to the *Kyr* and Oecumenic Patriarch Joseph. And the people
of Pskov received him honorably and he consecrated for them in
Pskov the Archimandrite Gelatius; and they gave him his dues,
according to tradition, and gave him all taxes according to tradition,
and presented many gifts to him. From Pskov he journeyed to the
Germans [Livonia], then to the Eighth Council, and the Germans
bade him farewell honorably. He came to the city of Iur'iev in the
German land[42] and all Orthodox Christians and all priests of the
Greek law who lived there met him with crosses. The Latins and
all Germans, however, met him with crucifixes, according to their

42. The city of Iur'iev, founded by Iaroslav the Wise, later situated
in the territory of the German Livonian Knights, is now in the Estonian
S.S.R. It is also called "Dorpat," or "Tartu" in Estonian.

1439   Roman law.[43] Isidore, breaking his oath—because he had sworn before Grand Prince Vasilii Vasilievich to be pious [Orthodox] first went and bowed and made the sign of the cross and kissed the crucifix of the Roman law. Thereupon he went to the holy crosses of the Greek law, and he accompanied the crucifix of the Roman law into the temple—that is to say, their church—and he rendered them honor and accompanied them, but he did not respect in the same way the [cross of the] Greek law.

ABOUT ABRAHAM, BISHOP OF SUZDAL'[44]

Seeing this, God-loving Abraham, Bishop of Suzdal',[45] and all those Orthodox Christians travelling with him were seized by fear because [Isidore] behaved in this [pro-Roman] manner before even viewing the Council.

The same spring on Palm Saturday the city of Kolomna burned and little was left of it. It burned during vespers and stopped at sunset, and the people began to move after the fire.

The same spring the Tatars campaigned against Riazan' and performed much evil, then returned home.

The same year the Tatars raided Lithuania and returned home with many captives. The same year Prince Iurii Semionovich of Lithuania came to Novgorod. The same year in Novgorod in the Vezhishchi section there was built a stone Church of St. Nicholas in place of the collapsed one and on the same foundation.

ABOUT METROPOLITAN ISIDORE

In the Year 6947 [1439]. Isidore the Greek, Metropolitan of Kiev and all Russia, came to Eugenius, Pope of Rome, to the vainacting Eighth Council in the Roman land in the city of Ferrara. He found there the Greek Emperor John, son of Manuel, of Constantinople, and with him the Oecumenic Patriarch Joseph. And with

43. The Russian cross differs from the Latin one in the number of crossbeams (three). The Latin cross, also, may have a sculptured figure of Christ.

44. The author of the Russian report on the Council of Ferrara and of Florence was Monk Simeon, who accompanied Bishop Abraham of Suzdal' to the Council. This report is strongly pro-Orthodox and anti-Roman.

45. Bishop Abraham of Suzdal' was the only Russian bishop to go with Metropolitan Isidore to the Council.

them were [Bessarion] the Metropolitan of the Emperor of **1439**
Trapizond[46] and Metropolitan of the Tsar of Iberia,[47] and there
were also many [other Orthodox] metropolitans from other lands.
And there were bishops, and their number was one hundred and
twenty. And there were many erudite people and many great elders,
and many philosophers, and simple Greek elders and lay people,
and a great many other Greeks. There were also archbishops,
bishops and monks from Latin lands: from Aquitania [South-West-
ern France], from the Latins, from Allemania [Germany], Italians,
people of Galata [West European section of Constantinople], and
French people, and people from Brabant and from Kafa,[48] and
there were a great many of them. But they did not start the Council,
only examined the books, waiting for advice from Metropolitan
Isidore of all Russia. Emperor and *Kyr* John, son of Manuel, told
Eugenius, Pope of Rome, and all others present, the following
words: "In the Russian eastern land there is a great Orthodoxy
and the highest Christianity is in this White Russian land, and there
as Sovereign is my great brother, Vasilii Vasilievich, to whom the
eastern rulers listen, and the grand princes with their lands serve
him. Only because of his humility, his piety and the magnitude of
his Orthodox mind he does not call himself 'Emperor' but only the
'Grand Prince' of his Russian Orthodox lands."

And therefore the Council did not meet for six months. When
Metropolitan Isidore came to them, then a great many of his people
met him with great honor for the sake of glorifying the name of
the great Tsar Vasilii Vasilievich of all Russia. After a few days the
Council began. The first time the council met in the month of
September.[49] Pope Eugenius entered the temple, which is called a

46. Bessarion, originally of Trapizond—at that time actually Metropolitan of Nicaea—was, together with Metropolitan Isidore, one of the
staunchest supporters of the Union of the Orthodox church with Rome.
He was a rather limited man but apparently considered that the preservation of Constantinople from the Turks was more important than differences in dogma and rites. The Byzantine Emperor John and his court
hoped that after Union the Western powers would initiate a crusade against
the Turks to save Byzantium. The Union, although shortlived, was proclaimed but no crusaders came to help Byzantium.

47. Iberia: Medieval name for present-day Georgia in the Caucasus.

48. Kafa was an important trade city in the Crimea specialized in slave
trade, dominated by merchants from Genoa and Crimean Jews.

49. Actually, the Council opened October 8, 1438.

1439   church, and with him were Latin archbishops and bishops. And he stayed on the left side. The Emperor and Patriarch were on the right side, on the throne. Then there were brought the shrines of the Holy [Apostles] Peter and Paul, of silver and gold, and before them three candles were burned. And ahead of them [the members of the Council] were tables for the philosophers, and in front of the Emperor was the table for the theologians. And at the table of the philosophers were put the wise people: the Roman Cardinal Julian, and with him the Greeks—John of Bologna and Andrian of Crete.[50] And at the table of the theologians before the Emperor were Mark, Metropolitan of Ephesus, representing the Patriarch of Alexandria; Isidore, representing the Patriarch of Antiochia; and Bessarion of Nicea, representing the Patriarch of Jerusalem. And thereupon the Council commenced.

When the Pope entered the temple he fell slightly on one knee, according to the Latin way, and moved forward and took his place. Thereafter a bishop began [celebrating a Mass] loudly in the Latin language. And there were quite a number of singing seminarians. Thereafter [everyone] began to talk and the interpreters also talked, speaking in three languages: Greek, Italian, and philosophic.[51] And there were many books brought before them, and after their talk they parted.

And so they continued for three days, but nothing happened among them because when the Italians began to speak the Greeks were reveling. When the holiday of great John the Theologian arrived[52] the assembly met for the fourth time[53] and, according to the earlier rules, the Italians[54] were [again] the first to start speaking. And many books were brought, and there was a great argument among them, and they [the Italians and Greeks] could not agree.

Blessed Mark, Metropolitan of Ephesus, addressed them with peaceful intention and in accordance with divine reason, and tried to persuade them with salutary words. He told them meekly and reverently the following:[55]

50. Probably John of Colosses and Andrew of Rhodes.
51. "Philosophic"—apparently, Latin.
52. John the Theologian: May 9.
53. The fourth public session took place on October 30. There is some confusion in dating.
54. Their main speaker was Cardinal Cesarini.
55. The main speech of Metropolitan Mark occurred during the third session of the Council on September 3.

"Kind fathers! In agreement with the instruction of our [Greek]   **1439**
fathers who met in council in the Imperial City [Constantinople],
we question you about the *Articles of Faith*. Give us this [exact answer]
and you will receive [the same] from us. Who can be convinced by
your teaching should you not give [an exact answer]? What do you
accept? Proclamation and confession of faith which one accepts
does not allow any amendment or exclusion. It was decided and
sealed [forever by the Church Fathers] and then whosoever should
try to introduce anything new should be excommunicated, and
those who attempt to make more [changes] should be punished.
You regard the above-mentioned addition [*Filioque*] a small one.[56]
[In your] mind this is a small word and harms very little or even
not at all, and [you think] if you use it widely it will unite all Christians. But this addition is a major one and there is much to be said
concerning it, and we sin when we accept it. If it were added for
better understanding, it should [now] be removed for a better
[chance] of comprehension, and you would win brethren who are
tormented [by it] and who have so much love [for God]. We beseech
you [to do this], most honorable brethren and lords, just as we
beseeched you before. We do so for the sake of the grace of Our
Lord Jesus Christ, Who loved us and sacrificed His life for us who
were dissolute, sinful, and desperate.

"Let us return to the holy accord which we used to have between
us and which was in concord with the Holy Fathers, when all of us
confessed the same[57] and when there was no schism between us.
Try to understand each other. Let us be ashamed [of our disunity].
In [the spiritual presence of] our common Holy Fathers, let us
respect their rules, let us fear interdiction, let us preserve the tradition, and then in unanimous harmony and unity of spirit we can
glorify the Most Precious and Magnificent Name of Father, Son
and Holy Ghost. And now it would be salutary for you, Latins, to

56. Mark of Ephesus spoke here concerning the Procession of the
Holy Ghost. According to the Nicene Creed, which was preserved in integ-
rity by the Eastern church, the Holy Ghost proceeds from the Father. In
the eighth century the Roman Catholic church began to add the words,
"*Filioque*" ["and Son"] to this *Article*. This dogmatic difference about the
interpretation of the procession of the Holy Ghost, together with recogni-
tion of the supreme authority of the Pope, were the main problems which
separate the Eastern church from the Western one.

57. That is, when all Christians accepted the *Articles of Faith* without
the *Filioque*.

1439 learn the divine truth and not to tell a falsehood, not to lie about the Holy Fathers, not to claim any false writ, not to divide [the definition of the Procession] of the Holy Ghost, and not to use unleavened bread. Let us believe in the decision of the seven holy [Oecumenic] Councils and follow the covenant of the Holy Fathers. Let us not reject or blame them, and let us not convoke any eighth Council, or call it thus [as you do]. You would better study the teachings of the seven blessed Popes [of Rome], look into the Holy Book and follow the prescription of the oecumenic teacher, St. John Chrysostom, and adhere to the rules of the Holy Apostles and of the divinely blessed Fathers of the seven Holy [Oecumenic] Councils. And having adhered to the writ of the saints, put it [at the basis of your dogma] and do not speak from a seductive and erroneous one. Thus let us correctly, according to divine law of the holy rules, address our prayers to Almighty and Merciful God and celebrate the church service and glorify the memory of the Holy Apostles and Holy Fathers, Basil the Great, Gregory the Theologian, John Chrysostom, all the fathers of the seven Oecumenic Councils who were directed by God, and the most holy Oecumenic Popes of Rome, beginning with Sylvester and unto Hadrian. And all these saints will pray to God for us and will bring us to truthful reason. Then Lord God will open the mind of wisdom and will manifest to everyone His true divine word. And God will appease the feelings of the hearts of our souls so that all of us will hear and understand the truth and will follow the right path; and then the feet of our reason will not stumble.

"And you, honorable Pope Eugenius! You should correctly argue about all these [questions] and have a right mind because you summoned to this populous Council the pious Emperor John, son of Manuel, the Holy Oecumenic Patriarch Joseph, many eastern Metropolitans and bishops from everywhere, and the honorable Oecumenic[58] Councils and the upright archimandrites and abbots and numerous priests and monks, and the intelligent, very wise philosophers and virtuous and active monks!

"In the Name of God, act truthfully and verily and then the work of this Council will not be in vain. [Let us hope] that it was not about us that the Prophet David said, 'Tongues speak senselessly and the people teach in vain.' The princes of the people have met

58. Unclear—*Ed.*

here for [the word of] God and of His [Son, Jesus] Christ. Let us   **1439**
be careful. Let it not happen that the faithful Orthodox people
hear that you reject the truth but love temptation and wrongdoing
because then they will laugh at your vainly disputing meeting. And
if you do not want to contribute to the truth and will not follow
the path of God, then you should know, yourself, what the Prophet
said about such [untruthful people]: 'If you do not want to hear
me, weapons will strike you.' And this was spoken by the mouth
of God."

It was in such kind and enduring words that Mark, Metropolitan of Ephesus, argued and humbly addressed them. Then, however, the Roman Cardinal Julian[59] arose from his place and, being
mightily upset because he could not abide such words, went to Pope
Eugenius and said to him, "Honorable Pope, holy teacher, have
you heard this abuse which Mark has spoken about you? He has
called your books false, and he does not want to recognize your
Council as a Council. He does not mention your name before other
[patriarchs during the church sevice]; he does not want to call an
Eighth Council but wants only to follow the seven Councils, and
teaches us concerning them."

Hearing these words from him, Pope Eugenius became very
embarrassed and said to the Byzantine Emperor John and to the
Oecumenic Patriarch Joseph: "Emperor John, and you, Patriarch
Joseph, did you hear what abuse against me was spoken by Mark,
Metropolitan of Ephesus, and that he denies my books?" The Emperor then answered, saying, "We did not hear any detraction spoken by Mark and everything which Mark said before us was just."

And then Eugenius, Pope of Rome, ordered that a great many
books be brought which would embarrass Mark. Blessed Mark,
Metropolitan of Ephesus, became upset in heart and, greatly burning in mind about their Latin temptations and seeing that the people
of God were confused and ready to accept the seduction of their
[the Latins'] heresy, he began to speak angrily, saying the following:

"Oh, Latins! Oh, Latins! If you do not give up your wild insol-
ence, speaking untruth about the Fathers and teachers of the seven
holy Oecumenic Councils summoned by God, and against the seven

59. Not Julian, but John, or Giovanni di Montenero, provincial Patriarch of Lombardy, was the main Roman speaker on the dogma of the
Filioque.

1439   most blessed Popes, then you should know that soon you will stop speaking your insolent, lying speeches."

And at this very time Mark angrily said to someone, "Get out of here! Don't remain here!" And then a monk fled rapidly. At that time the Italians and the Latins were in consternation, and Pope Eugenius arose from his place and walked out, and so did all the cardinals, archbishops and bishops, Italians, Germans and all the Latins, who could not abide the words of Mark. There remained only the Greeks and the Russians. Then Emperor John, son of Manuel, and Patriarch Joseph questioned Mark, saying, "What evil thing did you say to Pope Eugenius and the cardinals? For they have left their places."

Mark, Metropolitan of Ephesus, answered, telling them, "Hear, pious Emperor John, and you, Oecumenic Patriarch Joseph. One who does wrong can not listen to the truth. Of such the Prophet said, 'The mouths of those who speak lies became stopped.' And I can only say to them, 'One who will step away from the Covenant of the Holy Apostles and Holy Fathers of the seven Holy Councils summoned by God and from the seven holy Popes who were Oecumenic teachers—those will be anathema. And therefore they ran from their places. Remember how you, yourself, said in Constantinople, that the Latins are not Christians, for how can they be Christians? Now and ever they can not listen to the truth. How can they follow the true path? What kind of unity can there be between us and them and how can there be one united church which rejects the truth of God? But you, Your Majesty, Emperor, should know that you should tell them that the Latins produced the schism in the holy divine Church, that they rejected the Orthodox faith. And then when they are exposed, they would not listen, and they would escape even from the city because of their wrongdoing. Now hear, Emperor John, what the Pope says. He does not want to pray [during the liturgy] for you, the Emperor. Neither does he want to call [our Eastern] Patriarchs his brethren, but he commands that his name, Pope Eugenius, be mentioned in all churches of the entire world. But if we first mention Pope Eugenius, then he will command us to celebrate the liturgy with unleavened bread. And I do not want to see an Emperor in this Council, nor do I want to name Pope Eugenius in the first place. But I order everyone not to reject the seven Holy councils and the covenant of the Holy Fathers because it is written in the holy rules, 'One who amends or rejects

the covenant of the Holy Oecumenic Fathers and teachers will be   **1439**
accursed.' And I am greatly fearful of this and therefore I do not
call [this meeting] the Eighth Council. And I do not want to mention
Pope Eugenius [during the church service] and I do not care for
his teaching. And if someone in an Orthodox church mentions
Pope Eugenius [during the church service] he will be anathema,
or accursed."

The Latin chaplains, hearing this, became ashamed and ran
away so as not to hear his words. Then the Greek Emperor John
told him, "Holy Father, cease." And he [Mark] arose and walked
out and went home.

Later the cardinals began coming often from Pope Eugenius
of Rome to the Greek Emperor John, son of Manuel of Constantinople, to the Oecumenic Patriarch, Joseph, to the Russian Metropolitan Isidore, telling them tempting speeches in which they
[tried to prevent] Mark, Metropolitan of Ephesus, from prevailing.
And the Latins said, "Do according to our will and you can have
as much gold as you want." And many people came to them and
did so with them and were tempted. And the Greek Emperor John,
and Joseph, Oecumenic Patriarch, decided that the continuation
of the council should finally be in the Latin city of Florence. Having
decided this and having received much gold, they went to the city
of Florence.

KHAN MAHMET [MOHAMMED] COMES TO MOSCOW

The same year on Friday, the third day of the month of June,
Khan Mohammed[60] came unexpectedly close to Moscow with large
forces. Grand Prince Vasilii Vasilievich intended to march against
him but did not have time to prepare. Nonetheless, he went forward
against him; but seeing how few men he had, he returned and
went beyond the Volga, leaving his voevoda, Prince Iurii Patrikeevich, in Moscow with an endless multitude of Christians. Khan
Mohammed came close to Moscow, sojourned there ten days and
returned. He did not do anything to the city; but he did much evil
to the Russian land; and, returning, he took Kolomna, burned it,
captured many people and slaughtered others.

The same year in Novgorod Lord Euthymius, Archbishop of
Novgorod, built a stone granary in his court. The same year in

60. "Makhmet," in *Nik.*

1440   Novgorod Bishop Euthymius renovated the Church of Holy Sophia
and had it whitewashed. The same year in Novgorod Bishop
Euthymius built a stone belfry in the city in place of the old one.
The same year in Novgorod Lord Euthymius, Archbishop of Novgorod, found the body of Bishop John of Novgorod, in whose time
the Suzdalians campaigned against Novgorod. The same year in
Novgorod the Great Lord Euthymius gilded the casket of Prince
Vladimir Iaroslavovich, grandson of great Vladimir, who Christianized the Russian land, and he made an inscription on it. Likewise
he made an inscription on the casket of the latter's mother and put
a cover on it, and he established the fourth day of the month of
October as a memorial day for each year.

THE ASSASSINATION OF SIGISMUND

In the Year 6948 [1440]. In the month of September, Sigismund,
Grand Prince of Lithuania, brother[61] of Vitovt, son of Keistut,
grandson of Gedimin, was killed in Lithuania by Prince Aleksandr
Czartoryski and his brother, Prince Ivan; and he reigned for nine
years. He was a cruel and merciless prince who loved gold and
silver more than people, and he was the undoing of many Lithuanian princes, and he slaughtered them, drowned them in water
and put them to die in prisons. He killed without mercy great lords
and boyars and commoners and merchants in great number, and
therefore Lord God brought this cruel death on him. After his
death they did not come out in favor of his son, Prince Mikhail,
because of [their] hatred for his father, Sigismund. And his son,
Prince Mikhail, wept, saying, "My father, my father, Sigismund,
Grand Prince! You destroyed yourself because you were merciless
for your own purposes and you left me a memorial of the hatred
of all the people because of your mercilessness." The entire Lithuanian land and the Russian cities of the Lithuanian state assembled
and elected as their grand prince Kasimir, the royal son, the son
of Iagailo, grandson of Olgerd, great grandson of Gedimin; and
they set him on the throne in Wilno quietly and without dissension.

The same fall Khan Mahmet [Mohammed] of the Great Horde
killed Marsup, an important lord of the Horde, and many Tatars
at that time were massacred in the Horde. Not only there, but also
in the other hordes there were disturbances, dissension, fratricidal
feuds and fighting.

61. Actually, cousin.—*Ed.*

EMPEROR AND PATRIARCH AND METROPOLITAN ISIDORE
WENT TO FLORENCE

The same winter the Greek *Kyr* and Emperor John, son of
Manuel of Constantinople, and Oecumenic Patriarch Joseph of
Constantinople, and many Metropolitans and bishops came to the
German [*sic!*] city of Florence; and with them came Isidore, Met-
ropolitan of Russia, who was of the same mind with them, in order
to commit his evil intrigue, hoping that with his flattering he would
satisfy Mark. Mark, Metropolitan of Ephesus, however, told the
Emperor and Patriarch, "Do not go to the Latin city of Florence.
You can not achieve there the intention which you have in mind;
and it [Byzantium's fate] will happen in the way God wills." They
did not heed him and went, and because of this journey Pope
Eugenius could impose his will on them. Mark, however, told them,
"Did I not tell you that the Latins are just liars? When they speak,
they only lie."

And from that time Emperor John, himself, with Isidore, Metropolitan of Russia, began going very often to the Pope to deal, in
order to conclude the affair. And they began to take counsel by
themselves, trusting that they would impose their will on Mark,
Metropolitan of Ephesus. He, however, told them the harshest
words, addressing them all, "Latins," [and particularly] the Emperor, the Patriarch and all the Greek Metropolitans, bishops and
philosophers, as well as Isidore, Metropolitan of Russia, who was
of the same mind with them. And he accused them daringly, without
any restraint, and without hesitation called them "Latins." The
Emperor and the Patriarch told him, "O Mark! Since you spoke so
harshly there, please speak peacefully here." And responding to
them, Mark, Metropolitan of Ephesus, said, "From now on, Emperor and Patriarch, I will not obey you and it will happen according
to the will of God."

The Council convened many times without him but did not
achieve anything, and thereafter the Greeks with Isidore, Metropolitan of Russia, began recording in their books [what he said]
so as to be able to overcome him or catch some word from his
mouth because they wanted to lead him away from the truth. But
he [Mark] did not pay any attention to their censure and reproached
them and their philosophers, and took no heed of the speeches of
the Emperor and Patriarch or of Isidore, Metropolitan of Russia,
as well as of all the Greek Metropolitans, bishops, priests, monks,

1440   and all the Greeks who were of the same mind with them. And he did not give his blessing either to the Pope or to the Council, and walked out to his house.

They did not dare to continue the Council without him, however, because that could cause much talk among the people. On many occasions on the advice of Isidore, Metropolitan of Russia, the Emperor and the Patriarchs confronted him [Mark], saying, "Heed Pope Eugenius and you will be blessed and you will not suffer from your stubbornness." And on many occasions he was interdicted severely by the Emperor and the Patriarch, as well as by Isidore, Metropolitan of Russia. Following them, Pope Eugenius, himself, instigated by Isidore, Metropolitan of Russia, threatened him with torture; but he did not fear anything and, recalling the prophet David, he said,"One who lives with the help of the Almighty will find shelter under the Heavenly God." And, also, "One will appeal to Me, and I will hear him and be with him in his grief. And I will take him up and glorify him and grant him long days, and I will show him My salvation." Mark, Metropolitan of Ephesus, relying on the Lord God, Who provides salvation, found his consolation in God. Later he was greatly entreated and importuned by the Pope, who sent him much gold so that he [Mark] would obey him and do his will; but he paid him no attention and told them, "I came hither not in order to share gold or silver but only for the purpose of the truth of God," and they could not seduce him.

John, the Greek Emperor of Constantinople, the Oecumenic Patriarch Joseph, Isidore, Metropolitan of Russia, and all other Metropolitans and bishops, and all present, beginning with the day of Alexis, Man of God—the seventeenth day of the month of March— and to the day of Sisoes the Great—the sixth day of the month of July[62]—discussed and kept counsel among themselves, and accepted that [gold and silver] so as to do what was sought of them [that is, to agree to the Union].

Mark, Metropolitan of Ephesus, did not always come to them [that is, to the meetings] to participate in their deliberations because they could not get anything from him and were not able to overcome him in the dispute. Then the Emperor, the Patriarch, all the Metropolitans and bishops, and Isidore, Metropolitan of Russia, together with Pope Eugenius, met in the Great Council, questioning,

62. In *Ioasaf.* and *Obol.*, incorrectly June 6.

discussing and holding counsel for many days. The Latins, arguing **1440** and putting forward their [opinions], said, "The head of the Roman church is the head of all churches. The Christian faith is the same as we, the Romans, hold it or as you, the Greeks. Only the rules and rites are not the same. Even among you, Greeks, there are not the same and concordant rules and statutes, but different ones. Those of Egypt, of Alexandria, of Antiochia, of Sinai, and of Jerusalem are not the same but different, and they celebrate not in the same way. Likewise, the rules and rites of Constantinople, of the holy Mountain [Athos], and of Studion [Monastery in Constantinople] and many others are not similar. And many other missals used by the Patriarchs in their dioceses, and many other books do not agree among themselves. The Christian faith, however, is the same in them all, and therefore you should submit yourself to the rules and statutes of our Roman church, and accept our rules and rites and keep them. If you do not want to have the rules and rites of our Roman church, you may keep your own Greek ones. But you should be together in spirit with the Roman church and you should unite the Christian church and not divide it." In this way, arguing and discussing, they unified the faith [the dogma and rites] and concluded their affairs among themselves, and they put it firmly in writing, all of them penning[63] the following in the Council with Eugenius, Pope of Rome, and with the Greek Emperor John.

[*ENCICLIQUE LAETENTUM COELI:* ACT OF UNION BETWEEN THE EASTERN AND WESTERN CHURCH, PROCLAIMED AT THE COUNCIL OF FLORENCE, 1439]

[I], Eugenius, Bishop and servant of the servants of Our Lord God Jesus Christ, the Only Begotten Son of God, sign [this act] in order to preserve the memory of this eternal event. [I do so] with the consent of our beloved son John, the Most Serene Emperor of the Romans,[64] as well as together with the delegates of our honorable brethren, Patriarchs, and all other heads of the Eastern church.

May the heavens rejoice and the earth exalt [Psalms 19:1], for the partition within the City [of God] that divided the Eastern church from the Western has been removed and peace and concord

---

63. Actually accepting.—*Ed.*

64. Here is meant John VIII Paleologue, 1425–48, Emperor of the Eastern Roman Empire, now usually called "Byzantium" by historians.

1440   have returned [to the church], Jesus Christ being its cornerstone [Ephesians 2:20]; the divided parts have come together into one unity and [the church] has become strongly united by love and peace; the once-divided [church] has become united and strengthened by the created Union. While during these years there was a longlasting grief caused by the clouds and mists of sadness, now the gentle ray of kind unity has shone forth; and although during the time of the former partition we wept grievously, at the present time we rejoice in unspeakable gladness about spiritual agreement and give our thanks to Almighty God.

Rejoice, ye faithful of the entire universe, and you, the conciliar Mother Church, because [of our] knowledge of Christ's call; rejoice together with all your elected children. For behold, after long years of disagreement, the Western and Eastern church fathers felt the need to expose themselves to the hardships and difficulties of travel by land and sea; they have assembled together happily and eagerly at this sacred Oecumenic Council and holy meeting in their desire to renew their original love; and they have not been thwarted in their intentions, for after long and difficult efforts they have at last gained, by the grace of the Holy Ghost, their cherished and holy desire [that is, to hold this Council].

Who, therefore, would not express his gratitude and praise for these divine benefits?

Who would not be astonished at the bounty of such divine generosity?

Whose heart, even if it were of iron, would not be softened by such measure of divine mercy?

Such a deed, indeed, is a sacred one because it could not be expressed by human mind; and for this reason we, with real boldness, accept it, singing the chants of the saints:

Praise to You!
Glory to You!
Thanks to You!

Christ, You are the fountain of generosity Who granted so many blessings to Your bride, the conciliar Church! In our time You demonstrated Your mercifulness by Your miracles, and permitted [us] to glorify and confess them. Oh! How great and indescribable is the gift granted to us by Christ and which I, a sinner, have been given to see [with my own] eyes. Prior to me, it was denied to so

many people who, crying, sought to see it but were not honored **1440**
with it.[65]

[*DECISIONS* OF THE COUNCIL]

[1. Procession of the Holy Ghost (*Filioque*)]

"Coming together at this holy and divine Oecumenic council,
the Latins and the Greeks have shared great confidence so that
among other problems the teaching concerning the Divine Procession of the Holy Ghost has been discussed with utmost diligence.
Indeed, evidence has been produced from divine Scripture and
from a great number of eastern and western holy teachers, of whom
some say that the Holy Ghost proceeds from the Father and the
Son, and some that It proceeds from the Father through the Son;
all of them, however, look to the same understanding; the difference is only in the wording.

"The Greeks say that the Holy Ghost proceeds from the Father,
but they do not assert this with the intention of ruling out the Son.
[They assert this] because it seems to them, as they say, that the
Latins teach that the Holy Ghost proceeds from the Father and the
Son as if from two [different] sources of creation. And for this
reason they abstain from saying that the Holy Ghost proceeds from
the Father and the Son as if from two [different] sources of creation.
And for this reason they abstain from saying that the Holy Ghost
proceeds from the Father and the Son.

"The Latins, however, explain for a better understanding that
they teach that the Holy Ghost proceeds from the Father and the
Son because the Father is the source and origin of all divinity,
including the Son and the Holy Ghost. They [the Latins] maintain
that they do not assert two origins and two Processions but that
they assert, and have up to now, that there is one Procession and
single Creation of the Holy Ghost, and they believe in this way.

"And now, out of all these views, one and the same sense of
truth has been elicited. They have at last unanimously accepted
and agreed to the Union described below.

"In the Name of the Holy, Indivisible Trinity—Father, Son
and Holy Ghost—this sacred, holy and Oecumenic Council which
took place in the above-mentioned and selected City of Florence,
decrees: this [teaching] is confessed by all Christians and is accepted
by them. We all confess it. We all believe in this way, and we all

65. Here is meant the Union of both churches.—*Ed.*

1440 confess in this way, and agreed to sign it. This is the faith of the
Holy Apostles. It is the faith of the Holy Fathers. It is the faith of
all Christians who sincerely believe in Christ. And in this way do
we think and confess:

"Since the Holy Ghost is of the same Essence as the Father
and Son, and the Son has [this Essence] from the Father from the
very beginning, and is of the same Procession, therefore [the Holy
Ghost] is of the same origin and same Procession. They [the members of the Council] assert that in the same teaching as of the Holy
Fathers and teachers. . . .[66] The Holy Ghost [also proceeds] from
the Son, still is eternally connected with the Father. We stipulate,
furthermore, that the aforementioned words "and from the Son"
[*Filioque*] were legitimately added to the *Creed* for the sake of making
clear the truth, especially in view of the necessity of the time.

[2. Use of bread in the Eucharist]

"Likewise we state that both unleavened and leavened wheat
bread may be used [for Communion] to be consecrated as the Body
of Christ; the priest has to abide by the statutes and rules of the
church, eastern or western.

[3.Purgatory]

"As far as the deceased are concerned, we considered that
those who have passed away being true believers but who did not
manage to atone for their sins with worthy fruit of penitence as
they were taught by their spiritual fathers, their souls are cleansed
by punishment [of purgatory] after their death, as well as by memorial liturgies, alms, and other offerings offered on behalf of these
[deceased] believers, according to [the teaching] of the church.

"And the souls of those who, after their baptism, have not
incurred any stain of sin, as well as those become clean by their
atonement, are received into heaven and they will [enjoy] seeing
the Three Hypostasies [Father, Son and Holy Ghost]; but in view
of the difference of their merits, some of them will see them [the
Trinity] more perfectly than another.

"The souls[67] which go to hell are to be punished with different
punishment.

[4. Primacy of the Pope]

"Likewise we declare that the Holy Apostolic See of the Arch-

66. Part of the sentence is missing, and the remaining text is unclear.
67. Missing words. In Latin text, "of the sinners."

bishop of Rome and the Roman Pope hold primacy over all parts of the world, and that he, himself, is the successor of blessed Peter, leader of the Apostles, and he is the true vicar of Christ and head of all the churches and the father and teacher of all Christians. And that to him through blessed Peter full power has been given by Our Lord Jesus Christ to lead, rule, and care for all the churches, as also is written and determined by the holy rules of the Oecumenic Council and in the sacred canons. Furthermore, we renew the order of the other venerable Patriarchs which has been handed down in the canons whereby the Patriarch of Constantinople is second after the most holy Roman Pope; and the third is the Patriarch of Alexandria; and the fourth, the Patriarch of Antioch; and the fifth, the Patriarch of Jerusalem; and that all their privileges and rights remain unchanged.

"Given in Florence in the Oecumenic Council held in the cathedral church.[68] In the year of Our Lord's Incarnation, 1439, sixth of June, the ninth year of our pontificate. We all confess and think this way, and having agreed to it, all of us have signed [this document] in the year 6948, the sixth day of June."

And the Greek Emperor John of Constantinople signed it, and so did the Russian Metropolitan Isidore. The Oecumenic Patriarch Joseph of Constantinople passed away the same month of June, the tenth day, and his [body] was placed in the temple which they call the church in which the Pope had his Council. Blessed Mark, Metropolitan of Ephesus, who did not sign these vain and seductive articles, as well as Metropolitan Gregory of Iberia [Georgia], and Isaac of Nitra, and Sophronius of Gaza—[all] escaped from the city and started their journey home. The Emperor, however, brought them back from their journey, but Gregory of Iberia escaped to Venice and then by sea to his king, and managed not to be returned and not to go thither, and did not obey the Emperor and did not fear his anger or his interdiction. And their Council came to an end in the City of Florence on the sixth day of the month of June in the Year 6948.

THE END OF THE ACCURSED COUNCIL

Eugenius, Pope of Rome, and all the Romans rejoiced greatly, and he very much honored the Emperor and all the Greek Met-

---

68. I.e., "*La chiesa maggiore*," the biggest of the churches in Florence.

1440   ropolitans, bishops, monks, philosophers, and all the Greeks who participated in that Council. And he honored them and gave lots of gold and silver to the Emperor, to the Metropolitan [Isidore], to the bishops, to the philosophers, and to all the Greeks because he induced them into his temptation.

ABOUT THE ROMAN SERVICE

Thereafter Pope Eugenius served a mass in vestments of scarlet velvet and in gloves, and with golden rings on his hands. On his head was a hat with high crowns which was [adorned] with gems and pearls of great value. And when he went to the cathedral he carried before him in golden shrines the relics of the saints, having the form of human body made of gold and silver, and having images of Holy Peter and Paul. And when he entered the cathedral which they call a church he dropped slightly on one knee, together with his archbishops and bishops, and then, entering, he took a place on a throne having a scarlet velvet cushion for his head. And they trumpeted in trumpets and played music on organs and harps according to the Italian tradition. The Pope celebrated his Mass in Italian, and before it a thanksgiving service, while Isidore, Metropolitan of Russia, with his Greeks, celebrated in Greek, and after the thanksgiving service they all went to Pope Eugenius. They prostrated themselves before him and received a blessing from him according to the Latin tradition, and he blessed them and took leave. Thereafter they [the Greeks and the Russians] remained with them as guests until the twenty-sixth day of the month of August, and then they departed, having covered themselves with the darkness of want of faith. Alas! It was a pernicious temptation! Alas! It was the union of Greek Orthodoxy with abomination. How could it happen that in place of the Light of Life there came the darkness of darkness? How could [men] of a pious faith come together with the Latins? The Emperor and Patriarch of Orthodoxy fell into the temptation of the Latin heresy and perished, caught in a net of gold. Because through Isidore's lie they accepted gold. They broke from God and joined the Latins. What good did you see in the Latins, Emperor? And how could there be honor in their divine churches when they raised their voices as if mad, and there was much shouting and noise, and they sang too loud? Could this be ecclesiastic beauty when people play on drums with their hands, on trumpets and organ, dance and stamp with their feet, and have [mystery] plays from which the devil has joy? Is it humility and **1441** pious decorum in the holy church when the Pope kneels slightly on one knee, brings unleavened bread and officiates in gloves, and has rings on his glove? And so did their archbishops and bishops and teachers and chaplains fall slightly on one knee; and so do all the Poles and all the Latins, both male and female, small and tall, they all fall on one knee before the end of their service, which is repellent to God. And so did the Jews when they abused Christ Our Saviour, Who, during his holy passion, suffered from their offenses and ignominy. Besides all that, they outraged the image of God: their ecclesiastic teachers and clergy shave their beards and mustaches so as to win female attention. And to that they claim such whoredom: "It is right to come thus to the Sacrament." And during the church service and Eucharist they are accompanied by dogs. Everywhere they praised Isidore for his speeches, and therefore Isidore received great honor from the Pope, and received fair presents and much wealth.

*

* *

The same year the city of Polotsk burned entirely.—The same year Prince Iurii Simeonovich Lugvenev of Lithuania left Novgorod for Lithuania and the Grand Prince of Lithuania, Kasimir Iagailovich, gave him Mstislavl' as a patrimony, as well as Krichev and quite a few other towns and districts. He became very ambitious and took Smolensk, Polotsk, and Vitebsk; but it was not useful for him because there were rebellion and fighting. The same year he took great fright, seeing his senseless daring which he had committed by his unreason, and he fled to Moscow.—The same year Lord Euthymius of Novgorod built the stone Church of Holy Anastasia.— The same year he built a small stone mansion in his court.

In the Year 6949 [1441]. Eugenius, Pope of Rome, rejoiced in the Council because of his agreement with John, the Greek Emperor of Constantinople, the son of Manuel, and with all the Greek Metropolitans and bishops, and with monks, with philosophers, with princes and boyars, and with all the Greeks. And they [Latins] especially greatly honored Isidore, Metropolitan of Russia. They let the Emperor go to Constantinople with all his people, and they also let Isidore, Metropolitan of Russia, go with great honors. When Isidore left Rome on his way to the Russian Metropolia he came

1441   on the fifth day of the month of March to the city called Budin
[Budapest], and from thence he sent a message to the lands of the
Poles, Lithuanians, Germans,[69] and to all Russian Orthodox Chris-
tianity. The following was written:

THE *EPISTLE* OF ISIDORE, METROPOLITAN OF RUSSIA

"I, Isidore, by the grace of God Most Venerable Metropolitan
of Kiev and all Russia, legate from the rib of the Apostle [*legatus
latere*] for Poland, Lithuania and the Germans. Peace and blessing
to all and to every faithful and true Christian who believes in eternal
salvation from the Lord Jesus Christ. Rejoice and be of good cheer,
all of you, concerning God because the Eastern church and the
Roman church, which long were divided and were hostile one toward the other, now have become united in true unity according
to their original union and peace, and there is quietude and love
and the ancient single authority without any division. You all, people
of Christ, whether you be Latin or Italian, or whether you be under
the Holy Conciliar Greek Church of Constantinople to which the
Russians, Serbs, Walachs[70] and all other Christians belong who truly
believe in Christ Jesus, Son of God, and God, Who created all—
heaven and earth—and in Whom is all our life and all our hopes,
now and ever, accept this holy and most sacred Union and single
authority with great spiritual joy and honor.

"I beseech you all for the sake of Our Lord Jesus Christ, Who
provided us with His grace, that there should not be any division
between the Latins and you because everyone is the servant of God
and Our Saviour Jesus Christ, and is baptized in His Name. There
is One God, One Father, one baptism and there should be among
you common agreement and tranquility and peace and love because
of Jesus Christ. And you, people of the Latin faith, you should
accept without any hesitation all those who are of the Greek faith.
They all are baptized and their baptism is holy and recognized by
the Roman church because it is true and it is the same as the one
of the Roman church and one of the Eastern church. Beginning
with now, there is not among us any mean mind or dissension in
these matters. Both the Latins and the aforementioned Greeks
should go to the same unified church with a pure and humble

---

69. Here and later are apparently meant the lands of the German
Orders of the Teutonic and Livonian Knights.
70. Rumanians.

heart, and they should bring their prayer and their supplication to **1441** be united in one unity unto the Lord God. And when the Greeks are in the Latin land and in case there are [only] Latin and Roman churches in some parts of these lands, they should go thither to the divine service with daring but humble heart and accept the Body of Christ with humble heart, and render honor there as they do in their own churches in their lands in which they live; and [in such cases] they have to come for confession to the Latin priests and accept from them the Body of Lord Jesus Christ, Our God. The Latins, likewise, have to go to the Greek churches and participate in their divine services with a warm faith and with humble heart, and venerate the same Body of Christ, because the One consecrated by the Greek priest in leavened bread is truly and wholly the Body of Christ as is That One Which is consecrated by the Latin priest in unleavened bread. And therefore we have to venerate both the leavened and the unleavened. And the Latins have to come for confession to the Greek priests and accept from them the holy and divine Communion because both are the same and true. And so it was decided by the great Oecumenic Council in their final meeting after many consultations and investigations of holy, divine writings in the honorable and great church in which was celebrated the church service and which is in the city of Florence. And it was on the sixth day of the month of June in the year 1439 after the Incarnation of Our Lord."

ABOUT THE PASSING OF PRINCE DMITRII IURIEVICH THE HANDSOME

The same fall on the twenty-second of September Prince Dmitrii Iurievich the Handsome passed away, and there was something unusual in his illness. First of all, he became almost deaf and there was an illness in him and his disease was very hard on him because for many days he could not eat anything with his mouth and he could not have any sleep. Then he wanted to make his Communion. It was Sunday, the eighteenth of September. A liturgy was celebrated and a priest came with the sacred Sacrament but at that moment bleeding commenced from both his [the Prince's] nostrils and the bleeding was so strong that he could not make his Communion, and the priest with the Communion remained waiting in the porch. Thereafter the bleeding began to lessen and his spiritual father, the priest-monk by name Hosea, put some paper into his nostrils and the Prince arose, accepted the divine Communion in the doors of his chamber, and he had Communion with great awe

1441   and fearfulness; and he accepted the Communion and the water
from the service and lay down in his bed. Thereafter he ate some
meat and fish soups and drank a cup of wine, and told his people,
"Leave me alone in peace. I want to sleep." And they were very
happy because they thought this blood was sweat [*sic?*] and they
went to eat and to drink at Dionisii Fomin's.

When evening came someone who remained with the Prince
rushed to Hosea, his spiritual father; and Dementii, the Prince's
deacon, was also there. He told them, "Go quickly. The Prince is
dying." They came and found him at his last gasp. And they read
the prayer on the occasion of the departure of a soul, and the
canon. And so he passed away. Hosea closed his eyes and covered
him. There was very much crying and lamenting and disconsolation.
But thereafter they drank some mead and lay down, and a number
of them [lay down] in the bedchamber of the Prince and slept. Only
his deacon did not drink anything but lay across from the Prince
on the other bench, and looked around because he could not sleep.

About midnight when he was looking about, the Prince, with
his own hands, removed the cover from his head and said very
loudly, "And Peter recognized Him, that He was Lord." Seeing
this, Deacon Dementii froze with fear, but the Prince repeated the
same words. The Deacon, recovering somewhat and becoming
stronger, awoke those present. And the Prince repeated always the
same words. Then he began to sing in the manner of *demestvo.*[71]
"Sing to God and praise Him for ages, alleluia." And then the chant
to the Holy Virgin according to the fourth tone: "The Living One
finds His dwelling in Heaven." And also the other chants in honor
of the Virgin. And while singing he closed his eyes, and it was
possible to see that his body was like that of a living one. Before
matins he became quieter. After matins his spiritual father, Hosea,
brought him the Reserve Sacrament, but the Prince did not even
look at it. Then he [Hosea] touched his lips with the [Communion]
spoon and the Prince looked; and seeing it, he accepted Communion, saying from the depth of his heart, "Rejoice, Womb of the
Divine Reincarnation." And so he received Divine Communion.
Thereafter, on Monday and then on Tuesday, he intoned from
the Scripture, chanted hymns, could recognize people, talked with

71. *Demestvo*—a new way of harmony in church singing in the fifteenth
century.

them about what he wished but not very coherently. And when **1441** people spoke to him, whatever they said he could not hear. On Wednesday he stopped talking but still recognized people. On Thursday during the liturgy when [the priest] began to read the Holy Gospel, he finally gave up his soul. This was on the twenty-second day of the month of September.

At once the boyars sent to Uglich for his elder brother, Prince Dmitrii Iurievich Shemiaka. In the meantime they prepared the dead as was fitting, and bore him to the Church of Holy Leontius. In this church there was no regular service but they celebrated a [Eucharist] service and the memorial service, as is proper for the dead. On the eighth day after his death his brother, Prince Dmitrii Shemiaka, arrived, and they celebrated for him the burial service, put him in the casket, wrapped the casket with linen, and pitched it. And they took him to Moscow by horse-drawn sledge. But carrying him, they dropped him twice. They brought him to Moscow on the fourteenth day of the month of October, and it was the twenty-third day after his passing. They carried him to the Church of Archangel Michael in the Square and celebrated the burial service, and he was still in the casket. Thereafter they split the casket, expecting to find only the bones, and opened it. They found him completely intact, and nothing was changed, as well as the burial vestments which had been put on him. And his face was white like one in sleep, and there was nothing black or blue. And so, rendering thanks to God, they laid him in the grave next to his father, Prince Iurii Dmitrievich.

The same winter Isidore the Greek, Metropolitan of all Russia, came from the Eighth Council, from Rome, from the Pope, to Russia, to Kiev, and began to call himself legate from the rib of the Apostle [*legatus latere*].

The same winter Grand Prince Vasilii Vasilievich marched toward Novgorod with an army, and from Novgorod the Novgorodian Bishop Euthymius came to him, and with him the boyars and commoners; and they met him near the town of Diemon in Dereva. And they petitioned him and they made peace with him according to the old tradition, and gave him eight thousand Novgorodian rubles. In the meantime the Pskovians, coming to the aid of the Grand Prince, campaigned in many Novgorodian lands and perpetrated much meanness and evil. At the same time the Novgorodian voevodas with the people from the Trans-Volokh campaigned

1441   in the patrimony of Grand Prince Vasilii Vasilievich, and did much evil.

The same winter Prince Iurii Vasilievich the senior [son of the Grand Prince] passed away and the other prince, Iurii Vasilievich, also son of the Grand Prince, was born on the twenty-second day of June. One year before this very day, on the twenty-second of June, when the memory of Holy Apostle Timotheus is celebrated, Grand Prince Ivan Vasilievich was born[72] and he was baptized by Abbot Zinovius of the Monastery of the Trinity and St. Sergius.

ABOUT ISIDORE

The same spring Isidore came to the Russian land and went to Moscow, announcing that in the great Council the Eastern church had joined the Western; therefore he wanted that Orthodoxy and the great dominion of the Muscovite Grand Prince Vasilii Vasilievich be united with the Latin Faith; but Lord God did not allow him to do this. Already earlier in his messages he called himself "legate from the rib of the Apostle [of the Pope]" for Poland, Lithuania, and the Germans [Livonian and Teutonic Orders of German Knights] and had ordered that there be carried before him the Latin crucifix and three silver staffs, to honor the Italian tradition. In the prayers and service of the divine liturgy he would pray not for the Holy Oecumenic Patriarchs but, first of all, mention and glorify and praise Eugenius, the Roman Pope, to whom for gold he had surrendered the holy Orthodox Greek faith. He arrived in Moscow in the third week of great and holy Lent, and the same day he celebrated a *Te Deum* for the Grand Prince, for all Orthodox Christianity, and then officiated at the divine liturgy, in which he mentioned Pope Eugenius of Rome in the first place. At the end of the divine liturgy he ordered his protodeacon to go to the ambo in surplice and stole and to read loudly the epistle of the vain and rejected Council, in which [all] is written in a manner displeasing to God and in apostasy: this was [about] the Latin heresy in which the Holy Trinity is divided and in which it is said that the Holy Ghost proceeds from the Father and that the Holy Ghost also proceeds from the Son. In it are also confused the discussions about the Host, claiming that both leavened and unleavened bread may be Transubstantiated into the Body of Jesus Christ. There also was

72. Ivan Vasilievich: the son of Grand Prince Vasilii Vasilievich, future Ivan III.

written in it [concerning] the dead: those who die in true faith and confessing God, and with humility, but not having had time to confess or repent of their sins, about which the Holy Father taught—those will be cleansed after their death through torment.[73] But all this sophistication was done in order to seduce the true Orthodoxy and then, seducing it, to break Christianity away from divine law. And Eugenius, Pope of Rome, himself sent with him a writing about all this last proceeding, to the pious Grand Prince Vasilii Vasilievich, and in this message was written:

THE *MESSAGE* OF EUGENIUS, POPE OF ROME, TO THE GRAND PRINCE ABOUT METROPOLITAN ISIDORE

"I, Eugenius, Bishop, the servant of the servants of God, send my Apostolic blessing and grace to Your Highness, Grand Prince Vasilii Vasilievich of Moscow and Grand Tsar of all Russia. We thank Almighty Lord God that after many labors with the help of the grace of the Holy Ghost, the Eastern church is united with us, which will lead to the salvation of the souls of many people and which is written for your glory and your praise.[74] And to our most honorable brother, Isidore, your Metropolitan of Kiev and all Russia, I send this from the Apostolic See in order to help and support this union and agreement because he labored very much for a strong union. Therefore everyone should help him in all his deeds and, especially, in the deeds of Union which is deemed to his honor and to his ecclesiastic rank which he received. For the sake of Our Lord Jesus Christ, we ask you, Supreme Highness, to accept piously this aforementioned Metropolitan Isidore, who did so much for the good of the Church. And we command you to be his active helper in all the deeds which he will do for the good of the Church, and to do so with all your power, and then you will receive praise and glory from men; and from us, our blessing; and from God, the Eternal Gift. Given in Florence in the ninth year of our priesthood."

When Grand Prince Vasilii Vasilievich heard that the Pope of Rome, and not the Patriarch of Constantinople, was mentioned first during the divine liturgy, and saw and heard many other things not in accord with the custom of the Russian land, he was astonished, and Grand Prince Vasilii Vasilievich said, "Neither in the time of

73. This sentence is unclearly formulated.
74. The exact meaning of this sentence is unclear.

1442   our forefathers and fathers nor of our brothers, the grand princes of the Russian land, have such things happened, and I do not wish them."

And he commanded him [Metropolitan Isidore] to live in the Monastery of the Miracles and he arrested him on Wednesday during great, holy Lent, when the holy cross is venerated; and he was imprisoned in this monastery the entire year. It is worthy to wonder at the wisdom and great mind of Grand Prince Vasilii Vasilievich because everyone else—princes, boyars and many others, and especially the bishops of the Russian land—remained silent and became sleepy [passive] and slept [remained passive] concerning this Isidore. Only this Christ-loving sovereign, Grand Prince Vasilii Vasilievich, wise in God, recognized Isidore's pernicious temptation and very rapidly exposed him, shamed him, and called him an evil, destructive wolf instead of shepherd and teacher. Then all the Russian bishops who were then in Moscow became aroused, as well as the princes, boyars, lords, and a great many Christians. They remembered and confirmed the law of the Greeks as it used to be heretofore, and began to preach from Holy Writ, and called Isidore a heretic. And so Grand Prince Vasilii Vasilievich rejoiced concerning the agreement of his bishops, princes, boyars, and all Orthodox Christians, and commanded him [Isidore] to remain in the monastery while an investigation of him be made according to the Sacred Rules of the Holy Apostles and Seven Holy Councils of the Holy Fathers. Then he was to be brought to the just court of truth before archbishops and bishops, and before the entire Sacred Council, and his heresy to be exposed so that his shame should be brought about and he put away union with the Latins and agreement with heresy, and accept his guilt, repent, and then be pardoned.

Isidore, however, being filled with the evil Latin heresy, did not want to break away from the Union and agreement with the Latins, and did not want to obey either the Grand Prince or the entire Sacred Council. And the Grand Prince placed him under his bailiffs' supervision and ordered him to be guarded so long as he not break away from the Union and from agreement with the Latins and not return [to Orthodoxy] or repent, when he would then receive mercy. And so he lived in the Miracle Monastery under arrest.

In the Year 6950 [1442]. The Tatars of the Great Horde came to the Riazan' *ukraina* [frontier] and caused much evil, retreating **1442** with captives.—The same fall Grand Prince Vasilii Vasilievich developed a dislike for Prince Dmitrii Iurievich Shemiaka and marched against him toward Uglich. And the latter fled to the Novgorodian Bezhetskii Verkh, and the Grand Prince returned to Kiasov and thence to Moscow.—And Koludar Irezhskii[75] was whipped with the *knut*.—Thereafter Prince Dmitrii Iurievich Shemiaka, together with Prince Aleksandr Czartoryski [campaigned and] almost reached Moscow. But Abbot Zinovius of the Trinity brought them [Grand Prince and Shemiaka] to peace and mutual love.—The same fall there was a fire in Moscow.—The same winter, fearing Grand Prince Vasilii Vasilievich, Prince Dmitrii Iurievich Shemiaka sent to Great Novgorod asking them if they would be willing to accept him; and the Novgorodians answered, "If you wish, Prince, to come to us, come, and we will be glad to have you."

This same winter was extremely fierce, and the great freezes were unbearable and there was much damage to the cattle and to the people.—The same spring there were great thunderstorms and terrifying lightning, and storms, and tornadoes, and all the people were seized with fear.—The same spring there were sudden late freezes and a deep snow fell, and hardly did it pass than again the storm commenced and there were great freezes and great winds, and there was great grief among the people.—The same summer rye was very costly.

The same summer in the town of Rusa, Lord Archbishop Euthymius of Novgorod erected a stone Church to the Holy Transfiguration of Our Saviour. It was erected on the old foundation, and he consecrated it himself and organized a monastery and supplied it with icons, books, church vessels, all the necessary provisions for its needs.—The same summer Bishop Euthymius built in Novgorod in his own court a stone Church to St. Nicholas.—The same summer in Novgorod there was a very grave conflagration in Podolié, and twelve stone churches burned and the whole section burned as far as [the Church of] St. George. And a great many Christians burned, and it stopped only at Liubianitsa. Later the same month there was a fire in Novgorod and the Zapolié of Nikita's Street burned; and much harm was done to the people. Those who were fleeing with their possessions from the first fire all burned [in

75. Koludar Irezhskii, unknown to other sources.

1443   the second] together with their belongings, and there was great
distress among the Christians.

Then, because of this distress, these Novgorodians who suffered from the conflagration caught many people unjustifiedly,
saying, "You set fire secretly, you wanted it because of your greed,
and in this way you brought misfortune and calamity!" And so
many Christians were executed by fire and others were thrown
from the bridge over the Volkhov River, and some were stoned to
death. But God is alone to know the mystery of the human heart
[and He Alone knows] whether it was just or not, that [those people]
suffered from such evil punishment. Such misfortune happens because of our sins in order to show us that we should give up our
evil doings and change our lives, and repent and live according to
the will of God so that we may have reward in the present and in
the future.

ABOUT ISIDORE, HOW HE ESCAPED FROM MOSCOW TO ROME

In the Year 6951 [1443]. On the fifteenth day of the month of
September Metropolitan Isidore was enveloped by the darkness of
his faithlessness and did not want to reject or repent the Union
and agreement with the Latins. And he could not abide staying
[under arrest] and waiting in the Monastery of the Miracles in
Moscow and therefore, being faithless, he escaped secretly at night
and fled with his pupils, Monks Gregory and Athanasius. And from
Moscow he went to Tver', from Tver' to Lithuania, and from thence
to Rome to his Pope because he was conducted and instructed in
his perdition by the devil. Grand Prince Vasilii Vasilievich, who
was wise in God and greatly intelligent, did not send anyone to
force him to return and did not want to keep him as a vain madman
disgusting to God, and he did not want to be connected with the
latter's sins, and did him no harm.[76] And so Isidore went to Rome
to Pope Eugenius, and from that time far away he continued to
deal like an evil and destructive viper-devil, cruelly persecuting the
Holy Church, which was blossoming in piety in the Russian dominion, and he [continued] to turn Christians to the Latin Faith and
to Union and compromise. And Lord God and the Purest Mother

76. Apparently, the Grand Prince, Muscovite government, and the
church were quite happy about Isidore's escape since they did not know
exactly what should be done with him. Therefore Isidore was neither
pursued nor sought out.

of God protected the Holy Church of Russia from such an enemy **1443**
smart in evil, and it will remain without blemish and discord. This
occurred thanks to the great sovereign, Vasilii Vasilievich, who was
a man of great sense and who was instructed by God. This most
wise Tsar of all Russia greatly blossomed in piety; Lord God very
wisely showed him how to understand everything, how to reckon
and how to do the will of God, and how to preserve all His coven-
ants.[77]

77. On pages 43 to 61 of this twelfth volume of *PSRL* are quoted
various decisions of Oecumenic Councils, interpretations of the same, and
citations from the writings of the Holy Fathers. Since these quotations deal
exclusively with differences between Catholic and Orthodox churches and
have no bearing on Russian history, they are not translated here. For the
benefit of readers, however, a list of these quotations follows:

    p. 43, The First Decision of the Seventh Oecumenic Council, which
        met in Niceae;
    pp. 43-49, From the Epistle of Nikon of the Black Mountain;
    pp. 49-50, The 55th Decision of the Sixth Council, which met in Trull;
    pp. 49-50, From the *Vita* of the Holy Wonderworker Simeon of the
        Miraculous Mountain;
    p. 50, The Fifth Decision of the Holy Apostles;
    p. 50, Interpretation of the same;
    pp. 50-51, The Twelfth Decision of the Sixth Oecumenic Council,
        which met in Trull;
    p. 51, Interpretation of the same;
    pp. 51–52, The 13th Decision of the same Council.
    p. 52, Interpretation of the same.
    p. 52, The 33rd Decision of the Occumenic Council, which met in
        Carthagen;
    p. 52, The Fourth Decision of the same Council;
    pp. 52–53, Interpretation of the Third and Fourth Decisions of the
        same Council;
    p. 53, Interpretation of the same by Alexis and Aristinus;
    p. 53, The 66th Decision of the Holy Apostles;
    pp. 53–54, The 69th Decision of the Holy Apostles;
    p. 54, Interpretation of the same by Holy Ignatius;
    p. 54, The 42nd Decision of the Holy Council in Laodicea;
    pp. 54—56, The Short Story about the Latins, how They Broke from
        the Orthodox Patriarchs, how They were Expelled from their
        Primacy, from the Books (Which Indicate How the Patriarchs
        Should be) Mentioned (during the Church Service) and about
        the Iconoclastic Emperors Who Reigned in Constantinople;
    p. 56, Chanting by St. Theophilus;

1444   *In the same Year 6951 [1443].* Archbishop Euthymius of Novgorod built in his court a service building [for his churches] and a guard house.

In the Year 6952 [1444]. On the fifteenth of September Grand Prince Ivan Vladimirovich, grandson of Olgerd, came from Lithuania to Novgorod at Novgorod's request in order to rule over the junior cities[78] in which Prince Semion Lugven Olgerdovich and his son, Prince Iurii, grandson of Olgerd [earlier ruled]. Prince Iurii Semionovich, grandson of Olgerd, went to the Germans[79] but the Germans did not permit him to travel, and he went to Moscow.

The same fall the Germans [of the Livonian Orders] burned the suburbs of the Novgorodian city of Iama and campaigned along the shore, and they sent to Novgorod [saying] "We do not fight with you. It is Prince Gregorii of Kiev from overseas who fights on behalf of Rugodivets [Narva], his guide and interpreter." But all this was the Germans' lie.[80]

The same fall the Grand Prince of Tver' campaigned from his patrimony into many Novgorodian districts and towns. The people of Tver' campaigned in the districts of Bezhetskii Verkh and Novotorzhok, captured many people, burned, and returned home with great wealth.

The same fall the Grand Prince of Lithuania, Kasimir, son of Iagailo, sent to Novgorod saying, "Take my governors into Gorodishche and I will protect you. Because of you I did not conclude any peace treaty with the Grand Prince of Moscow." But the Novgorodians did not accept this.

---

p. 56, Interpretation of the same;

p. 56, Continuation of the previous (Short Story about the Latins);

p. 57, About Pope Formosus;

pp. 57–58, How the Latins were cursed;

p. 58, Epistle about Patriarch Michael Siggelus of Constantinople;

pp. 59–60, Epistle of Patriarch Photius of Constantinople to the Romans about the Holy Ghost and unleavened bread;

p. 60, From the other books about Pope Peter, whose voice was nasal;

pp. 60–61, About Brittany and about the Allemanian prince.

78. Each principality—in this case, Novgorod—had the *gorod*, which was the capital of the principality, and *prigorody*, which were the "junior" remaining cities and towns of the given territory.

79. Apparently, Prince Iurii Semionovich went to the territory of the Livonian or Teutonic orders.

80. This text is unclear.

The same summer the Khan's son, Mustafa, was killed on the **1444** Listan River in the [region] of Riazan'. And the winter was fierce and evil, and hay was very expensive, and many horses died.

STORY OF MUSTAFA, THE KHAN'S SON

The Khan's son, Mustafa, came campaigning into the Riazan' [region] with an army of a large number of Tatars; and he occupied many districts and towns of Riazan', and caused much evil to the Riazan' [principality]. And he retreated with a large number of captives and stood in the *polé*[81] and he sent to Riazan' to sell them captives. The people of Riazan' paid the ransom to the Tatars for their captives. Thereafter Mustafa came openly and peacefully to Riazan' desiring to pass the winter there. It was very difficult for him [to remain in the *polé*] because the whole *polé* was burned by fire during the fall, and the winter was fierce and very bad. There was much snow and wind and many violent storms. Therefore he came peacefully to Riazan' and wanted to winter there because he greatly needed this.

When Grand Prince Vasilii Vasilievich of Moscow heard about this he sent against him Prince Vasilii Obolenskii and Andrei Fedorovich Goltiaev, and with them his retinue, as well as the Mordva [militia] on skiis. [He did this] because the winter was very fierce with much snow, and the Tatar horses died from cold and the severe freezes, and they were in great misfortune, and hay was very expensive. The Khan's son, Mustafa, at that time was in the city of Pereiaslavl' of Riazan' [principality], because the people of Riazan' dislodged him from the city. He departed from the city and then stayed close to the city of Pereiaslavl'. Then from Moscow the voevodas of Grand Prince Vasilii Vasilievich came against him, and they met on the Listan River. The Tatars were in miserable condition and half frozen, and had no horses, and from the cold and freeze, strong winds and storms their bows and arrows were of no help. And the snows were very deep. Mordva on skiis, with maces and bare spears and sabers, attacked them [the Tatars]. The Cossacks of Riazan'[82] also on skiis with maces and bare spears and sabers, came from the other side; and the voevodas of the Grand Prince came with their forces. There was assembled a large number

81. *Polé*, or, quite often, *ukraina*, designated the prairie in southern and southeastern Russia when the Tatars roamed there.
82. *Cossacks* at that time denoted free people, mostly runaway serfs, living along the frontier (*ukraina*) in the *polé*.

1444 of foot soldiers with lances, axes and bare spears, and there was a great and very fierce battle on the Listan River, and the Christians began to overcome [the Tatars]. The Tatars, however, did not surrender and fought fiercely with sabers and knives. Many Tatars were killed, and the Khan's own son, Mustafa, was slain, and many Tatar lords were killed with him. Prince Ahmet Murza and Prince Azerbei, son of Misherevan, were captured, and many other Tatars were taken. The Tatars, however, killed Ilia Ivanovich Lykov from the Grand Prince's regiment.

The same winter the Novgorodians of Great Novgorod campaigned in the German [Livonian] land beyond the Narva River. [They were under] Prince Ivan Vladimirovich, grandson of Olgerd. They campaigned and captured and burned around Rugodiv, up to Purdozn, and around the Narva River up to Lake Chudskoe. They campaigned everywhere and captured everyone, submitting all to death and to the sword, and returning home with great booty.

The same spring Prince Ivan Andreevich of Mozhaisk, grandson of Ivan, great grandson of Danilo Aleksandrovich of Moscow, caught Andrei Dmitrievich and his wife and burned them at the [Church of the] Myrrh-bearing Women in Mozhaisk.

The same summer the Grand Master of the Germans [Livonian Order] with all his troops marched against the Novgorodian [lands]. Coming to the city of Iama, they fired at the city with cannon and guns and caused much evil. He remained five days and fought in the Vot land, on the Izhora River and on the Neva River. He captured many people and massacred them, burned much, but did not take the fortress. Many Germans were killed before the fortress and many were ill. At that time Prince Vasilii Iurievich from the Suzdal' branch of princes was in the fortress of Iama. And the Germans returned to their land with great booty. The Novgorodians under their Prince Ivan Vladimirovich, grandson of Olgerd, wanted to send an army to the Narva River to fight the Germans, but at that time the horses started dying in the Novgorodian cities and districts, and many people became ill. Therefore the Novgorodians gave up the campaign and did not march toward the Narva River. At that time the people of Pskov sent their envoys to Novgorod to strengthen peace and love. Having heard that there was an epidemic in Novgorod among the horses, and that the people were very ill and that the Novgorodians had given up fighting the Germans, the envoys of Pskov departed from Novgorod without concluding a peace.

The same year the Karela people campaigned against the Mur-   **1445**
man people and killed many, fought, and returned home.[83]

In the Year 6953 [1445]. In the month of September Tatars
campaigned in the Riazan' *ukraina* [frontier]. The same fall the
Tatars campaigned against Mordva. The same winter Khan Ulug
Mahmet [Mohammed] came with an army from the old city of
Nizhnii Novgorod to Murom, and Grand Prince Vasilii Vasilievich
marched against him and the Khan fled to the old Nizhnii Novgorod. At that time Aleksandr, son of Ivan Konstantinovich, was
shot, and during the battle his hands were hurt.

Seven thousand Lithuanians came against the city of Kaluga,
and Prince Mikhail Andreevich with four hundred people fought
against them, and at that time Prince Andrei Lugvitsa of Suzdal'was
killed, while Sudok and Kaninskii were taken to Lithuania.

FROM ANOTHER CHRONICLE ABOUT THE SAME[84]

The same winter Grand Prince Vasilii Vasilievich sent two sons
of the Khan to campaign against the Lithuanian cities of Viazma,
Briansk, and other unmentioned cities, and they went forward,
campaigned much, and put [many people] to death, and burned
a great deal. They came almost to Smolensk, taking captives and
causing vast evil to the Lithuanian land, and returned home with
great booty. The Grand Prince of Lithuania, Kasimir Iagailovich,
hearing of this, sent his lords to fight Mozhaisk and other cities.
Arriving there, they took five cities, captured, burned, and caused
much evil, returning home with great booty. Grand Prince Vasilii
Vasilievich at that time went against the Tatar Khan Ulug Mahmet
[Mohammed], who was in Murom, and many Christians died from
the freeze and others were killed by the Tatars, and the land was
rendered barren. But God helped Grand Prince Vasilii Vasilievich,
and the Tatars ran to the old Nizhnii Novgorod, from whence they
had come, and others were killed.

FROM OTHER CHRONICLERS ABOUT THE SAME[85]

The Lithuanians came to Kaluga under Lord Sudivoi, Lord
Rodivil Osikovich, Andriushka Mostilovich, Iabub Ralovich, Andrei
Isakovich, Nikolai Nemirovich, and Zakharia Ivanovich Koshkin

---

83. Both the Karela and Murman tribes are Finno-Ugric people.
84. This is the title in *Nik.*
85. Title as in *Nik.*

1445   with seven thousand warriors, and they roamed around Kozelsk
and Kaluga but did not succeed, and from thence they came to
Sukhodrov. The people of Mozhaisk, whose Prince was Ivan Andreevich—but Prince Ivan Andreevich was not at that time in
Mozhaisk—assembled one hundred people from Mozhaisk, and
their voevoda was Prince Andrei Vasilievich Lugvitsa from the
[branch of the] princes of Suzdal'. The people of his brother, Prince
Mikhail Andreevich, also heard about this and, despite the fact that
Prince Mikhail Andreevich was not in his Vereia, they also gathered
a hundred, and their voevoda was Sudok. The people of Prince
Vasilii Iaroslavlovich also heard about it, and although Prince Vasilii
Iaroslavlovich was not in Borovsk they gathered sixty people, and
their voevoda was Zhynev. They met the Lithuanians at Sukhodrov
and battle took place there; there was killed Prince Andrei Vasil-
ievich Lugvitsa, who was from the Suzdal' princes and who was the
voevoda of Prince Ivan Andreevich of Mozhaisk. And there was
killed Karacharov and four other people. And [the Lithuanians]
captured Iarobka and Simeon Rzhevskii, who were voevodas of
Prince Ivan Andreevich of Mozhaisk, and [they also captured]
Sudok, Filip Shchokin, and Kaninskii, the voevodas of his brother,
Prince Mikhail Andreevich of Vereia, and five other young men.
And two hundred Lithuanians were also killed.

THE GRAND PRINCE CAMPAIGNED AGAINST
KHAN ULUG MAHMET [MOHAMMED]

At that time Grand Prince Vasilii Vasilievich went with all his
brothers and cousins to [the city of] Vladimir. [With him were]
Prince Dmitrii Iurievich Shemiaka, Prince Andrei Ivanovich of
Mozhaisk, Prince Mikhail Andreevich of Vereia, and Prince Vasilii
Iaroslavlovich and all his princes, boyars, and warriors. And they
marched against Khan Ulug Mahmet [Mohammed], who came and
settled in the old city of Nizhnii Novgorod.[86] He came from the
prairie because before that he had been chased away from the
Great Horde by his brother, Kichik Ahmet [Mohammed]. And he
went to Belev and settled there. The Grand Prince sent against him
his princes, boyars and voevodas but for our sins God allowed the
Tatars to slay many of us, although there were few of them. From
Belev the Khan went to Nizhnii Novgorod, where he settled in the
old city, and much evil emanated from him. From old Nizhnii
Novgorod he marched to Murom. Learning of this, Grand Prince

86. The fortress of Nizhnii Novgorod still was in Russian hands.

Vasilii Vasilievich spent the holiday of Epiphany [January 6] in **1445** Vladimir and went toward Murom against [the Khan] with all his brothers, cousins, and all his people. Receiving this news, however, Khan Ulug Mahmet ran back to old Nizhnii Novgorod, where he had been living. The vanguard regiments of the Grand Prince defeated the Tatars at Murom, at Gorokhovets and other places, but the Khan remained in Murom. While the Khan campaigned around Murom, the Tatars fought in the *lug*.[87] The Grand Prince, returning, went to Suzdal', from thence to Vladimir, from thence to Moscow, where he arrived the evening of Good Friday. The same year in the city of Suzdal' in the Cathedral Church of the Most Pure Virgin a great sign occurred.

ABOUT THE BATTLE AT SUZDAL'

The same spring Grand Prince Vasilii Vasilievich received the news in Moscow that Khan Ulug Mahmet had sent his children, Mamutiak and Iakob, from the old city of Nizhnii Novgorod, where he was residing. Having fasted and made his communion during St. Peter's Fast, the Grand Prince moved against them from Moscow. When he arrived at Iur'iev there came to him the [Nizhnii] Novgorodian voevoda, Prince Fedor[88] Dolgoldov, and Iushka Dranitsa, who set fire at night to the fortress and escaped by night because they were exhausted from the great famine. "Of all that they had as bread reserves, they ate all and could not withstand the famine and, wearied by the Tatars, therefore at night they set fire to the fortress and fled."

The Grand Prince Vasilii Vasilievich spent St. Peter's Day [June 29] in Iur'iev, from whence he marched to Suzdal'. From their patrimonies there came to him his brothers and cousins—Prince Ivan Andreevich of Mozhaisk, his brother, Prince Mikhail Andreevich of Vereia, and Prince Vasilii Iaroslavovich, grandson of Vladimir, great grandson of Ivan Danilovich of Moscow, and many other voevodas and warriors came with him. Grand Prince Vasilii Vasilievich marched with his brothers and cousins with all his forces, toward Suzdal', and camped on the Kamenka River. It was Tuesday, the sixth day of the month of July. The same day there was an alarm and they put on their armor, raised the banners and marched onto the battlefield; but the [Russian] troops there were not very

87. *Lug*: apparently, park land, the transitional area between the prairie and forest.
88. Origin and background unclear.

1445   numerous. Grand Prince Vasilii Vasilievich returned to his camp, supped with his brothers, cousins, and boyars, and wrote late into the night. This very evening [his voevoda] Aleksei Ignatievich, with his regiment, and several other voevodas, came to the Grand Prince.

Morning came, the sun rose, and the Grand Prince awoke and commanded that matins be celebrated. This was Wednesday, the seventh day of the month of July. After matins the Grand Prince wanted to rest and at that very time the news arrived that the Tatars were fording the Nerel' River. Thus he began to send [the alarm] to all the camps, and at that very time set about donning his armor. Raising the banners, he marched against the Tatars. His cousins, Prince Ivan Andreevich of Mozhaisk, Prince Mikhail Andreevich of Vereia, and Prince Vasilii Iaroslavovich, brother-in-law of Grand Prince Vasilii Vasilievich, marched with him. All the princes, boyars and voevodas, and all the regiments followed him, having donned their armor, and marched eagerly against the Tatars.

They moved onto the battlefield but there were few warriors with them, hardly one and a half thousand, because not all the regiments succeeded in joining them. Neither did the Khan's son, Berdedat, manage to join the Grand Prince because he spent the night in Iur'iev and, likewise, Prince Dmitrii Shemiaka did not come or send his regiment. They marched onto the battlefield on the left side of St. Euthymius Monastery and met the accursed sons of Hagar there. And there was a large number of them opposing the Christian regiments. They commenced fighting, and in the beginning the regiments of the Grand Prince were victorious and the Tatars fled. Our men, however, pursued them and some ran alone, while others set to robbing the dead Tatars. The Tatars, however, returned against the Christians, and in this way overcame them. They captured by hand even the Grand Prince and Prince Mikhail Andreevich, and many other princes, boyars, and minor boyars, and many other warriors. Prince Ivan Andreevich, who was wounded many times and fell from his horse, got another mount and escaped. The Grand Prince, however, received many wounds on his head and hands, and his whole body was badly mutilated because he fought very courageously. This evil happened to the Christians on Wednesday, the seventh day of July.[89]

89. The reason for this detailed dating is probably the fact that it was the first time that a Muscovite Grand Prince was taken prisoner by the Tatars; but it was also the last time that it happened.

There were many Tatars killed, more than five hundred, and **1445** they were about three and a half thousand. The Tatars pursued and slew many, robbing and burning the towns and slaughtering people and taking [others] into captivity. The Khan's sons remained in St. Euthymius Monastery and took the body cross from the Grand Prince and sent it with the Tatar, Achisan, to Moscow, to his mother, Grand Princess Sofia, and to his [wife] Grand Princess Maria.[90] And when he [Achisan] came to Moscow there was great wailing and lamenting not only by the grand princesses but by all Christians. The Tatars remained at Suzdal' for three days, then went to the city of Vladimir. Crossing the Kliazma River, they stopped before the city but could not get into the city, so they went to Murom and from thence to Nizhnii Novgorod.

ABOUT THE BURNING OF MOSCOW

On Wednesday, the fourteenth day of the same month of July, a fire started in the inner city of Moscow. This happened at night, and everything burned so that not a piece of wood remained in the city. The stone churches collapsed and even the stone walls of the fortifications collapsed in many places. A great many people burned: the monk-priests and priests, monks and nuns, and men, women, and children because this fire issued from thence [from the inner city], and they were afraid to go outside the walls because they feared the Tatars. And great wealth and an endless amount of all sorts of goods burned because a great number of people from many cities had taken refuge in Moscow. When the city burned, the Grand Princess Sofia and Grand Princess Maria with their children and boyars went to the city of Rostov, and the citizens were in great despond and became agitated. Those who could sought to leave the city. The common people assembled, however, and began to restore the city gates and started catching and thrashing those who wanted to escape from thence, and even put [some] in irons. And so the panic came to an end and everyone together set to fortifying the city and building houses for themselves.

On the twenty-fifth of August of the same year, after the day of the Dormition of Our Lady, Khan Ulu Mahmet [Ulug Moham-med] with his children and his entire horde went from [Nizhnii]

90. This article was sent as proof of his captivity and in order to get a ransom.

1446 Novgorod to Kurmysh, taking with him the Grand Prince and Prince Mikhail. He sent his envoy, Bigich, to Prince Dimitrii Shemiaka. The latter was very happy and rendered him [to Bigich] great honor because he wanted to become Grand Prince. And he let him go with all manner of calumny about the Grand Prince. He sent with him his [own] envoy, *diak* Fedor Dubinskii, in order to prevent the Grand Prince from getting back the Grand Principality. Thanks to the All Powerful, Merciful and Blessed, Man-loving God Who witnessed such merciless malevolence again of [Shemiaka's intended] fratricide and betrayal of the Sovereign, this [envoy] was prevented from reaching the Tatars in Murom and the hearts of the godless, lawless, Christian-killing sons of Hagar were turned toward mercy, for [the Khan] thought that his envoy was killed by Shemiaka.

ABOUT THE RELEASE OF THE GRAND PRINCE FROM KURMISH

In the summer of the year 6954 [1446] Khan Ulu Mahmet [Ulug Mohammed] and his son, Mamutiak, rendered honor to the Grand Prince. Receiving from him a pledge on the cross that he would pay as large a ransom as possible, they let him go from Kurmish on the first of October, the day of the Protection of the Most Holy Mother of God. With him were Prince Mikhail and others, whosoever [had been captured] with him. At the same time [the Tatars] sent with them their envoys, several of their lords with many warriors, Prince Seid Assan, Utiesha, Kuraisha, Dyl-Hodja, Aidar, and many others. The Grand Prince, after a two-day march from Kurmish, sent a *seunch*[91] with Andrei Pleshcheev to his mother, Grand Princess Sofia, and to [his wife] the Grand Princess [Maria] with the children, as well as to his brothers and boyars, and to all other people [informing them] that the Khan had honored him and released him to his patrimony to be Grand Prince.

In the meanwhile [Shemiaka's] *diak*, Fedor [Dubinskii] with the Khan's envoy, Bigich, came by boat from Murom and let the horses go onto the shore. Andrei [Pleshcheev] approached Ivan's [?] town of Kiselev, which is located between Nizhnii Novgorod and Murom, and there met Plishchka Obraztsov, who was with the horses of [*diak*] Fedor [Dubinskii] and Bigich. Andrei [Pleshcheev] told them that the Grand Prince was released to reign in the Grand Principal-

91. *Seunch*: "happy message."

ity. They [Plishchka Obratsov with his people] returned from thence   **1446** and met at the Dudin Monastery with [*diak*] Fedor [Dubinskii], who was going [to the Khan] with Bigich on the Oka River. Hearing this, Fedor returned to Murom with Bigich. When they arrived in Murom Prince Vasilii Ivanovich Obolenskii caught Bigich and put him in irons. Learning this, Prince Dmitri [Shemiaka] fled to Uglich.

The Grand Prince came to Murom, remained there a short time and then went to Vladimir, and there was great joy in all the cities of Russia. On St. Demetrius' Day [October 26] the Grand Prince came to Pereiaslavl', where were his mother, Grand Princess Sofia, and his [wife] Grand Princess Maria, and his sons—Prince Ivan and Prince Iurii—and all his princes, boyars, lesser boyars, and a great many of his retinue from all cities.

ABOUT THE EARTHQUAKE

On the first of October of the same fall, the very day the Grand Prince was released from Kurmish, at six o'clock at night, the earth shook in the city of Moscow, in the Kremlin, in the suburbs, and all the churches shook. Many people who were asleep at the time did not hear it at all. Others, who were not sleeping, heard it and were greatly distressed, afraid for their lives, and in the morning they told of it tearfully to those who had not heard. The same fall during St. Philip's Fast[92] the Grand Prince confessed and had Communion, and came to Moscow on the seventeenth day of November, staying at the court of his mother in Vagankovo, outside the city. Thereafter he journeyed into the city to the mansion of Prince Iurii Patrikeevich.

ABOUT SHEMIAKA'S EVIL PLOT AGAINST GRAND PRINCE VASILII

The devil put into the mind of Prince Dmitrii Shemiaka the desire for the [Grand] Principality, and he began to send to Prince Ivan of Mozhaisk, telling him of this: "The Khan released the Grand Prince and the latter has pledged on the cross to the Khan that the Khan will rule in Moscow and in all Russian cities and in our patrimonies, and himself [the Grand Prince] will rule in Tver'." And in such a manner at the devil's instigation, and having taken counsel with his evil advisors—at that time there were the present Konstantinoviches and their other boyars who did not wish any

92. St. Philip's Fast: the week before November 14.

1446   good either to their Sovereign or to all Christianity—they sent the above-mentioned speech to Grand Prince Boris of Tver'. The latter, hearing this, became sore afraid [to lose Tver' to the Grand Prince] and became their co-conspirator. There were, however, many people from Moscow conspiring with them—boyars and great merchants, and also monks were at that council. And so the princes and their councils secretly began to arm themselves and to look for a convenient time to dislodge the Grand Prince.

They found an opportunity which furthered their evil plan: at that time the Grand Prince wanted to go on a pilgrimage to [the Monastery of] the Lifegiving Trinity and to the relics of Wonder-maker Sergius, and he journeyed thither with his honorable children, Prince Ivan and Prince Iurii, as well as with a small number of people because they did not intend anything other than to provide gifts and supplies to the friars of this great monastery. The traitors who were in Moscow every day sent information to Prince Dmitrii Shemiaka and Ivan of Mozhaisk, and they, assembling their forces in Ruza, prepared themselves like dogs for a hunt or like savage beasts thirsting to taste human blood.

Having received the news that the Grand Prince had left the city, they immediately hurried to Moscow and arrived there on Saturday at nine o'clock, on the eve of Sunday, the twelfth day of the month of February—the day of the Prodigal Son—and they took over the city. There was no resistance to them because no one knew of it except their co-conspirators, who opened the city to them. Entering therein, they captured the Grand Princesses Sofia and Maria and robbed the treasury of the Grand Prince and of his mother. They arrested and sacked the boyars who were there, as well as many other inhabitants of the city.

That very night Prince Dmitrii [Shemiaka] sent Prince Ivan of Mozhaisk in haste after Grand Prince Vasilii, who was at the [Monastery of the] Trinity, and with them there were many of his own people and his [Ivan's]. This Sunday of the Prodigal Son, during the very liturgy, there hastened to the Grand Prince a man called Bunko, who told him that Prince Dmitrii Shemiaka and Prince Ivan of Mozhaisk were moving against him with an army. But [the Grand Prince] did not believe him because this Bunko quite recently had abandoned him for Prince Dmitrii, and he said, "They just want to confuse us. My cousins and I pledged on the cross [to abide in peace] so how could it be?" And he [the Grand Prince] said to throw

Bunko out of the monastery and dispatch him home. He was turned **1446** out and treated like a thief because the armed guards arrested and beat him.

Although the Grand Prince did not have faith in his message, he nonetheless sent guards toward Radonezh. They took up a position watching from the mountain at Radonezh. The scouts [of Shemiaka's] recognized these guards from afar but the guards did not notice [Shemiaka's] men because they had no faith in this information. [Shemiaka's] scouts told Prince Ivan [of Mozhaisk] that there were guards on the mountain near Radonezh. Then he ordered that many sledges be prepared, some covered with bast mats, some with linen, and [in each sledge] under them were two armed warriors, with a third walking behind as if accompanying the sledge. When the forward [sledges] passed the guards, then all the warriors jumped out of the sledges and caught them. The guards were unable to flee because there were nine feet of snow. Very soon they [Shemiaka's men] came to the monastery, riding horses from the mountain to the town of Klementievskoe, just as if it were a pleasure hunt.

When the Grand Prince saw them, he ran to the stable but there were no horses at hand because he had taken [Bunko's] information for a lie, relying on [Shemiaka's] pledge on the cross, and he had not ordered that anything be prepared for himself. All his people were in despair and frightened because they were greatly surprised. The Grand Prince, seeing no help withal, went to the monastery, to the stone Church of the Holy Trinity. The bell-ringer, a monk named Nikifor, hastened to unlock the church. The Grand Prince entered and he [Nikifor] locked it, and the Grand Prince went to hide. Then the murderers, like vicious wolves, rode into the monastery on horseback. Ahead of all was Nikita Konstantinovich [a boyar of Prince Shemiaka], and he rode his horse up to the front door of the church, and up the steps. When he dismounted, he [slipped and] struck a stone just before the church doors of the porch. The others hastened to lift him up, and he could hardly breathe, appearing as if drunk, and his face was like death.

Thereupon Prince Ivan [of Mozhaisk], himself, rode into the monastery with all his warriors. Prince Ivan began to ask, "Where is the Grand Prince?" Inside the church the Grand Prince heard Prince Ivan's voice and cried out in a loud voice, "Brother, be

1446   merciful to me. Don't deprive me of the ability to see the icons of God and His Purest Mother, and of all His Saints. And then I will not leave this monastery and I will be shorn [a monk] here." He went to the southern doors, opened them, took from the grave of St. Sergius the Icon of the Apparition of the Holy Mother of God and the Two Apostles to St. Sergius, and he met Prince Ivan [of Mozhaisk] in those church doors, saying, "Brother, let us both pledge on the Life-Creating Cross and on this Icon in this church of the Life-Begetting Trinity, at the grave of this Wonderworker Sergius, that we shall hold no bad thoughts nor wish none of our brothers or cousins any harm. And now I don't know what may happen to me."

Prince Ivan told him, "Sovereign lord, in the case we harbor evil toward you, then let there be evil upon us. We do this, however, because of the Christian [Russian] people and your ransom. When the Tatars who accompanied you see it [that is, that you are no longer Grand Prince], they will reduce the ransom which you must give the Khan."[93]

GRAND PRINCE VASILII IS TAKEN PRISONER BY SHEMIAKA

The Grand Prince put the icon back in its place and fell upon the grave of Wonderworker Sergius. He wept inconsolably and sighed deeply, praying loudly, gasping, and all present marvelled at his tears and themselves wept. Even these evil robbers did likewise. Prince Ivan [of Mozhaisk] bowed slightly in the church, walked out and said to Nikita [Konstantinovich], "Seize him." After long prayer, the Grand Prince arose, looked about and said, "Where is my brother, Prince Ivan?" Nikita, the evil servant of the bitter and merciless tormentors, approached the Prince and seized him by the shoulder, saying, "You are captured by Grand Prince Dmitrii Iurievich." And the other [the Grand Prince] said, "The will of God be done." And the other, evildoer, bore him out of the church

93. When Grand Prince Vasilii Vasilievich was released by Khan Ulug Mohammed he was forced to promise a very great ransom. The Tatar officers who accompanied him to Moscow extorted this ransom in a most harsh and pitiless manner, really impoverishing the Russians. Consequently many princes, boyars, merchants, and commoners participated in the conspiracy in the hope that once Grand Prince Vasilii Vasilievich ceased being the ruler, the ransom would be reduced. Shemiaka, however, was actually attempting to take over the power in the Grand Principality of Muscovy.

and from the monastery and put him in an empty sledge with a   **1446**
monk opposite him, and went with him to Moscow. All his boyars,
together with all the others, were captured, robbed, and left naked.
The Grand Prince's children—Prince Ivan and Prince Iurii—hid
in the same monastery and they [Shemiaka's] bloodsuckers, left,
since they had already caught a sweet booty and therefore did not
care for the latter, nor did they ask about them. These sons of the
Grand Prince, Ivan and Iurii, that same night escaped from the
monastery with those who remained, and succeeded in hiding. They
escaped to Prince Ivan Riapolovskii, to his town of Boiarevo, near
Iur'iev. Prince Ivan [Riapolovskii] with his brothers, Semion and
Dmitrii, with all his people, hurried with them to Murom, and then
they fortified themselves there with many people.

THE GREAT EVIL

On the fourteenth of February, Monday night of Shrovetide,
Grand Prince Vasilii was brought to Moscow and was guarded in
Shemiaka's estate, while Prince Dmitrii Shemiaka, himself,
sojourned in a court on Popovkina. On Wednesday of the same
week, at night, the Grand Prince was blinded and was sent with his
[wife] Princess to Uglich Pólé. And his mother, Grand Princess
Sofia, was deported to Chukhloma. Learning of this, Prince Vasilii
Iaroslavovich [of Serpukhov] and Prince Semion Ivanovich
Obolenskii fled to Lithuania. The other lesser boyars and all the
people greeted and pledged to serve Prince Dmitrii, and he led
them to pledge on the cross.

ABOUT BASENOK

Only Fedor Basenok did not want to serve him. Prince Dmitrii
[Shemiaka], however, ordered him to be put in heavy irons and
kept under guard. But he [Basenok] persuaded his guard [to release
him] and escaped from the irons, hastening straightaway to
Kolomna, where he stayed with his friends. After convincing many
people to go with him, he raided the district of Kolomna and departed for Lithuania with many people.

ABOUT IAROSLAVOVICH

He [Basenok] came to Debriansk because the King [of Poland
and Grand Duke of Lithuania] gave to Prince Vasilii Iaroslavovich
[of Serpukhov] as patrimony Debriansk, Gomel, Starodub, Mstis-

1446   lavl', and many other places; but Prince Vasilii Iaroslavovich gave Debriansk to Prince Semion Obolenskii and to Fedor Basenok.

Prince Dmitrii [Shemiaka] learned that the Grand Prince's children had arrived and settled in Murom with many people but did not want to send for them fearing because all the people were indignant about his rule and thought [badly] of him because they wanted to see Grand Prince Vasilii ruling his state.

ABOUT THE CHILDREN OF THE GRAND PRINCE

And Prince Dmitrii [Shemiaka] plotted the following. He summoned to him, to Moscow, Bishop Jonas of Riazan', and when the latter arrived he promised him the Metropolia, telling him, "Father, you should return to your diocese, to the city of Murom, and take under your mantle the children of Grand Prince [Vasilii], and I will be glad to bestow them and release their father, the Grand Prince; and I will give them a patrimony so they will be able to be together."

ABOUT LORD JONAS OF ROSTOV

Lord Jonas went on boat to Murom considering these speeches of Prince Dmitrii [Shemiaka]. Arriving in Murom, he started deliberating with the boyars of the Grand Prince's children; with three Princes Riapolovskii and others with them. The boyars considered at length and came to the conclusion, "If we don't follow the Bishop and do not go to Prince Dmitrii [Shemiaka] with the Grand Prince's children, he [Shemiaka] may come with an army, take the city, capture whomsoever he wants, and do [whatsoever he wants] to them, to their father, the Grand Prince, and to all of us. In what will our strength consist then if we do not heed the Bishop's words?" And they told Bishop Jonas, "Since you have come to our lords, the children of the Grand Prince, as well as to us, with the proposal of Prince Dmitrii [Shemiaka], we will not venture to do otherwise than to release to you the Grand Prince's children without assurance. Let us go, however, to the Cathedral Church of the Nativity of the Most Holy Mother of God, cover them with the icon cloth and then take them under your Bishop's mantle, and then we will let them go with you and we, ourselves, will go with them." Bishop Jonas promised to do thus, went to the church, started a service to the Most Pure [Virgin Mary] and after the service he took them under his mantle from the icon cloth of the Most Pure and went

with them to Prince Dmitrii [Shemiaka], to the city of Pereiaslavl',   **1446**
where he was; and he came to Pereiaslavl' on the sixth day of the
month of May.

ABOUT SHEMIAKA'S SYCOPHANCY

Prince Dmitrii [Shemiaka] received them with some flattery,
invited them to his table and gave them gifts. On the third day
after that he sent them with Bishop Jonas to their father [Grand
Prince Vasilii Vasilievich], into captivity in Uglich. And he [the
Bishop] accompanied them to their father and left them there,
then returned to Prince Dmitrii. The latter ordered him to go
to Moscow and take over the court of the Metropolia, and Jonas
did thus.

When the [Princes] Riapolovskii—Prince Ivan and his brothers,
Prince Semion and Prince Dmitrii—saw that Dmitrii Shemiaka had
betrayed his word and lied to the Bishop in everything, they began
to plot how to liberate the Grand Prince. Prince Ivan Vasilievich
Striga, Ivan Oshchera, with his brother, Bobr, and Iushko Dranitsa,
and many other junior boyars of the Grand Prince's court were in
the same plot, and together with them in the plot was Semion
Filimonov with all children, Rusalka and Runo, and many other
junior boyars. They determined the term to assemble at Uglich at
noon on St. Peter's Day [July 29]. Semion Filimonov with all his
people came on time; however, Prince Dmitrii Shemiaka had tidings
concerning the Riapolovskiis and, not daring to go to Uglich at that
time, they [the Riapolovskiis] all went beyond the Volga to Beloozero. Thereupon Prince Dmitrii sent after them from Uglich an
army of many regiments under the command of Vasilii Veprev
and Fedor Mikhailovich. They were to assemble at the mouth of
the Sheksna on the day of All Saints. Fedor [Mikhailovich] did not
succeed in joining up with Vasilii [Veprev] on time, while the
Riapolovskiis turned against Vasilii [Veprev] and defeated him at
the mouth of the Mologa River. At that time Fedor [Mikhailovich]
crossed the Volga at the mouth of the Sheksna with all his troops.
Riapolovskii learned of this and moved against him. Seeing them,
Fedor [Mikhailovich] hastily recrossed the Volga, while the
Riapolovskiis marched through the Novgorodian land to Lithuania
and reached Prince Vasilii Iaroslavovich in Mstislavl'. Having no
tidings of their [movements], Semion Filimonov went toward Moscow with all his people. Only Runo did not go with him but followed

1447   the Riapolovskiis. The Princes Riapolovskii and Prince Ivan Striga
with many other junior boyars, as well as those aforementioned
and unmentioned, came to Prince Vasilii Iaroslavovich [of Ser-
pukhov][94] and started deliberating with him about how to free the
Grand Prince.

Prince Dmitrii Shemiaka, realizing that very many people had
abandoned him for the Grand Prince, sent for Bishop [Jonas] and
began to discuss with Prince Ivan [of Mozhaisk], with the bishops
and boyars, whether to release him or not. Bishop Jonas repeated
uninterruptedly every day, "You have done wrong. You have led
me into sin and shame. You were supposed to release the Grand
Prince but you confined his children with him. You gave me your
word of honor and they obeyed me, and now I am a liar. Liberate
him, take [these sins] from off my soul and from your own; consider
eternity: his children are small. You must strengthen [an agreement
with him] by [pledging on] the Most Honorable Cross and before
us, brethren bishops." Many, however, spoke contrariwise. Prince
Dmitrii [Shemiaka] pondered this at length and decided to release
the Grand Prince and to give him a patrimony where he could abide.

The same year in Uglich, on the thirteenth of August, a son,
Andrei, was born to Grand Prince [Vasilii Vasilievich].

ABOUT THE RELEASE OF GRAND PRINCE VASILII BY SHEMIAKA

In the Year 6955 [1447]. Prince Dmitrii Shemiaka went to Uglich
with the intention of releasing the Grand Prince and his children.
All the bishops, archimandrites, and abbots were with him. Arriving
in Uglich, he released the Grand Prince and his children, repented
and apologized, begging for pardon. The Grand Prince made peace
with him and took all the guilt upon himself, saying, "I should have
suffered much more because of my sins and my many lawlessnesses
and many trespasses of my pledge on the cross to you, as well as
because of [my sins] against the senior cousins and all those Orthodox Christians whom I have ruined or intended to ruin altogether. I deserve capital punishment but you, my Sovereign, you
have shown me your mercifulness and have not ruined me despite
my lawlessness. I will have to repent for all my evildoings." He said
all this and many other words so numerous that it is impossible to
write them all. When he spoke the tears streamed from his eyes

94. Prince Vasilii Iaroslavovich was in the city of Mstislavl' in
Lithuania.

like brooks, and all present were astonished by such humility and   **1447**
emotion and they all shed tears, looking at him.

Thereafter Prince Dmitrii gave a banquet for the Grand Prince,
the Grand Princess, and their children, and present were all the
bishops of the Russian land, many boyars, and many lesser boyars.
He greatly honored the Grand Prince, giving numerous gifts to
the Grand Prince, to his Grand Princess, and to their children. He
gave the Grand Prince [the land of] Vologda with all [lands] as his
patrimony, and let the Grand Prince, Grand Princess, and the children go thither.

The Grand Prince arrived [in Vologda] and thereafter went
with his entire [family and retinue] to the Kyrillo [-Beloozerskii]
Monastery, where he gave supplies and alms to the brethren. Such
a sovereign, however, is not meant to remain in exile in such a
remote and sparsely inhabited land. When the boyars, the junior
boyars, and the people of the Grand Prince became aware of this,
very many of them left Prince Dmitrii [Shemiaka] and Prince Ivan
[of Mozhaisk] and went to the Grand Prince. The latter, after
sojourning in Beloozero, left it and at that time very many people
joined him. The Grand Prince, however, did not return to Vologda
but went to Tver' to meet with Boris Aleksandrovich, Grand Prince
of Tver'. When he arrived in Tver' the Grand Prince of Tver' let
him rest there, rendered him great honors and gave him numerous
presents. There Grand Prince Vasilii Vasilievich betrothed his
senior son, Prince Ivan, to Maria, the daughter of Grand Prince
Boris. And many boyars with numerous men joined the Grand
Prince [Vasilii Vasilievich] in Tver'.

When Prince Dmitrii [Shemiaka] released the Grand Prince
[Vasilii], Prince Vasilii Iaroslavovich [of Serpukhov] was unaware
of it. And he decided with the boyars of the Grand Prince [Vasilii]
to leave their wives and children in the Lithuanian land and go to
find a way to liberate the Grand Prince [Vasilii] from Uglich. They
decided on a date when they would assemble in the Lithuanian
district of Patsyn'. Just before the time when they—Prince Vasilii
Iaroslavovich [of Serpukhov], who was in Mstislavl' with the three
[princes] Riapolovskii, Prince Ivan Striga [Obolenskii], Oshchera
and many lesser boyars, as well as those who were in Briansk, to
wit, Prince Semion Obolenskii, Basenok, and many [other] junior
boyars—were to leave the Lithuanian land, the news came to Prince
Vasilii [Iaroslavovich] in Mstislavl' that the Grand Prince had been

1447   released and had received Vologda. This news was brought by Danilo Bashmak.

At the same time a certain Kyianin [man of Kiev] named Poltinka came to Briansk to Prince Semion [Obolenskii] [with the same news]. This [Poltinka] was sojourning in Moscow in the service of Princess Olelkova, daughter of Olelko[95] in order to get tidings about the Grand Prince [Vasilii]. From Briansk he journeyed to Kiev and told them the same news which had been brought by Bashmak. Then Prince Vasilii Iaroslavovich [of Serpukhov] with all the boyars and people, with wives and children, moved from Mstislavl'; [simultaneously] Prince Semion [Obolenskii] and Basenok departed from Briansk, similarly with everyone, and they all assembled in Patsyn'. And hither came Dmitrii, son of Andrei, to them bearing word that the Grand Prince had gone from Vologda to Beloozero, and from thence to Tver'. And so from thence [from Patsyn'] all of them, with many people, went farther.

When they came to Elna they encountered Tatars and started shooting at each other. Thereupon the Tatars, however, began to shout at the Russians, "Who are you?" And those answered, "We are the people of Moscow and we are going with Prince Vasilii Iaroslavovich [of Serpukhov] to aid our Sovereign, Grand Prince Vasilii Vasilievich. They say he is already released. And who are you?" The Tatars responded, "We have come from the Cherkess land with Khan Mahmet's [Ulug Mohammed's] two sons, Kasim and Iakub. We heard [concerning Grand Prince Vasilii], that his brothers betrayed him, and we went to aid the Grand Prince because of his earlier good deeds and his bread. We have received many good things from him." And so they joined each other and made an agreement and proceeded farther together, seeking how to aid the Grand Prince.

Prince Dmitrii Shemiaka and Prince Ivan of Mozhaisk were then still in Volok. In the meantime the Grand Prince dispatched his boyar, Mikhail Borisovich Pleshcheev, to Moscow hurriedly with a small number of people so as to ascertain how they could bypass the army of Prince Dmitrii [Shemiaka]. And they passed through [Shemiaka's] army unnoticed by anyone and at night on Christmas

95. The Princess was the daughter of the Lithuanian Prince Olelko Vitovtovich. Thus she was the cousin of Grand Prince Vasilii Vasilievich and the niece of his mother, Grand Princess Sofia, who, herself, was the daughter of the famous Lithuanian Grand Prince Vitovt.

Eve arrived in Moscow, during matins, at the St. Nicholas Gate. At **1447**
that time because of the holiday Princess Uliana, wife of Prince
Vasilii Vladimirovich, was riding into the city [of Moscow] to matins,
and therefore the gates were open. So they [boyar Pleshcheev with
his men] entered the city at once. [Learning of this] Fiodor
Galichskii, lord lieutenant of Prince Dmitrii [Shemiaka], who was
also at matins at that time in the Church of the Most Pure [Virgin
Mary], fled. The lord lieutenant of Prince Ivan [of Mozhaisk], a
certain Vasilii Cheshikha, attempted to flee the city on horseback
but Rostopcha, servant of the Grand Princess in charge of heating
the palace, caught him, put him in irons and brought him to the
voevodas. And other of Prince Dmitrii's and Prince Ivan's supporters were arrested, put in irons and sacked. The citizens were
brought to pledge to Grand Prince Vasilii, and they started fortifying the city.

In the meanwhile, the Grand Prince moved with large forces
toward Volok against Shemiaka and the Prince of Mozhaisk. The
latter were taken aback. How could it be that the Grand Prince was
moving against them from Tver'? At the same time they had word
that [from the other direction] the Khan's sons and Prince Vasilii
Iaroslavovich [of Serpukhov] were marching against them with
large forces, that Moscow was already taken, and that the people
were fleeing from them. So they, themselves [Shemiaka and the
Prince of Mozhaisk] fled to Galich, and some [of their men] to
Chukhloma. They took with them Grand Princess Sofia, mother
of the Grand Prince, and retreated to Kargopol'.

The Grand Prince followed them, having sent his Grand Princess to Moscow. He marched, and camped before Uglich. Here he
was joined by Prince Vasilii Iaroslavovich [of Serpukhov], with
whom were the above-mentioned boyars of the Grand Prince. They
camped before Uglich and took it; there, before the city, Iushka
Dranitsa, a courageous Lithuanian man, was killed. From thence
the Grand Prince moved to Iaroslavl', where he was joined by the
Khan's sons, Kasim and Iakub. From Iaroslavl' the Grand Prince
sent his boyar, Vasilii Fedorovich Kutuzov, to Prince Dmitrii
[Shemiaka], asking him to release his mother, Grand Princess Sofia,
and telling him the following: "Brother, Prince Dmitrii Iurievich!
What honor and pride is there in it for you to hold your aunt, my
mother, in captivity? I am already on my throne of the Grand
Principality, so why do you want revenge?" Having sent this [envoy],

1448   he [the Grand Prince] journeyed to Moscow, arriving there on
Friday, the seventeenth of February, the day when the Oecumenical
Council is remembered.

When the Grand Prince's boyar arrived, he addressed Prince
Dmitrii [Shemiaka] and the many who were with him. Prince Dmitrii
took counsel with the boyars and said, "Brothers, I should not
torment my aunt, who was also my Sovereign Grand Princess. I,
myself, am fleeing. I need people and they are tired, and we still
have to guard her. It were better to release her." And so, having
consulted, they released her from Kargopol'. With her Prince Dmitrii sent his boyar, Mikhail Fedorovich Saburov, and some lesser
boyars. When Grand Prince [Vasilii Vasilievich] learned that his
mother had been released and was nearby, he went to meet her.
They met in the Monastery of the Holy Trinity and St. Sergius,
from whence they journeyed to the city of Pereiaslavl'. Mikhail
Saburov with his escort petitioned the Grand Prince so as not to
return to Shemiaka but to remain in the service of the Grand Prince.

In the Year 6956 [1448]. During St. Philip's Fast, Mamutek,
Khan of Kazan,[96] sent all his princes with great forces to campaign
against the cities of Vladimir, Murom, and others in the patrimony
of the Grand Prince. Hearing of this, Grand Prince Vasilii
Vasilievich sent his army against them.[97]

The same winter the Grand Prince marched against Prince
Dmitrii Shemiaka, who was in Galich, and came with strong forces
to the city of Kostroma, and there they began sending envoys to
each other. Prince Dmitrii took fright and began suing for peace:
he pledged on the cross and under oath gave the "anathema char-

96. In 1445 Khan Ulug Mohammad, who, himself, had been driven
out of the Great Horde by his brother, Kichik Mohammed, took Nizhnii
Novgorod, and in 1446 he defeated and captured Grand Prince Vasilii
Vasilievich. After the Grand Prince was released, Ulug Mohammed left
Nizhnii Novgorod and settled on the Volga near the place where the Kama
River becomes its tributary. There he founded the city of Kazan' and thus
became the first Khan of the Tatar state of Kazan' on the upper Volga.
The population of this state consisted of Tatars, who came with him;
Turkic Bulgars (now Chuvash), who were already Moslem and had their
own rather advanced state; and the Finno-Ugric tribe of Cheremis. During
the century of its existence, this Tatar state became a source of endless
conflicts with and raids against the Russians. Mamutek was Ulug Mohammed's son. Grekov, pp. 415–18.

97. This paragraph is in *Litsevoi svod* only, not in *Obol.* or *Ioasaf.*

ter" against himself[98] wherein he declared that from that time on **1449** he would never wish any evil to the Grand Prince, to his children, nor to the whole Grand Principality, nor to his patrimony. "In the case I should trespass this charter or what is written herein, I will nevermore have God's grace upon me, nor [that] of His Purest Mother, nor of the Honorable and Life-creating Cross. And there will be for me no prayer or intercession by any of the saints or great wonderworkers of our land, nor by the Most Holy Metropolitans Peter and Alexis, nor any others. And there will be for me no blessing by any bishop of the Russian land, neither of those who are presently in their dioceses nor of anyone in the entire clergy who are with them."

The Grand Prince listened to his petition, granted him peace, and returned to Kostroma on Maundy Thursday, spending Easter in Rostov; and the next day he celebrated the Annunciation, also, in Rostov, and banqueted at Bishop Ephraim's. The same day he departed for Moscow, where he arrived during the week of St. Thomas' Fast. His son, Ivan, was in Vladimir.

The same spring on Easter Day the Lithuanian ambassador, *Pan* Semion Icdigoldov, was received by the Grand Prince.

In the summer there was a plague among the horses and other animals, and among the people, but not very severe.

The same year Prince Vasilii the One-Eyed passed away.

ABOUT THE ASCENSION OF JONAS, BISHOP OF RIAZAN', TO THE RUSSIAN METROPOLIA

In the Year 6957 [1449]. On the fifteenth day of the month of December he [Jonas] was elected by the Russian bishops to Metropolitan of all Russia. [There were] Ephraim of Rostov, Abraham of Suzdal', Barlaam of Kolomna, and Pitirim of Perm'. Novgorodian Archbishop Euthymius and the Bishop of Tver' sent their charters expressing their agreement to elect Jonas, Bishop of Riazan', to Metropolitan. Earlier, when he was in Constantinople about the appointment to the Metropolia, he received the blessing of the Holy Patriarch and of the entire Holy Council to become Metropolitan after Isidore.[99] After his consecration he gave the Diocese of Rostov

98. "Anathema charter" (*Prokliataia gramota*) means that the person who gives such "charter" will be accursed if he breaks his word.

99. In 1437 after the death of Metropolitan Photius, Bishop Jonas indeed was elected as the Russian candidate to the Metropolia of Kiev and

1449   to Bishop Ephraim because previously [before Jonas] Archbishop Theodore had been there, having been appointed from Constantinople.[100]

This very spring Prince Dmitrii Shemiaka, breaking his pledge on the cross and his "anathema charter," moved on Kostroma with large forces and arrived there on Easter Day. He fought for a long while against the city but did not succeed in the least because the garrison there was under Prince Ivan Vasilievich Striga [Obolenskii] and Fedor Basenok, and with them were many lesser boyars and the retinue of the Grand Prince. Learning of this, the Grand Prince moved against him, taking with him the Metropolitan, the bishops, his cousins and the Khan's sons, and all forces. When he drew near the Volga the Grand Prince sent his cousins and the Khan's sons with all their forces. When he arrived at Rudino, Prince Dmitrii [Shemiaka] crossed [the Volga] to the opposite shore and made peace [with the Grand Prince].

This very year a son was born to the Grand Prince in the month of July and he was named Boris.

The same year the rapidly advancing Tatars of Seid-Ahmet moved to Pokhra, captured the wife of Prince Vasilii Obolenskii and caused much evil to the Christians, massacred them and took captives. When the Khan's son, Kasim,[101] learned of this he moved against them [with his own Tatar troops] from Zvenigorod, and those [Tatars of Seid-Ahmet] were scattered over the land. And whomever he met, he defeated and took away captives. Seeing this, the Tatars fled.[102]

Moscow and of all Russia. He went to Constantinople to receive the investiture from the Patriarch but in the meantime Patriarch Joseph sent Isidore to Russia to become Metropolitan there. It is possible that in view of the tradition that there would be appointed to the Russian Metropolia alternately a Greek, and after him a Russian, as Metropolitan, the Patriarch promised Jonas that he would become the Russian Metropolitan after Isidore. No documents containing this promise have been preserved, however. Kartashov, Vol. I, pp. 357–77.

100. This last sentence is in *Litsevoi svod* only; the names of the bishops are not mentioned in *Obol.* or *Ioasaf.*

101. See year 1447.

102. In the reign of Vasilii II a great many Tatar princes and khans' sons (*tsarevichi*) left the Great or Golden Horde, moved to the Muscovite land, settled there with the permission of Grand Prince Vasilii Vasilievich, and became "service Tatars" of the Muscovite rulers. A considerable

ABOUT THE BATTLE OF GALICH

In the Year 6958 [1450]. The Grand Prince campaigned against Prince Dmitrii [Shemiaka] and wanted to advance to Galich but received tidings that [Shemiaka] had gone to Vologda. And the Grand Prince moved toward Iledam[103] toward Obnora and intended to advance against him toward Vologda. When he was at the [Monastery] of St. Nicholas on the Obnora [River], he received tidings that [Shemiaka] had returned to Galich, so the Grand Prince went back down the Obnora and then up the Kostroma River. And he came to [the Monastery of] St. John on Zheleznyi Borok and there received the message that Prince Dmitrii was in Galich and that he had many people with him, that he was fortifying the city and preparing cannons, and that there was infantry with him, and he stood before the city with his entire force. The Grand Prince, hearing this and relying upon Lord God, His Most Holy Mother, and on the great wonderworkers and the power of the honorable cross, sent his princes-voevodas with all his forces. The main voevoda was Prince Vasilii Ivanovich Obolenskii, and there were many other princes and voevodas. Therafter he dispatched the Khan's sons and all their princes with them. They came to Galich on the twenty-seventh of January. Prince Dmitrii took up a position on the mountain before the city with all his forces, without moving from the spot. The voevodas of the Grand Prince advanced from the lake to the mountains, but they did so cautiously because the mountain was very steep. They advanced from the ravines, climbed the mountains, and the armies met: and there was a terrible massacre but God helped the Grand Prince. Many [of his enemies] were killed, the best people were captured by hand, and Prince [Shemiaka] barely escaped, while nearly all his infantry was destroyed. But the fortified city [of Galich] remained closed. The Grand Prince, who was in

---

number of them were later Christianized and Russianized, thus becoming founders of many aristocratic Russian families. Kasim settled in the Riazan' land and founded there the town of Kasim, or Kasimov. The Kasimov Tatars kept the Islamic faith and their own language into the twentieth century, despite the fact that they lived completely surrounded by the Russian population. They formed a tiny Tatar territory some one hundred miles southwest of Moscow. Grekov, pp. 418–22. Vernadsky, pp. 331, 389.

103. Perhaps "Iledam" is a scribe's error. This could be *po sledam*— "following his tracks."

1451   Borok, received news that the victory was his and he thanked God and His Purest Mother and the great wonderworkers, and commanded that a *Te Deum* be sung in the Church of St. John the Precursor. And thereafter he went to Galich. When he arrived in Galich the citizens surrendered; he pacified the city and put his lords lieutenants in this entire patrimony, and returned to Moscow, where he arrived in Shrovetide; and Shemiaka escaped to Great Novgorod.

The same summer Volodimir Khavrin erected on his estate in Moscow a stone church in honor of the holiday of the Exaltation of the Cross. It was erected in the place of the earlier stone church which collapsed during the fire in the Suzdal' section.—Metropolitan Jonas laid in his estate the foundation of a stone palace with a church in honor of the holiday of the Deposition of the Vestments of the Holy Mother of God.

The same year on the fifth of August there was a tremendous cloud over Moscow and horrifying thunder, and the lightning struck the stone Cathedral of Archangel Michael. On the thirteenth of August there was a tremendous storm which broke the cross on the same Church of the Archangel Michael.

The same year when the Grand Prince was in his patrimony in Kolomna, word came to him that the Tatars were advancing from the *polé* under Mali Berdei Ulan, and with them were other princes with numerous Tatars. The Grand Prince sent against them Kasim, the Khan's sons who served him, with his Tatars and with his voevoda, Konstantin Aleksandrovich Bezzubtsov, with warriors from Kolomna. And they caught them on the Betiuka River in the *polé* and killed many Tatars. The other [Tatars] ran away. On that occasion Romodan Zinoviev was killed.

In the Year 6959 [1451]. Prince Semion Olel'kovich visited his grandmother, the Grand Princess Sofia, in Moscow, and his uncle, Grand Prince Vasilii. The same spring the day of the great martyr George happened to be on Holy Friday.

ABOUT THE TATAR RAIDS

The same year the Grand Prince received tidings that the Khan's son, Mozovsha, from the horde of Seid-Ahmet, was advancing against him. And the Grand Prince moved against him toward Kolomna without having time [to gather] an army. He was near Brashevo when the news came that the Tatars were already on the shore [of the Oka River]. The Grand Prince returned to Moscow **1451** and sent the people with him under the command of voevoda Prince Ivan of Zvenigorod toward the shore of the Oka River with the order to prevent a rapid crossing of the river by the Tatars. But the latter took fright and retreated, though by another route than the Grand Prince's. The Grand Prince came to Moscow on St. Peter's Day, prepared the city for a siege and left his mother, Sofia, there, as well as his son, Prince Iurii, and a great multitude of boyars and lesser boyars, together with his [spiritual] father, Metropolitan Jonas, Ephraim, Archbishop of Rostov, and all the clergy and monks and a great many people of Moscow. He, himself, left the city of Moscow with his son, Grand Prince Ivan; and he let his Princess with the smaller children go to Uglich. He passed the night in Ozeretsk and moved toward the Volga.

Coming to the shore [of the Oka], the Tatars halted there, expecting an army against them, but there was no one. Expecting that the army was hidden or was letting them cross [the river], they sent scouts to the other side of the Oka. They reconnoitered everywhere there, found nothing and returned, saying that there was no resistance. And so they crossed the Oka River and hurried toward Moscow, where they arrived at one o'clock on Friday the second of July on the holiday of the Deposition of the Vestments of the Most Holy Mother of God. And then they burned all the suburbs at once and started advancing toward the city from all sides. There was a great drought and fire encompassed the city from all sides. The churches began to burn and it was impossible to see, because of the smoke, how to attack the city or move to the gates or to places where there were no stone walls. In the city [people] were in great sorrow and sadness and in great despondency, having no help from anywhere. [They] could only pray tearfully to Lord God, to His Purest Mother, Strong Intercessor and Interceder, with Her Son and Our God, because it was Her holiday as well as the holiday of the great wonderworkers.

When the suburbs burned those who were in the city rested from great exhaustion, from the fire and smoke, made a sortie from the city and started fighting with the enemy. Toward sunset the Tatars retreated from the city and the citizens started preparing for the next morning against the godless all the weaponry of the fortress—cannons, guns, catapults, crossbows, and arms and shields and bows and arrows—which were needed for battle with

1451   the enemy. When the sun rose the citizens were ready against the enemy but could not see anyone. They went out of the city, looked here and there but saw no one. When they sent their scouts to the Tatar camps, they found no one: the Tatars had abandoned the heavy materials made of copper and iron and much other goods, and the bonfires were dead.

[The Tatars] retreated from the city because they were seized by fear and trembling. They fled, imagining that a great army was against them, and they ran away because of the wrath of God and the prayers of His Most Holy Mother, as well as thanks to the intercession of the great wonderworkers and all the saints. They fled [so fast] that they abandoned the captives and would turn neither to the left nor to the right in order to flee as quickly as possible from the wrath which was coming upon them. Hearing this, everyone in the city rendered praise to God and to His Purest Mother, this Ready Intercessor, and to all the great wonderworkers, and they sang a *Te Deum* to celebrate escape from all the evils which had been advancing against them.

Grand Princess Sofia at once sent for her son, Grand Prince Vasilii, who, the same Friday at sunrise, crossed the Volga at the mouth of the Dubna River. When he heard it the Grand Prince first of all shed tears and thanked Lord God and His Purest Mother and all the saints, and returned immediately to Moscow. Coming to the city, he went to the Church of the Most Holy Mother of God and fell prostrate before the icon of the Lord, shed many tears and said, "Thank You, Lord, that You did not turn this, Your flock of Orthodox Christians, over to the godless eaters of raw [flesh]!" He also prostrated himself before the icon of the Most Holy [Virgin], wept and prayed, and then before the grave of the wonderworker [Metropolitan] Peter. And he sang a *Te Deum* and received a blessing from the hand of his [spiritual] father, Metropolitan Jonas. Thereafter he walked out of the church, embraced his mother and his son, Iurii, and the others. Likewise he went to all the cathedrals, which were celebrating a *Te Deum*, shedding tears and thanking the Man-loving God, His Purest Mother and all the saints for the miracle which had happened. Thereafter he comforted the people of the city, saying, "This happened to you because of my sins, but do not be despondent. All of you should build houses on your places and I will give you compensation and remission of taxes." He also went for dinner with the Metropolitan, with his mother, his children, and the boyars. And after the sorrow which had come **1453** upon the city because of our sins, there was great joy on this day.

In the Year 6960 [1452]. The news came to the Grand Prince that Prince Dmitrii Shemiaka was marching toward Ustiug. The Grand Prince passed Christmas in Moscow, and on St. Basil's Day [the first of January] advanced against him. On the day of the Baptism of Our Lord [the sixth of January] he was in the Monastery of the Holy Trinity and St. Sergius. From thence he went to Iaroslavl'. From Iaroslavl' he sent his son, Grand Prince Ivan, against Prince Dmitrii toward Kokshenga, and he, himself, went to Kostroma. From Kostroma he sent the Khan's son, Iakub, son of Mamutek, to join his son against Prince Dmitrii [Shemiaka]. And before that he sent toward Ustiug Prince Vasilii Iaroslavovich of Serpukhov, and with him his boyars, Prince Semion Ivanovich Obolenskii and Fedor Basenok, and many others, and his retinue. Prince Dmitrii, who was in Ustiug, learned that the armies were advancing against him; he burned the suburbs of Ustiug and fled.

ABOUT KOKSHENGA

Grand Prince Ivan and the Khan's son moved to Kokshenga,[104] conquered their cities, occupied all this land and took captives. He went to Ust' Vaga and to Osinovo Polé, and from thence all of them returned in good health, with many captives and booty. The same year, the fourth day of the month of June, the Grand Prince married his son, Grand Prince Ivan, to Maria, daughter of Grand Prince Boris Aleksandrovich of Tver'. The same year on the first day of the month of August a son, who was named Andrei, was born to Grand Prince Vasilii.

In the Year 6961 [1453]. On the ninth of April Moscow and all the Kremlin burned.

*

* *

[Hereafter under the same year, 6961 (1453), the information about Russian history is interrupted by various stories concerning Constantinople and its fall, not having any immediate significance

104. Kokshenga was partially populated at that time by Finnic tribes of Chud'-Zavolochskaia. This was a region beyond the Volok portages between the northern Dvina and the northern tributaries of the Volga, the region of the Vaga and northern Dvina rivers between the Onega and Mezen' rivers. This Kokshenga region was part of Shemiaka's appanage.

1454   for Russian history. (*PSRL*, Vol. XII, pp. 78–108): the story about the founding of Constantinople (pp. 78–81), a list of the emperors of Constantinople (pp. 81–83); a story of the fall of Constantinople by Nestor Iskander (pp. 83–97); another version: a short story about the taking of Constantinople (pp. 97–100); and the story of Sultan Mahmet [Mohammed] by Ivashka Peresvetov (pp. 100–08). The story of the reign of Vasilii II is resumed on page 109 of *PSRL*, Vol. XII.]

*
* *

The same Year 6961 [1453]. On the fifteenth of June Grand Princess Sofia [mother of Vasilii II] and the widow [of Grand Prince] Vasilii Dmitrievich passed away. [Before dying] she became a nun, and the same day she was buried in the Monastery of the Resurrection in Moscow, where her mother-in-law, Eudoxia, named Euphrosenia when she became a nun, was also [buried].

The same year, on the twenty-third of July news of the passing of Shemiaka was brought from Novgorod to the Grand Prince, who was at vespers at that time in the Church of the Great Martyrs Boris and Gleb over the Moat in Moscow. [The news was] that Prince Dmitrii Shemiaka had passed away unexpectedly in Novgorod and was buried in St. George Monastery, and this news was brought by *pod'iachii* Vasilii Beda, who subsequently became *diak*.[105]

In the Year 6962 [1454]. On the twenty-ninth of March Euthymius, Archbishop of Rostov, passed away. The same year Theodosius, who was previously Archimandrite of [the Monastery] of Archangel Michael near [the Monastery] of the Miracles, was consecrated Archbishop of Rostov by Metropolitan Jonas, the bishop of his diocese and the Holy Council.

ABOUT THE PRINCE OF MOZHAISK

The same year Grand Prince Vasilii marched against Mozhaisk, against Prince Ivan Andreevich of Mozhaisk because of his disloyalty.[106] The latter, hearing of it, fled with his wife and children and

105. It seems that Shemiaka was poisoned. In 1453 *diak* Stepan Borodatyi was dispatched from Moscow to Novgorod. Apparently, he conspired with Shemiaka's boyar, Ivan Kotov, to instigate the Prince's cook to poison him. Shemiaka died after having eaten a poisoned hen.

106. Prince Ivan Andreevich of Mozhaisk was disloyal toward his suzerain Grand Prince in supporting Shemiaka.

with all his [followers], and went to Lithuania. The Grand Prince **1456** came to Mozhaisk, occupied it and was merciful toward everyone residing in the city: he honored them, and after appointing his vice-regents, he returned to Moscow.

The same year on the thirty-first day of August there was terrifying thunder which hit the stone Church of the Nativity of the Most Holy Mother of God in Moscow and which had the Church of St. Lazarus attached to it.

In the Year 6963 [1455]. The holy Bishop Pitirim was killed by the godless Pechora Voguls.[107]—The same year the Tatars of Seid Ahmet came to the Oka River and crossed it below Kolomna. The Grand Prince sent Prince Ivan Iurievich with many warriors against them; and they met him, and there was a battle and the Christians routed the Tatars. On that occasion Prince Simeon Babich was killed, but this happened not during the skirmish but just by chance.

ABOUT THE ICON OF THE MOST PURE [MOTHER OF GOD] OF SMOLENSK

In the Year 6964 [1456]. In January Bishop Misail of Smolensk came from Smolensk to Moscow to Grand Prince Vasilii Vasilievich with many citizens of Smolensk, and petitioned him to permit the release of the icon of the Most Holy Mother of God which had been taken by voevoda Iurga. The Grand Prince conferred with his [spiritual] father, Metropolitan Jonas, with the other bishops and boyars. "How is it possible to hold captured [the icon] of the All Powerful Lady of the entire world?" He honored this Bishop Misail and others who came with him, and thereafter Grand Prince Vasilii arranged a celebration for the return of the wonderworking icon of the Most Holy Mother of God. And he asked Metropolitan Jonas with all his Holy Council to come to his court, to the Church of the Annunciation which was there, because that icon was located in that church on the ambo to the right of the Holy Lord's gate. The Metropolitan and all the above-mentioned came thither and celebrated, first of all, a *Te Deum* before the icon of the Most Pure, then a liturgy. After the liturgy the Grand Prince, the Metropolitan, Grand Princess Maria and their children—Grand Prince Ivan, Princes Iurii, Andrei and Boris, and Prince Andrei the lesser, who

107. The Voguls, now called Mansi, in the fifteenth century occupied the region of the Pechora River, the northern Urals, and the southern part of the Ob' River. They are a tribe of Finno-Ugric origin and the closest relatives of the Hungarians, who likewise lived there until the Hunnic invasion in the fourth century A.D.

1456   was still a little child in arms—all approached the icon of the Most
Pure. And everyone made the sign of the cross and the Grand
Prince shed tears, and so did the Metropolitan and the others. And
they removed from its frame the wonderworking icon of the Most
Holy Mother of God, the Virgin Mary, and rendered it over unto
Bishop Misail of Smolensk, who asked for it. And besides that,
many other icons, much smaller but decorated with gems and pearls,
which had been captured and which were not requested by the
Bishop, were given to him by the Grand Prince.

Metropolitan Jonas took up one of them, the icon of the Most
Holy Lady with the Infant, and said, "Bishop, you are the son and
brother of our humility. Leave this one icon of the Most Holy
Mother of God in commemoration of this day on which you came
and on which you received a priceless treasure which was inaccessible
to you for many years. [Leave] it here as a blessing to my lord
and son, the Grand Prince, to his princess and to their children so
that they will remember these days." And he [Bishop Misail] with
joy did according to the words [of the Metropolitan]; and in this
way the Metropolitan asked the Bishop [to assist him] and both
took [this icon] in their hands and blessed the Grand Prince, Princess,
and their honorable children with it; and they gave it into the
hands of the Grand Prince. The Grand Prince accepted the icon
of the Most Holy Mother of God, kissed it tearfully and told them
to depart from the church with the icon of the Holy Mother of
God, which was to be returned to Smolensk. And all departed,
carrying the wonderworking icon of the Most Holy Mother of God;
and they followed the Metropolitan with his Holy Council, who
also carried the [other] icon which was left as a blessing on the
Grand Prince. Behind them went the Grand Prince with his children
and with the princes and boyars. At that time there was a large
number of troops in Moscow, and all of them and all the people
of the glorious city of Moscow followed them. The Grand Prince
accompanied the [icon] to the Church of the Annunciation which
is located in Dorogomilov, two miles outside the city, and from
thence he returned with the other icon remaining with him. During
this procession they celebrated a *Te Deum* and, approaching the
Church of the Annunciation [in the Kremlin], he commanded that
the icon be placed on the same spot where earlier had stood the
one released [to Smolensk]. And on this very spot he commanded
that [a copy] of this icon be made, to take its measurements, and

he gave it a name.[108] And he commanded the priests to celebrate **1456** a *Te Deum* every day before this remaining icon, and to chant the *acathysts* and the *ikoses*. This happened on the eighteenth of January, on Sunday, the day our holy fathers Athanasius and Cyril are remembered.

ABOUT THE WAR WITH NOVGOROD AND THE BATTLE OF RUSA

The same winter on the nineteenth day of January, on Monday, Grand Prince Vasilii Vasilievich marched against Novgorod with an army because the Novgorodians did not behave loyally. When he was at Volok, he was joined by his brothers, by all his princes and voevodas, with a great many warriors; but from Novgorod posadnik Vasilii Stepanov came to him, to Volok, petitioning that the Grand Prince forgive them, not go against Novgorod, and put aside his wrath. The Grand Prince did not accede to the petition and marched against them. When he came to the Novgorodian land he sent Prince Ivan Vasilievich Obolenskii-Striga and Fedor Basenok against Rusa. When they arrived there they took a great amount of booty because the people living there had time neither to escape nor to take away their goods nor to hide them. The commanders remained there with their voevodas and lesser boyars and with minor people, without whom they could not be; but they sent all their other people back with the great booty.

They sent them ahead of them [of the commanders] whilst they, themselves, wanted also to march back to the Grand Prince. At that time, however, they received the news and themselves noticed that a very large army of Novgorodians was moving against them. There were about five thousand of them [of Novgorodians], while with them [that is, with the Grand Prince's commanders] about two hundred remained. Seeing this, they took fright; but then they started discussing among themselves. "What should we do? In case we do not move against them to fight, we will be punished by our sovereign Grand Prince because we took booty and sent the warriors away with it. Better, let us die for loyalty to our sovereign and not for treason." And they marched against them [against the Novgorodians]. There was a wattle fence between them and on [both sides] were high snowbanks, so that they could not come

108. All miraculous icons have names, usually determined by their location: i.e., Our Lady of Vladimir; of Smolensk; of Kazan; of Kursk, etc.

1456 together [to fight]. The warriors of the Grand Prince noticed that the Novgorodians had very heavy armor and started shooting arrows at their horses. The horses took fright and began to rush about under them and to throw them out of their saddles. The latter [Novgorodians] did not know how to fight in such conditions and were as dead, and their hands grew weak. Their lances were so long that they could not raise them, as was the usual manner of doing battle. They dropped them onto the ground and the horses rushed about, and they fell from the horses because they could not master them. And the words of the Prophet were fulfilled concerning them, to wit, "Do not rely upon your horse for salvation; and even when there is a multitude, power cannot save itself." And soon they began to flee, chased by the wrath of God. A great many of them were killed, and the others were captured. On that occasion their main posadnik, Mikhail Tucha, was captured, and Osip Nosov with many others was killed. But not many of them were captured because there were no people to take captives since the troops of the Grand Prince were few. They were pursued by the voevodas of the Grand Prince, and by the warriors who were with them. They were slaughtered, robbed, and captured; and so they [the Grand Prince's voevodas] returned and came to their sovereign Grand Prince, all in good health.

The Novgorodians, escaping back to Novgorod, related what had occurred to them, and in Novgorod were grief, sorrow, and great lamentation because of the many killed or captured and because of their treason against the Grand Prince. According to their habit, they began ringing the *veché* bell, and the entire city came to the *veché*, as well as the posadniks, tysiatskiis, and all the other people; and they did not know what to say, were confused, trembled as if drunk, and spoke foolishly. Then all of them, having held counsel, began to petition their Archbishop Euthymius that he should go and ask the Grand Prince to pardon his patrimony and turn aside his fierce wrath so that they not perish because of their treason against him, their lord, the Grand Prince.

The Archbishop, seeing that the people were truly in trouble, told them, "My children, for your misdeeds and your crimes I can not even come before the eyes of my lord Grand Prince. There is also my sin. But [the Prince] may be merciful. I will go and entreat him to forgive us all for these evil deeds, because, indeed, there was not only our treason against him, but you even ventured to raise your hands against him."

And so he went to the Grand Prince, and with him were the   **1458**
posadniks, tysiatskiis, and commoners, as was their habit. Archbishop Euthymius approached the Grand Prince, began to petition him and to pray for his patrimony, for Novgorod. And before
that he importuned his brothers and his boyars. After listening to
the intercession of this man of God, Archbishop Euthymius, and
all of his [the Prince's] brothers and boyars, as well as those Novgorodians who accompanied the Archbishop, the Grand Prince pardoned them. For his efforts the Grand Prince took from them ten
thousand Novgorodian silver rubles, and there was more for his
brothers and boyars. And he sent his boyars to Novgorod, and they
brought all Novgorod under oath that they should obey the Grand
Prince and not keep evildoers or traitors. And so the Grand Prince
returned to Moscow.

ABOUT [THE PRINCE] OF RIAZAN'

Grand Prince Ivan Fedorovich of Riazan' died the same spring,
being tonsured before and receiving the name of Job [as monk].
Shortly before him, his princess passed away; and he [before dying]
asked Grand Prince Vasilii Vasilievich to care for his principality
of Riazan' and for his son, Vasilii. Grand Prince Vasilii took his son
and the latter's sister, Feodosia, to Moscow, sent his namestniks to
Riazan' and to other [of the Riazan'] cities and districts. At that
time his son [Prince of Riazan'] was eight years of age.

ABOUT PRINCE VASILII IAROSLAVOVICH

The same year on the tenth day of July the Grand Prince in
Moscow arrested Prince Vasilii Iaroslavovich [of Serpukhov] and
sent him to prison in Uglich. Ivan, the latter's son by his first wife,
and his second wife-Princess, however, escaped to Lithuania.[109]
    [*No entry for the year 6965 (1457).*]
    In the Year 6966 [1458]. On the twenty-ninth day of the month
of September the city of Murom and all its Kremlin burned.—The
same fall on the twentieth of October at nine o'clock at night inside

109. Prince Vasilii Iaroslavovich of Serpukhov fought for many years
on the side of the Grand Prince of Moscow, and during the wars with
Shemiaka was one of the Prince's main army commanders. Apparently,
after the death of Shemiaka he became overly-ambitious and too powerful,
and therefore the Grand Prince decided to get rid of such an influential
person, at the same time thus eliminating an important appanage prince
within the Grand Principality of Moscow.

1460   the city of Moscow near the Church of Vladimir Khovrin a conflagration started and much [of Moscow] burned—about a third of the
city. The rest was preserved by God.—The same winter on the
fifteenth day of February, on Wednesday of the week of St. Theodore when [in the churches] they started celebrating the hours, a
son was born to Grand Prince Ivan [son of Grand Prince Vasilii
Vasilievich] and was named Ivan. The same winter Archbishop
Euthymius of Great Novgorod passed away.

ABOUT VIATKA

The same year the Grand Prince sent an army under Prince
Semion Riapolovskii against Viatka, but he, not succeeding in the
least, returned.—The same year in Moscow in the Semion court at
the St. Nicholas Gate a stone church was built in honor of the
Presentation of the Most Holy Mother of God.

In the Year 6967 [1459]. The Annunciation fell on Easter Day.—
The same year the Tatars of Seid Ahmet boasted and went to raid
Russia, but Grand Prince Vasilii sent against him to the shore [of
the Oka River] his son, Grand Prince Ivan, with strong forces. The
Tatars came to the shore but Grand Prince [Ivan] did not allow
them to cross, fought them, and they fled. And in order to praise
[God] for this, Metropolitan Jonas built a stone Church to the Praise
of the Most Holy Mother of God, and it was added to the Cathedral
of the Most Pious near its altar at its southern gate. The same winter
in the month of February the priest-monk Jonas was consecrated
Archbishop of Great Novgorod by Metropolitan Jonas and the
Russian bishops. This same year the Grand Prince sent Princes
Ivan Iurievich, Ivan Ivanovich, and Prince Dmitrii Riapolovskii
with great forces against Viatka. They campaigned, took two
towns—Orlov and Kotelnich—and the other [towns] he led to
pledge to the Grand Prince. Thereafter they returned to Moscow.

THE GRAND PRINCE SOJOURNED IN NOVGOROD

In the Year 6968 [1460]. The Grand Prince went in peace to
Great Novgorod and with him were his children, Prince Iurii and
Prince Andrei the senior. The Novgorodians rendered great honor
to the Grand Prince and his children. From Novgorod during
Shrove Week the Grand Prince sent his son, Iurii, to Pskov because
they [the people of Pskov] were hurt by the Germans [of the Livonian Order]. When Prince Iurii arrived, the people of Pskov re-

ceived him with great honor, put him on a throne in the Church of the Holy Trinity, and put into his hand the sword of Prince Dovmont, and gave him many gifts.[110] Prince Iurii sent his army to campaign against the German cities. When the Germans heard that the Grand Prince had sent his son against them with strong forces, they sent their envoys to Prince Iurii, and they [the envoys] petitioned him and [promised] that they would make peace with the people of Pskov according to the terms of Pskov. The Grand Prince returned from Novgorod to Moscow on the day of the Forty Martyrs of Sebastian [the ninth of March] and Grand Prince Iurii came from Pskov on Friday of the sixth week [of Lent], on the eve of the day of the resurrection of Lazarus.

The same year on the thirteenth day of the month of June at six o'clock there came from the western land a fearsome and dreadful cloud, extremely dark, and there was a strong storm, and the people became desperate and fled so as to escape such a fright because it was very dark and the storm was terrifying. And because of this duststorm it was impossible to see anything. The people began to supplicate Lord God and the Purest Mother to deliver them from this cloud. And the Almighty and Man-loving God heard the prayers of His servants and at once the clouds passed over the city and there was quiet and light as before. The next day, on the fourteenth, it was very quiet throughout the day. In the evening, however, on the fifteenth there came from the south a frightful cloud of gray color, followed by a terrible tempest and strong wind, and there were great lightnings and the earth and churches looked as if they were on fire, and there was terrifying and very loud thunder. The strong tempest shook many stone churches, and many churches in the city of Moscow were damaged, their tops were scattered, and the battlements of the walls of the fortresses were ruined and blown away, and throughout the towns and countryside many churches were torn out from their foundations and carried afar off. And many buildings were destroyed and scattered, and all the forests and woods, as well as great oaks, were uprooted, while the tops of others were broken off, and yet others were broken in half, and some to one-third and down to the roots, and even such as were very sturdy.

110. Dovmont, a Lithuanian prince, left his country, went to Pskov, became the prince of this city-republic—1265–99—and was remembered for his heroic fight against the Livonian Order and against the Lithuanians.

1461   The people were distraught and greatly aggrieved, and all were in great sorrow and were desperate for their lives, and could not save their belongings for their own good. However, they begged each other for forgiveness, and such a love for man by Our God, Jesus Christ, was demonstrated that none among the people were injured either in the cities or in the towns or on the highways or in the fields or in the forests. And those who were in the churches which were scattered or hit by wood, thanks to the love of God toward man, all were saved. It was a chastisement from Our God, Jesus Christ, upon us sinful ones so that we leave off our evil ways and learn how to live according to His will. And at once the tempest was over, as well as the thunder and lightning, and all became quiet as before.

The same year and the same month, on the eighteenth of June at two o'clock on Friday, the sun began to disappear and a [five-day-old] moon appeared. But when the fourth hour passed, the [sun] was full as before. This same month at night the moon disappeared.

The same year the godless Khan Ahmet [Seid Ahmet] of the Great Horde came with his entire force toward Pereiaslavl' of Riazan', and stood before it for six days during the fast of the Dormition of the Most Holy Mother of God. Many of his warriors were injured by the citizens, many were slaughtered, and many wounded. And having achieved nothing before the city, he retreated with shame and went into the *polé*. The same year in Moscow was erected a stone Church of the Manifestation of Our Lord[111] by the abbot of the Monastery of the Holy Trinity and St. Sergius.

In the Year 6969 [1461]. In the month of February Grand Prince Boris Aleksandrovich of Tver' passed away and his son, Mikhail, ascended [to the throne] of Tver'.

ABOUT THE PASSING OF METROPOLITAN JONAS

The same spring at two o'clock on the thirty-first day of the month of March, on Tuesday of Holy Week, His Holiness Jonas, Metropolitan of all Russia, passed away and was buried in the Cathedral Church of the Dormition of the Most Holy Mother of God in Moscow. [He is buried] behind the left ambo across from [the graves of] Their Holinesses, Metropolitans Cyprian and

111. Manifestation of Our Lord of the Holy Spirit during Christ's Baptism—Theophany—January 6.

Photius, who were before him. The Grand Prince was not in Moscow **1462**
at that time. He was in Vladimir because he was conducting a war
against the Khan of Kazan'. The same spring Archbishop Theodosius of Riazan' was elected Metropolitan by the [Council of] Russian bishops of our Muscovite land, [in which participated] Philip
of Suzdal', Euphrosinius of Riazan', Gerontius of Kolomna, and
Bassian of Sarai.[112] Archbishop Jonas of Novgorod and the Bishop
of Tver' sent their envoys with charters in which they declared,
"Our Metropolitan will be he, whosoever is desired by Lord God
and His Most Pure Mother and the great wonderworkers, as well
as by our lord Grand Prince Vasilii Vasilievich and our brethren,
the Russian bishops, and by the entire Holy Council with them."
And all signed unanimously.

The same year Grand Prince Vasilii Vasilievich built in Moscow
a stone Church of the Nativity of St. John the Precursor. [It was]
near Borovietskii Gate and earlier there had been a wooden one:
people say that it was the first church in Moscow, that on that place
there used to be a forest, and in this forest was built a church, and
at that time it used to be the Cathedral Church of Metropolitan
Peter; and the residence of the Metropolitan was also there. And
now the palace of Prince Ivan Iurievich is there.—The same year
the Grand Prince marched to the city of Vladimir and wanted to
campaign against the Khan of Kazan'; when he was in Vladimir
the envoys from Kazan' arrived and made peace.

THE MIRACLE OF SAINT ALEXIS

In the Year 6970 [1462]. In the month of January in the Monastery of St. Archangel Michael [constructed] in honor of his miracles,
near the grave of Saint Wonderworker [Metropolitan] Alexis, a
monk of the same monastery whose name was Naum was miraculously cured. From his youth he had a dried out leg, and he had to
walk on a wooden leg. And he worked in the kitchen and in the
bakery of that monastery. Once at night he came to the icon of the
Saint, which is located near the grave of the Saint, and started
praying to the Saint; but, becoming angry, he said, "Many miracles
and cures were wrought upon many people by you, thanks to God;

112. The bishop of Sarai, capital of the Golden Horde, cared for the
spiritual needs of Orthodox Christians who resided in Sarai and other
places of the Golden Horde. Since the fifteenth century he resided primarily in Moscow.

1462   but I have been laboring since my childhood in this monastery of your monks, and I have worked for many years, yet you have no mercy upon me!" Forthwith he shook his leg and threw away the wooden limb on which he walked, and he went whole to his cell in which he lived.

The same year Euphrosinius Zvinets, Bishop of Riazan', passed away, and in his place as Bishop of Riazan' they consecrated David, who before was treasurer of Metropolitan Jonas; and this happened on the first day of February.

The same winter several lesser boyars of Prince Vasilii Iaroslavovich [of Borovsk and Serpukhov][113] conspired and pledged to each other on the cross that they would raid Uglich, liberate the prince and escape with him. This conspiracy became known to the Grand Prince, who commanded that they be arrested and punished. Some were whipped with the *knut* and their hands and noses were cut away, and some had their heads cut off. And with this capital execution were punished Volodia Davydov, Parfen Brein, Luka Posiviev, and others.

ABOUT THE PASSING OF GRAND PRINCE VASILII VASILIEVICH

About the same time, on Friday of St. Theodore's week, the Grand Prince began to suffer from the drying-out disease,[114] and he commanded that his wounds be burned with tinder in many places because he did not foresee that he had a serious illness. But his wounds began to rot and his illness became very grave, and he wanted to be tonsured but he was not so permitted. And from this illness he passed away at three o'clock in the night on Saturday, the twenty-seventh day of the month of March. And the next morning, Sunday, he was buried in the Church of St. Archangel Michael in Moscow, where all the grand princes and their entire families are buried.

*
* *

113. Prince Vasilii Iaroslavovich's principality was confiscated by Grand Prince Vasilii Vasilievich, and he, himself, was put under arrest in Uglich.

114. *Sukhotnaia bolest'*—apparently, a kind of infection of the flesh, probably gangrene or very large boils.

[THE REIGN OF IVAN III VASILIEVICH]
[1462–1506]

ABOUT THE REIGN OF GRAND PRINCE IVAN [III] VASILIEVICH

In the same Year 6970 [1462]. After the passing of the Grand Prince [Vasilii (II) Vasilievich] and with his blessing, his senior son, Grand Prince Ivan, ascended to the throne of the Grand Principality. And to his second son, Prince Iurii, he left Dmitrov, Mozhaisk, Serpukhov, and other districts and towns, and the treasury with which he was blessed by his late grandmother, Grand Princess Sofia. And Prince Andrei the senior [third son of Vasilii II] received a blessing and received Uglich, Bezhetskii Verkh, and many other districts and towns. And Prince Boris [the fourth son] was given Volok-Lamskii, Rzhev, Rusa, and all the districts and villages of his great grandmother, Maria Goltiaeva, as she ordered. And Prince Andrei the junior [the fifth son] was given Vologda with all [districts] and Zaozer'e, and with it many other districts and towns.[115] And he left to his Grand Princess Maria all his treasury and the town of Romanov and many districts and towns all over the Grand Principality, all of which used to be [the possessions] of previous grand princesses, as well as a great many which he took from those who were traitors or which he bought.

ABOUT THE DISCOVERY OF THE WONDERWORKERS OF IAROSLAVL'

In the Year 6971 [1463]. In the city of Iaroslavl' in the Monastery of St. Saviour there were found the relics of Prince Fedor Rostislavovich and his sons, Konstantin and David. They were under the church in the basement and were preserved in all their entirety, and were not at all decomposed. Archimandrite Christophorus of this monastery took them from there with great honor and brought them into the Church of the Great Saviour and put them in the same grave, and put on them new monks' vestments because they died having been tonsured. And there were many miracles and

115. It is of interest to note that the junior sons of Vasilii II Vasilievich received as appanages only territories which up till then had been the lands of appanage princes outside the main Muscovite patrimony and which had belonged either to Shemiaka and his brothers or to the princes of Mozhaisk, Serpukhov, and others. Thus, the central territory of Muscovy came entirely into the hands of Grand Prince Ivan III, heir of Vasilii II.

1465   many cures done unto those who came to them with faith, and
likewise to this day

In the Year 6972 [1464] . Grand Prince Ivan and his mother,
[dowager] Grand Princess Maria, permitted Prince Vasilii Ivanovich
[of Riazan'] to go rule in his patrimony, the grand principality [of
Riazan'].[116] The same winter in the month of January Prince Vasilii
of Riazan' returned to Moscow and married the sister of the Grand
Prince [Ivan III] by the name of Anna; and he wed her in the
Church of the Purest [Virgin Mary] in Moscow in the week when
they celebrate the memory of the Three Hierarchs;[117] and, together
with the Princess, he returned to his patrimony of Riazan'.

ABOUT THE CONSECRATION OF JOSEPH, METROPOLITAN OF CAESAREA PHILIPPICA [IN PALESTINE]

The same winter on the fourth of March Metropolitan
Theodosius consecrated a certain man from Jerusalem by the name
of Joseph, who was the brother of the Patriarch of Jerusalem, to
Metropolitan of Caesarea Philippica. The latter brother, the Patriarch, went to Moscow for alms as they were in dire need because
of the Sultan of Egypt. He did not arrive [in Moscow] but passed
away in Kafa. And this Joseph wanted to be in his place and therefore he let himself be consecrated by our Metropolitan and by the
bishops of the Russian land. Having collected a large amount of
alms, he went back but did not arrive in his land.

In the Year 6973 [1465]. On the thirteenth of September Metropolitan Theodosius resigned from the Metropolia and went to
the Monastery of the Miracles of [Archangel] Michael.

ABOUT THE ELECTION OF PHILIP TO METROPOLITAN

Grand Prince Ivan sent for his brothers and for all the bishops
of his land, as well as for the honorable archimandrites and abbots.
And so there assembled the princes, the Grand Prince's brothers,
all the bishops of the Russian land and all the Holy Councils, archimandrites, abbots, archpriests, and other priests. Bishop Philip of
Suzdal' was elected Metropolitan of all Russia according to the will
of the Grand Prince and his brothers and all the bishops who
participated in the elections, and the whole Holy Council. In the

116. See the year 6964 (1456).
117. St. John Chrysostom, Gregory the Theologian, and Basil the
Great were the celebrated Three Hierarchs.

Council were the following bishops: Bishop Tryphon, Archbishop **1466** of Rostov; Bishop Euthymius of Debriansk, who on that occasion received the See of Suzdal'; David of Riazan'; Gerontius of Kolomna; and Bassian of Sarai. Those who could not come to the elections sent their envoys and charters, and signed unanimously. And he was elevated to Metropolitan of all Russia in the month of November.

Grand Princess Maria of Tver' passed away on the twenty-second of April, and on the twenty-fourth of April she was buried in the Church of the Ascension.[118] The same year Tryphon, Archbishop of Rostov, relinquished his archbishopric.

The same year[119] the godless Khan Mahmut[120] went against Russia with the entire Horde and arrived at the Don. But thanks to the mercy of God and His Purest Mother, Khan Gazi-Girei defeated him and occupied the Horde.[121] And they started fighting among themselves, and in this way God delivered the Russian land from the pagans.

In the Year 6974 [1466].[122] On the fifth day of October at one o'clock at night the moon perished for two hours.—The same spring on the eighth of April Bishop Bassian of Sarai passed away.—There was a very great plague in Pskov and Novgorod which started on Easter and began to diminish toward St. Philip's Fast.—The same year on the fourteenth of May it began to snow and there was one foot of snow. It remained for two days, and on the twenty-sixth of the same month the snow stayed over the day. And on the eighteenth of August there was a freeze, and another freeze happened the same month on the twenty-seventh which destroyed the spring sowing.—The same summer the princess dowager of Prince Petr Dmitrievich passed away. She had been a nun for a long while and accepted the *schema*[123] in Moscow on the day of Ascension, and she received the nun's name of Euphrosinia.

118. Princess Maria was the wife of Ivan III and daughter of Grand Prince Boris Aleksandrovich of Tver'.

119. This following paragraph is from *Litsevoi svod*, but not found in *Obol.* or *Ioasaf.*

120. Mahmut: Should be Ahmet, son of Kichik Mohammed, who became Khan of the Golden Horde in 1415 after the eclipse of Seid Ahmet. Grekov, p. 421.

121. Gazi-Girei was Khan of the Crimea.

122. The first part of the annual entry under the year 6974 (1466) is found only in *Litsevoi svod*, not in *Obol.* or *Ioasaf.*

123. *Schema*: a second tonsure with very severe rules.

1468   *In the Year 6975 [1467].*[124] On the first of November Lake Rostov froze and began to howl, and it lasted for two weeks, and this did not let the people in the city sleep. [It sounded] as if six or eight people were thrashing; and thereafter there was a long knocking noise.—The same winter of the fourteenth of January there was a severe freeze and many people died on the roads in Moscow, as well as in other cities, districts, and towns.—The same spring on the fourteenth of April, Sunday evening, a son, Ivan, was born in Moscow to Prince Vasilii of Riazan'.

The same year[125] in Moscow the stone Church of the Ascension was renovated by Grand Princess Maria [widow of Vasilii II]. This church was founded sixty-two years ago by Grand Princess Eudoxia, [wife of Prince] Dmitrii Ivanovich [Donskoi]; but during her lifetime not very much was done because she passed away the same year and was buried in the same church. Later, after many years Grand Princess Sofia undertook the completion of this church and built up to the drum, and started work on the dome, but the dome was not finished. During many fires some of its stones were damaged and the arches became unstable. Therefore Grand Princess Maria wanted to pull it apart and build a new one; but inside everything was in very good condition. Considering this, the master stonecutters of Vasilii Dmitriev Iermolin, together with his masters, decided not to pull it apart. They cut away the burned stones that were outside and pulled apart the unstable arches, and they finished building all of it with new stones and baked bricks, and reassembled the arches and completed the building; and so everyone was amazed at such an unusual deed.

ABOUT KAZAN'

In the Year 6976 [1468]. The day of the Exaltation of the Cross [the fourteenth of September] the Khan's son, Kasim,[126] started campaigning against Kazan', and with him were large forces under the voevodas of the Grand Prince: Prince Ivan Vasilievich Obolenskii-Striga and others. When they came to the Volga and wanted to cross it, they encountered Ibrahim, Khan of Kazan', with all his lords and all his forces—which did not permit them [the

124. The first paragraph of this annual entry in the year 6975 (1467) is found only in *Litsevoi svod*.
125. Here the text of *Ioasaf.* and *Obol.* is resumed.
126. Kasim was a Tatar lord.

Russians] to cross to their shore. Then the Khan's son [Kasim] was **1468** invited and tempted by the Kazan' lords and by Abdul-Mamun to rule them. Believing them and not realizing that it was a deception, he [Kasim] asked and received permission from the Grand Prince, expecting to receive what was promised him. Not succeeding in the least, he returned [to the Russian army]. They [the Russian troops] were very tired by their advance because the fall was very cold and rainy, and there was not enough food, and many Christians would have eaten meat even on a fast day. Many of their horses died of starvation, and many of them abandoned their armor; but they all returned home in good health. After their retreat the Kazan' Tatars forthwith raided Galich and took a small number of captives, but they did not succeed in the countryside or towns because all of them were besieging the city [of Galich]. The Grand Prince sent advance troops to Murom, to Nizhnii Novgorod, to Kostroma and to Galich, and commanded them to hold the cities and to beware of the Kazan' [Tatars].

The same fall on the third of November Metropolitan Philip consecrated the Church of the Ascension.

ABOUT THE CHEREMIS[127]

The same fall Grand Prince Ivan sent Prince Semion Romanovich against the Cheremis and with him were many lesser boyars of his retinue. When they all met together they marched on the sixth of December, the day of St. Nicholas from Galich, and went through the forest without any highroad, and the winter was very cold.

The same winter on the seventeenth of December Bassian, Archimandrite [of the Monastery] of the Saviour, was consecrated Archbishop of Rostov; some time before, he was Abbot of the Monastery of the Holy Trinity [and St. Sergius].

The same winter on the day of the baptism of Our Lord [Epiphany], the sixth of January, the army of the Grand Prince entered the Cheremis land and did much evil to it. People were massacred, others were captured, and others were burned, and their horses and all manner of animals which they [the Russians] could not take along—all was killed; and whatever sort of wealth

127. *Cheremis*, presently *Mari*, is a Finno-Ugric tribe north of Kazan' which was under the strong influence of the Kazan' Tatars.

1468   they had was taken; and they campaigned in the land, and what remained they burned; and they came as far as a day's march from [the city of] Kazan'. They all returned in good health to the Grand Prince. And the Grand Prince commanded the people of Murom and of Nizhnii Novgorod to campaign along the Volga, and they marched occupying the hills and *barata* on both shores.[128]

The same winter three weeks before Lent the Grand Prince journeyed to the city of Vladimir, and with him were his brothers— Prince Iurii and Prince Boris—and his son, Prince Ivan; and Prince Vasilii Mikhailovich of Vereia; and all their princes, boyars, and voevodas with their men-in-arms. Prince Andrei, senior, and the other Prince Andrei were left by the Grand Prince in Moscow.—The same spring during Lent there came to Moscow [Chancellor] Iakub Pisar', ambassador of King Kasimir [of Poland], and Ivashenets; and the Grand Prince requested him to come to him in Pereiaslavl'; and he, himself, with his son went from Vladimir. When he arrived in Pereiaslavl' he let the ambassador return and he, himself, went back to Vladimir.

The same spring the Kazan' Tatars seized and burned Kichmenga, and the Grand Prince sent [his forces] to catch them.— The Grand Prince came to Moscow in the evening on Holy Friday, and the same spring after Easter he sent many lesser boyars and his retinue to the Kama River to campaign in the Kazan' lands: Runa with the Cossacks went from Moscow to Galich; the grandchildren of Semion Filimonov—Gleb, Ivan Shusta, and Vasilii Guba— went from Galich; and on St. Nicholas' Day they went with the people of Vologda to Ustiug, and Prince Ivan Zvenets marched with the people of Ustiug from Ustiug; and Ivan Ignatievich Glukhoi marched with the people of Kichmenga; and all of them met near Kotel'nich on the river Viatka. And from thence many people of Viatka marched with them, but the people of Viatka learned that the [Tatars] of Kazan' were moving against them[129] and they returned to Viatka. Three hundred of them, however, marched with voevodas of the Grand Prince. The [Tatars] of Kazan' came with such strong forces to Viatka that the people of Viatka were unable to resist them and they surrendered to Ibrahim, Khan of Kazan'.

128. *Barat* (Tatar): a market where various products are traded. Dal', Vol. I, p. 48.

129. Actually, against their city.

[At that time] the Grand Prince's voevodas were campaigning **1468** on the river Viatka against the Cheremis, and then marched from Viatka down the river Kama. They campaigned as far as Tamluga and they killed many [Tatar] merchants and seized lots of their goods. They went as far as the Tatar ferry and returned up the river, campaigning in the same Kazan' lands; and they went campaigning to Belaia Volzhka.

In the meantime the Kazan' Tatars, two hundred men, went on a raid and arrived at Volzhka on their horses. They left their horses with the Cheremis and went up the river Kama in boats. The Grand Prince's forces arrived there and fought with those Cheremis and massacred the people and the horses and all the animals, and killed the horses of those Tatars who had gone up the river Kama; and they followed the Tatars along the Kama. When they learned that they had come very close to those Tatars they stopped, and the voevodas, selecting seven boats of their men [at-arms], sent them with voevoda Ivan Runa. They caught up with the Tatars. Seeing them, the Tatars leaped onto the shore, and Runa also ordered his men to land on the shore after them. But the Tatars entrenched themselves behind a small river and started fighting behind it. Thanks to God's mercy the Christians began to overcome them and they crossed this small river, marching against the Tatars; and they so defeated them that they took their voevoda, Ish-Tulazi,[130] the son of Lord Tarkhan, and another *berdyshnik*.[131] And among the Russians two men were killed in this battle, and about sixty people were wounded; but by the mercy of God all of them remained alive. From thence they marched against Velikaia, Perm' and Ustiug, and all arrived in Moscow in good health, bringing the captured Tatars to the Grand Prince.

The same year on the twenty-third day of May, at two o'clock at night, a conflagration began in a suburb of Moscow and everything along the moat burned up beyond Bogoiavlenskaia Street, past the Vesiakov estate. And five streets burned along the street of Bogoiavlenié to St. John [church], and down from St. John as far as Vasilievskii meadow, and from Bol'shaia Street to the Ostryi Konets, up to the river; and down to [the Church of] Cosma and Damian at Ostryi Konets. It was very exhausting inside the city because there was a strong wind and many storms, but God pro-

130. Ish-Tulazi, or Thei Tulaz.
131. *Berdyshnik*: a commander armed with a halberd, "*berdysh*."

1469   tected it. The same year the promised Church of Simeon of Miracle
Mountain was built by the Grand Prince.

The same year on the fourth of June the Grand Prince's advance troops of the men of Moscow campaigned from Nizhnii Novgorod, under Prince Fedor Khripun; and they went up the Volga
and defeated the Kazan' Tatars, the Khan's retinue, and many
good [warriors]; and at that time they killed Kolupei [Halib Bey?]
and captured Prince Hozium Berdei [Hodja Berdei?] and brought
him to Moscow to the Grand Prince.

ABOUT TSAREVNA SOFIA

In the Year 6977 [1469]. The same winter on the eleventh of
February a man named Iurii came from Rome, from the Greek
Cardinal Bessarion.[132] [He came] to the Grand Prince with a message
in which was written, "There is in Rome [a princess] named Sofia,
daughter of the [former] despot of Morea, Thomas [Paleologue],
of the Imperial [family] of Constantinople. She is an Orthodox
Christian. If you want to marry her, I will send her to your realm
because already the French King and the Grand Prince of Milan
are wooing her; but she does not want to become Latin."[133] At that
time some Italians also came [with Iurii]: one named Charles, who
was the older brother of Ivan the Italian, a Muscovite financier;
and their nephew, Antonio, son of their oldest brother. The Grand
Prince began to contemplate these words [of Bessarion's] and discussed this matter with his [spiritual] father, Metropolitan Philip,
with his mother and with the boyars. The same spring on the
twentieth of March he sent Ivan the Italian to Pope Paul and to
Cardinal Bessarion to see the Tsarevna [Zoë–Sofia]. Ivan the Italian
went thither to the Pope and saw her and [did] what he was

132. Cardinal Bessarion, a Greek, played an important role at the
Council of Florence.
133. Sofia, whose original name was Zoë, was the niece of the last
Byzantine Emperor, Constantine, and daughter of the last despot of Morea
(Peloponnesus), and she was Catholic. The Russian sources obviously make
her Orthodox because to marry a Catholic would have been unacceptable
to the Muscovite mind. Indeed, Zoë embraced Orthodoxy before marrying
Ivan III and took the name, Sofia. In this way the Muscovite dynasty became
connected with the last Byzantine dynasty. Her family resided in Italy
under the protection of the Pope. In the *Chronicle* she is called "Tsarevna"
("daughter of the Emperor") because she belonged to the family of the
last Byzantine Emperor, or Tsar, in Russian.

sent for, and he talked to the Pope and the Cardinal. The Tsarevna, **1469** hearing that the Grand Prince and all his lands were of the Orthodox Christian faith, wanted to marry him. The Pope greatly honored Ivan the Italian, the Grand Prince's ambassador, and let him return to the Grand Prince, saying that he would give him the Tsarevna in marriage but that he should send his boyars for her. And the Pope gave to Ivan the Italian letters that the Grand Prince's ambassadors may travel freely for two years in all lands which are under the authority of the Pope of Rome.

GRAND PRINCE IVAN SENT AN ARMY IN BOATS BY RIVER AGAINST KAZAN'

In the Year 6977 [1469]. The same spring, one week after Easter Week, the Grand Prince sent against the lands of Kazan' an army in boats under voevoda Konstantin Aleksandrovich Bezzubtsev, and with him were the many lesser boyars, the retinue, the lesser boyars from the entire land, from all his cities and from the patrimony of his brothers; and from Moscow he sent the Surozhane merchants[134] and the wool merchants and other merchants and other Muscovites who were fit according to their strength, and they were placed under the command of voevoda Prince Petr Vasilievich Obolenskii-Nagoi. And they went along the Moskva River to Nizhnii Novgorod and the others along the river Kliazma, and the people of Kolomna and all those who were living on the upper Oka went along the river Oka, and with them the people of Murom; and the people of Vladimir and Suzdal' went by the river Kliazma. And at the same time the people of Dmitrov, of Mozhaisk, of Uglich, of Iaroslavl', of Rostov, of Kostroma, and others from all the Volga went by the Volga to Nizhnii Novgorod. And all of them met in Nizhnii Novgorod. And the Grand Prince sent to Istiug a voevoda, Prince Daniil Vasilievich of Iaroslavl', and with him his retinue and his lesser boyars: Ivan Gavrilovich; Timofei Mikhailovich Iurla; Gleb and Vasilii, grandchildren of Semion Filimonov; Fedor Borisovich Briukho; Saltyk Travin; Nikita, grandson of Konstantin; Grigorii Pervushkov; Andrei Burdak. And from Vologda voevoda Semion Peshek Saburov marched with the people of Vologda. Arriving in Ustiug, they went in boats to Viatka and the people of Ustiug were with them.

134. Surozh, or Soldaia, was an important trading city of the Crimea. Muscovite merchants who dealt with Surozh were called "Surozhane."

1469   When they came to Viatka they started talking to the people of Viatka, telling them the message of the Grand Prince that they should campaign with them against the Khan of Kazan'. The latter responded, "We have been submitted to the Khan and we promised him that we would help neither the Khan against the Grand Prince nor the Grand Prince against the Khan."

At that time there was in Viatka an envoy of the Khan of Kazan' and he sent a message to Kazan' that from thence, from Viatka, the Grand Prince's army was advancing in boats but they were not very numerous. [Meanwhile] Konstantin Bezzubtsev joined all those who were ordered thither and he was staying in Nizhnii Novgorod. The Grand Prince sent him a letter saying that he should remain in Nizhnii Novgorod but that those lesser boyars and other warriors who were willing may be released to fight against the Kazan' lands. He read the letter and sent for all who were under him. And all the princes and voevodas came to him, and he told them that the Grand Prince had sent him a letter saying, "And he [Grand Prince] commanded that all those who were willing may campaign in the Kazan' lands on both shores of the Volga, and he commanded him [Bezzubtsev] to remain in Nizhnii Novgorod. And you may campaign, but do not go to the city of Kazan'." Those who heard this—the Grand Prince's warriors—told their voevoda Konstantin, "We all want to march against the accursed Tatars for the holy churches, for our sovereign Grand Prince Ivan, and for all Orthodox Christians." And they all went and Konstantin [Bezzubtsev] remained in Nizhnii Novgorod.

They went from the river Oka to the old city of Nizhnii Novgorod, and they stopped at St. Nicholas on Bechev, left their boats, and went into the city to the old Church of the Transfiguration of the Lord and asked the priests who were there to celebrate a church service for the Grand Prince and his warriors. And they went from thence and also prayed at St. Nicholas and gave alms according to their possibility. Thereupon all of them assembled and began to consider who should be their voevoda because they must obey the command of a single person. After conferring at length, they selected, according to their will, Ivan Runa. The same day they made sixty verstas from Novgorod and passed the night. In the morning they dined at Roznezh and passed the night in Cheboksary, and from Cheboksary they advanced the whole day, and they advanced the whole night and arrived at the city of Kazan' at early **1469** dawn on the twenty-second of May, on Whitsuntide.[135]

They left the boats and entered the suburbs while the Kazan' Tatars were still sleeping, and ordered the trumpets to sound and began to hack to pieces, rob, sack, and capture the Tatars. And all those [Christians] who were there [in Tatar captivity], people from Moscow, from Riazan', from Lithuania, from Viatka, from Ustiug, from Perm', and from other cities—all those were liberated from captivity. And fire was set in all these Tatar suburbs from all sides. Many Moslems and Tatars who did not want to fall into the hands of Christians, and especially those who cared for their great wealth, locked themselves up in their houses with their goods, their wives and children, and with everything which they had. And so they burned. When the suburbs burned, the [Russian] army retreated from the city and they were very tired, and they embarked in the boats and went to Korovnich Island, where they stayed for seven days. Then from Kazan' a man escaped thither to them, a man of Kolomna who had been there in captivity, and he told them that Ibrahim, Khan of Kazan', had gathered against them all his land and the land of Kama and the Syplin land and the Kostiak land[136] and the Belovolzhskii land and the Votiak land and the Bashkir land: "And he will be here against you at early dawn with his army in boats and on horses."

Hearing this, the voevodas of the Grand Prince and all his warriors started sending away young people with big boats and they, themselves, remained in a rear guard on shore to protect them; and they ordered them to stop at Irykh Island on the Volga, and not to go through the narrows. But they did not heed them. They went to the narrows on the big boats, and the Tatars arrived there on horses and started shooting because they wanted to kill them. But they started shooting against them [against the Tatars] and were able to beat them back. The Tatar army that was in the boats with their most distinguished lords and warriors advanced against the army of the Grand Prince, which was also in boats, as if they wanted to swallow them because they could see only a few of the remaining [Russians in the rear guard]. But those [Russians]

135. That year Whitsuntide was May 21, not May 22. *Nik.*, p. 122.
136. Kostiak land: Postiatskii, in *Ioasaf.*, p. 59.

1469   were unafraid and advanced against the Tatars although the latter were numerous. And they fought for a long time, chasing the Tatars to the very city of Kazan', through the fields and up to the walls; and they returned, went to Irykh Island and joined those who were with the big boats.

While they were on that island, their main voevoda, Konstantin Aleksandrovich Bezzubtsev, came thither to them. As soon as he arrived he sent to the people of Viatka a message from the Grand Prince, saying that they must go to Kazan' to fight. He gave them a deadline, to be at Kazan' in three and a half weeks. The people of Viatka answered, "If the Grand Prince's brothers will go to Kazan', then we will go also."

Konstantin [Bezzubtsev] remained there with all forces the designated three and a half weeks, but there was no news forthcoming either from the Grand Prince's voevodas or from Viatka. And the food supplies were coming to an end since they had little with them because they had advanced in a hurry. Then Konstantin went up the river from Irykh [Island] to Nizhnii Novgorod. And they rowed the whole day and half the next morning, and were met there by the [Tatar] wife of Kasim, who was also the mother of the Kazan' Khan Ibrahim, and she told the Grand Prince's voevodas, "The Grand Prince permitted me to go to my son with all honor and all my possessions, and there will be no more evil among them [that is, between the Grand Prince and the Khan of Kazan'], and all will be free." And she passed them on the river and they [the Russian troops] went up the river. They came to Zvenich, and spent the night there from Saturday to Sunday.

In mid-morning they asked that a mass be served by the priests who were with them, and started preparing their food. Having attended the mass, they wanted to go to eat, but in some churches the mass was not yet at an end; and at that time there came the Kazan' Tatars, all their lords and warriors from all their lands, some troops in boats and some on horseback. Seeing this, the Grand Prince's voevodas and all his warriors boarded the boats and moved against the Tatar army in the boats, and started fighting with them. And the Christians overcame the Tatars, who retreated to the shore where their horse troops were. And those mounted Tatars started shooting at our men from that shore. And they [the Russians] retreated from them to their own shore. Then the Tatars who were in the boats returned, behind them. Those [Russians], however,

turned and chased them back to their own troops. And so they   **1470**
fought the whole day till the very night and, finally, went to their
respective shores to pass the night. Thereafter Prince Fedor
Semionovich Khripun, who was one of the Riapolovskii princes,
defeated the Tatars on the Volga on the fourth day of June.

The same year there was a battle and fierce fighting on the
Volga near the mouth of the Kama between the people of Ustiug
and the Grand Prince's retinue, and the Kazan' Tatars; and many
of them were killed on both sides. On that occasion Nikita Konstantinovich was killed, and Iurla Pleshcheev and his companions were
taken prisoner, but the remainder of the people of Ustiug fled,
fighting, to [Nizhnii] Novgorod. The same year Grand Prince Ivan
Vasilievich of all Russia sent his brothers, Prince Georgii and Prince
Andrei, senior, as well as Prince Vasilii Andreevich, grandson of
Mikhail, with his other voevodas and many troops on horseback,
to Kazan', to fight.

In the Year 6978 [1470].[137] On the first of September Prince
Iurii Vasilievich [the brother of Ivan III] came to Kazan' with all
the Muscovite warriors, and the troops that came in boats marched
toward the city. The Tatars made a *sortie* from the city and, after
fighting, ran back into the city. The Muscovites chased them,
camped at the city, and cut off their water. Khan Ibrahim, seeing
that he was in a bad plight, sent his envoys to Prince Iurii Vasilievich,
petitioning for peace, which was concluded according to the will
of the Grand Prince. And they returned to Moscow with all the
troops.

The same year on the fifteenth day of April, which was Palm
Sunday, at twelve o'clock after vespers there was an occurrence
with the sun. A circle appeared in the sky. One edge of this circle
was in the middle of the sky and the other one descended toward
the west. That part of the circle which was toward the west was
scarlet within and green next to it up to the middle of the upper
part of the circle along its edges, and it was of the same colors as
a rainbow in the sky. And the other part, the upper one, was white;
and under the circle there were two bows which looked the same:
around, they were green, and the inside was scarlet, and one end
of these bows was in the west. And in the middle toward the west
there was something like the sun. And between the bows under

137. In the *PSRL* edition of *Nik.*, the events from September 1, 6978,
are dated as 1470; in the printed *Ioasaf.* and *Musc. Late 15th* still as 1469.

1471   the very circle there were two horns—the end of the one toward the south, the end of the other toward the north. And between them was something shining very brightly as if it were the sun; and it was located directly above the real sun. And below that sun between the horns, as well as between the bows, there were on each side another sun across from the real sun.[138] And it could be seen for two hours, and thereafter the circle and the bows turned and all three unusual suns merged together and became a single one, and followed the real sun slightly above it. Thereafter they also merged together—the real one and the unusual one. Around this circle, of which the edge was in the middle of the sky, on both sides above it was something white but on the top these white things did not merge, and below up to the semi-circle were their ends. This sign was seen by many people in Moscow; however, it is said that it was not seen in any other cities.

The same spring on the twenty-seventh day of May, during the week of the Blind,[139] Prince Andrei Vassilievich [brother of Ivan III] of Uglich married in Moscow Princess Elena Romanovna, daughter of Prince Mezetskii. They were wed by Metropolitan Philip in the Church of the Most Pure.

The same year on the thirtieth day of the month of August toward the end of the second hour a conflagration started inside the city of Moscow, in Posol. [It commenced] from the east of Bogdanov, in the household of Nosov near [the Church of] St. Constantine and St. Helen. Toward vespers it burned entirely because there was a very strong wind from the north; and beyond the river, many households burned; but the others were saved. And the burning logs and birch bark were blown away many miles.[140] The Grand Prince at that time was in Kolomna. There remained unburned in the city only the palace of Prince Ivan Iurievich, two estates of his nephew and one of Irina Alekseevna, because the wind was blowing from that side.

In the Year 6979 [1471]. King Kasimir [of Poland] sent to Khan Ahmed of the Great Horde a Tatar named Girei Krivoi. This Girei was a slave bought by the Grand Prince, and he escaped from

138. This was probably an electrical phenomenon or polar lights, unusual so far to the south.

139. Week of the Blind: Sunday of the Blind is the fifth after Easter.

140. Birch bark was used as shingles.

Grand Prince Ivan [III] to the King. Grand Prince Vasilii Dmit-   **1471**
rievich [of Moscow] had already bought Girei's grandfather, named
Misiuria, from his father-in-law, Grand Prince Vitovt. This Misiuria
had a son, Amurat, and this Girei Krivoi was Amurat's son. This
Girei came to the Khan and started telling all manner of untruths
and calumny about the Grand Prince as he had been told by the
King; and he brought him many presents from the King, as well
as to his lords, to Temir, and to others. And he petitioned, saying,
"[The King asks] that the sovereign Khan be so gracious as to
campaign against the Muscovite Grand Prince with his entire Horde
and he [the King] will fight from his side with his entire land because
my country is in a difficult situation from him [Ivan III]." And Lord
Temir and the others, having accepted the gifts from the King,
incited the Khan against the Grand Prince. But the intention of
those accursed ones did not materialize because without the will of
God man cannot create troubles. The Khan kept Girei at his palace
for this whole year because he had nothing to tell the King through
him, and there were no other questions.

PORTENTOUS SIGNS IN GREAT NOVGOROD

In this year, as well as in the previous time, in Great Novgorod
there occurred many portentous signs about which the people who
lived there told stories. They say there was once a great storm which
broke the cross on Holy Sophia. And then blood appeared on two
tombs. Thereafter the following occurred: at the Church of St.
Saviour of Khutyn all the bells of Korsun' began to ring by themselves. Another portent that was terrifying and worthy of attention:
in the convent of the Holy Martyr Euthymia there were tears on
the icons of the Most Holy Mother of God which flowed from Her
eyes. Seeing this, many people of Novgorod who were God-fearing
wept and prayed to God. Others who had petrified hearts did not
fear God and did not pay attention to anything. They only made
fun of everything, not understanding their perdition and the wrath
of God that was to come upon them. Such manner of signs never
happened to foretell anything good but, rather, starvation or plague
or bloodletting or capture, as occurred in the olden times when
there were the kings of Israel and the Prophets, and others before
them and after them and up to the present day. And when there
is an apparition on the sun or on the moon, or a portent in the

1471   stars or in any other [planet or] creature which is not habitual, all this is usually written in the chronicles which are called *Krinitsa*[141] and later in the chronicle-writing, in the days when there will be a king or a prophet, and it will be said, "In the years and in the days of King David, or Solomon, or Isaiah, the Prophet, or Hezekiah the King, there happened such and such." Such things also happen in the present time, and our eyes can see them.

ABOUT THE PASSING OF BLESSED ARCHBISHOP JONAS OF NOVGOROD, ABOUT BISHOP THEOPHILUS, AND ABOUT THE CAPTURE OF NOVGOROD

The same fall on the eighth day of November in the Cathedral of Archangel Michael, the blessed Archbishop and Wonderworker Jonas of Great Novgorod appeared to God.

And there was a prophecy by Wonderworker Metropolitan Jonas to Grand Prince Vasilii Vasilievich that his honorable spiritual son, Grand Prince Ivan, would destroy all the traditions of freedom of the people of Novgorod and would bring everything under his will, and so will it happen.[142] And his body was buried in the Oten Hermitage. After the death of this perspicacious and most holy Bishop Jonas, the people of Novgorod as of old, as was their custom, met in *veché* to select a candidate from among the priest-monks to be archbishop. And having selected three of them, they cast lots, and the lot fell to a certain priest-monk by the name of Theophilus, and he was enthroned in the Archbishop's palace. And they sent their envoy, Nikita Larionov, to petition Grand Prince Ivan Vasilievich for safe conduct and that he should kindly request the nominated monk Theophilus to come to Moscow, be consecrated there by his [spiritual] father, Metropolitan Philip, to the archbishopric of Great Novgorod and of Pskov, as it used to be in the time of the previous grand princes. The Grand Prince, receiving the petition, did not make any obstacle, treated them honorably and sent them back, agreeing with everything which they had petitioned him for on behalf of all Novgorod; and his answer was the following:

141. *Krinitsa* denoted both "lily" or, generally, a "flower" and "spring"; in this case, it means *"florilege"*—a collection of flowers of Divine Truth or Piety. Dal', II, p. 138.

142. This last sentence is in *Litsevoi svod* only, not in *Obol.* or in *Ioasaf.*

"My patrimony, Great Novgorod, sent you to me to inform   **1471**
me that after God took their father and our prayerful man, Archbishop Jonas, they have elected the priest-monk Theophilus, according to the old [way] by casting lots; and you petition that I,
Grand Prince, honor this nominated Theophilus and request him
to come to me to Moscow and to my spiritual father, Metropolitan
Philip, so as to be consecrated to the archbishopric of Novgorod
and Pskov without hindrance. And that I do it according to the old
tradition as it used to be under my father, Grand Prince Vasilii,
and under my grandfather and my great grandfather, and all the
grand princes who were before, since we are of the same stock of
Vladimir, Great Novgorod and all Russia."

ABOUT THE DISTURBANCE IN NOVGOROD AND THE TURMOIL AMONG THEM

When their envoy, Nikita Larionov, came to them to Novgorod
and told them the decision of the Grand Prince, many of the best
people who were there, the posadniks, tysiatskiis, and commoners,
as well as their nominated [Archbishop] Theophilus, were very
happy about it. Some of them, however, some children of the late
posadnik Isaak Boretskii[143] with their mother, Marfa, and with other
traitors who were instructed by the devil—because worse than devils
were those who tempted the destruction of their land and their
own ruin—started shouting during the *veché*, speaking senseless
and depraved things: "We do not want to be under the Grand
Prince of Moscow. We do not want to be called his patrimony. We
are free people of Great Novgorod and the Grand Prince of Muscovy has caused us many offenses and has perpetrated many injus-
tices; but we will be with Kasimir, King of Poland and Grand Prince
of Lithuania."

And so the entire city became restless and they behaved as if
drunk. Some wanted the Grand Prince according to the old [ways]
and to be with Moscow. Others were for the King and Lithuania.

Thereafter the traitors began to hire poor commoners, members of the *veché*, who are always, according to habit, ready to do
that for which they are [paid]; and, coming to the *veché*, they started

---

143. The Borestskii family opposed Moscow and expected that the
Polish King would protect this republic's independence and maintain the
dominating position of its boyar class.

1471   ringing the bells and shouting, "We want to be under the King!"
The others answered them, "We want to be under the Grand Prince
of Muscovy according to the old [way], as it used to be before!"
The hirelings of these traitors started throwing stones at those who
were for the Grand Prince and there was such a disturbance among
them that they started fighting among themselves, rising up against
each other.

Many among them—former posadniks, tysiatskiis and better
men, as well as commoners—said to them, "It is impossible,
brothers, to be thus, as you claim—to be under the King and to
receive an archbishop from his Metropolitan who is a Latin. From
the very beginning we were the patrimony of those grand princes—
beginning with our first grand prince, Rurik—whom, according to
our own desire, our land got as prince together with his two
brothers, from the Varangians. Thereafter his great grandson,
Grand Prince Vladimir, became Christian and Christianized our
Russian lands [and us Slovenians and the land of Mer][144] and the
land of the Krivichi; the Ves', as the Beloozero land was called; the
land of Murom; and the land of the Viatichi; and others. And since
this holy and great Prince Vladimir and up to our present lord,
Grand Prince Ivan Vasilievich, we have not been under the Latins
and we have never received a consecrated archbishop from them;
and you wanted to have the consecration [of our bishop] from
Gregory, who called himself "Metropolitan of Russia" and who is
the pupil of Isidore, a real Latin."[145]

These dissolute people, just as the earlier heretics, were instructed by the devil, wanted everything to be done according to
their own will, and dared to be against piety, and did not want to
obey the Grand Prince but only shouted, "We want to be under
the King!" And the others said, "We want to be with Moscow, with
Grand Prince Ivan, with our father, Metropolitan Philip, with
Orthodoxy!"

Those evildoers who made themselves the enemies of Orthodoxy, who did not fear God, dispatched their envoys, Panfil Selifon-
tov and Kyril, son of Makarii, grandson of Ivan, to the King with
many presents and they said the following: "We are the free people

144. "And us Slovenians and the land of Mer:" not in *Ioasaf.*, but in
Obol.
145. See the year 1440.

of Great Novgorod and we petition you, most honorable King, that **1471** you become sovereign of our Great Novgorod and our lord, and that you instruct your Metropolitan Gregory to consecrate our bishop, and that you give us a prince from your realm."

The King accepted their presents with love and was very happy with their speeches. He honored them greatly and let their envoy return home, [having accepted] all their conditions; and he sent them a prince, Mikhail, son of Olelko of Kiev. The Novgorodians received him honorably but they did not send away from the *gorodishte*[146] the Grand Prince's namestniks. In Novgorod there was also Prince Vasilii, brother of Gorbatyi [Shuiskii], from the princes of Suzdal', and they sent him off to the troops which were in Zavoloch'e on the Dvina.

Grand Prince Ivan Vasilievich, hearing this—that in his patrimony in Great Novgorod there was a great mutiny—sent them his envoys, saying the following:

"People of Novgorod, your land is my patrimony, and so it was beginning with our grandfathers and forefathers, since the time of Grand Prince Vladimir, who Christianized the Russian land, who was the great-grandson of Rurik, the first grand prince in your land. And from this Rurik up to the present day you have known only one dynasty of grand princes, from the Kievan princes to Grand Prince Dmitrii Iurievich, who was also called [Grand Prince] Vsevolod of [the city of] Vladimir.[147] And from this Grand Prince up to me it was the same lineage. We rule you and we bestow honor on you, and we defend you from everyone and we are free to chastise, in the case you begin to regard us differently than as of old. You have never been under any king [of Poland] or under any grand prince of Lithuania, and it was this way since our land came into being. And now you break away from Christianity and go to the Latins, despite your pledge on the cross. And I, the Grand Prince, apply no force upon you and I do not tax you higher than was done under my father, Grand Prince Vasilii Vasilievich, or under my grandfather or my great-grandfather, or under other

146. *Gorodishte*: the residence of the ruling prince and/or the namestniks (administrators) of the Grand Prince.

147. "Dmitrii" was the Christian name, "Vsevolod" the clan name, of Vsevolod Great Nest, Grand Prince of Vladimir and N.E. Russia, who died in 1212. He was a son of Iurii Dolgorukii.

1471   grand princes of our lineage. And I intend in future to bestow my good will upon you because you are my patrimony."

Hearing this, the people of Novgorod, their boyars and posadniks, their tysiatskiis and burghers who did not want to break the tradition or their pledge on the cross, were happy about this and wanted to be ruled by the Grand Prince as of old.

MESSAGE OF METROPOLITAN PHILIP TO NOVGOROD[148]

His Holiness Philip, Metropolitan of all Russia, sent to them, the people of Novgorod the Great, not one but several admonitions according to holy writ in which he said, "I hear, my sons, that some among you are supporting grave agitation and disorder in your land because they are willing to start a great rebellion and a great schism in the holy church of God, breaking away from Orthodoxy and from the ancient dominion, and want to join the Latins. And you, yourself, should bring to order these mindless people and prevent the evil undertakings because, my sons, it is distasteful to God that you relinquish the light of piety and join the darkness of the Latin temptation, as if you were not thinking about God's just Judgment, or were not afraid of receiving from Him many eternal torments. And you should fear God's wrath and His terrible scythe, which the great Prophet Zacharias saw coming from the heavens upon the rebellious sons [of Israel]; and therefore you should chastise the lawless ones who create among you dissent and temptation. You should show them how to be good according to the ancient way in which their fathers used to walk and live, in the former piety and tranquility. Many unavoidable evils confront you in such undertakings, in the case you relinquish the law of piety and way of salvation according to the Commandments of the Living God, and join the Latins—in such case there will be great and unavoidable retribution because Lord God will summon all those God-rejecting seducers who seduce the souls of the faithful. You must eschew such evildoings according to the saying, 'Flee sin as you flee a warrior; flee heresy as you flee a snake, so as to avoid being stung by the sting of eternal perdition.' My sons, you, yourselves, know about those great kingdoms and great lands, numerous cities and places which existed in former times; which, because of the trespas-

148. The text of this message is in *Litsevoi svod* only, not in *Obol.* or *Ioasaf.*

sing of the Law and trespassing of the obedience of the prophets, **1471**
Apostles, and teachings of the Holy Fathers, fell into eternal sin
and devastation. And those cities and lands which did not submit themselves to the God-appointed ruler were shaken and destroyed. The great, imperial Constantinople, which used to be
famous above all other realms for its piety—was it not ruined because of the Latin heresy and because of the annihilation of piety?
Was it not submitted to the pagan Turks? And you, sons, should
fear the wrath of God because not just one or two of you, but a
great many people, have become seduced, desiring to renounce
the truth and depart from the right path, forgetting the great and
ancient dominion and law of your fathers which they received from
grandfathers and forefathers. And you, sons, you must submit to
a strong hand of the law-abiding and pious sovereign Grand Prince
Ivan Vasilievich of all Russia because you are submitted to him by
God. You should be submitted to your father and grandfather,
according to the saying of the great light of Christ and oecumenic
teacher, Apostle Paul. He said, 'Everyone who obeys the power of
God obeys the authorities. And one who resists the authorities
resists God's law.' And he also said, 'Fear God and obey the Prince
because he is the servant of God. He does not carry a sword for
anything but to avenge the enemy and support virtue.' And you,
children, try to understand this and submit yourselves therefore,
and then God's peace will be with you."

THEOPHILUS' ADMONITION[149]

The monk-priest, Theophilus, who was nominated Archbishop
[of Novgorod], from the very beginning forbade them [the Nov-
gorodians] such evil intentions and commanded them to keep away
from these wicked instigations; but they did not heed his words
and therefore he wanted to return to the monastery and to remain
silent in his cell, but they did not let him go. Those Novgorodians,
boyars, and posadniks, tysiatskiis and other citizens who did not
want to betray their original traditions or trespass their pledge on
the cross, hearing the words of the Grand Prince's envoys and the
Metropolitan's epistle, as well as the instruction of their nominated
Bishop Theophilus, rejoiced very greatly and wanted to set themselves aright and abide under the grand prince as of old.

149. The text of this following paragraph is only in *Litsevoi svod*, not
in *Nik.* or in *Ioasaf.*

1471   But these aforementioned children of Isaak [Boretskii] and their mother, Marfa, with their supporters and their hirelings, became like mad people, like beasts which have no human mind. They did not want to heed the words of the Grand Prince's envoys or of Metropolitan Philip's envoy, but began hiring evil leaches, murders, gossipmongers, and other disreputable men who sooner resemble cattle because they are mindless and could only shout in such a manner as even speechless animals do not growl. And those ignorant Novgorodians were calling him [the King of Poland] Lord of Great Novgorod, and those people would come to the *veché*, ring the bell, yowl and howl like dogs, and speak sheer nonsense: "We want to be under the King!" And there was a tumult among them as used to be in ancient Jerusalem when the Lord gave up [that city] into the hands of Titus.[150] Such people there were at that time, and the same fight now among themselves.

The Grand Prince, hearing this, was very aggrieved, grew sad and thought, "It appears as if there has never been any Orthodoxy [in Novgorod]. Since Rurik and Grand Prince Vladimir they never accepted any other sovereign, and from the time of Vladimir they have known only one dynasty which has ruled them—first, by the Grand Prince of Kiev, then of Vladimir. But in the last years they now want to spoil everything which they have had, to betray Christianity for the Latin faith." [And the Grand Prince thought] "I know not what to do, and I will lay all my hope only on Lord God."[151] He contemplated at length and then announced to his [spiritual] father, Metropolitan Philip, and to his mother, Grand Princess Maria, and to the boyars who were with him, that he wanted to go against Novgorod with an army. Hearing him, they advised him to carry out his thought about the Novgorodians and to rely upon God, in view of the latters' disobedience and betrayal. Thereupon the Grand Prince sent for all his brothers, for all the bishops of his land, for the voevodas and all his warriors.

When everyone had come to him he announced his intention of campaigning against the Novgorodians because they had in every respect betrayed [him] and there was not the slightest truth in their

150. Titus, the son of Emperor Vespasian, in A.D. 70 seized and destroyed the city of Jerusalem after the Jews' uprising there. He was Emperor in A.D. 79–81.

151. The Grand Prince's thoughts appear as in *Ioasaf* in *Nik.*, only the last sentence is in quotes.

behavior. [And he asked,] "But should we go now against them or **1471** should we not? Because now it is summertime and the land has much water in it, and there are vast lakes and rivers and numerous very impassable marshes. Previously, none of the grand princes campaigned in such season, and whosoever did lost many people."

They pondered this at length and finally decided to rely upon Lord God, His Purest Mother, on the power of the honorable and life-giving cross on which the Novgorodians had pledged [their loyalty] before their betrayal. The Grand Prince received a blessing from Metropolitan Philip and from all the bishops of his land, and from the entire Holy Council, and began to arm his forces in order to campaign against them. And thus did his brothers and all the princes, boyars and voevodas, and all his warriors. He [Ivan III] secretly sent letters of persuasion [to Novgorod] concerning their misdeeds for distribution among the Novgorodians, and he sent to Mikhail, Grand Prince of Tver', asking his aid against the Novgorodians. And *diak* Iakushka Shatbaltsev was sent to Pskov on the twenty-third day of May, the holiday of the Ascension of the Lord, to tell them [on behalf of the Grand Prince]: "My patrimony, Novgorod the Great, is breaking away from me to join the King [of Poland] and they want the Archbishop to be consecrated by Metropolitan Gregory, who is a Latin. And I, Grand Prince, am definitely going to campaign against them. And I relinquish my pledge on the cross [given to Novgorod]. And you, my people in my patrimony of Pskov, posadniks and commoners of the entire land of Pskov, you must give up your pledge on the cross [given to Novgorod] and campaign against your brother, Novgorod, and you will march against them and your army will be under my voevoda, Prince Fedor Iurievich Shuiskii, or under his son, Prince Vasilii."

On the thirty-first day of May, on Friday, the Grand Duke sent Boris Slepets to Viatka commanding him to campaign with his levies in the Dvina land: and he dispatched an order to [voevoda] Vasilii Feodorovich [Obrasets], who was in Ustiug, commanding him, also, to march with the levies of Ustiug against the Dvina land and to meet there Boris [Slepets] with his levies of Viatka. On Thursday during the week of the Trinity, the sixth day of the month of June, the Grand Prince sent his voevodas, Prince Daniil Dmitrievich Kholmskii and Fedor Davydovich, with a great many warriors, and with them were many lesser boyar warriors of Princes Iurii Vasilievich and Boris Vasilievich [brothers of Ivan III], and the Grand

1471 Prince commanded them to march toward Rusa. On Thursday, the thirteenth day of the same month, the Grand Prince sent Prince Vasilii Ivanovich Obolenskii-Striga with many warriors: and with him were the [Tatar] lords, sons of Daniar, with many Tatars; and he commanded them to march toward Volochok along the Msta River.

GRAND PRINCE IVAN VASILIEVICH CAMPAIGNS AGAINST GREAT NOVGOROD

Thereafter the Grand Prince commanded a celebration of church services and the distribution of vast alms in the churches throughout his land, in the monasteries, among the priests and monks and among all the poor. The Grand Prince went to the Cathedral Church of Our Most Holy Lady, the Mother of God, Virgin Mary, up to the miraculous icon of the Purest Mother of God of Vladimir, and celebrated many services there, and shed many tears. "My Lord God, Most Holy and Eternal King, Thou knowest the mysteries of human hearts and Thou knowest that much Christian blood will be shed on earth; but I dare it not because I desire or so wish; rather, I do so only because I endeavor to fulfill Thy true, divine law."[152] [And then he prayed] also before the miraculous icon of the Most Pure which had been painted by Wonderworker [Metropolitan] Peter, himself. Thereafter he went to the grave of Our Holy Father, Wonderworker Metropolitan Peter, where a *Te Deum* was also celebrated, and where he shed tears and begged for help and intercession. And he did likewise at the [graves] of the other metropolitans who were buried in the same church—their holinesses Metropolitans Theognostus, Cyprian, Photius, and Jonas. Upon leaving, he went to the Monastery of the Miracles and of the Blessed Archangel Michael, where, entering the church, he attended a *Te Deum*. And this observer of piety prayed to Lord God and the Most Pure Mother of God, appealing for help, the invincible power of the honorable and life-giving cross of the Lord, as well as the great intercessor and ready helper of all Christians in battle, the most glorious voevoda of the heavenly power, Archistrategos Michael; and the holy and great John the Precursor; and the Holy Council of the prophets, Apostles, bishops, saints, martyrs, holy abbots, and all just saints, and he prayed piously.[153] And then

152. This last sentence is in *Litsevoi svod* only, not in *Obol.* or *Ioasaf.*
153. This last sentence is in *Litsevoi Svod* only, not in *Obol.* or *Ioasaf.*

he entered the bay altar of the same Church of the Annunciation **1471** of the Most Holy Mother of God, where the grave with the miraculous relics of our holy father Alexis, Metropolitan of Russia and Wonderworker, were located. And he prayed, shedding many tears, and thereafter went to the Church of Archistrategos Michael and of the Holy Council of Angels, and there also he had a *Te Deum* celebrated, asking them for help and intercession. He also went to the graves of his forefathers, Grand Princes of Vladimir, Novgorod and all Russia, which are in another bay of the same church. [They were] his forefathers, beginning with the grave of Grand Prince Ivan Danilovich and ending with that of his father, Grand Prince Vasilii. And he prayed to and beseeched saint Grand Prince Vladimir of all Russia and his blessed sons, the passion martyrs Boris and Gleb, and he also prayed to all his saintly [princes], his ancestors, asking them, "Although you are far away from here, nonetheless help me by your prayer [in my struggle] with the apostates of your Orthodox nation."

And from thence he went to all cathedral churches and monasteries, everywhere ordering a *Te Deum* be served and distributing considerable alms. Afterwards he also came to his [spiritual] father, Metropolitan Philip of all Russia, asking for a blessing and pardon. His Holiness blessed him with the cross, fortified him with prayer, and blessed him and all his warriors against the enemies, in the same way as Samuel blessed David against Goliath. Grand Prince Ivan Vasilievich received the blessing from his father, Metropolitan Philip, and all the bishops of his land, and from the entire clergy, and left Moscow the twentieth day of the month of June,[154] which was a Thursday when the memory of holy father Methodius, Bishop of Patar, is celebrated; and he started the campaign against his adversary. With him were [the Tatar] Lord Daniar and other warriors of the Grand Prince's, numerous princes, and voevodas with large forces, which he had prepared against the adversary.

And so pious Grand Prince Ivan [started campaigning] against those apostates, in the same manner as his great grandfather, pious Grand Prince Dmitri Ivanovich, campaigned against godless Mamai and his Tatar army which was repulsive to God. Indeed, despite the fact that they called themselves Christians, their deeds were worse than those of the infidels. They were always betraying, tres-

154. In *Ioasaf.*, the date is incorrectly July 20, not June 20 as in *Obol.*

1471   passing their pledges on the cross, and, worst of all, they began behaving like madmen, as it was written above. They were Christianized five hundred and four years ago, and have been under Orthodox Russian grand princes, but in this latter time, only twenty years before the end of the year 7000,[155] they wanted to break away, to join the Latin king, and to have their archbishops consecrated by the latter's Metropolitan Gregory, who was Latin. The Grand Prince, as well as Metropolitan Philip, sent them many messages warning them to avoid such a deed, instructing those [Novgorodians] as if they were their children: "According to the Lord's words, as written in the Gospel, 'If thy brother sinnest against thee, show him his fault between thee and him alone; if he hearest thee, thou hast gained thy brother. If he hearest not, take with thee one or two more, that at the mouth of two witnesses or three every word may be established. And if he refusest to hear them, tell it unto the Church; and if he refusest to hear the Church, also, let him be unto thee as the gentile or the publican.' " [Math. 18:15–17] These Novgorodian people, however, did not heed it but persisted in the evildoing. Were they not worse than infidels? The infidels did not know God from the beginning because they could not learn Orthodoxy from anyone, and they adhered to their original way of paganism. Those, however, were Christian for many years, but at the end started breaking away and finally started joining the Latins. Therefore the Grand Prince marched against them not as against Christians but as against pagans and apostates of Orthodoxy.

The Grand Prince arrived in Volok on the same day of the Nativity of [St. John] the Precursor [the twenty-fourth of June]. Similarly, the Grand Prince's brothers marched forward, each on his own road: Prince Iurii Vasilievich from his patrimony [of Dmitrov], and Prince Andrei Vasilievich, also from his patrimony [of Uglich]; Grand Prince Boris Vasilievich, from his patrimony [Volok Lamskii and Rusa]; and Prince Mikhail Andreevich [of Tver'] with his son Prince Vasilii, from his own patrimony.

[The Grand Prince] left in Moscow his son, Grand Prince Ivan, and his own brother, Prince Andrei the junior. On the holiday of the Apostles [Peter and Paul, the twenty-ninth of June] the Grand Prince arrived in Torzhok. And the voevodas of the Grand Prince

155. The year 7000 equals A.D. 1492 and was considered a critical year in the life of Christians, as many people expected it would be in the year of the end of the world.

of Tver' came to him there—Prince Iurii Andreevich Dorogobu- **1471**
zhskii and Ivan Nikitich Zhito—and with them were many people
to help the Grand Prince against the Novgorodians. To Torzhok
there came to the Grand Prince the envoy of the city of Pskov,
Vasilii, with Bogdan and Iakushka Shebaltsev. They came [to say
that Pskov] had given up its pledge on the cross to Novgorod and
that all were in readiness [to fight]. From Torzhok the Grand Prince
sent Bogdan back to them [and with him] Kuzma Korobin, also,
asking them to march straightaway against Novgorod; but he did
not let Vasilii go. Then the Grand Prince left Torzhok [for Nov-
gorod]. The Grand Prince's brothers with all their great forces,
each coming [with men] from his own patrimony, marched against
Novgorod from different routes, taking prisoners, towns, and taking people into captivity. The Grand Prince's voevodas, Prince
Danilo Dmitrievich [Kholmskii] and Fedor Davydovich, who
marched with the advance troops, sent their warriors to many Novgorodian places, as they were commanded, to burn [towns], take
captives and chastise [the people] mercilessly for their disobedience
to their sovereign Grand Prince. When the voevodas came to Rusa,
they occupied and burned those places, captured people and
burned, and marched against Novgorod toward the river Shelon'.
And they came to a place called Korostin on the shore of Lake
Ilmen'.

And there, unexpectedly, a Novgorodian army in boats came
against them. Usually in summer the lakes and marshes of the
Novgorodian land are greatly flooded, and therefore in summertime horse troops would never have been sent thither by any earlier
grand princes. Therefore, living in the fall, winter, and spring
obediently, the cunning [Novgorodians] would fearlessly commence
their troublemaking in summer because their land would be protected then by the floods. This time, however, by God's will and
for their chastisement and amendment, their land was quite dry
since not a drop of rain had come from the sky onto their land
over the entire summer, from the month of May till the month of
September. And because of the sun's heat, all their land and all
their marshes dried out. Such was the grace which was given from
above by the Lord to his pious servant, Grand Prince Ivan Vasilievich of all Russia, so that he could subdue his enemies by his
strong hand. From all sides and from everywhere his armed forces
were advancing through the Novgorodian land without hindrance

1471   and could fight unimpeded, chasing cattle everywhere where usually were impassable places and marshes. But this time they were dry.[156]

They [the Novgorodians] left their boats and stealthily approached the [Grand Prince's] camps but the latter became alarmed in time because the sentries of the Grand Prince's voevodas, noticing them, warned their voevodas. The latter took up arms straightaway and went against them, and many Novgorodians were killed, while many were captured by hand. [The Grand Prince's voevodas] ordered those who were captured to cut away each other's noses and lips and send them back to Novgorod; and they took away their armor and either threw them into the water or burned them because they did not need any of them since they had sufficient arms and weapons of their own.

[BATTLE ON THE RIVER SHELON']

From thence the same day they [the Novgorodians] returned to Rusa, where was another foot army which was more numerous and stronger, and which had come to Lake Ilmen' in boats on the Pola River. But the Grand Prince's voevodas also marched against them and defeated those who arrived, and they sent Timofei Zamytskii with this news to the Grand Prince. And Timofei came on the ninth day of July to the Grand Prince, who was on Lake Kolomna. [In the meantime] the voevodas, themselves, marched from Rusa to the town of Diemon. The Grand Prince sent to them, commanding them to go beyond the river Shelon' with the purpose of joining the levies of Pskov. And he commanded Prince Mikhail Andreevich and his son, Prince Vasilii, to remain at Diemon with all their warriors. The Grand Prince's voevodas went to the river Shelon' and when they started fording it the Novgorodian army approached from the opposite side. And there were a great number of them. They had come from their city to the same river Shelon', and there were so many that the Grand Prince's regiments took fright because they were few. The rest of the [Grand Prince's] troops who had come with them were unaware of [the Novgorodians'] arrival because they had been campaigning around Novgorod.

All the Novgorodian posadniks and tysiatskiis and, speaking

---

156. The foregoing paragraph is taken from *Litsevoi svod,* and is not found in *Ioasaf.* or *Obol.*

plainly, the carpenters and potmakers, and those who, since their   **1471**
birth, had never ridden a horse and had never had the intention
of raising a hand against the Grand Prince—they were all forced
by the traitors to march [against the Grand Prince]. Those who did
not want to fight were sacked and beaten, and some among them
were thrown into the Volkhov River. They, themselves, claim that
there were forty thousand of them in this battle.

The Grand Prince's voevodas, although they had few [troops]—
it was said that there were only five thousand of them—and despite
the fact that they saw that there were a great many [of the enemy]—
did not take fright, however, relying upon Lord God and His Most
Pure Mother and on the truth of their sovereign's [cause]. They
advanced headlong against them in the manner of roaring lions,
crossing this large river—the Novgorodians, themselves, say that
there has never been a ford there—but those [warriors of Ivan III],
without looking for a ford, crossed and were all alive and healthy.
Seeing this, the Novgorodians became confused and hesitant, as
if drunk; but those [soldiers of Ivan III] marched against them
and started shooting at them, and the [Novgorodians'] horses
started rearing and throwing off their soldiers. Soon the Novgorodians began to flee, driven by the wrath of God for their misdeeds
and for their betrayal not only of their sovereign but also of Lord
God, Himself. The Grand Prince's regiments pursued them, stab-
bing and chopping them, and those [Novgorodians] ran away, push-
ing and stomping each other, whosoever could whomsoever.

A great many of them at that time were killed; they, themselves,
claimed that there were twelve thousand men who perished in these
battles, and more than two thousand were taken captive by hand.
[Among] the prisoners were their posadniks, Vasilii Kazimir, Dmitrii Isaakov Boretskii, Kuzma Grigoriev, Iakov Fedorov, Matvei Selezenev, Vasilii Selezenev, two of Kazimir's nephews—Pavel Teliatev
and Kuzma Gruzov—and a multitude of wealthy burghers.[157]

And the words of the prophet were fulfilled about them: "And
five of you will defeat a hundred, and the hundred will move ten
thousands." They fled for so long that their horses became
exhausted and they abandoned them so as to scatter into the valleys,
the water, the marshes, and the forests. God made them so blind

157. Wealthy burghers were a class of prominent patrician citizens
below the boyars but above the merchant class.

1471   that they were unable to recognize their own land or find the road to the city from which they had come; and so they wandered, lost in the forest; and those who emerged from the forest were taken prisoner by the [Grand Prince's] soldiers; and those who were wounded and wandered into the forest died from exhaustion; and some drowned in the water. And those who were not thrown off their horses were carried by their horses to the city, but they appeared as if drunk or asleep; and many of them bypassed the city, believing that it was already taken, and they were despondent and unsure, as if drunk, and all their wisdom disappeared.

And the Grand Prince's warriors drove them for twenty versts and returned greatly exhausted. The Grand Prince's voevodas, Prince Danilo Kholmskii and Fedor Davydovich, stepping on the bones [of the slain], joined their troops and, seeing that all their warriors were sound, rendered their thanks to God, to His Most Pure Mother and to all the saints. And the voevodas started asking the captured Novgorodians, "Why, with such a multitude of your own warriors, did you stand so weakly after you saw that our army was very small?" And the latter answered them, "We saw an endless multitude of you marching against us, and not only did we see those who were advancing against us but we also saw other regiments which were outflanking us from the rear, and these regiments had yellow banners and great lances, and we heard the speech of many voices and a terrifying stomping of horses, and a great fright came upon us and we were seized by fear, and awe entered into our hearts."

This happened in the morning on Sunday, the fourteenth of the month of July, when Holy Apostle Aquila is remembered. And after this battle the army of the Grand Prince continued to campaign in many towns near Novgorod, up to the German border on the river Narva; and the larger city called Novoe Selo was occupied and burned. In the meantime the Grand Prince's voevodas, having somewhat relaxed after this action and having joined other of their troops, sent Zamiatnia to the Grand Prince with word that God had helped him [Ivan III] and they had defeated the Novgorodian army. He came quickly to the Grand Prince in Iazhobilits on the eighteenth of the same month of July, and it was a great joy for the Grand Prince, for his brothers and for all his warriors.

At that time [the Tatar] Lord Daniar was with the Grand Prince, as well as the latter's pious brothers, Iurii, Andrei, and Boris, with their boyars and with their armed forces. On this occasion the **1471** Grand Prince promised to build a church in Moscow dedicated to Saint Apostle Aquila, which was [later] done, and voevodas Danilo [Kholmskii] and Fedor [promised] to build another church dedicated to the Resurrection of Christ. And at that time a certain Luka Klementiev arrived from Novgorod, coming to the Grand Prince from the nominated Archbishop and from the entire city of Novgorod, asking for safe conduct. The Grand Prince granted it to him and sent him away from Selishche, which was across from Diemon.

The Novgorodian voevodas who were besieged in the town of Diemon petitioned Prince Mikhail Andreevich [Vereiskii] and his son, Prince Vasilii, and surrendered, promising that if they were released alive they would contend nothing and would give up all their wealth. And the city [of Diemon] gave him [Prince Vereiskii] a ransom of one hundred Novgorodian rubles.

From the people of Pskov there came to Ignatichi, to the Grand Prince, posadnik Nikita with Kuzma Korob'in, to say that the Pskovians with all the levies under voevoda Prince Vasilii Fedorovich [Shuiskii] had started advancing to serve him, their sovereign. During their march they sacked and burned Novgorodian towns and slew people and burned them, locking them up in their houses. The Grand Prince sent Sevastian Kuleshov to them from the Pola River and with him their earlier envoy, Vasilii.

THE PROPHECY OF BLESSED ZOSIMA OF SOLOVKI BECAME TRUE

The same month, the twenty-fourth of July, the day of the memory of Holy Martyrs Boris and Gleb, the Grand Prince came to [Staraia] Rusa and commanded that [the following] Novgorodian posadniks should be punished for their treason and for their apostasy with capital punishment: Dmitrii Isakovich Boretskii, Vasilii Selezenev Guba, Eremei Sukhoshchok, and Kiprian Arzubiev.

And he sent many others to Moscow in order to imprison them. And he commanded the inconsequential people be released to Novgorod. Vasilii Kasimir, Kuzma Grigoriev, Iakov Fedorov, Matvei Selezenev, Kuzma Gruzov, Fedor Tabazin and others he sent to Kolomna to be put in irons. The Grand Prince, himself, came on the twenty-seventh of July, a Saturday, to Lake Ilmen at the mouth of the river Shelon', to the place between the shore and Korostyn.

ABOUT THE BATTLE ON THE DVINA

The same day [the twenty-seventh of July] there was a battle between the voevodas of the Grand Prince—Vasilii Fedorovich Obrazets with the levy of Ustiug and other men; and Boris Slepets with the levy of Viatka [on one side]—and [the Novgorodian] levies of Zavolochie and Dvina under Prince Vasilii Shuiskii [on the other]. The Grand Prince's voevodas had four thousand less thirty people, and the other [Shuiskii] had an army of twelve thousand. The battle was fought in this way: both left the boats, both were on foot, and they started fighting at the third hour of the same day, and fought till sunset. And from the fighting their hands became numb and they took the banner of the Dvina levies, although under it three banner bearers were killed. When the first was killed, a second picked it up; when he was killed it was taken up by a third. But they [the soldiers of Ivan III] killed the third and seized the banner. And the levies of the Dvina became confused, and toward evening they were overcome by the Grand Prince's regiments. And a great many people of the Dvina and Zavalochie were killed while others were trampled, and their Prince [Shuiskii] was wounded. He jumped into a boat and escaped to Kholmogory, while many [of his men] were taken prisoner. Thereafter their towns were occupied and their entire land was submitted to the Grand Prince. And in the Grand Prince's army fifty from the Viatka levies were killed, one from the Ustiug [levies], and a man of Boris Slepets's, called Migun. All the others were preserved by God.

[ABOUT THE NOMINATED BISHOP THEOPHILUS AND THE
NOVGORODIANS WHO CAME TO THE GRAND PRINCE WITH
A PETITION]

The same day there came to the mouth of the Shelon' River in boats the nominated Archbishop Theophilus with the posadniks, tysiatskiis and other wealthy burghers from all sections of the city. First of all they solicited the Grand Prince's boyars and voevodas, asking them to intercede with the Grand Prince's brothers so that the latter would intercede with the Grand Prince; and that [thereafter] they, together with the boyars themselves, would also intercede with the Grand Prince. The boyars went with them and solicited the Grand Prince's brothers; and the Grand Prince's brothers, Prince Iurii, Prince Andrei, and Prince Boris, as well as Prince Andrei Mikhailovich with his son and their boyars, petitioned

the Grand Prince for them [that is, for the Novgorodians]. And **1471**
for the sake of his brothers and his boyars, the Grand Prince accepted their entreaty and bestowed mercy upon them, and permitted the nominated Monk Theophilus, posadniks, tysiatskiis, and
the others to come to him and appear before his eyes. And they
came to the Grand Prince, bowed to the earth because of their
crimes and because they had raised their hands against him. [They
begged] the sovereign to pardon them, to be merciful toward them,
to turn aside his wrath, and to do so not because of their petition
but in order to show his good heart toward those who had sinned,
and that he order no more executions, sacking, burning, or capturing. And the Grand Prince became merciful. He showed them his
mercy and accepted their solicitation, stilled his wrath and commanded forthwith to stop burning and taking prisoners, and to
release those who had been captured. And those who had been
sent away and taken off were to be returned. And so [they] entreated
the Grand Prince, [providing] him sixteen thousand Novgorodian
silver rubles [as indemnity] besides [giving] to the Grand Prince's
brothers, to the other princes, to the boyars and voevodas, and to
all others who had interceded for them.

And their land was occupied and burned to the sea. This was
done not only by those who had campaigned under the Grand
Prince and his brothers but also by those levies from the other
lands which had marched against them [the Novgorodians]. The
land of Pskov campaigned [against Novgorod] at its own will; there
have never been such wars since their [Novgorodian] state existed.
Sevastian Kuleshov, who was sent by the Grand Prince to meet the
Pskovian levy, met them at Porkhov, and from thence marched to
their own Pskovian town of Dubkov; they took six cannons thither
and advanced to Porkhov. Sevastian told them that the Grand Prince
was in good health, that there had been a victory over Novgorod,
and said that the Grand Prince had commanded them to proceed
at utmost speed to Novgorod. The Pskovian levies let Sevastian go
from Porkhov to the Grand Prince and, together with him, they
sent their envoys, Kuzma Sysoev and Stefan Afanasiev Vinkov; and
they, themselves, went with all their forces to Novgorod, camping
there at the [Monastery of the] Saviour on the Milich, twenty versts
before Novgorod.

Sevastian with the envoys of Pskov, Kuzma and Stefan, reached
the Grand Prince at the mouth of the Shelon' on the thirty-first

1471   day of July, just before Our Lady's Fast. And Prince Vasilii Fedorovich Shuiskii, who was a voevoda of Pskov,[158] came with other posadniks and wealthier burghers to the Grand Prince [but] first sent
him his envoys, [and met him] on the same spot at the mouth of
the Shelon'. After their arrival the Grand Prince remained there
eleven days on the same place, giving instructions to the Novgorodians; and he pardoned them and granted them peace according to
his will, as he wanted it. He arranged for Pskov an agreement with
Novgorod which was better than the earlier one, and in the way
the people of Pskov wanted it.

Then the Grand Prince granted the Novgorodians peace, love
and mercy, honored their nominated [Bishop] Theophilus and their
posadniks, tysiatskiis, and others who came with them, and let them
return to their city. He sent with them to Novgorod his boyar,
Fedor Davydovich, to bring everyone in Novgorod the Great, from
the small to the great, to swear on the cross and to receive silver
from them. And they went to Novgorod and did as they were
commanded.

On the thirteenth day of the month of August Grand Prince
Ivan Vasilievich of Vladimir, Moscow, and Novgorod and all Russia,
returned from thence to Moscow with a great victory; and with
him were all his brothers, princes, all the voevodas and all their
warriors, bringing with them great booty.

The same year the Grand Prince, when he started campaigning
against Novgorod, had sent Nikita Beklemishev to search in the
polé for [the Tatar] Lord Murtaza, son of Mustafa, to invite him
into his service. Nikita found him in the *polé* and invited him to
the Grand Prince, and went to the Grand Prince's son in Moscow,
where he arrived before the Grand Prince returned from
Novgorod.

ABOUT THE PEOPLE OF VIATKA

The same summer the people of Viatka descended on the river
Volga in boats, captured Sarai,[159] took much goods, and captured
many prisoners. Hearing of this, the Tatars of the Great Horde

---

158. This Vasilii Fedorovich Shuiskii was Ivan III's voevoda and a
distant relative of Prince Vasilii Vasilievich Shuiskii-Grebenkov (Suzdalskii),
the last Novgorodian "service prince-voevoda," who fought against Ivan's
troops on the Dvina.

159. Sarai was the capital of the Great, or Golden, Horde.

who were roaming in the vicinity one day's journey distant, went   **1472**
with a large number of warriors to catch them. And they took the
boats and closed the entire Volga with their boats, wishing to kill
those [people of Viatka]. They, however, broke through the Tatar
[fleet] and escaped with everything. At Kazan' [the Tatars] also
wanted to catch them but they passed by, avoiding them, and went
to their own land with the entire [booty].

In the Year 6980 [1472]. At the beginning of the indiction—that
is, at the beginning of the new year when blessed Simeon the Stylite
is remembered [the first of September], the Grand Prince came to
his patrimony, to the glorious city of Moscow. [After] having defeated all his evil foes, after having chastised his stubborn enemies,
and after having submitted to his will those who did not want to
obey, he won great wealth and glory. He was met by Metropolitan
Philip, accompanied by the Sacred Council with crosses in the vicinity of the church, just before the large stone bridge and the well
on the square. And the people of Moscow came to meet him far
distant from the city, some as far as seven versts. People came on
foot, young and old, famous and simple, and there was a great
multitude of them. His honorable son, Grand Prince Ivan, and his
brother, Prince Andrei the junior, and the other princes, boyars
and junior boyars, *gosti*[160] and merchants and the better people[161]
assembled to meet him on the eve of St. Stephen's Day [the thirty-
first of August], and they waited for him all night. And there was
great joy then in the city of Moscow.

[ABOUT THE NOVGORODIANS WHO DROWNED IN LAKE ILMEN']

The same year on the second day of September a great many
people with their wives and children left Novgorod and its towns
and went in large boats on the lake, and each one was in his place.
It is said that there were one hundred and eighty of these large
boats, and in each vessel there were fifty people and more. And
when they were on the deepest place of the lake a very strong and
unexpected wind arose and the water of the lake overturned them
and all the ships were sunk. None of them remained alive and all
the people with their goods were drowned.

160. *Gosti*: either very rich merchants, who received this extremely
rare title from the ruler of Moscow, or merchants engaged in foreign trade.
161. *Luchshie liudi* ("better people"): upper class, highly respected city
dwellers.

1472   The same fall Girei came from the Horde to the King of Poland, accompanied by the Khan's envoy. But at that time the King was waging war against the King of Hungary.

[THE VENETIAN AND THE POPE'S ENVOYS CAME TO MOSCOW]

The same year on the tenth day of the month of September Antonio the Italian came to the Grand Prince from Venice and with him came a certain man, Giovanni by name, Trevisano by surname, the envoy of Nicola Trona, Doge of Venice. And he was sent to the Grand Prince by this Doge and by all the lands which were under him, with a request that the Grand Duke permit this Trevisano to be accompanied to Khan Ahmet of the Great Horde. He was sent thither to him [the Khan] with many presents to ask for [the latter's] help in [the Venetians'] fight against the Turkish Sultan of Constantinople. When this Trevisano arrived in Moscow he went, first of all, to Ivan the Italian, a Muscovite financier, because this Ivan had been born in that land [Italy] and was well-known there. And he told him all the reasons for his coming to Moscow, and did so before going to the Grand Prince. And the Italian financier told this Trevisano not to speak of it [that is, of his mission to the Khan] to the Grand Prince, and not to give him the great presents: "And I can do this [journey to the Horde] without [the permission of] the Grand Prince, and I will accompany you to the Khan." This Ivan the Italian came to the Grand Prince with this Trevisano, calling him a minor Venetian prince, claiming that [Trevisano] was his nephew, and he said, "He has come to me on his own business and to visit." And he concealed it [Trevisano's mission to the Khan] from the Grand Prince. On that occasion Antonio [the Italian] brought the Grand Prince word from the Pope that the Grand Prince's envoys might travel freely to Rome in all the Latin lands—that is, in Germany, Italy and all the other lands which are under the authority of the Pope, and so on to the end of the ages, and that he [Ivan III] may send for Princess Sofia, the daughter of Emperor Thomas of Morea [now Peloponnesus].[162]

The same fall Metropolitan Philip ordered that stone be prepared for building a church to the Holy Mother of God.

The same fall on the eighth of the month of November Philotheus was consecrated Bishop of Perm' by Metropolitan Philip.

162. This Thomas is previously mentioned, correctly, as "Despot" and not as "Emperor." See the beginning of the annual entry for the year 1469.

The thirtieth day of the same month the nominated [Arch-   **1472**
bishop] Theophilus came to Moscow to be consecrated to the
archbishopric of Great Novgorod; and with him came posadniks
Aleksandr Samsonovich and Luka Fedorovich. The same winter
on the eighth of December Archimandrite Theodosius of the
[Monastery of the] Miracles [of Archangel Michael] was consecrated
Bishop of Riazan' by Metropolitan Philip, and at his ceremony were
present Archbishop Bassian of Rostov, Archbishop Euthymius of
Suzdal', Gerontius of Kolomna, Prochorus of Sarai, and Philotheus
of Perm'.

ABOUT THE CONSECRATION OF THEOPHILUS AS ARCHBISHOP OF GREAT NOVGOROD

In the same year 6980 on Sunday, the fifteenth of the same
month [December], the previously nominated Theophilus was consecrated to the Archbishopric of Great Novgorod, and at this ceremony were the above mentioned Russian bishops, the archimandrites, archpriests, honorable abbots, and the entire Sacred Council
of the glorious city of Moscow. After his consecration he petitioned
the Grand Prince in his own name and in the name of all Great
Novgorod, as well as in the name of the posadniks and tysiatskiis
and all those who came with him about the prisoners—about
Kazimir and his other associates. The Grand Prince accepted their
petition and released all those [prisoners] with honor; and there
were thirty of them in Moscow; and he let the Archbishop, himself,
go home on the twenty-third of the same month.

The same winter they started bringing stone to Moscow for
building the Church of the Most Holy Mother of God.

ABOUT THE STAR

After Christmas during the same month of December a great
star appeared in the skies and behind this star was a very long and
wide ray. It shone very much, more than the [other] stars. And it
would come out at the sixth hour at night after the summer sunrise.
Then it would go to the southwest, and the ray would extend
forward. The end of the ray was extended like the tail of a great
bird. In the month of January, after the day of the Baptism of Our
Lord [the sixth of January], there appeared, however, another star
with a tail above the southwest. Its tail was very thin and not very
long, and its shining was less bright than the ray of the first star.
The first star also moved toward the west and would appear three

1472   hours before the rise of the sun, and the second one would appear in the same place three hours after sunset.

The same winter the Grand Prince sent Prince Fedor Pestryi to fight Great Perm' because of their disobedience.

THE GRAND PRINCE SENT TO ROME FOR PRINCESS SOFIA

The same winter the Grand Prince, having consulted with his [spiritual] father, Metropolitan Philip, and with his mother, Grand Princess Maria, and with his brothers and boyars, sent Ivan [Giovanni] the Italian to Rome. He sent him on the sixteenth of January to get Princess Sofia, and he sent charters and an embassy to the Pope and to Cardinal Bessarion. In the meantime the former Pope died and they were told that there is another Pope by the name of Calistus. When they arrived in that land, they learned that the Pope's name is not Calistus but Sixtus, and having discussed this among themselves, they rewrote the name: they erased out the name of that Calistus and they wrote Sixtus.

ABOUT THE BUILDING IN MOSCOW OF THE CHURCH OF THE ASSUMPTION OF THE MOST PURE [VIRGIN MARY] BY METROPOLITAN PHILIP

The same year in the month of April, according to the will and great desire of His Holiness, Metropolitan Philip of all Russia, and with the gracious agreement and on the command of the faithful and Christ-loving Grand Prince Ivan Vasilievich of all Russia, the building of the Church of Our Most Holy Lady, Mother of God, was started in Moscow. He wanted to build a very great church with one dome, according to the dimensions of the Church of the Most Holy Mother of God in Vladimir, which was built by the faithful Grand Prince Andrei Iurievich Bogoliubskii, grandson of Monomakh. His Holiness, Metropolitan Philip, who saw this very large, high and beautiful church on many occasions, had a burning idea and desire to see built in Moscow a similar church, in honor of the Most Holy Mother of God, which would be the burial place of His Holiness and Wonderworker, Metropolitan Peter, and other Metropolitans of Russia. First of all he summoned the master stonemasons and sent them to the city of Vladimir to see the church and to take its measurements. They went thither, saw the Church of the Most Pure, marvelled greatly at the beauty of the building and its majesty and height, measured its width, height, and its

sanctuary, and returned to Moscow. And they began taking their   **1472**
measurements in Moscow in the vicinity of the [old] Church [of
the Virgin]. That church was ramshackle and its vaults were crack-
ing and were supported by wooden scaffoldings. In the month of
April they began excavating the ground for the foundation. Having
excavated the ground for this, they strengthened the bottom of the
foundation with wood, and then they filled the excavation with
stones.

After finishing, they pulled apart the small sanctuary and the
bays [of the old church], and the same month on the thirtieth day,
when the memory of Holy Apostle Jacob, brother of St. John the
Theologian, is celebrated, at the second hour of the day His Holiness, Metropolitan Philip, with the entire Sacred Council, put on
ecclesiastic vestments, took the honorable cross and holy icons and
went to the foundation [of the new] church, and he ordered that
all the bells be rung. And there had also come the pious and Christ-
loving Grand Prince Ivan Vasilievich of all Russia with his son,
Grand Prince Ivan, his mother, and his brothers, boyars, and nobles,
and a great multitude of people of the glorious city of Moscow.
And so they celebrated a *Te Deum*, and then the Metropolitan with
his own hands laid [the stones in the place] where the sanctuary
was to be, as well as on the sides and in the corners, and thereafter
the master started working on the building. The [foundation] of
this church was laid in the vicinity of the foundation of the first
church, which had been laid by His Holiness, Metropolitan Peter,
under Prince Danilo Ivanovich, and it was one hundred forty-six
years ago less three months. And when they built up to the height
of a man they began to dismantle the first one down to the foundation; then they removed the stones and bases of the burial places
of Their Holinesses, the Russian Metropolitans Cyprian, Photius,
and Jonas, and they dug around their tombs.

On Friday, the twenty-ninth day of the month of May when
the most honorable martyr, Theodosia the Virgin, is remembered,
at the beginning of the second hour of the day the Metropolitan
ordered that the bells be rung, and with him came the entire Sacred
Council, Prochorus, the Bishop of Sarai, the archimandrites, the
archpriests and abbots, and all the priests of the city of Moscow;
and they started to sing burial chants. Then the pious Grand Prince
Ivan came with his son, with his mother, with his brothers Georgii

1472   [Iurii], Andrei [the senior], Boris and Andrei [the junior], and with their princes and boyars and the entire multitude of Orthodox Christians of the glorious city of Moscow—men and women, young and old. And having sung [the memorial chants], as is fitting for the dead, the Metropolitan ordered that the shrines with the honorable relics of the bishops be moved from the disassembled church to the places prepared in the newly-founded one. And they took the shrine with the relics of Metropolitan Cyprian and put it into a niche in the wall on the right side [of the new church]. Thereupon they took the shrine with the relics of Metropolitan Photius and put it into the same niche with Cyprian.

Thereafter they came to the tomb of His Holiness, Metropolitan Jonas, and when they removed its top there emanated forthwith throughout the entire church a powerful fragrance, and all who were there could smell it. His relics were in their entirety and were not decayed, and the flesh adhered to his bones, and nothing had altered its structure. And all the vestments and shrines of these three bishops had not decayed after so many years since their passing. And the entire multitude of Orthodox Christians who saw this shed many tears then at this glorious sight, and thanked God and His Most Pure Mother, Who had glorified Their saintly servants. And they took up the shrine of His Holiness, Metropolitan Jonas, and put it with its most honorable relics into a niche in the left wall. And this translation of their relics took place that day. It was sixty-five years and nine months less eighteen days after the passing of Metropolitan Cyprian. And it was forty-one years less thirty-four days after the passing of Photius. And it was eleven years and two months after the passing of Jonas.

And when they disassembled the church they removed from the wall of the church of the great martyr, St. Demetrius, the remains of Prince Iurii Daniilovich, Grand Prince of all Russia, and put them into a wooden casket above the tomb of Metropolitan Theognostus, where they had been in the Church of the Veneration of the Most Honorable Fetters of the Apostle Peter. And then they prepared a place in the same Church of Great Demetrius in the wall on the same side, and they brought the remains into the prepared place, and they sang the burial chants and put them there.[163]

163. The last two sentences are somewhat unclear. It is difficult to ascertain whether the remains of Prince Iurii were taken to the Church of St. Demetrius or to the new Cathedral of the Assumption.

And during this transfer the Metropolitan was there with the above **1472** mentioned council of the clergy, the Grand Prince with his son, and a great many people; and it was one hundred and forty-seven years after his murder.[164]

Thereafter came the time for the churchbuilders to disassemble the wall at the sanctuary [of the old church], where the tomb of our holy father, Wonderworker [Metropolitan] Peter, was supposed to be. And then Metropolitan Philip asked the Grand Prince to remove the relics of His Holiness and put them higher in the new church, but in the same location [within the sanctuary]. The Grand Prince told him, "You, my father, know, yourself, what should be done; but, better, send for the bishops of our land because, my father, it is a deed which surpasses our authority. But it is a matter for you and for your children, other bishops and clergy."

Metropolitan Philip, relying on Lord God and His Most Pure Mother, and on the prayers of the great Wonderworker [Metropolitan] Peter and all the other saintly metropolitans,[165] sent for all the bishops and summoned to him those who were already there, as well as the archimandrites and other clergy, in order to discuss it. And he told them his thoughts and the words of the Grand Prince, saying, "He relies upon me and upon you, my children." And they all agreed with great respect with the speech of Metropolitan Philip and the Grand Prince. And the Metropolitan was filled with great joy and took great daring because he wanted to see the relics of the saint [that is, of Metropolitan Peter].

ABOUT THE TRANSLATION OF THE RELICS OF
METROPOLITAN AND WONDERWORKER PETER

On the fourteenth of the same month, at night from Sunday to Monday, he came to the grave of His Holiness and holy father, Metropolitan Peter, and ordered the priests to pull apart the structure above the shrine, while he, himself, was seized with awe and shed many tears, [wondering] whether it would be pleasing to the saint. And they pulled apart the structure over the tomb of the saint, and they saw that his relics were shining with light and that a great fragrance emanated from them; but the coffin in which he

164. Iurii, Grand Prince of Vladimir and Moscow (1320–25) was killed by Dimitrii of Tver'.

165. Here were meant Metropolitans Peter (1308–26), Cyprian (1390–1406), Photius (1408–31), Jonas (1448–61), Theognostus (1328–53), and Alexis (1353–78).

1472   had been laid was broken apart from the fire, although the fire
had not touched the relics [of St. Peter] in the least.

People say that it was the fire when the evildoing Khan
Tokhtamysh cunningly took the city of Moscow, and that his tomb
was broken at that time because they were looking for something
hidden in it; but they found nothing and burned it upon leaving
the city. The coffin had burned but his relics were not even harmed
by smoke because they were protected by the grace of God. But
the vestments which had been on him had burned in the fire although those which were under his relics remained preserved. Seeing this, the Metropolitan marvelled at the measureless love for
man of Our Lord Jesus Christ, Who in such a manner glorified
His saintly servant. And they prayed at length with tears and with
great awe, and joyfully took up the relics from this shrine and put
them into a new stone one, which they placed in about the same
location [in the new church].

When the time came to prepare a niche [in the new church]
in which his shrine would be provisionally placed, the Metropolitan
came at night with the people who were ready for this; they did it
and translated the shrine with the relics of the saint into this niche,
which was built on the left side of the new church near its northern
entrance—where, also was already located the tomb of Metropolitan
Jonas. And [in the new church] this niche was built in exactly the
same location as that in which the relics of the saint had formerly
lain [in the old church]. And they put it on a higher elevation in
the new church because the floor of the new church was about a
man's height higher than that of the earlier church; and a place
for the shrine was made at this level and the relics of this saint
were placed there.

And there assembled the bishops—Archbishop Bassian of Rostov, Bishop Euthymius of Suzdal', Theodosius of Riazan', Gerontius
of Kolomna, Prochorus of Sarai—and on the thirtieth day of the
same month the Metropolitan informed the Grand Prince that the
time had come to translate the saint's relics, and it would be in the
morning of the first of July. The Grand Prince relied on this decision, as well as on the decision of the Sacred Council. On that day,
on the thirtieth of June, at the eleventh hour of the day they ordered
[the bells] rung for vespers, and the Metropolitan was joined by all
the bishops, archimandrites, archpriests, abbots, and priests. And
they entered the new church and went to the tomb of His Holiness,

Metropolitan Peter the Wonderworker. Then there came pious **1472** Grand Prince Ivan Vasilievich, his mother, Grand Princess Maria, and his son and his brothers, the two Princes Andrei, and the boyars and lords and all Orthodox Christians.

Then it was decided to celebrate both the day of the translation [of the relics] of the saint [Metropolitan Peter], and the day of his passing, which was on the twenty-first of December. After the celebration of vespers and a prayerful service to the Most Holy Mother of God and to the Wonderworker, they departed. The same night the Christ-loving princes came, one at a time, to the shrine of the saint, attending the service, and so did the lords and the others who loved God; and they left at the fifth hour at night, when the bellringing for matins had already begun.

All the abovementioned who attended vespers also attended matins in honor of the celebration of the day of the passing of the Wonderworker. At the second hour of the same day, the first of July, after having celebrated matins, they ordered that all the bells be rung, and started a thanksgiving service. The Grand Prince with his son and his brothers came to the shrine of the saint and touched and venerated it with awe and trembling, and many princes, boyars and priests were with him. And so they took up [the reliquary] and conveyed it to the prepared place which was in the same location [in the new church as in the old one]. The previous place was inside the sanctuary ambo near the altar; but in the new church it was before the gate and the holy sanctuary, in the same place of honor as before.

They deposited the reliquary with the relics of the saint, celebrated the thanksgiving service, made the sign of the cross with awe and joy at the relics of the saint because the saint's reliquary was uncovered and everyone could see his holy relics. Thereafter the bishops, princes and lords departed, and all the Orthodox Christians who wanted to come thither to touch and venerate the shrine of the saint went to the saint's tomb.

During the translation of the venerable relics of the saint, one of the pious clergymen saw above the tomb a white dove which was flying extremely high, which it did over the shrine until the saint's relics were covered, and then it became invisible. When the time for the liturgy came, the Metropolitan himself celebrated it in the palace of his court in the Church of the Deposition of the Vestments, and he ordered the bishops and all the clergymen to celebrate [the

1472   service in the Cathedral] of the Archangel [Michael]. After that the
Grand Prince commanded that considerable alms be distributed to
all, in all the cathedrals, and that they be given to the clergymen
of the city, to the monasteries and to the poor. The bishops,
princes—the Grand Prince's brothers—archimandrites, the leading priests, and a great many boyars sat at the Grand Prince's table,
and everyone gathered in his residence and ate and drank. And
so from that day was established the holiday of the Translation of
the Relics of His Holiness, Our Metropolitan and Wonderworker
Peter, who was our holy father.

[ABOUT PRINCESS SOFIA]

The same year on the twenty-third day of the month of May
Ivan [Giovanni] the Italian came to Rome to Pope Sixtus and Cardinal Bessarion, and this Ivan the Italian and those who were with
him were greatly honored by the Pope and by Princes Andrew and
Manuel, the children of Thomas [Paleologue, Despot of Morea]
[and the brothers of Sofia]. And they received valuable gifts and
sojourned there thirty days and two.

On the twenty-fourth of June they let Princess Sofia go from
Rome to the Grand Prince, and the legate Antonio was sent to her
as the Pope's envoy, and with them many Romans. And the envoy
of the [Paleologue] Princess was Dmitrii Manuilovich [Trakhaniote]
with many Greeks. And many other Greeks who served her accompanied her. They did not go the same route as the Italian had come
to Rome but by the lands of the Pope, toward the sea. And the
Pope sent his charters to all the cities and to all the places where
they had to travel to the dominion of the Grand Prince, to the city
of Pskov. And he wrote that all the princes of those lands and all
the honorable lords and bishops of all the countries, whitherso-
ever the Princess would come, should meet her, honor her, provide her with provisions and give her carriages and guides. And
they should do the same to all the others who were traveling with
her to the dominion of the Grand Prince. And in accord with this
missive of the Pope's, all the countries rendered great honor to
Princess Sofia and to all those who were with her.

The same year [6980, or 1472] on the twenty-sixth of June the
Grand Prince received word from Perm' that his voevoda, Prince

Fedor Pestroi, had occupied the Permian land.[166] He arrived there   **1472**
at the mouth of the Chernaia River on Thursday of St. Thomas'
week, and from thence he proceeded further with horses on rafts.
Arriving at the town of Anfalov, he left the rafts and went on by
horse to the upper land, toward the town of Iskora. And he sent
Gavrila Nelidov to the lower land, toward Uros, Cherdin, and
Pochka [against the troops of the Permian chieftains] to meet Prince
Mikhail. Before Prince Fedor reached Iskora he was met on [the
river] Kolva by the Permians. They engaged in battle and Prince
Fedor won, and in this battle they seized their [Permian] voevoda,
Kacha. And from thence Prince Fedor marched to Iskora and captured it, as well as the [Permian] vocvodas, Burmot and Michkin,
while their [voevoda] Zynar surrendered to him [to Prince Fedor]
and received safe conduct. Then [Prince Fedor] seized other [Per-
mian] towns and burned them.

[In the meantime] Gavrila [Nelidov] proceeded forward and
conquered the lands whither he was sent. Thereafter Prince Fedor
came to the mouth of the [river] Pochka where it merges with the
Kolva and was joined there by all his troops. The prisoners of war
were all brought thither. [Prince Fedor] built a fort there, made it
his headquarters and submitted the entire land for the Grand
Prince. From thence Prince Fedor sent Prince Mikhail with [cap-
tured] Burmot, Michkin, and Kacha to the Grand Prince and he,
himself, remained in the fort of Pochka. And the booty which he
seized from these Burmot, Michkin, and Kacha he also sent to the
Grand Prince: sixteen *sorok*[167] of sable; a sable furcoat; twenty-five
pieces of broadcloth; three coats of armor; one helmet; and two
swords of damask steel.

The same year the ill-famed Ahmet, Khan of the Horde, incited
by the Lithuanian King Kasimir, moved into the Russian land with
a large force. Hearing of this, the Grand Prince sent his voevodas
to the shore [of the Oka River] with many troops.[168] As their vanguard commander he sent Fedor Davydovich, with the levies of
Kolomna; also, Prince Danilo and Prince Ivan Obolenskii-Striga

166. The Permians, a Finnic tribe now called "Komi," inhabit the
extreme northeastern part of European Russia near the Ural Mountains.

167. *Sorok*: a counting unit for 40. (From the Greek, *tessarakonta*).

168. The Oka River till the time of Ivan IV formed the southern
border of Russia.

1472   were dispatched to the shore [of the Oka] with numerous troops on the day of the Deposition of the Vestments [of the Holy Virgin Mary].[169] The very same day the Grand Princess Maria went to Rostov; thereafter, the Grand Prince dispatched his brothers with numerous troops to the shore [of the Oka].

The same year on the twentieth of July at three o'clock in the night a conflagration commenced in the Moscow suburb of the [Church of the] Resurrection, located on the Moat, which lasted all night and the next day till dinner.[170] A vast multitude of households burned, among them twenty-five churches. It burned along the shore [of the Moscow River] up to the [Church of the] Exaltation of the Cross on the Sharp End[171] and to Vasilii's Meadow and to the Kulichka; [and the conflagration] spread from the suburb of the Resurrection to that of the [Church of the] Ascension on the Moat up to Yar and to the stone Church of the Manifestation of the Lord; and from the Church of the Resurrection in Dmitrii Street to the Church of St. Eupatia and to Kulichka. At that time there was a severe storm and the flames were spread by the wind over eight households and more. Roofs were torn away from churches and mansions. It was very miserable then for the city; but by God's mercy and the prayers of His Most Pure Mother and the intercession of the great wonderworkers, the wind blew away from the city, itself, and in suchwise it was protected. The Grand Prince, himself, was in the city and went to several places with the lesser boyars, extinguishing and tearing apart [the burning constructions].

The thirtieth day of the same month, on Thursday, the eve of the fast, the Grand Prince received news that the Khan with his entire horde was marching toward Aleksin. At the second hour of

169. The date of the celebration of the Deposition of the Vestments of the Holy Virgin Mary was July 2. According to tradition, this holiday commemorated the translation of the vestments of the Virgin Mary in A.D. 458 from Palestine to Constantinople, where they were deposited in the Church of St. Mary of Blachernae, and her apparition there. Roty, p. 87.

170. The sections and suburbs of Moscow were usually named after the main churches. In this case, it was the Church of the Resurrection built at the fortifications on the moat.

171. Exaltation of the Cross: this holiday and the churches devoted to it commemorated, according to tradition, the finding in A.D. 313 by Empress Helen, mother of Emperor Constantine, of the Cross on which Christ was crucified.

the same day the Grand Prince ordered that a liturgy be celebrated. **1473**
After attending a *Te Deum* and fasting, he moved rapidly to
Kolomna and ordered his son to journey to Rostov. Khan Ahmet
came with great forces to the town of Aleksin. There were very
few people there and there were no firearms in the fortress: neither
cannon nor guns nor crossbows; but they nontheless killed a great
many Tatars at the city. On Friday, however, they returned to the
city with great forces and set it afire, so that all the people remaining
there were burned, and those who escaped from the fire were taken
captive. From thence the Tatars marched forthwith to the shore
of the Oka with great forces, and rushed into the river, wanting to
cross over to our side because there were no Russians there in that
place and because they were guided by some of our men. There
were only Petr Fedorovich and Semion Beklemishev, with very few
people.

When the many Tatars forded [the Oka] toward them, they
began shooting at each other and fought till just a few arrows
remained, and they [the Russians] considered retreating. At this
time, however, they were joined by Prince Vasilii Mikhailovich with
his regiment, and after him there came the regiments of Prince
Iurii Vasilievich, and at the same time came Prince Iurii, himself.
And so the Christians began to overcome the Tatars, who, seeing
so many Christian regiments, fled beyond the river. And the regiments of the Grand Prince and all the princes came to the shore,
and there was a great multitude of them as well as of [the Tatar]
troops in Russian service under Prince Daniar, son of Tregub.[171a]
Then the Khan, himself, came to the shore and saw the numerous
regiments of the Grand Prince's moving like a sea because their
arms were very clean and shone as silver, and they were very well
armed; and he began to retreat little by little from the shore.

The same night awe and trembling overcame him and he ran
away, chased by the wrath of God; but not one single man of the
Grand Prince's regiments was behind him across the river, because
Our Merciful and Man-loving God cared for His Christian people,
He sent a deadly plague upon the Tatars and very many started
dying in their troops. Taking fright, they fled so rapidly that in six

171a. Daniar was the head of the Kasimov Tatar territory on the Oka
River, controlled by Moscow. See footnote 102.

1473 days they reached their *katuns*, from whence they rode all summer.[172] It was the mercy of Our Lord Jesus Christ for us sinners,
and such was the victory over the repugnant raw flesh eaters. This
occurred because of the prayers and intercession of His Most Holy
Mother, Our Lady Theotokos, the Most Honorable Virgin Mary,
as well as because of the intercession of the host of venerable incorporeal powers of Heaven, of all the saints, and the saintly wonderworkers of Russia, their Holinesses, Metropolitans Peter, Alexis,
Jonas, and all the others.

The Grand Prince, learning that the Khan had retreated, began
to send his people after the Tatars along their route, taking those
who remained behind as well as those Christians who were captives.
When the news reached the Grand Prince that the Khan had returned to his *katuns* and to his winter camp, he thanked the Lord
God, His Most Pure Mother, Ready Helper in misfortunes, as well
as the intercessors, Archangels Michael and Gabriel, and all the
other heavenly incorporeal hosts and all the saints because, thanks
to their prayers, the Lord preserved the Christian people from the
raid of the godless sons of Hagar. And the Grand Prince returned
to Kolomna, and with him was [the Tatar] Prince Daniar, son of
Tregub. There he honored him and let him depart to his town;
and he, himself, journeyed to Moscow, arriving at the city on Sunday, the twenty-third day of the month of August.

In the Year 6981 [1473]. On the first day of September the
Italians and the Greeks from Rome arrived with Princess Sofia in
the German city of Luebeck, and they sojourned there for eight
days. On the ninth of the same month they took boats to the ship
and on the tenth day they boarded it.

ABOUT THE PASSING OF PRINCE IURII VASILIEVICH

On the twelfth day of the same month, on Saturday at the
tenth hour of the day, pious and Christ-loving Prince Iurii Vasilievich passed away in Moscow at the age of thirty-one years, seven
months and twenty-two days. At that time neither the Grand Prince
nor his mother nor his brothers were present: all of them were in
Rostov because their mother, the Grand Princess, was ill there then.
Metropolitan Philip sent to the Grand Prince announcing the pass-

172. *Katun* is the Tatar word for wife. This means that in six days
the Tatars ran from the Oka to the lower Volga, or at least to their grazing
grounds to the north of the Caspian Sea, some five hundred miles.

ing of his brother and [asking] what his wishes were: to bury him   **1473** in his absence or wait to bury him. On Sunday after matins the Metropolitan with the bishops of Sarai and of Perm', and the entire Sacred Council, arrived at the Prince's palace, took up his body and bore it to the Church of Archangel Michael, where they chanted the burial prayers and placed him in a stone sarcophagus, which they put in the middle of the church. Four days after, on Saturday, Grand Prince Ivan Vasilievich came from Rostov and shed many tears and sobbed greatly. Also, his other princely brothers, the other princes, and the boyars and all Orthodox Christians shed many tears; and even those who, since their birth, had never shed a tear—even they, regarding the lamenting people, began to weep. Metropolitan Philip with the above-mentioned bishops and with all the Sacred Council celebrated the burial service and entombed the body of pious Prince George[173] in the Church of Archangel Michael, where all the pious Grand Princes are buried, and all their family; and this happened on the sixteenth day of the same month.

ARRIVAL OF PRINCESS SOFIA IN MOSCOW

On the twenty-first of the same month the Princess, after a storm of eleven days at sea, arrived by ship in Kolyvan'.[174] And they departed from Iur'iev[175] on the sixth of the same month. On the eleventh of October they arrived in Pskov, where the people rendered great honor to the Grand Princess and to all those who accompanied her, and gave presents to the Princess. They remained there seven days and arrived in Novgorod the twenty-fifth of October, and they left it on the thirtieth of October, and there were great honor and gifts from the Archbishop and all Novgorod.

When they were in the vicinity of Moscow the Grand Prince was told that the Pope's envoy, legate [Cardinal] Antonio, who accompanied the Princess, had a Latin [Crucifix] carried before him because the Pope had said that he should journey with great honor in all countries and to Moscow, through the lands of his great realm [under the Pope's authority], and a long distance. Hearing this, the Grand Prince deliberated with his mother, with his brothers and with the boyars and some said, "Let us not prohibit

173. Russians frequently used two forms of the same name: the Greek "George" and the Slavic "Iurii."

174. Kolyvan', later called Reval, now Tallin.

175. Iur'iev: also called Dorpat or Tartu.

1473   him this." And others said, "Such a thing has never been in our land, that the Latin faith should be honored. The only one who tried to do so was Isidore and yet he perished." The Grand Prince, however, sent to his [spiritual] father, announcing it to him. The Metropolitan replied, "It is not possible that such [a procession headed by the Latin Crucifix] should enter this city or approach it. If you do permit it, he would even enter the gate of the city. I, your Father, would leave through the other gate. We should neither hear nor see this, because if one loves and praises a foreign faith then it means that he offends his own." Hearing this from His Holiness, the Grand Prince sent to the legate [saying] that he should not have a [Latin] cross borne openly before him and should order that it be hidden. The other resisted for a time concerning this but did according to the will of the Grand Prince. Ivan the Italian, our financier, was especially insistent that honor be rendered the Pope and his envoy, and to all their land, in the same way as had been rendered to him there [in Italy]. He abandoned the Christian faith and called himself an Italian of their [Latin] faith! He had concealed [while in Rome] that he was baptized in our [Orthodox] faith and did everything there [in the West] in the same manner as those [Catholics] did.

Thereafter, on the twelfth day of November, Thursday, they entered the city. The Metropolitan, himself, entered the church, put the vestments on her, blessed the Princess with the sign of the cross, as well as the other Christians accompanying her, and let her go from the church. And with her [everyone] went to Grand Princess Maria. Soon thereafter Grand Prince Ivan also came to his mother, and he became betrothed to the Princess according to custom, as is due Their Majesties' honor; and they went to church to the liturgy. Metropolitan Philip celebrated the liturgy that day in the wooden Church of the Assumption of the Most Pure which was [provisionally] constructed within the Cathedral of the Most Holy Mother of God, of which the construction was recently begun. Having celebrated the liturgy, he united in marriage the pious Grand Prince Ivan Vasilievich of all Russia with the Orthodox Princess Sofia, daughter of Thomas, Despot of Morea; and this Thomas was the son of the Emperor Manuel of Constantinople and brother of [the Byzantine] Emperor John VIII [1425–48], and of the last Byzantine Emperor, Constantine IX [1448-53].

At the wedding there were present the mother of the Grand   **1473**
Prince, Grand Princess Maria; his son, Ivan; his pious brother,
Andrei [the senior], Boris, and Andrei [the minor]; and all other
princes and boyars; and a great multitude of people, as well as the
Roman envoy, legate [Cardinal] Antonio with all his Romans, and
Dmitrii the Greek [Trakhaniote], envoy of the Princess' brothers,
Andrei and Manuel; and with him the other Greeks, because many
Greeks had come to serve the Princess. The next morning the same
legate of the Pope's embassy reported to the Grand Prince and
gave him the Pope's gifts; and with him were Dmitrii [Trakhaniote]
the Greek, who was the envoy of the brothers-in-law of the Grand
Prince—of Andrew and Manuel.[176]

ABOUT THE VENETIAN ENVOY, TREVISANO

After this, this legate Antonio and other Italians and Greeks
met in Moscow with the Venetian envoy, Giovanni Trevisano, and
asked him why he had been sent to the Grand Prince, and began
inquiring why he was staying there. And he told them differently
from what he had agreed with our Ivan the Italian.[177] And they
told the Grand Prince, "This Trevisano was sent to you from the
Doge of Venice, Nicola Trona, with a petition and gifts, and was
instructed to ask you to send him [Trevisano], together with your
own envoy, to the Khan of the Great Horde; and he was sent to
the Khan with the proposal of this Doge and that of other countries,
as well as with vast gifts, that [the Khan] should agree to help them
with his army against the Turkish Sultan." The Grand Prince, hearing this, forthwith investigated what was what, and what Ivan the
Italian had sought to conceal from him, because the latter had

176. This marriage of Ivan III to Sophia Paleologue had considerable
political implication. From her and from the Greeks accompanying her,
Ivan III learned the autocratic ways of the Byzantine Emperor. Instead of
discussing political matters with the boyars, as had his father and
forefathers, he started deciding them alone or in consultation with a few
of his advisers; and his son, Vasilii III (1506–33), and grandson, Ivan IV
(1533–89), did likewise. This novelty was thereby resented by the boyars
and service gentry, princes who were still semi-independent, and it resulted
in the confrontation between Ivan IV and the aristocracy in the 1560s, for
which the latter paid dearly. The same trend toward autocratic rule occurred in the same period in France, England and Spain. Kartashov, Vol. I,
p. 388 ff.

177. Ivan the Italian: the Muscovite financier.

1473 suggested [to Trevisano] that he, himself, conduct this Trevisano to the Khan. And [Ivan III] became wroth with them, commanding that the Italian [financier] be arrested, put in irons and sent to Kolomna. And he commanded his house to be destroyed and his wife and children to be put under arrest. And he also wanted to execute Trevisano, after he had been caught, but this envoy and the others with him interceded with the Prince that he should be merciful toward him until he receive information from the Venetian Doge. The Grand Prince, however, commanded that he be put in irons, and he remained under arrest [on the estate] of Nikita Beklemishev.

The Grand Prince permitted this legate Antonio, Dmitrii the Greek, and the other Italians and Greeks to sojourn with him for eleven weeks, rendering them great honor and giving them many presents, and he let them return [home] on the twenty-sixth day of January. And he sent many gifts to the Pope, as well as to his brothers-in-law. And his son, Grand Prince Ivan, as well as Grand Princess Sofia, did the same from themselves. And so they journeyed from Moscow to the Lithuanian and Polish lands, and to many other lands, to their great city of Rome.

THE FIRE IN MOSCOW AND THE DEATH OF METROPOLITAN PHILIP

The same spring on the fourth day of April in the fifth week of Lent, called the week of Praise, at the fourth hour at night, a fire started inside the inner city of Moscow in the Church of the Nativity of the Most Holy Mother of God, near the place where is the side chapel of the Resurrection of Lazar. And many households burned, [including] the palace of the Metropolitan and the palace of Prince Boris Vasilievich. [It burned up to the Church] of the Manifestation of the Trinity and to the city barns, and to the grain barn of the Grand Prince. His large palace was saved with difficulty. At that time the Grand Prince was in the city. It burned up to the stone storage near the city wall, which was on the estate of Prince Mikhail Andreevich. The roof of the Church of the Nativity of the Most Pure was burned, as well as the roofs of the city walls and all additional city construction; and all the households which were in the vicinity burned, up to the city grain storage.

It was already the end of the last hour of the night and the fire started coming to an end, when Metropolitan Philip came from outside the city to the Church of the Most Pure [Theotokos], because

during the fire he had left the city for the old Monastery of St.   **1473**
Nicholas. Upon entering the Church of the Most Pure he started
celebrating a *Te Deum* at the shrine of Wonderworker [Metropoli-
tan] Peter, and shed many tears. At that time the Grand Prince
approached him and, seeing him weeping, told him, "My father,
lord! Do not grieve. It was the will of God that your palace burned.
I will give you as many buildings as you want and if any of your
supplies burned, you can get everything from me." He addressed
him while he wept, and after long lamenting, the Metropolitan
began to suffer bodily, and his arms and legs grew feeble. Since
the Grand Prince was present, the Metropolitan told him, "My son,
as far as I am concerned, it was God's will. Permit me to retire to
a monastery." The Grand Prince, however, did not want to accept
his desire because he wanted to go to a remote monastery; but he
took him to the nearby Monastery of the Manifestation of Our
Lord Trinity Court. As soon as he had brought him thither he
forthwith sent for his [the Metropolitan's] confessor, and he [the
Metropolitan] received communion and unction.

And he [the Metropolitan] spoke to the Grand Prince and
asked only one thing: that the Church [of the Assumption] be
completed. At that time it was built half-way up the walls, and they
had already built the shrines for the saints in all three walls.[178]

Thereupon he spoke of his concern for this same church construction, summoned Vladimir Grigorievich and his son, Ivan
Golova, and told them that everything had been prepared for completion of the church's construction: "You should just take care
and it will be completed." Also, he spoke with other people involved
in the building of the church, and spoke uninterruptedly about it.
[He spoke also about] the people whom he had obtained for this
ecclesiastic undertaking, instructing that they be set free after the
end of his life. And he blessed all the princes and princesses, boyars
and priests, and all the Orthodox Christians who came to him,
wishing them peace and pardoning them and giving them a final
embrace, and asked forgiveness from all of them. And so passed
his [last] day, and it was on the fifth of April, and toward the end
of the first hour of the night he passed away to God. And many
people remarked about this, saying that they had had a vision in
church. After his death they found under his robe iron fetters,

178. The sanctuary is located at the fourth, or eastern, wall.

1473 which can be seen in his tomb up to now. No one before, neither his spiritual father nor his servant, had known about this.

On the seventh day of the month of April he was buried in the tomb in the Church of the Most Pure Mother of God, which he had begun to build; and he was buried with the singing of psalms, and there was much weeping. Present at his burial were the Grand Prince, his mother and his son, a multitude of boyars and lords, and all the people of the city of Moscow. There was only one bishop at his burial, Prochorus of Sarai, as well as the archimandrites of Moscow [monasteries], archpriests, abbots, and all the priests of the city of Moscow. And his tomb is located near the northern entrance of the church, where the shrine of His Holiness, Metropolitan Jonas, is situated. Upon entering the church from the northern door, it is located on the right side.

The same month during the same Palm Week, Grand Prince Ivan Vasilievich summoned his brothers and all the bishops of the land, announcing to them the passing of his Metropolitan Philip, and summoned them to come to him on St. George's Day. The same month on the twenty-third of April there came Archbishop Bassian of Rostov, Bishop Euthymius of Suzdal', Bishop Theodosius of Riazan', Bishop Gerontius of Kolomna, and Bishop Prochorus of Sarai. The Novgorodian Archbishop Theophilus and Genadius, Bishop of Tver', sent their envoys and unanimously signed, together with the other bishops, the following [statement]: "The one who shall be wanted by Lord God, by the Most Pure [Theotokos] and by the great wonderworkers, as well as by Grand Prince Ivan Vasilievich, by our brothers, the bishops, and by the Sacred Council shall become our Metropolitan." The Council took place in Moscow.

ABOUT THE CONSECRATION OF GERONTIUS TO BE METROPOLITAN

And they elected Bishop Gerontius of Kolomna as the most deserving to be the shepherd of the flock entrusted to him by God, and he was conducted to the palace of the Metropolitan on the fourth of June. And on St. Peter's Day, Tuesday, the twenty-ninth of the same month, he was elevated [to Metropolitan]. The same year on the twenty-fifth of July, the priest-monk, Nikita Semeshkov, son of the archpriest [of the Cathedral] of Archangel [Michael] in Moscow, was consecrated Bishop of the diocese of Kolomna by Metropolitan Gerontius. The same year Metropolitan Gerontius built in his court in Moscow gates constructed of baked bricks, and laid the foundation of a palace in his court.

The same year an envoy from Pskov came to the Grand Prince **1474**
to petition him that he help protect them from the Germans because
the armistice was over and the Germans were marching against
them.

In the Year 6982 [1474]. The Grand Prince sent Prince Danilo
Dmitrievich Kholmskii with many regiments to aid Pskov. When
they came to Pskov and the Germans learned that the Grand Prince's
voevodas with many warriors had come to aid Pskov, they sent their
envoys to Pskov requesting peace, and a peace for twenty years was
concluded according to the will of Pskov.

The same year the troops of Moscow took Liubutsk, and seized
many captives.[179] The same fall the people of Liubutsk unexpectedly
went against Prince Semion Odoevskii and started fighting with
him; and since he had very few men-at-arms, they killed Prince
Semion, but him only. All the others remained alive.

The same winter on the thirty-first of December [the Tatar]
Lord Murtoza, son of the Kazan' Khan Mustafa, came to Grand
Prince Ivan Vasilievich. The Grand Prince took him into his service
and as a patrimony gave him the town of Novogorodok on the Oka
River, and many districts. The same winter there came to the Grand
Prince an envoy of the Khan of the Crimea, Mengli-Girei, son of
Hadji Girei, by the name of Hadji Baba. He was sent to the Grand
Prince to express his affection and brotherly feelings. And the
Grand Prince honored this envoy and sent him back to his country.
And the Grand Prince sent along with him Nikita Beklemishev, his
envoy, to Mengli-Girei, Khan of the Crimea, likewise with expres-
sions of affection and brotherly feelings. This happened on the
thirty-first of March.

The same spring on the eighteenth of April at the seventh
hour at night a daughter by the name of Elena was born to the
Grand Prince by Grand Princess Sofia.

The same month on the twenty-fifth of April Antonio the
Italian came from Doge Nicola Trona [of Venice] to petition the
Grand Prince on behalf of the Doge and to ask the Grand Prince
kindly to release their envoy, Giovanni [Trevisano], from prison,

179. Liubutsk was a town near Mtsensk and Orel. It was a territory
contested between Moscow and Lithuania because the Russian population
of this region, which felt the pressure of the Catholic church in Lithuania
and in Poland, was breaking off its feudal relations with Lithuania and
was joining Russia, while some others remained in Lithuania. Prince
Odoevskii was from this contested region.

1474   thus aiding them all [Trevisano and his aids] as he had asked in his first request, and to send him [Trevisano] to Khan Ahmet of the Great Horde. The same day the Grand Prince showed his mercy to Giovanni Trevisano and commanded that he be released from irons and to appear before his eyes.

THE COLLAPSE OF THE CHURCH OF THE ASSUMPTION

The same year on the twentieth of the month of May at the first hour at night the Church of the Most Holy Mother of God, whose building was started by Metropolitan Philip of all Russia, collapsed. It was marvelous in its appearance, extremely high, and was already constructed up to the vaults. Only the cupola, the great dome, remained to be built. The northern wall, which was built over the tombs of Their Holinesses Metropolitan Jonas and Metropolitan Philip, consisted actually of two separate walls, an outside and an inside one, each built the thickness of only one stone layer; and between them was constructed a staircase which reached the top of the edifice. Because of its great height and heavy vault and staircase, which rested on this double wall, it was not strong enough and broke, pulling down with it the front, or western, wall. This caused great damage in the church. Half of the [front, or] western wall collapsed, and the [entire] northern wall up to the sanctuary, as well as the scaffolds, pillars, and vaults, also collapsed. And the shrine of Wonderworker [Metropolitan] Peter was buried [under the stones] but they did not damage it. The tomb of Metropolitan Jonas split but did not break entirely. Only a structure over the tomb of Metropolitan Philip was destroyed. Of the wooden church which was [provisionally] built inside this stone one, the roof was destroyed but the icons, the holy vessels, books, candles, chandeliers, and many other items were not hurt at all. From this entire church there remained only half of the front [western] wall with the front entrance, the whole southern wall with its pillars and vaults, and the entire santuary [eastern] wall; but because of this great wreck, the [remaining] pillars and walls became unsteady and some cracked without collapsing.

There was no small grief for Grand Prince Ivan Vasilievich and Metropolitan Gerontius, and for all Orthodox Christians, because this was already the third year that the original church had been dismantled; and now this one collapsed because of our sins. But it was a real miracle of the Most Holy Mother of God and the

intercession of the great wonderworkers [that no one was hurt] **1474**
because on that day the stonecutters who had been working in the
church were building up the vaults, others were carrying stone,
mortar, and wood, and some had climbed up to view the construction work. One hour before sunset all those who were working
came down, and even those who had gone up to look also came
down at the first hour of the night. And some came down only in
the last fifth of the first hour. And before the first hour struck, the
edifice collapsed. A young man, the son of Prince Fedor Pestroi,
who was walking on those vaults and heard the crashing and falling
of the stones, became frightened, ran in confusion to the southern
wall, and after the collapse [of the northern and part of the western
walls] he came down from [the wall of] the church, not at all harmed.

After this occurrence the Grand Prince ordered the disman-
tling of the remaining vaults and pillars of the southern side and
the front wall, as well as the southern wall, because it was dangerous
to enter to worship the icon of the Most Pure, the tomb of the
Wonderworker Peter and the other Metropolitans. And he sent to
the Roman land for master stonecutters, and others he ordered
brought from his patrimony of Pskov because they had learned
such work, the stonecutting craft, from the Germans.[180]

The same summer in the month of June posadniks Ivan
Agafonov, Kosma Sysoev Ledov, and Zinovei Sidorov came from
Pskov to the Grand Prince to petition Grand Prince Ivan Vasilievich,
their Sovereign, to defend them from the Germans. The Grand
Prince became displeased with them and did not let them appear
before his eyes because they were slow to come with the petition,
and they had forgotten to send their taxes to their Sovereign, as if
they had forgotten him. And they brought only insignificant gifts,
not according to the way their Sovereign had honored his patrimony. And they returned in shame to Pskov.

The same year on the seventh day of the month of July Nikifor
Basenkov came from the Horde with Kara Kuchuk, the envoy of
Khan Ahmet of the Great Horde, and with him were a multitude
of Tatars: there were six hundred of them who were part of the
embassy and who were supposed to be fed; and with them were
three thousand two hundred merchants with horses for sale and

180. Indeed, during more than two centuries of the Tatar Yoke, no
large edifices were built and Russians forgot how to build them.

1475 other goods. And they brought for sale more than forty thousand horses and a great deal of other merchandise.

On the twenty-fourth of the same month the Grand Prince sent Semion Tolbuzin as the head of his embassy to Venice, to the Venetian Doge Nicola Trona; and [with him was] Antonio the Italian [to announce] that he [the Grand Prince] had mercifully released their ambassador, Giovanni Trevisano, from prison as they had petitioned him; and, having supplied him with everything, he had let him go to Khan Ahmet of the Golden Horde. With them [that is, with the Venetian envoys] was his own envoy [to support] their proposal that he [Ahmet] be gracious enough to help them against the Turkish Sultan, who was in Constantinople.

On the fourteenth of the same month there came with gifts to the Grand Prince from Rome, from the princes—the children of Thomas of Morea, brothers-in-law of the Grand Prince—an envoy by the name of Demetrius the Greek, and he returned [to Venice] the same year.

The nineteenth of the same month[181] the Grand Prince allowed Kara-Kuchuk, ambassador of the Great Horde, to return, and with him he sent his own envoy, Dmitrii Lazarev, and the Venetian envoy, Giovanni Trevisano, whom he permitted to go [thither], and he supplied them all with men, horses, and gifts.

In the Year 6983 [1475]. On the first of September Bogdan, the ambassador of King Kasimir, came to the Grand Prince from Lithuania.

On the nineteenth of the month of September or on the eighth of the Heavenly One [?] at the sixth hour of the day it sleeted and then snowed heavily. That night and the next it froze, then [the rain and snow] disappeared and on the sixth of November it started snowing and the ground froze and the river stopped on the eighth of November. On the ninth of the same month of November at the second hour Grigorii Pereushkov, the Grand Prince's hunting master, saw two suns while he was riding to the hunt. The real sun was moving in its usual path while the unusual one was higher, in the middle of the sky, where it usually moves in midsummer; and there was much light, but you could not see any rays from it. And it was seen not only by him but also by the others who were with him.

181. The dating is confusing: apparently, the 24th, 14th, and 19th are all of the month of July.

The same winter Metropolitan Gerontius built a brick palace **1475**
on four stone basements at his estate, and he moved thither on the
thirteenth of November.

The same day Nikita Beklemishov, the Grand Prince's ambassador, came from the Crimea, from Khan Mengli-Girei, son of
Khan Hadji Girei, and with him was the Khan's ambassador, Dovletek Murza, with many gifts. And he [Dovletek] was received by
the Grand Prince on the sixteenth of the same month, [and he said]
"The Khan sends the Grand Prince his love and his brotherhood:
'Whosoever is your friend, Grand Prince, so he is my friend; and
whosoever is your enemy is my enemy. And our children and grandchildren should also abide in the same concord and brotherhood.'"
The same spring on the twenty-sixth of March, Easter Sunday, the
Grand Prince's envoy, Semion Tolbuzin, came from Rome, bringing
with him a master builder of churches and houses, and his name
was Aristotle; he was also a cannonmaker, and he could cast and
found them; and he was highly able to cast bells and all other things.

On the twenty-seventh in the morning of Easter Day the Grand
Prince sent Aleksei Starkov, his great ambassador, to the Crimean
Khan Mengli Girei, and with him went Dovletek Murza, the Khan's
ambassador.

On the second of April the Grand Prince sent Vasilii Kitai, his
envoy, and with him Fedets Mansurov, to Lithuania.

ABOUT THE PRINCES OF ROSTOV

The same winter the Princes of Rostov—Prince Vladimir Andreevich and his brother [cousin] Prince Ivan Ivanovich—with all
their children and nephews, sold to Grand Prince Ivan Vasilievich
their patrimony, half of Rostov, with everything. Having bought
this half from them, the Grand Prince gave it to his mother, Grand
Princess Maria.[182]

The sixteenth day of the same month, with the ringing of bells,
was the transposition of the relics of Wonderworker [Metropolitan]
Peter from the Church of the Most Pure [Theotokos] to the Church
of St. John, as well as the relics of the other metropolitans, Theognostus, Cyprian, Photius, and Jonas. And on the seventeenth the
Venetian master Aristotle began to tear down those walls of the

182. This paragraph is found in *Litsevoi svod* only, not in *Obol.* or in
Ioasaf.

1476   Church of the Purest which had fallen before, and the same day
he tore down two pillars, the front door, and the great part of the
front wall.

The twenty-third of the same month after vespers came a cloud,
and first there was a mild thunderstorm, then, beginning at noon,
there was a very strong one with lightning, and there was also a
mighty downpour; and there were freezes and frosts till the second
of May, and from that day it rained every day.

On the twenty-eighth of May at night a daughter, Theodosia,
was born to the Grand Prince; she [subsequently] became [the wife
of Prince] Kholmskii.

In the month of June the Venetian wall-builder Aristotle
started digging moats for the foundation of the Church of the Most
Pure Mother of God, and the depth of these moats was twelve feet
and in some places still deeper.

The tenth of the same month at the first hour of the day a
conflagration started beyond the Moscow River in the vicinity of
the Church of St. Nicholas, which is called the Borisov Church,
and many households and churches burned on that occasion.

In the Year 6984 [1476]. On the sixth of September there came
to the Grand Prince a certain Bogdan, ambassador of King Kasimir
[of Lithuania and Poland], and with him was Vaska Lubich.[183]

The twelfth of the same month at midnight a conflagration
started in Moscow, in the suburb behind Neglinnaia, between the
churches of St. Nicholas and All Saints.[184] Many households and
these two churches burned.[185]

The same day the ambassador of Lithuania left Moscow.

On the twenty-seventh of the same month at the third hour
of the night the estate of Nikifor Basenkov, located on the Arbat,
burned, and they all jumped out headfirst.

The thirtieth of the same month, on Saturday at the second
hour of the day, the sun perished. One-third of it perished, and
the moon looked as if it had horns. And this was seen by many in
Kolomna and its region, but no one could see it in Moscow. The
second day of the month of October, at the fourth hour, a fire

183. Vaska Lubich: the last name appears only in *Obol.*, not in *Ioasaf*.
184. "Neglinnaia" was a river forming the western border of the
Kremlin. Later it was filled in.
185. The last part of this paragraph is in *Litsevoi svod* only.

started inside the city of Moscow near the gates of St. Timothy, **1476** and the Grand Prince, himself, came with many people and extinguished it, and from thence he went to his table for dinner. In the middle of his dinner another fire started inside the city of Moscow near St. Nicholas' Gate. This happened at the fifth hour of the day between the Church of the Presentation of the Mother of God and the Church of Cosmas and Damian, and almost the whole city burned. It burned as far as the court of the Grand Prince, St. Saviour Monastery, the residence of Prince Mikhail Andreevich; and on the lower side, as far as the household of Fedor Davydovich. It was stopped only at the third hour of the night because the Grand Prince, himself, was with his people in all places where he was needed. And ten stone churches burned from outside, while the eleventh, the Church of the Ascension, also burned from inside. And besides these, ten partly stone churches burned, and twelve wooden ones. Two wooden structures at the Cathedral of the Archangel [Michael]—the Chapel of the Resurrection and the Chapel of St. Aquila—were torn down.

On the twenty-first of the same month Dmitrii Lazarevich, envoy of the Grand Prince to the Horde, came back hurriedly.

ABOUT THE GRAND PRINCE'S JOURNEY TO NOVGOROD

On the twenty-second of the same month [October], on Sunday, Grand Prince Ivan Vasilievich started his journey of Peace to Great Novgorod. [And he went] with many people, leaving his son, Grand Prince Ivan Ivanovich, in Moscow. On St. Dimitrii's Day the Grand Prince arrived in Volok, and ate and drank at his brother's, Prince Boris's. On the first of November he arrived in Torzhok.

On the fifth, in Volochok, the Grand Prince was met by men from Novgorod who complained about their fellow Novgorodians. Then one hundred versts before Novgorod the Grand Prince was met by Archbishop Theophilus of Novgorod the Great. Together with him were Prince Vasilii Vasilievich Grebenka Shuiskii; Archimandrite Theodosius of the Iur'iev Monastery; Naphanail, abbot of [the Monastery of] St. Saviour in Khutyn'; Barlaam, abbott of [the Monastery of] Vezhychi; the Archbishop's treasurer, Sergius; [the bishop's] confessor Euthymius Meshkov; the present posadnik, Vasilii Onanin; former posadniks Ivan, son of Afanasii, and Olferei and Kiril, sons of Iakov; and many other [former] posadniks. [There also came with them] the present tysiatskii, Vasilii Esipov; the

1476   boyars, led by Vasilii Nikiforov; the wealthy burghers, Ivan Dmitriev, Iurii Marin, Martemian Bozhin; along with minor boyars,
elders, and merchants of Novgorod. The same day Archbishop
Theophilus, Prince Vasilii [Shuiskii], and all the posadniks of Novgorod attended a dinner at the palace of the Grand Prince. They
ate, drank, and then departed. And on the twenty-first, the day of
the Presentation of the Most Pure Theotokos, a Tuesday, the Grand
Prince came to Gorodishte [the Grand Prince's residence in Nov-
gorod] and attended the church service in the Church of the Annunciation.

The same month of November on the twenty-third, Thursday,
the Grand Prince entered his patrimony, Great Novgorod. Archbishop Theophilus, together with the entire Sacred Council, all in
ecclesiastical   vestments—archimandrites,   abbots,   priests   and
deacons and the entire clergy, and all the monks—met the Grand
Prince with crosses as they were commanded by the Grand Prince,
and they did so without any pride; and with them were a great
many posadniks, tysiatskiis, boyars, wealthy burghers, and all of
Novgorod the Great, which met him with great love. The Archbishop blessed the Grand Prince with the cross and then, together
with the entire Sacred Council, they all proceeded with crosses and
icons into the Cathedral of Holy Sophia, Wisdom of God. And the
Grand Prince entered this church and there was celebrated a *Te
Deum*, and he venerated the icons of the Saviour, of his Most Pure
Mother, and of the other saints, as well as the tombs of his forefathers, the former grand princes, who were buried there. The
Archbishop celebated the liturgy with the entire Sacred Council
and the Grand Prince attended this service piously, joyfully and
praying devoutly, asking Lord God and His Most Pure Mother for
remission of his sins and supplicating the aid of the saints, who
knew how to please God. After completion of the service the Grand
Prince went for dinner to the Archbishop, where he ate and drank
joyfully, and the Archbishop presented many gifts to the Grand
Prince. After passing time joyously, the Grand Prince returned to
Gorodishte, and the Archbishop accompanied him with great honor
and wine.[186]

And these were the Archbishop's presents: three pieces of
broadcloth, a hundred ducats, walrus tusks, a barrel of imported

186. The following paragraph is in *Litsevoi svod* only.

red wine, and another of white. On Friday, the twenty-fourth of   **1476**
November, as well as on the other days, the posadniks, tysiatskiis,
boyars and wealthy burghers, and plaintiffs came to petition the
Grand Prince and to greet him with gifts and wine. There were all
manner of craftsmen and elders and wealthy burghers from all the
Novgorodian districts, some coming with complaints and some to
see him; and all without exception greeted him.

On the twenty-fifth of the same month, on Saturday, the Grand
Prince came to Gorodishte, and many Novgorodians from both
Slavkov Street and Mikitin Street complained to the Grand Prince
about the [following] Novgorodian boyars: incumbent posadnik
Vasilii Onanin, Bogdan Esipov, Fedor Isakov, Grigorii Tuchin, Ivan
Loshyn'skii, Vasilii Mikiforov, Matvei Selezenev, Iakov Selezenev,
Andrei Isakov Teliatiev, Luka Afonasov, Mosei Fedorov, Semion
Afonasov, Konstantin Babkin, Aleksei Kashin, Vasilii Tutrium, Vas-
ilii Balaksha, Efim Revshin, Grigorii Koshurkin, Ofimen's people,
Esipov Goroshkov, his son, Ivan, and Ivan's people of Savelkov,
who came into these two streets with many people on horseback.
They killed people, robbed them, and took people's wealth worth
a thousand rubles, while many people were beaten to death.

And the same day the boyars, Luka and Vasilii Isakov, the
children of Polinar, complained to the Grand Prince about Bogdan
Esipov, Vasilii Mikiforov, and Pamfila, the elder of Fedorovskaia
Street, because they came into their estates, beat people, sacked
their wealth, and took goods worth five hundred rubles. The Grand
Prince gave to the petitioners his police officials, Dmitrii Chubanov,
Fedets Mansurov, and Vasilii Dalmatov [to investigate] those who
were accused. When all these complaints about these people were
presented to the Grand Prince there were present, together with
the Grand Prince's prayerful Archbishop Theophilus, posadnik
Zakharyi Ovin, his brother, Kosma, Kasimir with his brother, Iakov,
and Luka and Iakov Fedorov, and other Novgorodian boyars and
wealthy burghers.

And the Grand Prince spoke to the Archbishop and to the
posadniks in this way: "You, my prayerful intercessor [Archbishop]
and you, posadniks of our patrimony, must say the following to
Novgorod the Great: 'You are supposed to set your police officials
against these trespassers, to whom I have sent my police officials,'
and I will see what happens. And you, my prayerful intercessor,
you posadniks who were with me, we must give justice to those who

1476 have been offended." And concerning this matter [he] sent to his patrimony, Novgorod, his boyars Fedor Davydovich and Ivan Borisovich, with orders that they send police officials against those who had offended their brethren. And the Novgorodians sent against them their own police officials, Nazar and Vasilii Anfimov, and they ordered that those offending boyars be sent with the police officials to the Grand Prince. And they were summoned to the Grand Prince the same day, on Saturday, and they were there in the morning on Sunday before the Grand Prince.

In the morning on Sunday, the twenty-sixth of November, both the offenders and the offended all appeared before the Grand Prince in Gorodishte. [These were] the elders of Slavkov Street and Mikitin Street with all the people from these streets; and Luka and Vasilii Isakov, both children of Polinar, and posadnik Vasilii Onanin, together with all the above-mentioned against whom there were complaints. And they had to answer [for their trespasses]; at the time they were with the Grand Prince, his prayerful intercessor, Archbishop Theophilus, and the Novgorodian posadniks. And they started the trial, and they investigated and examined those who had complained and those against whom there were complaints; and those who had intruded, beaten, and sacked were accused. And the Grand Prince commanded that Vasilii Ananin, Bogdan Esipov, Fedor Isakov, and Ivan Loshynskii be arrested; and then the minor boyars arrested Vasilii Onanin, Ivan Tovarkov, Bogdan Rusalka, Fedor Isakov, Mikita Beklemishev, and Loshynskii-Zvenets. And the Grand Prince commanded his police officials to take their accomplices against a bond of one and a half thousand rubles to the benefit of those who had complained; and the Archbishop took them on his own charge. At the same time the Grand Prince sent away Ivan Afanasiev and his son, Alferii, and commanded that those be arrested who wanted to break Novgorod away from the Grand Prince so as to be under the King. Vasilii Kitai arrested Ivan, and Iurii Shestak arrested his son.

On Tuesday, the third day [after the Grand Prince's arrival] the Archbishop and posadniks went to the Grand Prince in Gorodishte to petition in the name of all Novgorod that mercy be shown the arrested boyars and that they not be punished but be released to them on bail. The Grand Prince did not accept this petition of the Archbishop's and of Novgorod, and responded the following way:

"It should be known to you, our prayerful intercessor, and to **1476** all Novgorod, which is our patrimony, how much evil has been done by these boyars. And now, whatever manner of evil there may be in our patrimony, it is all their doing. How can we bestow our mercy upon them?" And the same day he sent them in irons to Moscow, with his police officials.

On the first of December, Friday, the Archbishop came to the Grand Prince, to Gorodishte, with numerous posadniks: Vasilii Kasimir with his brother, Iakov; Zakharii Ovin with his brother, Kosma; Fefilat Zakharin; Afanasii Ostafiev Bruz; Luka and Iakov Fedorov; and other posadniks, tysiatskiis, boyars, and many wealthy burghers. And they petitioned the Grand Prince in the name of all Novgorod the Great concerning those guilty ones: Grigorii Tuchin, Vasilii Nikiforov, Matvei Selezenev, and their accomplices, who were released to the Archbishop on his bail. They asked that the Grand Prince bestow his mercy [on them], not punish these guilty ones, that their guilt be decided according to the charter, and that the plaintiffs be paid for their losses. For the sake of his prayerful intercessor, the Archbishop, and for the sake of the petition of his patrimony, Novgorod the Great, the Grand Prince bestowed his mercy upon these guilty people, commanded that they not be punished and that the losses of the plaintiffs [valued at] one and a half thousand rubles be distributed by the police officials, and that their guilt be treated according to the charter, separately from each other. And the police officials did all this to them. Many other boyars were tried and called to order, and the people who had been offended by the powerful were shown his mercy and were protected by him.[187]

On Wednesday, the sixth of December, the day of St. Nicholas, the Grand Prince dined at Prince Vasilii Shuiskii's and [received] gifts: three pieces of broadcloth and three pieces of *kamka*,[188] thirty ducats, two gyrfalcons, and one falcon.

On the tenth of December, there were brought to Moscow the posadniks Vasilii Onanin, Bogdan [Esipov], Fedor [Isakov], Ivan Loshynskii, and Ivan [Afanasiev] with his son, Alferii.

On the fourteenth of December, the Grand Prince banqueted at the Archbishop's. It was Thursday and there were [presented to

187. The next date, December 6, and the following paragraphs dealing with the period December 6—January 14, are in *Litsevoi svod* only.

188. *Kamka*: old silk brocade.

1476   him the following] gifts: a hundred and fifty ducats, five pieces of broadcloth, a stallion, one barrel of wine, and two barrels of mead. On the fifteenth of December, there was a banquet at Kasimir's and his gifts were a golden cup, two *grivna*,[189] a hundred ducats, and two gyrfalcons. On the seventeenth of December there was a banquet at Zakhary Grigoriev's and the gifts to the Grand Prince were twenty ducats, five pieces of broadcloth; and from his son, Ivan, ten ducats, one piece of broadcloth, and two tusks. On the nineteenth of December at the incumbent posadnik's, Vasilii Esipov's, there was also a banquet in honor of the Grand Prince and the gifts were thirty ducats and three pieces of yellow-red broadcloth.

On the twenty-first of December, Thursday, there was a banquet for the Grand Prince at Iakov Korob's, and the gifts were two hundred ducats, gyrfalcons, and tusks; and from his son, Ivan, gyrfalcons and a yellow-red broadcloth and tusks. On the twenty-third of December, Saturday, there was a banquet for the Grand Prince at Luka Fedorov's, and the gifts were twenty ducats, twenty gold pieces, three pieces of broadcloth, and two tusks.

On the twenty-fifth of December, Christmas, there was a banquet at the Grand Prince's residence and there were the Archbishop and Prince Vasilii [Shuiskii], posadniks, all the tysiatskiis and the wealthy burghers, and many merchants; and he banqueted with them late into the night. On the twenty-eighth of December, Thursday, there was a banquet for the Grand Prince in Gorodishte at the [mansion] of Anastasia Ivanovna Grigorieva and her son, Iurii, and the gifts were thirty ducats, ten pieces of broadcloth with pearls, twice forty sables, and two tusks. On the thirtieth of December, Saturday, there was a banquet for the Grand Prince at [former] posadnik Fefilat [Zarkhar'in's] and the gifts were thirty ducats, three pieces of broadcloth, and one tusk; and from his son, Kuzma, ten ducats and two tusks. On the first of January there was a banquet for the Grand Prince at Iakov Fedorov's and the gifts were forty ducats, three pieces of broadcloth, and four tusks. On the third of January there was a banquet at Aleksandr Samsonov's; gifts: forty ducats, five pieces of broadcloth, and a gray stallion. On the fifth of January, Saturday, there was a banquet at posadnik Foma's and

189. *Grivna*: a silver bar weighing about one pound, used as a monetary unit.

gifts were three pitchers with pearls, one skewbald horse, and two barrels of white wine. On the eleventh of January, Thursday, incumbent posadnik Foma and tysiatskii Vasilii Esipov greeted the Grand Prince with one thousand rubles from the city of Novgorod the Great.

While the Grand Prince was still in Novgorod on the twelfth of January there came to him the German[190] ambassador from the Swedish King Gerstur[191] and his sister's son, Orban. This happened on the twelfth of January, and he brought from the king a present, a brown stallion; and he greeted the Grand Prince from the King and told him that there had been a treaty of peace [between Sweden and Novgorod] for a number of years, and these years had long since passed. And they asked the Grand Prince to grant that his patrimony, Novgorod, conclude a new treaty of peace with them [the Swedes]. And the Grand Prince agreed to this and commanded his prayerful intercessor, Archbishop Theophilus, and his patrimony, Novgorod, to conclude an alliance with them as of old. And he honored this event and let him go.

On the fourteenth of January there was a banquet at Kuzma Grigoriev's. The gifts were twenty ducats, three pieces of broadcloth, and two tusks; and from his son, ten ducats, one piece of broadcloth with pearls, and two tusks.[192]

On the nineteenth of January there was a third banquet for the Grand Prince at Archbishop Theophilus'. The gifts were 1,000 Hungarian and Venetian gold pieces, one hundred ducats, a golden cup with pearls, three grivnas, two *tur* horns[193] encrusted with gold, a silver plate, twelve grivenkas, eighteen pieces of broadcloth of different colors, and ten times forty sables. As farewell the Archbishop greeted the Grand Prince with three barrels of white wine, two barrels of red wine, and two barrels of old mead. The same month, on the twentieth, the incumbent posadnik Foma and tysiatskii Vasilii, son of Esip, presented the Grand Prince on behalf of the entire city of Novgorod the Great with one thousand rubles. Those posadniks and tysiatskiis who did not manage to hold a banquet for the Grand Prince all came to him with the gifts which they were supposed to have presented to the Grand Prince during

190. "German" ("*Nemets*") denotes either "foreign" or "Germanic."
191. King Gerstur: probably, King Sten Stures.
192. End of the text added in *Litsevoi svod*.
193. *Tur*: a Russian variety of buffalo.

1476 their banquets. Likewise the merchants and wealthy burghers, without exception, came to him with gifts, and many common people
came to greet him and [bring him] presents.

The Grand Prince, himself, gave the posadniks, boyars,
tysiatskiis, the posadnik's children, the merchants, and wealthier
burghers expensive cloth of brocade, cups, silver pitchers, as well
as forty sables, and horses to those who deserved them.

THE GRAND PRINCE LEAVES NOVGOROD

On Friday, the twenty-sixth of the month of January, early in
the morning, the Grand Prince left Novgorod for Moscow and his
first stop was at St. Nicholas on the Volok. And the Archbishop
came to that place to greet him, and with him was Prince Vasilii
Shuiskii and posadnik Vasilii Kasimir with his brother, Iakov,
Zakharia Ovin Grigoriev with his brother, Kuzma, Luka and Iakov
Fedorov, and other [former] posadniks, many boyars, and wealthy
burghers. And the Archbishop, greeting the Grand Prince, presented him with two barrels of white and red wine. Prince Vasilii
[Shuiskii], the posadniks, and all those who came with them each
presented a wineskin. The Grand Prince invited them to eat at his
place, and they ate and drank at his place, and he gave gifts to the
Archbishop and to Prince Vasilii [Shuiskii]. On the eighth day of
the month of February, on Thursday, the Grand Prince came to
Moscow early in the morning before the liturgy and [thereafter]
ate bread and drank at his mother's.

ABOUT THE SUN'S DISAPPEARANCE, OR ABOUT THE DARKNESS

On the twenty-fifth of the same month, during Shrovetide,
toward the end of the first hour of the day the sky became cloudy
and the sun did not yet start to shine; and then it began to grow
dark and it was dark as at the somber second hour at night; but it
did not last long. Once more light clouds appeared from the south
and then it was light, as before. And the same week many people
saw shining light at night and there were circles in the sky. On the
tenth day of the month of March, or on Heavenly [*sic, unclear*]
February fifteenth, at night from Sunday to Monday at the third
hour, the moon began to disappear; and it disappeared completely,
and it was impossible to see it until midnight, when it reappeared.

Sunday, the thirty-first of the same month at night Archbishop
Theophilus of Novgorod the Great came [to Moscow] to the Grand

Prince to intercede in the name of all Novgorod the Great on behalf **1476**
of the arrested boyars who were imprisoned in Kolomna and
Murom. With him were posadnik Kasimir's brother, Iakov Korob;
Iakov Fedorov; Akinf Tolstoi; and many representatives of the
wealthy burghers. They petitioned the Grand Prince for those
posadniks who had been arrested by the Grand Prince in Novgorod
and had been sent to be imprisoned; three of them in Kolomna:
Ivan Afonasiev with his sons, Alferii, and Bogdan [Esipov]; and
three in Murom: Fedor Isakov, Vasilii Onanin, and Ivan Loshynskii.
The Archbishop brought many gifts to the Grand Prince, as did
the posadniks. And he dined at the Grand Prince's on Monday,
the first of April, with all the people; on the seventh of the same
month, on Palm Sunday, the Grand Prince offered a farewell banquet for the Archbishop but he did not release any of those arrested
posadniks. And the Archbishop left Moscow on Monday of Holy
Week.

ABOUT THE SIGNS

On the eleventh day of the same month,[194] on Maundy Thursday, at the first hour of the day, there was a sign on the sun. The
sun rose very bright and all eyes could see it from the city of
Moscow; and it rose directly over the top of the Church of the Icon
[of Christ][195] not Made by Human Hands, which is in Andronicus
Monastery. And around the sun there was a very great circle: it
looked like bows, red and green, scarlet and yellow, and afar off
from it on the side there were two shiny rays. One could be seen
behind the Church of Holy Elias Under the Pines, and the other
one behind St. Nicetas, which is beyond the Iauza River. And the
third ray was high above the sun in the same circle, and it stood
between the horns [rays] and from it there were also two other
horns, one to the right, another to the left, but these were white.
And above this ray between these horns there was a bow turned
toward the circle near the sun, and its ends extended to the middle
of the sky, and the colors were the same as in the rainbow during
the rain. And it could be seen till the end of the second hour.

On the twenty-second of April they started building the Church
of the Most Pure [Theotokos]. On the twelfth of May the Metropoli-

194. It was the month of April.
195. This type of icon is called "Mandelion" in Western churches.

1477 tan read the prayers on the occasion of the foundation of this Church of the Most Pure [Theotokos] and of the Veneration of the Cross.

This same year on Sunday, the nineteenth of May, after matins, a daughter, named Elena, was born to the Grand Prince.

The same month, on the thirtieth, many boyars and minor boyars from Tver' came to be in the service of Grand Prince Ivan Vasilievich: Gregory Nikitich, Ivan Zhito, Vasilii Danilov, Vasilii Bokeev, three Karpoviches, Dmitrii Kindyrev, and many others.

The same year on the eighteenth of the month of July an envoy by the name of Bochiuk came to the Grand Prince from Khan Ahmet of the [Great] Horde, inviting the Grand Prince to the Horde, and with him were fifty Tatars. And there were merchants with horses and all manner of goods, and their number was five hundred fifty.[196]

On the thirty-first of the month of August at the first hour of the night there was frightful thunder and great lightning, as if it wanted to set a fire. But there was a very heavy downpour. This lightning destroyed the top of the stone church in the Simeon Monastery, up to the windows. And moving around the church, it hit the arch and then it broke through the wall at the front entrance and destroyed many holy icons. The icon of the Dormition and the icon of the Prophets were destroyed, and the icon of *Deisus*[197] was singed by the lightning. And the icon of the Most Pure *Hadigitria*,[198] which stands protected on the left side, was not touched, although stone fell around at the *grivnas* which were attached to it.[199]

In the Year 6985 [1477]. On the third of the month of September, at night, the full moon disappeared during August.

The sixth of the same month the Grand Prince let the Tatar envoy, Bochiuk, go, and with him went his envoy, Matvei Bestuzhev.

The twenty-sixth of the same month the Church of the Ascension on the Moat in Moscow burned.

196. Six hundred, in *Ioasaf.*
197. *Deisus*: an icon in which Christ is depicted between the Virgin Mary and St. John the Baptist.
198. *Hadigitria* icon: the icon of Our Lady of the Infant Christ, in which She is pointing at Him as to the way of salvation.
199. *Grivnas*: in this case, silver or golden coins, or replicas of a part of the body which was cured after prayer before the icon. These were attached to icons either by cured persons or by their relatives in gratitude for their cures.

The same month there was a fire in Novgorod the Great. It **1477** started at St. Nicholas in Buevishche and several households burned, and many stone churches burned with the people's goods.[200] And some of them collapsed and people burned, and no one remembered such a conflagration.

This fall was very dry and very cold, and the river became covered with ice on the twelfth of November; but on the day of the Presentation[201] there was rain, and thereafter there were several severe freezes but no snow. On the ninth of January from Thursday to Friday it began to snow, and the same the next day, but very little; and there was not even a foot of it over the entire winter. The same winter on the sixteenth of February during Shrovetide, at the seventh hour at night, the refectory and the cell of Archimandrite Genadius burned in the [Monastery of] Miracles of [Archangel] Michael [in Moscow].

[THE NOVGORODIANS CAME TO MOSCOW]

The same winter on the twenty-sixth of February posadnik Zakharia Ovinov came to Zbor to the Grand Prince, from Novgorod the Great. He was with the Grand Prince's police officials and with many Novgorodians. Some had to explain whom they had offended, others looked for the offenders. This never happened before since their land existed, since Rurik or since the grand princes began to reign in Kiev and in Vladimir, up to the present time of Grand Prince Ivan Vasilievich; but this [Grand Prince] brought them to it. Thereafter during that same Lent several posadniks, Vasilii Mikiforov, Ivan Kuzmin and many other posadniks, and many other wealthy burghers of Novgorod, as well as villagers, came in order to complain about an offense or in order to be responsible for such. And with them were also widows and monks and all those who were offended, and there were a great many of them.

On the twentieth day of the month of March, on Wednesday of the fifth week of Lent, after vespers at the seventh hour of the night, a fire started in the estate of Prince Andrei the younger, and the estates of both Princes Andrei burned. And the small houses of the priests [of the Cathedral] of Archangel [Michael] were torn down because the Grand Prince, himself, came with his son and

200. In the Middle Ages the basements of stone churches were often used as storage rooms for valuable goods.
201. Presentation of the Virgin Mary in the Temple, November 21.

1477 with many minor boyars; he did this because the Grand Prince did not have time to go to bed after attending the vesper service of the great canon of St. Andreas [of Crete].[202]

ABOUT THE GOVERNMENT [IN NOVGOROD]
[THE FINAL STAGES OF STRUGGLE BETWEEN IVAN III AND NOVGOROD]

In the Year 6985 [1477]. In the month of March Theophilus, Archbishop of Novgorod, and all Novgorod the Great sent their envoys, *podvoiskii* Nazar and Zakharii, clerk of the *veché*, to Grand Prince Ivan Vasilievich and to his son, Grand Prince Ivan Ivanovich; and addressing him, they called him *"Gospodar'."*[203] And this never happened before, not since our land came into being. None of the grand princes was called *"Gospodar'"* but always *"Gospodin."*[204] The same spring on the twenty-fourth of April, a Thursday, the Grand Prince sent his envoys, Fedor Davydovich and Ivan Borisovich, and with them *diak* Vasilii Dalmatov, to Novgorod, to the Archbishop and to all Great Novgorod, to clarify "what manner of government does their patrimony, Great Novgorod, want?" And they [the Novgorodians] began arguing, saying, "We did not send them with it." And they called it a lie.

THE PASSING OF ST. PAPHNUTIUS OF BOROVSK

The same year on Thursday, the first day of the month of May, after vespers at fifteen of the clock, the venerable abbot Paphnutius of the honorable Monastery of the Nativity of the Most Holy Mother of God, which is on the river Porotva near the city of Borovsk—only two miles away—expired; he, himself, founded this monastery, coming from the Vysokii Monastery in Borovsk, where he used also to be abbot; and he did this at the time of the local prince, the uncle of Prince Vasilii Iaroslavovich [of Serpukhov and Borovsk]. In the morning of Friday at the first hour he was buried: there was no one from the city or from the villages at his burial, only the priests, his pupils, and the elders who were tonsured

202. Andreas of Crete (660–740) was one of the greatest hymn writers of Byzantium, the others being Roman the Psalmodist and St. John of Damascus. The great canon by Andreas is sung during Lent.

203. *Podvoiskii*: police official; *Gospodar'*: the title of rulers of semi-independent states in Turkey, primarily in Valakhia and Moldavia. Such a title was certainly taken as an offense by Ivan III.

204. *Gospodar'*: local ruler; *Gospodin*: lord.

by him; only one secular priest, named Nicetas, the confessor of   **1477**
Prince Andrei the minor, came thither. This Nicetas, as well as the
other brethren, Paphnutius' pupils, said that there was no chanting
or any choir during the burial, but only one of his pupils, by the
name of Innocent, with tears, spoke memorial words; and while
the others were weeping and because of their many tears, some of
them fell to the ground, sobbing. At that time there were eighty-five
brethren. It is said that he was born in the village of Kudinovskoe,
and was [the son] of the priest Ivan, that his spiritual teacher was
elder Nicetas, and that he had been tonsured a monk by Archimandrite Markel when he was twenty years old; and for thirty years he
was a monk-priest and abbot. When he came to that place he established there the Monastery of the Ever Blessed Nativity of Our
Most Holy Mother of God, and first of all he built a wooden church,
and thereafter he built a stone one; and he decorated it very beautifully, adorning it with icons and books and church vessels; and
even the autocrats [Grand Princes] of the Russian land, themselves,
wondered at it and used to come to him during his life for blessing
and prayers as [earlier princes] used to go to the ancient blessed
fathers of our land. And so did the other princes and boyars, as
well as Orthodox Christians from the Lithuanian land and from
other lands, asking him for a blessing and prayers. And he remained
in his monastery for thirty-three years.

On the thirty-first of the month of May in the night from
Friday to Saturday, on the eve of All Saints, there was an extremely
strong cold and even the ponds froze completely, and all the vege-
tables, all the fruit, and the entire harvest were damaged.

SEDITION IN NOVGOROD

The same month when the Grand Prince's envoy was in Novgorod there was a disturbance in Novgorod; they summoned the
veché and assembling, took Vasilii Mikiforov and brought him to
the *veché*, crying, "You traitor! You went to the Grand Prince and
swore to him on the cross against us." And he told them, "I pledged
on the cross to the Grand Prince that we want to serve him with
truth and good, and [I did not speak against] my lord, Novgorod
the Great, or against you, my elders, or my brethren." But they
killed him mercilessly, believing the calumny of Zakharii Ovin, and
thereafter they killed Ovin, himself, with his brother, Kuzma; and

1477 this happened in the court of the Archbishop. And from that time they became maddened, as if drunk, and spoke all manner [of nonsense] and wanted again [to be under] the King [of Poland].

The Grand Prince learned of this from his envoys and from their posadniks who were faithful to him and who escaped to him when the evil dissent arose, as occurred after their first crime and as had occurred before [the battle of] Shelon'; and he bemoaned them greatly [for the killings] and he wept. He went to his father, Metropolitan Gerontius, saying that the Novgorodians had broken their pledge on the cross, "And they complain about the administration and claim that which I did not want from them, and thereafter they denied it and claimed that we lied." And he said the same to his mother, to his brothers, to the boyars, and to the voevodas, and thus his wrath was aroused against Novgorod.

He started preparing his army against his patrimony, against the Novgorodians who had become apostates and had broken their pledge on the cross, and he did so with the blessing of Metropolitan Gerontius of all Russia and of his entire Sacred Council, of the Archbishop and bishops of the entire clergy, as well as having received the advice and prayers of his mother, his brothers, the boyars, princes, and voevodas. Relying in all these matters upon the Lord God and His Most Pure Mother, and on the power of the Most Holy and Life-begetting Cross on which those who had betrayed him swore, he ordered a *Te Deum* be celebrated in all the churches of Our God and Saviour, Jesus Christ, and His Most Pure Mother, as well as in the churches of the Cross, of the Apostles, of the Martyrs, and at the tombs of the wonderworkers, Their Holinesses Metropolitans of Russia Peter, Alexis, and Jonas, and other Metropolitans, and the monasteries of the city of Moscow and in the [Monastery of the] Life-begetting Trinity at the tomb of Wonderworker Sergius; and in his entire patrimony, his grand principality, he commanded that alms be distributed in the cathedral churches and monasteries and in all other churches.

And he appealed to Tver', to Grand Prince Mikhail, asking him for help against Novgorod; and the latter did not refuse to do this and sent Prince Mikhail Fedorovich Mikulinskii with his numerous warriors. Thereafter he sent to his brothers, who at that time were in their patrimonies, commanding them to march against Novgorod from their places. When the Novgorodians heard about this they sent Fedor Kalitin, the mayor of Danslavskaia Street, to

the Grand Prince, petitioning for safe conduct for their Archbishop **1478**
and the Novgorodian envoys, that they be allowed to come to him
with supplications; but the Grand Prince commanded this man who
requested safe conduct be kept in Torzhok by his namestnik, Vasilii
Ivanovich Kitai.

In the Year 6986 [1478]. On the thirtieth of the month of September the Grand Prince sent to Novgorod with a declaration of war[205] a certain Radion Bogomolov, a clerk.[206]

On the ninth day of the month of October, on Thursday when
the memory of the Holy Apostle Jacob Alphaeus is celebrated, the
Grand Prince set out from Moscow to Novgorod in order to chastise
them with war for their crimes, leaving in Moscow his son, Grand
Prince Ivan, together with the Grand Prince's [Ivan III's] brother,
Prince Andrei the junior. And he commanded [the Tatar] Lord
Daniar, son of Kasim, to march against the city of Klin and be there
four days before his own arrival, and then [to march] to Tver' and
to Torzhok. The Grand Prince, himself, marched toward Volok
and his brother, Prince Andrei the junior, accompanied him as far
as that place. And the Grand Prince attended a liturgy in Volok
on the fourteenth of October, and he ate and drank at his brother's,
Prince Boris Vasilievich's. When the Grand Prince was still in Volok,
Grand Prince Mikhail of Tver' sent his junior boyar, Khydryshchik,
to provide him with supplies from his domain. From Volok the
Grand Prince marched toward Mikulin and then to Torzhok, while
his brother, Prince Andrei the younger, marched to Torzhok by
way of Staritsa. In Latoshkino, his first camp after Volok, Prince
Andrei Borisovich Mikulinskii greeted the Grand Prince in the
name of the Grand Prince of Tver' and invited him to break bread.

On Thursday, the sixteenth of October, namestnik Vasilii Kitai
informed the Grand Prince that another envoy, the wealthy burgher
Markov, had come to Torzhok from the Archbishop and all Novgorod, requesting safe conduct [for the Novgorodian envoys]. The
Grand Prince ordered him detained in Torzhok until his own arrival
there. On Sunday, the nineteenth of the month of October, the
Grand Prince came to Torzhok, where the Novgorodian boyars

205. *Skladnaia* or *razmetnaia gramota*: a declaration of war. Pushkarev,
p. 25.
206. The description of the campaign against Novgorod in *Obol.* and
Ioasaf. is very close to the text in *Musc. Late 15th C.,* p. 311 ff.

1478 Luka Klimentiev and his brother, Ivan, approached the Grand Prince, petitioning him to receive them into his service.

On the twenty-first of October, Tuesday, the Grand Prince sent Prince Vasilii Vasilievich Shuiskii to Pskov to be voevoda and namestnik there, as well as to be prince in Pskov according to their petition. This petition was brought by Vasilii and Nikifor Pechatnikov. On the twenty-third of October the Grand Prince left Torzhok and moved against Novgorod with the army. From Torzhok he went to Volochok, and from thence he marched between the Iazhelbitskii highroad and the Msta River, and commanded [the Tatar] Lord Daniar to go from Torzhok beyond Msta, and with him was Vasilii Borisovich Obrazets as the Grand Prince's voevoda. He also commanded Prince Daniil Kholmskii to advance on his side of the Msta, and with him were numerous minor boyars of the Grand Prince's retinue, as well as all the levies from Vladimir, Pereiaslavl', and Kostroma. He commanded his boyars, Grigorii and Ivan Nikitich, to advance along the same route together with the levies from Tver', and those of Dmitrov and Kashin, who were in the Grand Prince's service. And he commanded Prince Semion Ivanovich Riapolovskii to advance on the right side from him, between his route and the Msta, together with the levies of Suzdal' and Iur'iev. And on the left side from him, from Torzhok toward Diemon, he commanded his brother, Prince Andrei the younger, to march with Vasilii Saburov, the Grand Prince's voevoda, and with the levies of Rostov, Iaroslavl', Uglich, and Bezhichi who were in the Grand Prince's service.

He also commanded his mother's voevoda, Semion Fedorovich Peshek, to march with them with her retinue. Prince Aleksandr Vasilievich and Prince Boris Mikhailovich Obolenskii were commanded to advance between the highroad of Diemon and Iazhelbitskii, and with Prince Aleksandr [Obolenskii] were the levies from Kaluga, from Aleksin, from Serpukhov, from Khatun, from Moscow, from Radonezh, from Novy Torzhok, from Bernov, and from Glukhov, while the Prince Boris [Obolenskii] advanced the levies of Mozhaisk, of Volokh, of Zvenigorod, and of Rusa which served the Grand Prince. He [Ivan III] commanded Fedor Davydovich to march along the Iazhelbitskii highroad, and with him were the junior boyars from the Grand Prince's retinue, and the entire levy of Kolomna. On the same highroad he commanded Prince Ivan Vasilievich Obolenskii to advance, and with him were his brothers,

all the Obolenskii princes, as well as numerous minor boyars from   **1478**
the retinue of the Grand Prince. And the Grand Prince commanded
that Fedor Kalitin and Ivan Markov, the Novgorodian envoys who
had requested safe conduct [for the Novgorodian embassy], to be
taken with him from Torzhok.

On the twenty-sixth of October at Volochok the Grand Prince
was met by the Novgorodian posadnik Grigorii Mikhailovich Tuchin, who petitioned to serve him. On the twenty-eighth of October
in Berezka the Novgorodian wealthy burgher, Adrian Saveliev,
came to the Grand Prince, also, to serve him.

On the second of the month of November a certain Khariton
Kachalov came to Turno with a missive from Pskov to the Grand
Prince, and in this missive from Pskov it was written, "To our lord
and sovereign Grand Prince Ivan Vasilievich, Tsar' of all Russia!
We, the incumbent posadnik of Pskov, as well as the former posadniks and the posadniks' sons, and the boyars, merchants, and
wealthy burghers, and all Pskov, your patrimony, petition you, our
sovereign Grand Prince and Russian Tsar'.[207] Following your command, our lord, we for the second time send a declaration of war
to Great Novgorod, and our agents have left their summonses in
Great Novgorod and have returned to Pskov. And now, because
of our sins, the whole city of Pskov has burned. We inform you
tearfully, our Sovereign, of our calamity and we rely upon God
and upon you, our lord; and we, the well-wishing people of your
patrimony, of the city of Pskov, petition you, our lord and Tsar'
of Russia." The Grand Prince commanded them to go with him.

On the fourth of November while camped at Bolblovy, the
Grand Prince was joined by Prince Mikhail Fedorovich Mikulinskii,
voevoda of Grand Prince Mikhail of Tver', with the regiments of
Tver', to help the Grand Prince campaign against the Novgorodians. And the Grand Prince honored him and commanded him to
advance along his [Ivan III's] route.

On the eighth of November at [the Church of] the Saviour in
Iaglino, the Grand Prince commanded the Novgorodian envoys,
Fedor Kalitin and Ivan Markov, who had asked for safe conduct,

207. It may be of interest to note that already in the so-called *Muscovite
Chronicle of 1475*, whose text was partially followed by the compilers of
Ioasaf. and *The Nikonian Chronicle*, the Grand Prince of Moscow was termed
"Tsar' of all Russia," although this title became official only in 1547, at the
coronation of Ivan IV.

1478 to appear before him. When they approached him they petitioned him in the name of the Archbishop of Novgorod, Theophilus, and in the name of Novgorod the Great, for safe conduct, calling the Grand Prince their "Sovereign" ["*Gosudar*'"]: "We ask you, our Sovereign, that you grant safe conduct to the Archbishop and to the Novgorodian posadniks so that they might come to petition you and return according to their intentions." The Grand Prince agreed to grant them safe conduct, and gave them his charter of safe conduct. On the tenth of November in Ivanichi the Grand Prince was met by Grigorii Mikhailov Sovkin, a third envoy requesting safe conduct; and on the eleventh at the Church of Nicholas in Lokotsk, the Grand Prince commanded him to come to him, and he petitioned in the name of the Archbishop and Novgorod, calling the Grand Prince "Sovereign" ["*Gosudar*'"] and requesting safe conduct. The Grand Prince commanded his *diak*, Vasilii Dalmatov, to answer, and he spoke the following words of the Grand Prince's: "There have already appeared people petitioning in the name of our prayerful Archbishop and our patrimony [of Novgorod] and I have agreed and given safe conduct [for the Archbishop *a.o.*] to Ivan Markov and Fedor Kalitin, to the envoys who asked for it, and according to this safe conduct the Archbishop and the Novgorodian envoys may come to us and may leave according to their intentions." And Grigorii Sovkin petitioned the Grand Prince, asking him to give him a police official with whom he could pass through his army. The Grand Prince agreed and gave him Mikhail Pogozhii as a police official, and let them depart together from Lokotsk.

On the nineteenth of November in Paliny the Grand Prince was met by Ivan Vasilievich, son of Nikiforov, and with him was Luka Klementiev. And to the same camp in Paliny the Grand Prince dispatched his regiments and commanded who should be where.

He commanded his brother, Andrei the younger, to be with the vanguard, and his voevodas were to be: Daniil Kholmskii with the levies of Kostroma; Fedor Davydovich with the levies of Kolomna; and Prince Ivan Vasilievich Obolenskii with the levies of Vladimir.

In the right-hand army the Grand Prince placed his brother, Prince Andrei the older and, together with him, Prince Mikhail Fedorovich Mikulinskii, the voevoda of Tver', with the levies of Tver'. And also [with him] he placed his voevodas, Grigorii and Ivan Nikitich Zhyto, with the levies of Dmitrov and Kashin.

And he commanded his brother, Prince Boris, to be in the **1478** left-hand army, and with him Prince Vasilii Mikhailovich Vereiskii and Semion Peshek, the voevoda of his mother, Grand Princess Maria.

And the Grand Prince commanded the voevodas Ivan Iurievich and Vasilii Obrazets to be in his army with the levy of Borovsk; and Prince Semion Riapolovskii with the levies of Suzdal' and Iur'iev; and Prince Aleksandr Vasilievich [Obolenskii] with the levies of Kaluga, Aleksyn, Serpukhov, Khutyn, Moscow, Radonezh and Novy Torzhok; as well as Prince Boris Mikhailovich Obolenskii with the levies of Mozhaisk, Vologda, Zvenigorod, and Rusa; and also Vasilii Saburov with the levies of Galich, Iaroslavl', Rostov, Uglich, and Bezhichi; and he commanded all the levies from Pereiaslavl' and Murom to be in his army.

And from the same camp of Paliny the Grand Prince sent his voevodas to occupy but not to burn the Gorodishche[208] of Novgorod, and the monasteries [nearby].

He also commanded Prince Kholmskii with the levies from Pereiaslavl' and Kostroma, and Prince Ivan Striga [Obolenskii] with the levies of Vladimir, and Fedor Davydovich with the levies of Kolomna, and Grigorii and Ivan Nikitich with the levies of Dmitrov and Kashin, and the Prince Semion Riapolovskii with the levies of Suzdal' and Iur'iev, to march toward Bronich; and he told them to await there his further orders. And the other voevodas were told to await his orders in Vozvadna on Lake Ilmen, and in Uzhin.

On the twenty-first of November, the day of the Presentation of the Most Holy Mother of God, the Grand Prince camped at [the Monastery of Saint] Nicholas in Tukhov; from thence he sent his envoy, Petiulia Paiusov, to Pskov, and with him were Khariton [envoy] of Pskov. The Grand Prince also commanded his namestnik [in Pskov], Prince Vasilii Vasilievich Shuiskii, to begin campaigning with the levy of Pskov against Novgorod, taking with him cannons, guns, and arbalests [crossbows], and all supplies needed to besiege the city. "When you arrive at the mouth of the river Shelon', send me, the Grand Prince, someone forthwith to inform me of it, and then I will tell you where you should be with the levies of Pskov."

On Sunday, the twenty-third of November, there came to the Grand Prince, who was in Sytino, the Archbishop of Novgorod,

---

208. *Gorodishche*: a suburb of Novgorod where the residence of the ruling prince and his administration was located.

1478   Theophilus, and with him the Novgorodian posadniks, Iakov
Korob, Fefilat Zakhar'in, Luka and Iakov Fedorov, Luka Isakov
Polarin; and from the wealthy burghers, Aleksandr Klimentov,
Efimyi Medvednov, Grigorii Kiprianov Arzubiev, Philip Kilskii, and
the merchant, Iakov Tsarishchev; and all of them petitioned the
Grand Prince, and the Archbishop said, "Our lord and sovereign
Grand Prince Ivan Vasilievich of all Russia! I, my lord, your prayer
ful bishop, as well as the archimandrites, abbots, and all the priests
of all seven cathedrals of Great Novgorod, we petition you, our
sovereign Grand Prince. You, our lord sovereign Grand Prince,
have turned your wrath upon your patrimony, Novgorod the Great.
Now your sword and fire go through the Novgorodian land and
Christian blood is shed. [We ask you] our sovereign lord, to be
merciful to your patrimony; stop your sword and extinguish your
fire so that Christian blood be no more shed. Grant it us, our
sovereign lord! My lord, I, your prayerful bishop, together with
the archimandrites, abbots, and all the priests of all seven cathedrals,
we petition you tearfully, you, our lord and sovereign Grand Prince!
You, our sovereign lord, became angry with our boyars of Novgorod
and you sent them to Moscow [when first you came to Novgorod];
and we petition you, our sovereign lord Grand Prince, to be merciful
and release these boyars to your patrimony, Novgorod the Great.
My lord, I, your prayerful Archbishop, and all the aforementioned
priests of the seven cathedrals—we beseech you, our Sovereign."

And the posadniks and wealthy burghers likewise petitioned,
saying, "Our sovereign lord Grand Prince Ivan Vasilievich of all
Russia! Your prayerful Archbishop, lord Theophilus, stands before
you and petitions you, our sovereign Grand Prince; and so, also,
does our lord, the incumbent posadnik, Foma Andreevich, and the
former posadniks, and the incumbent tysiatskii, Vasilii Maksimov,
and the former tysiatskiis, boyars and wealthy burghers, and merchants and common people and all Novgorod the Great, your whole
patrimony, free men. We petition you, lord sovereign Grand Prince,
to be merciful toward your patrimony," and so on, just as the
Archbishop said earlier, "Your patrimony, Novgorod the Great,
petitions you, our Sovereign."

After them posadnik Luka Fedorov also petitioned, saying,
"Lord, Prince, Grand Prince Ivan Vasilievich of all Russia! Your
prayerful Archbishop, together with the posadniks and wealthy

burghers of all Novgorod, have petitioned you, our lord Prince, **1478** and this plea is now before you. [We ask] that you, our Prince, deign to discuss these matters with your boyars. Your prayerful bishop and your patrimony, all Novgorod, entreat you, our Sovereign."

The same day the Grand Prince invited them to dine with him, and they dined at his place on that day. And in the morning the Archbishop with all the aforementioned went with gifts to the Grand Prince's brother, Prince Andrei the younger, whom he petitioned to intercede with the Grand Prince. Thereafter the same morning they came again to the Grand Prince to entreat him that he kindly discuss the matter with his boyars. And the Grand Prince sent them for discussion his boyar, Prince Ivan Iurievich, with Vasilii and Ivan Borisovich, and they met the Archbishop, posadniks, and the wealthy burghers.

And posadnik Iakov Korob said, "[We ask] that our sovereign Grand Prince be kind toward his patrimony, Novgorod the Great, that he be merciful to us, free men, that he relinquish his dislike and pacify his sword."

After him posadnik Feofilat said the following: "[We ask] that the Grand Prince be merciful toward the boyars under his arrest, that he release them and accept the petition of the Archbishop and of entire Novgorod the Great."

Posadnik Luka Fedorov said, "[We ask] that the Grand Prince be kind toward his patrimony, that he come to Novgorod the Great every fourth year, and accept a thousand rubles; that he command his namestnik and the posadnik of the city to execute justice, and what the namestnik and posadnik cannot decide themselves, then the sovereign Grand Prince execute justice when he comes every fourth year; and that the Grand Prince agree to discontinue summoning [us] to court in Moscow, that there be no more summoning."

And Iakov Fedorov said, "[We ask] that the Grand Prince agree that his namestnik not change the decision of the court of the Archbishop and of the posadniks." And the wealthy burghers and their associates complained "that the [Grand Prince's] subjects submit their litigations against Novgorodians to the namestnik and posadniks in the city [of Novgorod], and request compensation also [before the court] of the namestnik and posadniks in the city; but when the Novgorodians claim damages from them [the Muscovites],

1478   then they [the Grand Prince's subjects] do not accept litigation in the city [of Novgorod], but go to the court in Gorodishche.[209] And they ask that the Grand Prince agree that the namestnik and posadniks should execute justice [in such cases only] in the city [and not in Gorodishche]."

And after these speeches Iakov Korob said, "Our prayerful Archbishop and posadniks and wealthy burghers of Great Novgorod have petitioned our sovereign Prince, and this petition is before our sovereign Grand Prince; and now his patrimony petitions that the Sovereign kindly show his patrimony what God has suggested to his heart to do, and the patrimony has petitioned its Sovereign how they should be."

The same day, Monday, the Grand Prince sent his voevodas to Novgorod to occupy Gorodishche and the monasteries. He commanded Prince Danilo Dmitrievich [Kholmskii], Fedor Davydovich, Prince Ivan Vasilievich Striga [Obolenskii] and Grigorii and Ivan Nikitich to go with their regiments from Bronich toward the city; and to the other side of the city toward the Iur'iev Monastery, and toward the Arkazh Monastery, he commanded his voevodas, Prince Semion Riapolovskii, Aleksandr Obolenskii, Prince Boris Obolenskii and Vasilii Saburov to advance with their regiments; [and he commanded] Semion Saburov, with the troops of his mother, Grand Princess Maria, as well as the regiments of his brother, Prince Andrei the younger, and Elizar Gusev, to go forward with their regiments. And all these voevodas marched with their regiments across the ice of Lake Ilmen; all these voevodas of one and the other side arrived [in the suburb of Novgorod] the same night from Monday to Tuesday and occupied Gorodishche and all the monasteries located near the city.

On the twenty-fifth of November, Tuesday, being in Sytino, the Grand Prince commanded that his answer be given to the Archbishop and to the Novgorodian envoys through Prince Ivan Iurievich, and with the latter were Vasilii and Ivan Borisovich [Obolenskii]. Prince Ivan Iurievich said the following:

"Grand Prince Ivan Vasilievich of all Russia responds thus to you, his prayerful Archbishop, to the posadniks, and to the wealthy burghers. You, our prayerful bishop, and you, posadniks

209. *Gorodishche*: the residence of the Grand Prince and his administration in Novgorod.

and wealthy burghers, you have petitioned me, the Grand Prince, **1478**
that I, the Grand Prince, should turn aside my wrath from my
patrimony, Novgorod the Great."

Thereafter Vasilii Borisovich said, "The Grand Prince advises
you, his prayerful Archbishop, posadniks and wealthy burghers,
and all others with you: you know, yourselves, that you sent to us,
the Grand Princes [to Ivan III and his son, Ivan], from our patrimony, from all Great Novgorod, your envoys, the police official
Nazar, and the *diak* of the *veché*, Zakhar. They have called us, the
Grand Princes, '*Gospodar*.'[210] And after having received your message, we, the Grand Princes, sent to you, the Archbishop, and to
our patrimony of Novgorod the Great, our boyars, Fedor
Davydovich and Ivan and Semion Borisovich. And we commanded
them to inquire of you, our prayerful Archbishop, and our patrimony of Novgorod, what manner of government by the Grand
Princes you want in our patrimony, Novgorod the Great? And you
denied that you sent us your envoys [to call us '*Gospodar*']. And you
claimed that we, the Grand Princes, are responsible for using violence against our patrimony, and you not only tried to demonstrate
that I, your Sovereign, lied, but you also perpetrated many misdeeds
and dishonor upon us, the Grand Princes. And there was much
disregard toward us. But we restrained ourselves, awaiting your
appeal to us; but you behaved in the most evil way toward us and
we could not tolerate this, and we decided to make our anger
manifest to you, and decided to campaign with armies against you.
[This was] in accordance with the Lord's words, 'If one sins toward
his brother, go to him and expose him just before him and yourself.
If he heeds you, you gain your brother. If he does not heed you,
take with you two or three witnesses and then he must speak in
the presence of these two or three witnesses; and if he does not
obey, tell the church of it; and if he does not obey the church, then
he will be as a pagan and publican for you.' We, however, the
Grand Princes, told you, our patrimony, 'Give up your malevolence
and your evildoings, and you, our patrimony, as of old, will abide
in our good grace. But you did not want this and behaved as if you
were aliens to us. Then, relying upon Lord God and His Most Pure
Mother and all the saints, as well as on the prayers of our forefathers,

210. *Gospodar*: "ruling lord."

1478 we the Grand Princes of Russia, campaigned against you because
of your misdeeds."

Thereupon Ivan Borisovich told them, "The Grand Prince
advises you, his prayerful Archbishop, and posadniks and wealthy
burghers, the following: 'You petitioned me, the Grand Prince,
that I should give up my discontent toward my patrimony [Nov-
gorod], and you spoke words about the Novgorodian boyars, at
whom I was angry; and you asked me to release them. But know,
our prayerful bishop, and you, posadniks and wealthy burghers,
and all Novgorod, that these boyars about whom you petitioned
me, the Grand Prince, with all my patrimony, Novgorod the Great,
that there was much evil from them done to my patrimony, Novgorod the Great, as well as to its environs; that they raided and
sacked and carried off the people's wealth, and they shed Christian
blood. And you, Luka Isakovich, you, yourself, were then a plaintiff;
and so were you, Grigorii Kiprianov from Nikitina Street. And I,
the Grand Prince, investigated with you, our prayerful Bishop, and
with you, posadniks, and with my patrimony, Novgorod the Great;
I ascertained that a great deal of evil was perpetrated upon my
patrimony by them; I wanted to execute them. But you, Archbishop, and you, our patrimony, petitioned me and I repealed their
execution. And now you speak on behalf of these guilty ones; and
if I do not satisfy you, you will still petition [for an unjust cause];
and so how can I satisfy you?"

After these speeches, Prince Ivan Iurievich said, "The Grand
Prince tells you that in the case our patrimony wants to petition
us, the Grand Princes and your Sovereign, then you, our patrimony,
should know how to petition us, the Grand Princes."

Thereafter the Archbishop, posadniks, and wealthy burghers
asked the Grand Prince to furnish them a police official who would
conduct them to the city, and the Grand Prince commanded his
police official, Runa, to accompany them. He was the same who
had met them as the Grand Prince's police official when they had
come from Novgorod to the Grand Prince.

On the twenty-seventh of November, Thursday, the Grand
Prince came to the city over the ice on Lake Ilmen. With him was
his brother, Prince Andrei the younger; and the same day Prince
Vasilii Mikhailovich Vereiskii came to the city. Arriving there, the
Grand Prince camped at [the Monastery of] the Trinity in the
Poozerie in the village of Loshinskoe, and commanded his brother,

Prince Andrei the younger, to camp at the Monastery of the Annun-   **1478**
ciation. The Grand Prince commanded his voevodas to camp near
the city with their regiments: Prince Ivan Iurievich in the Iur'iev
Monastery; Prince Danilo Kholmskii in the Arkazh Monastery; Vasilii Saburov in the Monastery of St. Panteleimon; Prince Aleksandr
Obolenskii in the Monastery of St. Nicholas on Mostishch; Prince
Boris Obolenskii in Sokovo in the Monastery of the Manifestation
of Our Lord; Prince Semion Riapolovskii was to camp along the
Pidba and on the Stipa [rivers]. From the Gorodishche side, Prince
Vasilii Mikhailovich Vereiskii was commanded by the Grand Prince
to camp in the monastery on Lisich'ia Mountain. And he com-
manded Fedor Davydovich, Prince Ivan Striga [Obolenskii], and
Grigorii and Ivan Nikitich to camp in Gorodishche.

On the twenty-ninth of November Prince Boris Vasilievich approached Novgorod, three days later than his brother, the Grand
Prince; and the latter commanded him to be stationed in the Archbishop's village of Krechevo, down the Volkhov [River].

On Sunday, the thirtieth of November, the Grand Prince commanded all the voevodas to send half of the people through for
provisions and to keep the other half with themselves. And he gave
them ten days to look for provisions, and on the eleventh day,
Thursday after the day of St. Nicholas, everyone was to be at the
city, whosoever he may be. The same day, Thursday, the Grand
Prince sent Sevastian Kushelev to meet Prince Vasilii [Shuiskii], the
namestnik of Pskov, as well as the levies of Pskov, with the command
that they march forthwith with artillery and with all supplies as
soon as they received the command. Sevastian met them at Soltse
on the river Shelon'.

On the fourth day of the month of December, on Monday,
there came to the Monastery of the Trinity in Poozerie Archbishop
Theophilus of Novgorod with the [incumbent and former] posadniks Iakov Korob, Feofilat Zakhar'in, Luka and Iakov Fedorov, and
Luka Isakov; and the wealthy burghers, Aleksandr Klementiev,
Filip Kilskii, Grigorii Kiprianov Arzubiev, Efimii Medvednov, and
the merchant, Iakov Tsarishchev. The Archbishop petitioned the
Grand Prince: "Our lord, sovereign Grand Prince Vasilii Vasilievich
of all Russia! I, my lord, your prayerful Archhbishop, with the
archimandrites, abbots, priest-monks, monks, and priests of all
seven cathedrals of Great Novgorod, have come to petition you,
our sovereign Grand Prince, that you, our lord, be merciful toward

1478 the Christians, toward your patrimony, that you stop your sword and extinguish the fire so that no Christian blood be shed. And I, your prayerful Archbishop, and the clergy of all seven cathedrals, we ask this, our Sovereign, with tears." The posadniks and wealthy burghers also petitioned the Sovereign to be merciful, and petitioned that the Sovereign allow them to talk with his boyars. And the Grand Prince sent his boyars to them: Prince Ivan Iurievich, Fedor Davydovich, Prince Ivan Striga [Obolenskii]. The Archbishop, posadniks, and wealthy burghers petitioned the Grand Prince the same as they had before, that he be merciful and show his patrimony what they should do, as God might put it into his heart concerning his patrimony. And the Grand Prince commanded that his answer be as it was in his first response: "Why did you send Nazar and Zakhar, and why did you call us '*Gospodar*'?[211] We thereupon sent you our envoy to inquire what manner of government you wanted. And you denied this, and perpetrated a lie upon us. We could not abide this. So, praying to Lord God and His Most Pure Mother, and to all His saints, we marched against you, asking God and the power of the life-giving cross of the Lord to aid us. And in the case our patrimony, Novgorod the Great, wants to petition us, the Grand Prince, they are aware how to do so."

The Archbishop and all those with him petitioned the Grand Prince to give them permission to go to the city and then return [to Ivan III], using the same safe conduct. The Grand Prince permitted it them.

The same day [the Tatar] Lord Daniar came to the city and with him were Vasilii Obrazets, voevoda of the Grand Prince, with the levy of Borovsk. The Grand Prince ordered the Tatar [Lord] Daniar to camp in the Monastery of St. Cyril, as well as in the Monastery of St. Andrew in the vicinity of Gorodishche. The accompanying voevodas of Lord Daniar, Petr Obolenskii and Prince Ivan Zvenets, were ordered to camp in the monastery in Kovalev. And he commanded Vasilii Obrazets with the Borovsk levy to camp at the Monastery of the Saviour in Volotovo. The same day Prince Andrei Vasilievich the older, also, came to the city and the Grand Prince commanded him to camp in the Monastery of the Resurrection at Derevianitsa. And Prince Andrei Fedorovich, voevoda of [the Prince of] Tver', was commanded to camp with his regiment at the Monastery of St. Nicholas at Ostrovok.

211. Instead of "*Gosudar.*"

On Friday, the fifth day of December, there came to the Grand   **1478**
Prince from Novgorod Archbishop Theophilus with the posadniks
and wealthy burghers, who had already come to him earlier; and
at that time he had [present] his brothers, Prince Andrei, Prince
Boris, and Prince Andrei the younger. The Archbishop and all
those with them earlier petitioned that the Sovereign show his
mercy, and they accepted their guilt for having sent Nazar and
Zakhar as their envoys to the Grand Prince and that thereafter
they had denied it.

The Grand Prince answered, "In that case you, yourselves—the
Archbishop and our entire patrimony, Novgorod the Great—
accepted your guilt before us, the Grand Princes, and acknowledged
having sent them [Zakhar and Nazar] to us with those speeches,
and then denied it. And now you, yourselves, witness to this and
ask what manner of government there should be in our patrimony
of Novgorod. We, the Grand Princes, wanted [there] our own government. In the same manner as we are in Moscow, so we want to
be in Novgorod." And the Archbishop with all his posadniks and
wealthy burghers again petitioned that the Grand Prince be kind
and permit them to return to the city to think about this, and that
they use the same safe conduct and that he should give them a
term wherein they must return to him. And the Grand Prince
allowed them to do so, and commanded them to return to him on
the third day, a Sunday.

The same day there came to the Grand Prince from Prince
Vasilii Vasilievich [Shuiskii], namestnik in Pskov, Vasilii Epimakhov,
posadnik of Pskov [representing] the levy of Pskov. He announced
that the Grand Prince's namestnik, Prince Vasilii Vasilievich, had
come with the levy of Pskov to serve their Sovereign and that they
had arrived with everything which he had commanded them to
take with them. He asked where they should camp, and the Grand
Prince commanded Prince Vasilii to camp in Bezkupitsy and that
the posadnik of Pskov with his wealthy burghers camp in the town
of Fedotino, [which belonged to] the wife of Isakov Polinarin; and
that the other minor burghers of Pskov should camp in the Monastery of the Trinity at the Variazh and in Klopsk. On the sixth of
December the Grand Prince commanded his master, Aristotle the
Italian, to repair the bridges over the Volkhov River near Gorodishche. And this master built such a bridge on boats [pontoons]
on the river near Gorodishche that even after the Grand Prince
won and returned to Moscow, this bridge still stands there.

1478

THE SURRENDER OF THE NOVGORODIANS AND THE CONDITIONS OF THE GRAND PRINCE'S ADMINISTRATION

On the seventh of December there came to the Prince the Archbishop of Novgorod with the aforementioned posadniks and wealthy burghers, and with them five common people from five sections: from the Nerev section came Avram Ladozhnin; from Bornchavskii [*sic*, Goncharskii?] was Krivoi; from Slavenskii, Zakhar Brekh; from Zagorodskii, Khariton; and from Plotnicheskii, Fedor Lytka. The Archbishop, wealthy burghers, and commoners petitioned as before that the Sovereign show them mercy and suffer them to hold counsel with his boyars. And the Grand Prince sent to them his boyars, Prince Ivan Iurievich, Fedor Davydovich, and Prince Ivan Striga [Obolenskii], and the boyars Vasilii and Ivan Borisovich [Obolenskii]. And the Archbishop took counsel with them together with all his posadniks, wealthy burghers, and commoners.

The first speech was the petition of Iakov Korobov, that the Grand Prince command his namestnik to execute justice together with the posadniks. Posadnik Feofilat petitioned that the Grand Prince agree that every year he receive from all the districts of Novgorod a tax of half a Novgorodian *grivna*[212] from every *sokha*.[213] And posadnik Luka petitioned that the Sovereign rule the minor cities of Novgorod through his namestniks, and that justice be administered as of old. Posadnik Iakov Fedorov petitioned that the Grand Prince agree not to move any people from the Novgorodian land; he also petitioned concerning the landholdings and lands of the boyars, that the Sovereign not interfere with them and agree that the people of Moscow not settle on Novgorodian lands. And they all petitioned that "We Novgorodians should not perform military service in the Nizovskaia land on the shore, but serve where the foreign lands adjoin the Novgorodian land.[214] Then we would be glad to defend them, our patrimony, on command of our Sovereign."

212. *Grivna*: a monetary unit whose value differed in various periods and in various parts of Russia. In the fifteenth century in Moscow there were ten *grivna* to a ruble.

213. *Sokha*: This was a new tax to be paid by the Novgorodians to the Grand Prince.

214. *"Niz"* or *"Nizovskaia land"* was the Novgorodians' term for the central part of Russia, around and south of Moscow and on the lower Volga.

The boyars went to the Grand Prince and told him about these **1478** speeches, and the Grand Prince sent them the same boyars with an answer, commanding them to say the following: "You, Archbishop, and our patrimony, Great Novgorod, petition us, calling us your Sovereigns, that we kindly show our patrimony what manner of government there should be in our patrimony, in Novgorod the Great. And I, Grand Prince, told you that I want in my patrimony, Novgorod the Great, the same government as we have in the Nizovskaia land, in Moscow. And now you teach me what my government should be. How, then, can it be *my* government?"

The Archbishop, posadniks, and wealthy burghers petitioned and told the boyars the following: "We do not want to teach the Grand Prince how to govern, [but we expect] that our sovereign Grand Princes be kind toward their patrimony, that they show their patrimony, Novgorod the Great, what manner of government will be in their patrimony because, Sovereign, your patrimony, Great Novgorod, does not know what custom there is in the Nizovskaia land or what sort of government our Sovereigns, the Grand Princes, have in the Nizovskaia land." The boyars went to the Grand Prince and told him this, and the Grand Prince sent them back with an answer, commanding them to speak as follows.

AND PRINCE IVAN IURIEVICH SPOKE

"The Grand Prince says the following to you, his prayerful Archbishop, to you, posadniks and wealthy burghers, and to the common people: You petition me, the Grand Prince, that I should explain to you what manner of government there should be in our patrimony. And our government and our Grand Princes' government is the following:

"There will be no *veché* bell in our patrimony of Novgorod. There will be no posadniks, and we will conduct our own government.

"And the Grand Prince will govern in his patrimony [Novgorod], and in its environs and in its towns in the same way as in our Nizovskaia land. And all the lands of the Grand Prince which you keep now will be ours.

"You petition me, the Grand Prince, that your people should not be removed from the Novgorodian land, that we should not interfere with the land ownership of the Novgorodian boyars; and we grant you the following: no people will be taken from your

1478   land. We will not interfere with your land ownership; and justice in our patrimony of Novgorod will be as of old, in the same way as justice now is in your land."

The same day, Sunday, there came toward the city [of Novgorod] to the Grand Prince the levies from Pskov, under Prince Vasilii Vasilievich Shuiskii, the namestnik of the Grand Prince's in Pskov; and with him the posadniks of Pskov with many warriors: posadnik Aleksei Vasilievich Kochanov, Zinovii Sidorov, Stefan Maksimov and other posadniks, boyars, junior boyars, and numerous men of Pskov.

On the fourteenth [of December], Sunday, the Archbishop came to the Grand Prince with the posadniks and with the aforementioned, and they petitioned that the Sovereign show mercy to his patrimony and order his boyars to negotiate. And the Grand Prince sent his boyars to negotiate with them. And they petitioned him to delay the suppression of the *veché*, of the bell, and of the posadniks, asking the Sovereign to remove his dislike from his heart and not to move people away or interfere with their land ownership, with their lands and waters, or with their wealth; and that he kindly delay moving the Muscovites to Novgorod; also, [they asked] that he should kindly agree not to send [Novgorodians] into military sevice in the Nizovskaia land. And the Grand Prince granted them all this. Then they again petitioned that the Sovereign assure his patrimony, Novgorod, that he give [his oath] on the cross [not to take any of these actions]. But the Grand Prince responded, "There will be no oath on the cross by me." And then they petitioned that the boyars give them their oaths on the cross, and the Grand Prince rejected this, too. And then they petitioned that the namestnik who would be with them give his oath on the cross; but he [Ivan III] also did not accept this. Then they asked for safe conduct, but the Grand Prince did not give them even this.

On the twenty-eighth of December, Sunday, Prince Vasilii Vasilievich Shuiskii, cousin of Prince Ivan Gorbaty [Shuiskii], was in Novgorod to give an oath of fealty on the cross to the Grand Prince in the name of the Novgorodians. Fearing the Grand Prince, the Novgorodians dared not speak one single word to him. And he sojourned in the city for two days after that oath.

On the twenty-ninth of December the Archbishop, with the aforementioned, again spoke humbly to the Grand Prince's boyars: "The Sovereign bestows nothing on us. He has delayed his oath

on the cross. He does not grant us safe conduct. In what way does   **1478**
he demonstrate his good will? And we would like to learn of his
good will from his own lips, without being sent away." And the
boyars went to the Grand Prince and told him this. And the Grand
Prince showed his good will, told them to come to him, and told
them, "You, our prayerful Archbishop, as well as you posadniks,
wealthy burghers and common people; you petition me, the Grand
Prince, in the name of our hereditary domain, Novgorod the Great,
that I should deign to turn aside my wrath, that I should not move
your people out of the Novgorodian lands, that I should not interfere in land ownership or the wealth of the people, that I should
not settle Muscovites, and that justice should be done according to
the old way in Novgorod, the same way as justice is now performed
in your land. And [you asked] that I should not send you into
military service in the Nizovskaia land. And I granted all this to
my hereditary domain [Novgorod], my good will. And so I will do
all this."

[CONFISCATION OF SOME NOVGORODIANS' LAND AND ESTATES]

And they, hearing this, bowed deeply and departed from him.
Thereafter, however, the Grand Prince sent after them the boyars,
in order to say the following concerning the lands and towns: "I,
Grand Prince Ivan Vasilievich of all Russia, say, 'I am sending my
boyars to you, my prayerful Archbishop, posadniks and wealthy
burghers, concerning the *volosts* and the towns.[215] [I want] our patrimony, Novgorod the Great, to give us some *volosts* and towns
because we, the Grand Prince, must maintain our government in
our hereditary domain, Novgorod the Great, and without this [in-
come] it will not be possible.' "

The Archbishop, posadniks, and wealthy burghers replied,
"We will tell Novgorod, our Sovereign."

On the thirtieth of December, Tuesday, Prince Vasilii Shuiskii
came from Novgorod in order to serve the Grand Prince.[216] He
was received by the Grand Prince, was honored and given gifts.
On the first of January the Archbishop with the posadniks and
wealthy burghers came to the Grand Prince, offering him the fol-

215. *Volost*: an administrative division in Russia which included several
towns and villages. It is roughly equivalent to a U.S. county.
216. Prince Vasilii Shuiskii was the last service prince of Novgorod,
defeated in 1471 by Ivan III's troops on the Dvina River.

1478   lowing *volosts*: Velikie Luki and Pustoi Rzhev; but he did not take them. On the fourth, Sunday, the Archbishop with the aforementioned persons came to the Grand Prince and presented ten *volosts*: four of the Archbishop's; three of the Iur'iev Monastery; one of the Annunciation Monastery in Diemon; the entire Antonovskaia *volost*; and the entire Tubas *volost*. And, also, all the lands in Novotorzhok: the Archbishop's, the monasteries', and the boyars' lands; and all other lands [in Torzhok], whosoever owned them, would be ceded to the Grand Prince. And the Grand Prince did not accept these ten *volosts*. And then they petitioned that the Sovereign, himself, think what he should be given by his hereditary domain and how many *volosts* he wanted to take, and that his hereditary domain [Novgorod] relied upon God and upon him. And the Grand Prince ordered the boyars to tell them, "I want to take half of all the *volosts* of the Archbishop, [half] of [all] the monasteries, and all the lands of Novotorzhok, to whomsoever they belong." And they [the Archbishop and the others] responded, "Sovereign, we will report this to Novgorod."

On the sixth of January, the day of the Baptism of Our Lord, Tuesday, the Archbishop came with the posadniks and wealthy burghers to the Grand Prince, rendered him honor and offered him half of the Archbishop's *volosts* and all the districts in Torzhok [Novotorzhok]: the lands of the Archbishop, of the monasteries, of the boyars, and others, to whomsoever they belonged. And all were ceded to the Grand Prince. And they petitioned [him] concerning the monasteries, that he agree to take half the *volosts* and lands from six monasteries—Iur'iev, the Annunciation, Arkazh, St. Anthony, St. Nicholas near the Nerevskii "end," and St. Nicholas Monastery on Skovorodka—and that the Sovereign should agree not to take the land of other monasteries because those monasteries were poor and had little land. And the Grand Prince told the Archbishop and the posadniks to go to the city and provide the rolls of half of the *volosts* owned by the Archbishop and by the monasteries, and that they should not hide anything: and if they should hide something, it would become the land of the Grand Prince.

On the seventh of January the Archbishop came with the posadniks and wealthy burghers to the Grand Prince, bringing the rolls: half of the Archbishop's *volosts* and the same of those of the monasteries. And the Grand Prince kindly decided not to take half of the

Archbishop's districts, and took only ten: Porog Ladozhskii;   **1478**
the Porog land on both sides of the Volkhov; the Nagorie-
Emelegezhskii parish; and the Kolbalskii parish; and there were in
them forty and half of four *sokha*;[217] and fifty *sokha* in Dreglekh
and Kremenitskii parish; and half of forty in the Belaia Msta *volost*,
and fifty in Utomlia; and fifty-two and a half in Kirva and Okhona
volosts; and Peros *volost*, in which were eighty-two *kunitsa*.[218] And
he took all the lands of Novotorzhok, those of the Archbishop, of
the monasteries, of the boyars, and whosesoever there were in
Torzhok. And from the six above-mentioned monasteries, half of
their *volosts*. From the Iur'iev monasteries the Grand Prince received
half, which was 720 *obzha*.[219] And from Arkazh, 333; and from the
Annunciation, 253; and from St. Nicholas of the Nerevskii "end,"
251; and from the St. Anthony Monastery, fifty *sokha*; and from
the St. Michael Monastery, 100 *obzha* less three. And from those
towns which belonged to Prince Vasilii Shuiskii [the former Novgorodian service voevoda], he took six towns, and there were eighty
sokha in them, less two.

THE TAX PROBLEM

On the eighth of January, Thursday, the Archbishop came
with the posadniks, wealthy burghers, and commoners from Novgorod to the Grand Prince petitioning that the Grand Prince pardon
his patrimony so that Christians not perish because there were too
many people [from the countryside] in the [besieged] city, and the
people were beginning to starve and die. The Grand Prince told
the boyars to discuss the tax with them because they paid, in all
the Novgorodian *volosts*, half a *grivna* and seven *denga* from one
sokha. And he ordered them to ask what a *sokha* may be. And they
said, "One *sokha* consists of three *obzha*; and one *obzha* is as much
land as a man can plough with one horse. And when three men

217. *Sokha*: a measure of land used as a unit for taxation. It varied
greatly according to the condition of the land, as well as the taxpaying
duties of the owners, usually between 650 and 1,200 acres. In the city a
sokha comprised forty to eighty households.
218. *Kunitsa*: a tax unit paid by a household. It originated from the
marten fur, which used to be a monetary unit in early medieval Eastern
Europe.
219. *Obzha:* a territorial unit of taxation. An *obzha* was a piece of land
which one man was able to plough in one day with one horse.

1478   plough with three horses, this will be a *sokha*." And the Grand
Prince wanted to have half a *grivna* from each *obzha* but then the
Archbishop with all his people from the city petitioned him, "The
Sovereign should be merciful and should tax according to our
petition: seven *denga* from every *volost* of Novgorod, as well as in
the Dvina region and in Zavolochie; and it will be from everyone
who ploughs the land, including the estate managers, the starostas
and the *odernovatyis*.[220] Thereafter the Archbishop with all his people
again petitioned: "You, Sovereign, should kindly [agree] not to
send your scribes and your tax collectors into the *volosts* of your
patrimony, Novgorod, because, Sovereign, the Christians are in a
difficult situation. But you should rely upon the Novgorodian administration. They will report how many *sokha* there are and they
will collect the tax, themselves; and they will turn it over to those
indicated by the Grand Prince, pledging on the cross guilelessly.
And they will submit the tax in Novgorod, and if someone hides
even one *obzha*, we will report him and tell of him to our Sovereigns,
and the Grand Princes may punish him."

The Grand Prince bestowed his mercy on his patrimony [and
agreed] that they should collect the tax by themselves, and transmit
it to whomsoever he commanded; and, also, not to send his scribes
and tax collectors to them.

ABOUT THE CHARTER AND THE IAROSLAVL' COURT

On the tenth of January the Grand Prince ordered his boyars
to tell the Archbishop, posadniks, wealthy burghers, and commoners about the Iaroslavl' court, and that this court should be prepared
for him.[221] And the Archbishop, boyars, and wealthy burghers
answered, "Our Sovereign, we are going to the city and will tell
Novgorod of this." And he also ordered that they present on the
same day a charter which showed what Novgorod the Great promised to the Grand Princes, swearing on the cross. And they [the
Novgorodians] asked the Grand Prince to send this charter to the
city so they could show it to everyone in Novgorod the Great. And
the Grand Prince sent this charter to the city with his clerk, Odinets,

220. *Odernovatyi*: a man who depended on someone else and was
supposed to work for him.
221. The Iaroslavl' court was the city residence of the former princes
of Novgorod.

and ordered that it be shown to the Novgorodians in the Arch-   **1478**
bishop's palace.

On Monday, the twelfth of January, the Archbishop came to
the Grand Prince with the aforementioned posadniks and wealthy
burghers and asked him to permit them to consult with his boyars,
and the Grand Prince sent his boyars for this talk. And they talked
about the Iaroslavl' court of the Grand Prince in the following way:
"Our lord, this is the court of our sovereign Grand Princes. If he
[the Grand Prince] wants to have this court, it is up to him and to
God. But if you, our Sovereign, want to take a place in our neigh-
borhood instead of this court, then you, our Sovereign, should
decide. And, Sovereign, the charter which you, the Grand Prince,
commanded to be brought to Novgorod the Great in order to show
Novgorod what obligations it owes their sovereign Grand Princes,
they accept under oath on the cross—this charter was heard by his
patrimony. And they swore to us on the cross in all things desired
by their Sovereign. [And we expect] that our sovereign Grand
Prince will care for his patrimony in the way God inspires his heart.
And his patrimony, Novgorod the Great, honors its Sovereign and
places its hopes in God and in its sovereign Grand Prince."

The Grand Prince commanded the Novgorodian *diak* to write
another copy from his own charter, word for word, as to what the
Novgorodians had pledged to the Grand Prince on the cross; and
he commanded that this copy be given to the Archbishop to be
signed by his hand, and to have the seal imposed in the five places
on the charter. The Grand Prince also asked the Archbishop and
posadniks and wealthy burghers to come to him the following day,
Tuesday, to the Monastery of the Holy Trinity in Poozerie. On the
thirteenth of January, Tuesday, there came to the Grand Prince
the Archbishop, many Novgorodian boyars, wealthy burghers, and
merchants; and the Archbishop brought the copy of that charter
with him which was written by the Archbishop's *diak*. And the
Archbishop signed it with his own hand and imposed his seal,
sealing it in the five places. On [that day], Tuesday, the thirteenth
of January, in accordance with this charter, the Novgorodian boyars
and wealthy burghers and merchants [who had come to the Grand
Prince] gave oath on the cross to the Grand Prince in the Monastery
of the Trinity in Poozerie in the presence of the Grand Prince's
boyars.

During the pledging the Grand Prince's boyars told the Nov-

1478 gorodians about the people of Pskov. "The people of Pskov served the Grand Prince and therefore, according to your pledge on the cross, you should not seek revenge against them by any kind of guile. And you should not interfere either in the territories or the waters or the households or the shore of Pskov; and you should not cause them any offense. And the Grand Prince's namestnik in Novgorod must resolve with the Grand Prince's namestnik in Pskov all litigations about land and water. And the namestnik of Pskov should do the same with him [that is, with the namestnik of Novgorod], so that you have justice and its enforcement on both sides."

And they told them about the Novgorodian boyars, junior boyars, and wives of the boyars [who remained faithful and joined the service] of the Grand Prince, and that they [the Novgorodians] not attempt to avenge them with any guile. And they also discussed the minor cities, the Dvina, the Zavolochie, and said that all these minor cities, as well as the people of the Dvina and the Zavolochie, should pledge their fealty to the Grand Princes. And they discussed the Ivanovskii priests and the Prince's Sen'ka,[222] that they [the Novgorodians] should pay the dues to these priests for the past year which they had not paid them; and that they should pay them the dues in the future. And they must return to Priest John all the property they took from him. And they must also return the land, the house and the property of Sen'ka which they took from him. And all the Novgorodians pledged on the cross to the Grand Prince concerning this and concerning everything that had been written down, and concerning what had been told them.

And when the Novgorodian boyars, wealthy burghers, merchants, and the Archbishop swore on the cross, they petitioned the [Grand Prince's] boyars that they should intercede with the Sovereign [Grand Prince] that "He should relinquish his dislike and remove it from his heart, and with his own lips, according to the earlier bestowal, he should speak of it loudly. And his patrimony, Novgorod the Great, pledged on the cross here at the [Cathderal of the] Trinity, according to the charter; and that in the city all the Novgorodians [likewise] are in the process of pledging on the cross according to this charter." And the boyars told this to the Grand Prince, and the Grand Prince agreed and told them all he had said

222. It is unclear what is meant by the "Ivanovskii priests"—probably, the Church of St. John priests; or of the "Prince's Sen'ka" and Priest John.

previously on the twenty-ninth of December. And after this speech **1478**
he said, "God willing, in future we will bestow our grace on you,
our prayerful Archbishop, and on our patrimony, Novgorod the
Great."

On the fifteenth of January, Thursday, the Grand Prince sent
to Novgorod his boyars, Prince Ivan Iurievich, Fedor Davydovich,
Prince Ivan Striga [Obolenskii], and Vasilii and Ivan Borisovich
[Obolenskii], to bring all Novgorod to the oath according to the
charter about which the Novgorodians had petitioned the Grand
Prince. And the Grand Prince bestowed his grace on Novgorod.
The Grand Prince also ordered Prince Ivan Vasilievich [Striga-
Obolenskii] to go alone to the [Bishop's] palace as his envoy to the
Bishop and to the city of Novgorod [to say that] from this day on
there was no longer any *veché* in Novgorod. And Prince Ivan said,
"Our Grand Prince, Ivan Vasilievich, Sovereign of all Russia, says
the following to you, his prayerful Archbishop, and to his patrimony, Novgorod the Great: 'You, our prayerful Bishop, Archbishop Theophilus, with your entire Sacred Council, and his entire
patrimony, Novgorod the Great, has petitioned our boyars that he
should bestow on you his grace, be merciful, and remove his dislike
from his heart. I, Grand Prince, because of our boyars' [interces-
sion], bestowed my grace on my patrimony and have put aside my
dislike. You, our prayerful Archbishop, and you, our patrimony,
you have petitioned us, your Sovereigns, Grand Princes [Ivan III
and his son]. Thereupon a charter was written and you pledged
on the cross, and thereafter our entire patrimony of Novgorodians
pledged on the cross according to this charter, to rectify your attitude toward us. And since you corrected [your misdeeds] we will
bestow our grace on you, our patrimony." After this speech in the
Archbishop's court, the Grand Prince's boyars brought to pledge
on the cross the Novgorodian boyars, wealthy burghers, merchants,
and all others, concerning that which they had petitioned the Grand
Prince according to the charter written down by the Archbishop's
diak; and the Archbishop signed it with his own hand and affixed
his seal for each of all five sections [of the city], one seal for each.
Then the Grand Prince sent his junior boyars and his *diaks* to all
five sections [of the city] and they brought everyone thither to
pledge according to the same charter. And they pledged: the men,
the boyars' wives, the widows and people of the boyars. And this
charter was certified by the Novgorodians with fifty-eight seals, and

1478   the Grand Prince's boyars took this charter of pledge into the Archbishop's court.

On the eighteenth of January, Sunday, all the Novgorodian boyars, junior boyars, and wealthy burghers petitioned to be accepted into the Grand Prince's service; and having given the oath, they departed from thence. Thereupon the Grand Prince sent Ivan Tovarkov to Kasimir, to the latter's brother, Korob, to Feofilat Zakhar'in; to Luka and Iakov Fedorov; to Ivan Kuzmin; to Ivan Zakhar'in, the son of Grigorii; to Mitia Esipov; to Mikhail Berdenev; to Vasilii Esipov; to Fedor Teliatev; [and] to Rodion Norov.[223] The Grand Prince commanded that they be told the following: "You have pledged to the Grand Prince according to the charter, and you must abide as is fitting, according to your pledge on the cross and to the charter. And if anyone hears from his brother Novgorodian something about the Grand Princes, be it good or bad, you must speak of it to your Sovereign Grand Princes [Ivan III and his son]; and when the Grand Princes discuss such affairs with you, or in case the Grand Prince's boyars discuss with you the affairs of the Grand Princes, then you should not discuss these affairs with anyone, according to your pledge on the cross." And all the boyars confirmed everything which they had pledged on the cross to the Grand Princes.

The same day the Archbishop asked the Grand Prince kindly to send his police officials to the districts and towns because those Christians who had left those [places] did not dare depart from the city. And the Grand Prince commanded that police officials be sent thither.

On the twentieth of January the Grand Prince sent [his envoy], Prince Ivan Ivanovich Slykh, from Novgorod to Moscow to his mother, to the Metropolitan and to his son, the Grand Prince, to inform them that he had submitted Great Novgorod to his will and that he had become Sovereign there in the same way as in Moscow; and he [Slykh] arrived in Moscow with this on the twenty-seventh of the same month.

On the twenty-first of the same month the Novgorodian boyars, wealthy burghers, and merchants presented many gifts to the Grand Prince. On the twenty-second of the same month the Grand Prince

223. All of these persons had been either posadniks or some other high official.

sent to Novgorod his namestniks, boyars, Prince Ivan Vasilievich **1478**
Striga [Obolenskii], and the latter's brother, Iaroslav, and commanded them to take up residence in the Iaroslavl' court, [which
became] the Grand Prince's residence. The Grand Prince, himself,
however, did not go to Novgorod because a plague had arisen
among the Novgorodians.

On the twenty-ninth of January, Thursday of Shrovetide week,
the day when the *hieromartyr*, Ignatius the God-bearer, is remembered, the Grand Prince came to Great Novgorod and with him
were his brothers, Princes Andrei and Boris, and Prince Andrei
the younger, and Prince Vasilii Vereiskii. And they venerated Holy
Sophia, the Wisdom of God, and he attended a liturgy at Holy
Sophia with his brothers. And after the liturgy service he departed
from the city back to Poozerie, where he dined at his place, and
with him were all his brothers, the Archbishop, many boyars of
Novgorod, and the wealthy burghers, and he drank with them.
And the Archbishop presented before the table of the Grand Prince
the following presents: a blue *panagia*[224] decorated with gold and
pearls; and a silver-encrusted ostrich egg for a cup; and a cup of
cornelian stone covered with silver; and a barrel made of crystal,
encrusted with silver; and a silver plate with twelve *grivenkas*; and
two hundred ducats.

The first of the month of February, the Sunday of Shrovetide,
the Grand Prince commanded that they arrest Mark Pomfilicv, the
merchants' *starosta*, and he was arrested in the city.

On the second of February, Candlemas day, at night from
Sunday to Monday the Grand Princess Maria [dowager of the Grand
Prince] Vasilii Vasilievich, was shorn a nun. This happened on her
estate in Moscow, and she was shorn by the abbot of the Monastery
of St. Cyril, and he gave her the [monastic] name, Martha.

The same day, Monday, the first week of Lent, the Grand
Prince commanded that they arrest in Novgorod Marfa Isakova,
widow of Novgorodian boyar Boretskii, and her grandson, Vasilii
Fedorov, Isaak's son. On the third of February, Tuesday of the
same first week of Lent, the Grand Prince commanded his
namestnik, Prince Ivan Vasilievich Striga [Obolenskii], to take away
from the Novgorodian [archives] the treaty-charter [between Nov-

224. *Panagia*: an icon of Christ or of the Holy Virgin suspended on
a chain, to be worn on the breast.

1478   gorod and Poland-Lithuania] so that there be no treaty between Novgorod and the Grand Prince of Lithuania—King [of Poland]. Prince Ivan got this treaty-charter and brought it to the Grand Prince. On the fifth of February, Thursday, the Grand Prince appointed two other namestniks for Novgorod: Vasilii Kitai and Ivan Zinovievich. On the sixth of February the Grand Prince commanded the arrest of Grigorii Kiprianov Arzubiev and the confiscation of his property.

On the seventh of February the Grand Prince commanded they send to Moscow the arrested Novgorodians, Marfa Isakova with her grandson; Ivan Kuzmin Savelkov; Akinf with his son, Roman; Iurii Repekhov; Grigorii Arzubiev; and Mark Pomfiliev. And what they owned he ordered confiscated for his treasury. On the eighth of February, the Sunday of the Council,[225] the Grand Prince attended a liturgy in the Cathedral of Great Sophia in Novgorod, and he dined at his own place in Poozerie, and present were his brother, Prince Andrei the younger, and the Archbishop and many boyars and wealthy burghers of Novgorod. On the twelfth of February, Thursday before the liturgy, the Archbishop came to the Grand Prince from Novgorod and presented him with a golden chain of five *grivenkas*; a golden cup of ten *grivenkas*; a golden cup of one and a half *grivenkas* and ten ounces; and a golden pitcher of one *grivenka* and three ounces; and a silver gilt bowl of thirteen *grivenkas*; and a collapsable gold cup of fourteen *grivenkas*; and a silver bowl of eleven *grivenkas*; and a gilt cup of six and a half *grivenkas*; and a gilt belt and large bracelet of eighteen and a half *grivenkas*; and one hundred ducats.

On the seventeenth of February, Tuesday, early in the morning, the Grand Prince left Novgorod, and his first stop was in Iamny, and the Archbishop came thither to take leave of him and presented him with a barrel of wine and a stallion. And the Novgorodian boyars and wealthy burghers presented wineskins and mead, and they all ate and drank at his place. And the Grand Prince gave presents to the Archbishop and to the boyars and let them go. On the fifth of March, Thursday of the fifth week of Lent, the Grand Prince arrived in Moscow. After his departure the Grand Prince commanded the *veché* bell to be brought from Novgorod to Moscow;

225. Sunday of the Council: the first Sunday of Lent, when the restoration by the Church Council of veneration of icons in 787, is remembered.

and when it was brought thither it was put in the belfry on the   **1478**
square to ring with the other bells. And since the land of Novgorod
the Great and the whole Russian land came into being, there was
not such a punishment laid upon them [that is, upon the Novgorod-
ians] either by the Grand Prince or by anyone else.

The same winter the Khan of Kazan' campaigned against Viatka and took many captives, massacring and sacking despite his
pledge, and many towns surrendered to him.

The same winter on the sixth of December the priest-monk
Bassian, son of Prince Ivan Vasilievich Striga-Obolenskii, was consecrated Bishop of Tver' by Metropolitan Gerontius. The same
spring, the day of the Annunciation occurred on Easter Wednesday.
The same day the ice broke in the Moscow River, and the next day
people began to ford it on horseback. The same day in the year
6986 [1478] the monk Josef[226] started building his monastery in
the uninhabited place of Volok-Lamskii.

The same spring the Grand Prince sent by boats against Kazan'
an army under the main voevoda, Vasilii Fedorovich Obrazets. And
on Tuesday, the twenty-sixth of May, [the levies of] Novgorod
marched toward Kazan'.

The same spring the Grand Prince's namestnik in Novgorod,
Prince Ivan Vasilievich Obolenskii-Striga, passed away and was
brought from thence and buried in the Church of the Saviour in
the Monastery of St. Euthymius in Suzdal'.

ABOUT THE ARGUMENT BETWEEN METROPOLITAN GERONTIUS AND ARCHBISHOP BASSIAN OF ROSTOV CONCERNING ST. CYRIL MONASTERY

The same spring there was an argument about the Monastery
of St. Cyril[227] between Metropolitan Gerontius and Archbishop Bassian of Rostov. Gerontius, influenced by Prince Mikhail Andreevich,
decided to take it over from the diocese of Rostov. This happened
because the monks of the St. Cyril Monastery, who were filled by
their great pride, vanity, and wealth, did not want to remain under
the jurisdiction of their diocesan bishop of Rostov or to obey the
Archbishop of Rostov; and, forgetting the word of God that every

226. Josef Sanin, called Volotskii, became the founder of the so-called
Josephite faction of the Russian church.
227. The Monastery of St. Cyril on Beloozero (White Lake) was one
of the most important and wealthiest in Russia. Both Metropolitan Gerontius and Archbishop Bassian wanted to have it in their dioceses.

1479   proud man will be humbled and that a humble man is honored, rebelled and behaved as if drunk. According to the words of the prophets, all their wisdom disappeared: believing themselves wise, they became fools because they were blinded by their evil behavior.

And they instigated Prince Mikhail and Prince Mikhail started speaking about this matter with the Metropolitan. The Metropolitan heeded Prince Mikhail and gave him a charter that Prince Mikhail should assume custody of the monastery, and that the Archbishop of Rostov had no right to interfere in it. Archbishop Bassian asked him not to trespass the rules [of the Church] or interfere in his diocese, but the Metropolitan did not heed him. Then the Archbishop approached Grand Prince Ivan Vasilievich and asked for a trial with the Metropolitan according to the rules. The Grand Prince sent him to the Metropolitan, but the latter did not want to heed him. Then the Grand Prince sent [his envoy] to take away the Metropolitan's charter from Prince Mikhail, and summoned the Council with all bishops and archimandrites, and they started in Moscow a trial between the Archbishop and the Metropolitan. After a long investigation the Metropolitan became afraid of the Conciliar Court and supplicated the Grand Prince; the Grand Prince reconciled the Metropolitan with the Archbishop and tore the charter to shreds. And he commanded that the Monastery of St. Cyril be under the jurisdiction of the Archbishop of Rostov in all ways, as of old. And all this evil emanated from the innovator Niphontus, former abbot of the St. Cyril Monastery, who came thither from another one; and from such monks who came from other monasteries, as well as from some who came from outside. The older monks, however, holy people tonsured in this monastery, all prayed tearfully to God and to the Most Pure Mother of God and to the great Wonderworkers Leontius and Cyril, that God should end the quarrel and that they should live in obedience to their lord, the Archbishop of Rostov, just as had their [late] venerable elder, Cyril.

In the Year 6987 [1479]. On the twenty-fifth of March in the eighth hour of the night on the eve of the feast of Archangel Gabriel [Annunciation], a son was born to Tsarevna Sofia, [wife of] Grand Prince Ivan III Vasilievich, and he was called Vasilii, after St. Basil of Parea. He was baptized on the fourth of April, Palm Sunday, in the Monastery of the Holy Trinity and St. Sergius, by Archbishop Bassian of Rostov and Abbot Paisos of the Trinity Monastery.

On the eleventh of July of the same year pious and Christ-loving

Grand Prince Ivan laid the foundation of a stone Church of St. **1479** John Chrysostomos and the earlier, wooden one was dismantled. This church [monastery] was built by the Muscovite merchants but the monastery had begun to become impoverished. The Grand Prince designated the abbot of this Monastery of the Resurrection to be dean of all the suburban priests and of its Cathedral Church [of St. John] in order to keep his [earlier] vow. He had given [this vow] because he was baptized [Ivan—John] on the holiday of the Translation of the Saintly Relics of St. John Chrysostomos, which is celebrated on the twenty-seventh of January. Next to the wall of this church he ordered that another be built in honor of Apostle Timothy because he was born on the day [when the latter's memory is celebrated]. And he ordered that the old wooden, dismantled, church be moved to his Monastery of the Intercession [of the Mother of God] in the gardens. And the earlier, smaller, one was dismantled.

ABOUT THE CONSTRUCTION AND CONSECRATION OF THE CATHEDRAL CHURCH OF THE MOST PURE [MOTHER OF GOD] IN MOSCOW

In the Year 6987 [1479]. The same year the Church of the Assumption of the Most Pure Mother of God in Moscow was completed. This church was unusually beautiful in its majesty, its height, its brightness, and its size, and there was never such a church in Russia except that in Vladimir. And its builder was [the Italian master] Aristotle.[228] It was consecrated the same year on the twelfth of August, Thursday, by Metropolitan Gerontius.

ABOUT THE TRANSLATION OF THE RELICS OF WONDERWORKER PETER AND OTHER BISHOP-SAINTS

The same year, on the twenty-third day of the month of August, the relics of Wonderworker Peter were translated to the new large church. On the twenty-seventh day of the same month of August, Friday, in the ninth hour of the day, the relics of their holinesses Metropolitans Cyprian, Photius, Jonas, and Phillip were translated, and they were placed in the new church in the places prepared for them; and the relics of Metropolitan Theognostos were placed in the Church of the Holy Apostle Peter in the wall, which was common

228. His full name was Aristotele Fioravanti della Alberti, *Enciclopedia Italiana* xv, pp. 237–38, (ed., Instituto Trecanni), 1932–40.

1480   to the [church where repose the relics of] Wonderworker Peter [in the Church of the Assumption]. And the remains of Prince Iurii Danilovich were placed in the wall of the Church of St. Demetrius. And since that time there was established on the twenty-fourth of August the feast of the Translation of the Relics of Our Holy Father, Metropolitan Peter, the new Russian wonderworker.

In the Year 6988 [1480]. On the twenty-sixth of October, Grand Prince Ivan Vasilievich peacefully departed for Novgorod the Great, and in Novgorod he sojourned in the estate of Efimi Medvednov. And he left his son, Grand Prince Ivan, in Moscow.

The same autumn, when the Grand Prince had already left for Novgorod, two khans came from the *polé*[229] asking Grand Prince Ivan Vasilievich and his son, Grand Prince Ivan Ivanovich, to accept them into their service. These were Khan Merdulat with his son, Berdulat, and the former's brother, [Khan] Aidar—[both] children of the Crimean Khan Hadji Girei.

The same winter, on the nineteenth of January, the Grand Prince ordered the arrest of the Lord Bishop of Novgorod, Theophilus, and he was sent to Moscow on the twenty-fourth of the same month. He was imprisoned there in the Monastery of the Miracles of Archangel Michael and remained there for six and a half years, and passed away there.

ABOUT THE SEDITION OF THE GRAND PRINCE'S BROTHERS

That winter the Grand Prince's brothers, Prince Andrei the elder and Prince Boris, broke away from the Grand Prince and sent their wives-princesses to Rzhev. Prince Boris went from Volok to Uglech to his brother, Andrei, and sojourned there until the Grand Prince returned [from Novgorod] to Moscow.

The same winter on the thirteenth of February, a cheese fare Sunday, the Grand Prince returned from Novgorod to Moscow, while his brothers marched on the Tver' highroad from Uglech to Rzhev and Rzhev to Velikie Luki. The Grand Prince sent after them Bassian, the Archbishop of Rostov, and, together with him, his boyars, Vasilii Fedorovich Obrazets and Vasilii Borisovich Tuchek, as well as *diak* Vasilii Mamyrev, [ordering them] to say, "Return to your domains and I will reward you, and give to you, Prince Andrei, an addition to your patrimony, our mother's cities of Kaluga and Alexin." But they did not heed either the Grand

229. *Polé*: steppe, prairie, where the Tatars roamed.

Prince's reward or the Archbishop's speeches and sent the Arch-   **1480**
bishop and the boyars back to the Grand Prince. And the Grand
Prince relied upon Lord God and His Most Pure Mother.

[ABOUT THE END OF THE GOLDEN HORDE]
ABOUT KHAN AHMET, HOW HE CAME TO UGRA

The same year it was heard that Khan Ahmet and the Great
Horde were marching against Russia.

The same winter on the fifteenth of March, a Wednesday of
Lent, Khan Merdulat's son, Berdulat, had his head cut off by a
Tatar of his own clan. And Merdulat, the father of Berdulat, himself
cut off the head of this Tatar.

On the twenty-third of the month of March, Thursday of the
sixth week of Lent, at the fourth hour of the day, a son was born
to Grand Prince Ivan Vasilievich, and he was named after Saint
George of Mitylene.

The same spring, in May, Nicetas, Bishop of Kolomna, passed
away.

Around the same time Andreas, son of Thomas, Despot of
Morea, brother-in-law of the Grand Prince [Ivan III], arrived in
Moscow from Rome.

The same spring the Crimean Khan Aidar was captured and
sent to be imprisoned in Vologda.

The same year the old Church of the Theophany in the estate
of the Trinity Monastery in the city [of Moscow] was dismantled
and a foundation for a new one was laid.

The same year the godless Khan Ahmet of the Great Horde
started his campaign against the Orthodox Christianity of Russia,
against the holy churches, and against the Grand Prince, boasting
that he would destroy the holy churches and capture all, Orthodox
Christians and the Grand Prince, himself, as happened under Batu;
[he started his campaign] because he heard that the Grand Prince's
brother had dissented from him. And the [Polish] King joined the
Khan. And the Khan's envoys who went to the King agreed that
the Khan would attack from the *polé* [prairie], while the King [would
do] the same on his side. And together with the Khan was the entire
Horde and his cousin, Kasim, and the Khan's six sons and a numberless multitude of Tatars. Godless Khan Ahmet marched very
slowly, expecting to be joined by the [Polish] King, and sent the
latter's envoys back to him, and sent his own envoys with them.

Hearing of this, Grand Prince Ivan Vasilievich sent his voe-

1481   vodas with armed forces to the shore of the Oka [River]; and he sent his brother, Prince Andrei Vasilievich the younger, to the latter's patrimony, to Torusa, also against him [the Khan]. And he also sent on the eighth of the month of June his son, Grand Prince Ivan Ivanovich, to the shore of the Oka River, to Serpukhov; with him were many voevodas and a numberless army.

The Khan moved slowly, waiting for the King, and then approached the Don [River], and learning of this on the twenty-third of the month of July, a Sunday, marched against him toward Kolomna and there he remained till the holiday of the Intercession of the Virgin [the first of October]. When the accursed Khan learned that the Grand Princes were awaiting him on all the ways he wanted to go [into Russia], he moved toward the Lithuanian land, seeking to bypass [the Russian armies]. And he crossed the river Ugra. But Grand Prince Ivan Vasilievich ordered his son, Grand Prince Ivan Ivanovich, and his brother, Prince Andrei Vasilievich the younger, to go to Kaluga to [guard] the shore of the river Ugra.

ABOUT THE UGORSHCHINA[230]

In the Year 6989 [1481]. On the thirtieth of September the Grand Prince came from Kolomna to Moscow to take counsel with his [spiritual] father, Metropolitan Gerontius; with his mother, the dowager Grand Princess, nun Martha; with his uncle, Prince Mikhail Andreevich Vereiskii; and with all his boyars because they all were now preparing Moscow for siege. They prayed him with great insistence to stand firm for Orthodox Christendom against the Moslems.

At that time the envoys of his brothers, Prince Andrei and Prince Boris, came to Moscow suggesting peace. The Grand Prince honored his brothers, thanks to the intervention of his spiritual father, Metropolitan Gerontius; of his mother, Grand Princess nun Martha; of Bassian, Archbishop of Rostov; and of Prince Mikhail Andreevich. He let the envoys go, telling them that they [his brothers] should come forthwith. The Grand Prince, himself, ordered a *Te Deum* in all the holy churches and at the graves of the wonderworkers [Metropolitans], and received a blessing from the Metropolitan and from his mother. He fortified the city and left

---

230. The choncler called Ivan III's resistance to Khan Ahmed on the river Ugra the "*Ugorshchina.*"

Metropolitan Gerontius, Grand Princess nun Martha, and Prince   **1481** Mikhail Andreevich, as well as the Muscovite namestnik, Prince Ivan Iurievich, to lead the defense of the city of Moscow against the siege.

There was a great multitude of people [in Moscow] from various cities. On the third of October the Grand Prince marched from Moscow to the Ugra River. Arriving there, he took a position in Kremenets with small forces. He sent the majority of his men to Ugra to his son, Grand Prince Ivan. His son, Grand Prince Ivan, and his brother, Prince Andrei the younger, took a position on the Ugra against the Khan, who had a large army.

In the Year 6989 [1481].[231] In the month of October a candle began burning by itself in the Cathedral of the Most Holy Theotokos in Moscow, at the grave of Wonderworker Peter. Metropolitan Gerontius celebrated a *Te Deum* to the Most Holy, Most Pure Theotokos and Wonderworker Peter. He blessed the water, lit a candle, and put this water into a cup made of wax, and sent it to the Grand Prince, to the river Ugra. At that time there arrived in Kremenets at the Grand Prince's his brothers, Prince Andrei Vasilievich the elder and Prince Boris Vasilievich, who came with all their forces to aid the Grand Prince against Khan Ahmet. The Grand Prince received them with love.

Khan Ahmet marched forward with all his forces and passed the cities of Mtsensk, Lubutsk, and Odoev and, upon arriving there, took up a position at Vorotynsk, expecting help from the [Polish] King; but the King did not come to join him nor did he send him his forces because he was fighting [elsewhere]. At that time the Crimean Khan Mengli-Girei was invading the Podolian land because he was a friend of the Grand Prince's.

Thereafter Khan Ahmet marched to the river Ugra, where [on the opposite shore] the Grand Prince had already taken a position with his brothers, all the Princes, the voevodas, and a great multitude of men-at-arms. The Khan stopped on the [western] shore of the Ugra, also with large forces, because he intended to cross the river. On the other side, however, were the armed forces of the Grand Prince. When the Tatars arrived, they began to shoot, and our men also started shooting with bows and arquebuses. Many

231. The compiler of the chronicle here repeats the before-mentioned year 6989 (1481).

1481   Tatars were killed and they were thrown back from the shore. For many days they fought on both sides for the river.

When the river [froze over and] stopped, then the Grand Prince commanded his son, the Grand Prince, and his brother, Prince Andrei, and all the voevodas with all the armed forces to retreat from the shore and to join him in Kremenets because he was afraid that the Tatars would cross the [frozen] river [and encircle his army]. He was heeding evil people, lovers of silver, rich and big-bellied betrayers of the Christians, secret supporters of the Moslems, who advised the Sovereign to the detriment of the Christians, saying, "Retreat! You can not start to fight them." At that time the devil, himself, spoke with their lips, the same who in ancient times appeared as a serpent and seduced Adam and Eve. Therefore the Grand Prince with his son, brothers, and all the voevodas [retreated and] marched to Borovsk.

THE MIRACLE

At that time a miracle occurred of the Most Holy Theotokos, and it was marvellous to see. Each side retreated from the other and no one intervened. But as soon as the sons of Russia retreated from the shore, the Tatars fled, seized by fear, believing that the Russians were retreating from the shore so as to fight there with them, [attacking their rearguard]. At the same time our men, imagining that the Tatars had crossed the river, fell back to Kremenets. Khan Ahmet was frightened by God. Not pursued by anyone, he fled from the river Ugra into the Lithuanian land, into the dominion of the [Polish] King, fighting in his land because of his [the King's] treachery.

When in his flight Khan Ahmet reached the Horde, he was attacked by Khan Ivak of Nogai, who conquered the Horde. And godless Khan Ahmet was killed by the latter's brother-in-law, Nogai Murza Iamgurchei. One of the Khan's sons wanted to conquer the *ukraina* [frontier region] beyond the Oka but the Grand Prince sent his brothers, both Andreis; and when the Tatars heeded this, they fled. In such manner God delivered the Russian land from the pagan Tatars, thanks to the prayers of the Most Pure Theotokos and the great wonderworkers. The Khan fled on the eleventh of November.

The Grand Prince then came from Borovsk to Moscow with his son [and heir] Grand Prince Ivan, with his brothers and all his

forces, and he praised God and the Most Pure Mother of God and   **1481**
the great wonderworkers and all the saints. And all the people were
happy and rejoiced with very great joy, and praised God and the
Most Pure Mother of God and the great Russian wonderworkers
for this glorious salvation, which had delivered them from the
pagan Tatars. And since that time in the God-protected city of
Moscow the holiday has been established on the twenty-first of
June, when the Most Pure Mother of God is glorified and a procession with crosses takes place.

[ABOUT THE BROTHERS OF THE GRAND PRINCE
AND HOW THEY WERE ENDOWED]

At that time the Grand Prince endowed his brothers, and to
end their strife he gave Mozhaisk to Prince Andrei Vasilievich, the
elder, and he returned to Prince Boris Vasilievich the latter's [own]
lands. And they strengthened their peace through a pledge on the
cross and went home.

The same winter Grand Princess Sofia came from Beloozero;
the Grand Prince had sent her—his wife—to Beloozero because of
the Tatar invasion.

The same spring on the twenty-third of the month of March,
a Saturday, at the fourth hour of the night Archbishop Bassian of
Rostov and Iaroslavl' passed away. The same spring on the tenth
day of the month of July, at the fourth hour of the day, Prince
Andrei Vasilievich the younger passed away and was buried in
Moscow in the [Cathedral of] Archangel [Michael].

On the twenty-second of the same month Ioasaf, from the
family of the Obolenskii princes, was consecrated Archbishop of
Rostov by His Holiness Metropolitan Gerontius. On the twenty-
ninth of the same month Gerasimus was consecrated Bishop of
Kolomna. The same year Simeon was consecrated Bishop of
Riazan'. He used to be the confessor of Metropolitan Gerontius.

In the [same] Year 6989 [1481] the Grand Prince sent [troops]
to campaign against the Prince, Grand Master of the German lands,
because of their trespassing: they campaigned in his patrimony of
Pskov when Khan Ahmet was positioned on the river Ugra.[232] And

232. The German Livonian Order began this campaign in alliance
with King Kasimir of Lithuania-Poland and with Khan Ahmet of the Great
Horde. Ivan III sent his troops against Livonia only after the invasion of
Khan Ahmet and the possible attack by King Kasimir were over.

1482 the Grand Prince sent the army against them with his voevodas, Prince Ivan Vasilievich Bulgak and Prince Iaroslav Vasilievich Obolenskii, and the Novgorodian namestniks, Prince Vasilii Fedorovich Shuiskii and Ivan Zinovievich with the Novgorodian levies, as well as Prince Vasilii Vasilievich Shuiskii with the levy of Pskov. In the month of February the voevodas of the Grand Prince marched from Pskov with great forces against the German land, moving forward by various routes, burning and campaigning in the German land, and defeating the Germans and taking them into captivity. And they came to the city of Veliad[233] on the first day of the month of March, and the Prince Grand Master escaped from thence a day ahead of the arrival of the Grand Prince's forces in this city. The Grand Prince's voevodas commenced a shock attack against the city, firing at it from guns and arquebuses and mortars; and breaking the wall, they took a part of the fortress of Veliad. From the dungeon [the Germans] petitioned the Grand Prince's voevodas that they be merciful toward them, that they not take them captive but that they accept a ransom—as much as they could give. Prince Vasilii Fedorovich Shuiskii, as well as other of the Grand Prince's voevodas, pursued the Grand Master, following him for fifty versts, although they did not catch him; but they took much of his treasury. Prince Ivan Bulgak and Prince Iaroslav [Obolenskii] took two thousand rubles from the fortress of Veliad secretly, for themselves, and moved away from the city with the army, not taking the fortress. And from thence they returned with a great number of captives and great booty, and they returned to the Grand Prince all in good health. At that time the people of Pskov brought the Grand Prince eight bells from the city of Veliad, together with the other booty taken from the Germans.

The same year the Grand Prince arrested the Novgorodian boyars, Vasilii Kasmir and his brother, Iakob Korob, as well as Mikhail Berdenev and Luka Fedorov.[234]

In the Year 6990 [1482]. On the sixth of October, the day when Holy Apostle Thomas is remembered, a son was born to Grand

233. Veliad: Fellin, in German: Veliandi, in the Estonian S.S.R.
234. Apparently, in expectation of the victory of King Kasimir and Khan Ahmet over Ivan III, the Novgorodian boyars had once again begun conspiring against their ruler, the Grand Prince.

Prince Ivan Vasilievich [III], and he was baptized Dimitrii on the   **1483**
twentieth day of the same month.

ABOUT PRINCE FEDOR BELSKII

In the [same] Year 6990 [1482]. Prince Fedor Ivanovich Belskii
gave up [service to] King Kasimir and came [to serve] Grand Prince
Ivan Vasilievich. He did not have time to take his wife with him.
The Grand Prince honored him and as patrimony gave him the
city of Diemon and Moreva with several *volosts.*

The same year Grand Prince Ivan Vasilievich was in Vladimir.

The same year an ambassador named Ivan came to the Grand
Prince from the Hungarian King Matthias, with [a message of] love
and brotherhood; and the Grand Prince honored the ambassador
and let him go home with love to his Sovereign. And with him the
Grand Prince sent his own envoy, Fedor Vasilievich Kuritsyn. And
he went, taking with him to King Matthias a treaty of peace, brotherhood and love.

The same year the Sultan of Turkey captured the city of Belgrade from voevoda Stefan of Walachia.

[THE PASSING OF GRAND PRINCE VASILII OF RIAZAN' AND THE ASCENSION OF GRAND PRINCE IVAN]

In the Year 6991 [1483]. The same winter on the sixth of January
at the time of the Eucharist, Grand Prince Vasilii Ivanovich of
Riazan' passed away and his son, Ivan, became Grand Prince.

The same winter on the twelfth of January Grand Prince Ivan
Ivanovich of all Russia, son of Grand Prince Ivan Vasilievich of all
Russia, married Princess Elena, daughter of voevoda Stefan of
Walachia.

The same year on the seventeenth of July Grand Prince Ivan
Vasilievich of all Russia and his son, Grand Prince Ivan Ivanovich
of all Russia, held council with their [spiritual] father, Metropolitan
Gerontius, with Archbishop Asaph of Rostov, with Bishop Simeon
of Riazan', with Bishop Gerasimus of Kolomna, and with Bishop
Prokhorus of Sarai, and they cast lots for the throne [of the Arch-
bishop] of Novgorod between Elyseus, Archimandrite of St.
Saviour, Genadius, Archimandrite of the Monastery of the Miracles,
and Elder Sergius of the Monastery of the Holy Trinity. And the
Metropolitan celebrated a church service with all those bishops and

1484   archimandrites, and the lot fell to Sergius to be Archbishop of Great Novgorod.[235]

The same year the Grand Prince sent Novgorodian boyars to a council with the Germans near Rugodiv,[236] and they made peace with the Germans for twenty years, pledging on the cross.

The same year Archimandrite Genadius Gonozov of the Monastery of the Miracles laid the foundation for a church in honor of Wonderworker [Metropolitan] Alexis in the Monastery of the Miracles [of Archangel Michael], and he also laid the foundation for a stone refectory there.

In the Year 6992 [1484]. On the fourth of September following the prodding of Grand Prince Ivan Vasilievich of all Russia, the Khan of the Horde of the Crimea and Perekip, Mengli-Girei, marched with all his forces against the domain of the King [of Poland], took Kiev, and burned it with fire. And he captured *Pan* Ivashka Hotkiewicz, voevoda of Kiev, and took an endless number of captives. He made a wilderness out of the Kievan land, and this happened because of the misbehavior of the King, who brought Khan Ahmet of the Great Horde with all his forces against Grand Prince Ivan Vasilievich and wanted to destroy the Christian faith.[237]

On the fourth of the same month Sergius, formerly called [by his lay name of] Simeon, who used to be archpriest of the Cathedral

235. The bishop of Novgorod had traditionally been elected in Novgorod. Since 1480, when the Novgorodian Archbishop Theophilus was arrested, together with many boyars and other local ringleaders—apparently for conspiracy and contact with Moscow's enemies, Livonia and Poland-Lithuania—the choice of the Archbishop of Novgorod was made in Moscow, thus abolishing Novgorod's ecclesiastic autonomy. About the same time, in 1484, the last elected Novgorodian Archbishop, Theophilus, relinquished the archbishopric and gave a written statement in which he admitted his inability to perform his ecclesiastic duties.

236. Rugodiv: now Narva.

237. In the fifteenth century the Crimean Khan had become independent from the Golden Horde, but in 1475 he recognized the suzerainty of the Ottoman Sultan, who already controlled Kaffa (now Feodosia) and Kerch in Crimea, and Azov in the Don estuary. Hence, the Crimean khans were enemies of their former suzeraine khans of the Golden Horde and were involved in Polish-Turkish military conflicts. They also became the allies of Muscovy. In the sixteenth century the situation changed, however, and the Crimea started raiding Muscovy.

of the Holy Virgin, was invested to the archbishopric of Novgorod   **1485**
and Pskov.

The same fall on the tenth of October at the tenth hour of the
night on Friday, the day when Holy Martyr Eulampius is remembered, a son was born to Grand Prince Ivan Ivanovich the younger
[son of Ivan III] and he was christened Dimitrii.

ABOUT THE ARREST OF THE NOVGORODIAN BOYARS

The same winter the Grand Prince ordered the arrest of the
leading and important Novgorodian boyars and their wives, and
he ordered the confiscation of their treasuries and estates [in the
Novgorodian lands]. And he gave them estates in various cities of
Muscovy. The other boyars who were conspiring against him he
ordered imprisoned in the jails of various cities.

On the sixth of May of the same spring Grand Prince Ivan
Vasilievich laid within his own court the foundation for a stone
Church of the Annunciation of the Most Holy Mother of God, and
he [ordered to] pull down the first foundation, which had been
laid by his grandfather, Grand Prince Vasilii Dmitrievich. And behind the church he laid the foundation for a palace.

The same year on the twenty-seventh of June Archbishop Sergius of Novgorod gave up his archbishopric and went to the Monastery of the Holy Trinity and St. Sergius, where he was earlier
tonsured a monk.[238]

The same year Metropolitan Gerontius laid in his court a
foundation for a stone Church of the Deposition of the Vestments
of the Most Pure Theotokos.

The same year, on order of Grand Prince Ivan Vasilievich,
they started building on the St. Sophia side in Great Novgorod a
new stone fortress on the old foundation.

In the Year 6993 [1485]. On the ninth day of the month of
December, Niphontus, Archimandrite of the Monastery of St. Simeon, was consecrated Bishop of Suzdal'. On the twelfth of the same
month Archimandrite Genadius of the Monastery of the Miracles

---

238. In Novgorod this archbishop, elected and consecrated in Moscow, encountered such strong resistance on the side of local political and
ecclesiastic groups that he preferred to give up his diocese.

1486   [of Archangel Michael] was consecrated to the archbishoprics of Novgorod the Great and Pskov.[239]

The same spring on the twelfth of May, Tuesday, the city of Moscow burned.

The same spring on the twenty-ninth of May at the third hour of the night a daughter, Princess Feodosia, was born to Grand Prince Ivan Vasilievich.

The same year on the fourth of July the mother of Grand Prince Ivan Vasilievich, pious Grand Princess Maria—who, after tonsure, had received the monastic name of nun Martha—passed away and was buried in the Church of the Ascension in Moscow.

On the nineteenth of the same July, on the Moscow River, a foundation for a cannon tower was laid, and from under this tower was built a secret passageway; and it was built by Antonio the Italian.

The same year Giovanni Ralo Paleologue came from Constantinople with his wife and children.[240]

The same year on the twenty-first of August Grand Prince Ivan Vasilievich gave up his pledge on the cross to Grand Prince Mikhail Borisovich of Tver' because of the latter's deceit: he [the Prince of Tver'] sent messages to King Kasimir of Lithuania and invited him to march with his own army against Grand Prince Ivan Vasilievich. And therefore Ivan Vasilievich marched with his army to Tver', and with him were his son, Grand Prince Ivan Ivanovich, and his brothers, Princes Andrei and Boris, as well as the voevodas with great forces. And he ordered his boyar Ivan Zakhariich to march with the levies of Novgorod against Tver'.

ABOUT THE ANNEXATION OF THE LAND OF TVER'[241]

In the year 6994 [1486]. On the eighth day of the month of September Grand Prince Ivan Vasilievich, together with his son, Grand Prince Ivan Ivanovich, and with his brothers, voevodas, and all forces, reached the city of Tver' and besieged that city. The

---

239. Genadius was a much smarter prince of the church than his predecessor, Sergius, and despite his Muscovite origin and consecration, he rapidly adapted himself to the Novgorodian ways of church life, becoming quite a successful hierarch.

240. Giovanni Ralo Paleologue was a relative of Grand Princess Sofia, wife of Ivan III.

241. The year 1486 (6994) was put by error of the scribe between two entries for year 1485 (6993).

tenth of the same month, Saturday, the suburbs of the city of Tver'   **1487**
were set afire. On the eleventh day [of September], Sunday, there
came to the Grand Prince from the city of Tver' the princes and
boyars who conspired in Tver', and petitioned him to accept them
into his service. The same day at night Grand Prince Mikhail
Borisovich of Tver', seeing his weakness, fled from the city of Tver'
to Lithuania. On the twelfth day [of September], Monday, Bishop
Bassian of Tver' and Prince Mikhail Kholmskii with his brothers
and his son, as well as other princes and boyars and all the people
of the land [of Tver'], came to Grand Prince Ivan Vasilievich and
surrendered the city to him. And the Grand Prince sent into the
city Iurii Shestak and Konstantin Malichkin and his *diaks*, Vasilii
Dalmatov, Romodan Alekseev, and Leontii Alekseev, commanding
them to bring all the burghers to pledge on the cross and to keep
their forces [of Ivan III] under control so as to restrain them from
sacking. And on the fifteenth day [of September], Thursday, Grand
Prince Ivan Vasilievich, together with his son, Grand Prince Ivan
Ivanovich, were in the city of Tver' and attended the Eucharist in
the [Cathedral of the] Saviour, and [Ivan III] gave that land to his
son, Grand Prince Ivan Ivanovich. On the eighteenth day of September [Sunday], Grand Prince Ivan Ivanovich entered the city of
Tver' to reside there; and on the twentieth of this same month
Grand Prince Ivan Vasilievich returned to Moscow after having
taken the city of Tver'.

In the [same] Year 6993 [1485]. On the thirty-first of August
they consecrated the Church of the Deposition of the Most Pure
Vestments which is located in the estate of the Metropolitan.

The same year they started building a fortress in the city of
Vladimir, and it was *diak* Vasilii Momyrev who laid the foundation.

In the Year 6995 [1487]. On the twenty-first of the month of
May at the seventh hour of the day a son, named Semion, was born
to Grand Prince Ivan Vasilievich.

ABOUT THE TAKING OF KAZAN'

On the eleventh of April, Maundy Thursday of the same
spring, Grand Prince Ivan Vasilievich of all Russia sent against
Kazan' his voevodas, Prince Daniil Dmitrievich Kholmskii, Prince
Aleksandr Vasilievich Obolenskii, Prince Semion Ivanovich
Riapolovskii, and Prince Semion Romanovich; and on the twenty-
fourth of April, Tuesday of the Second Week after Easter, the

1488   Grand Prince sent Khan Mohammed Amin of Kazan' [against] the city of Kazan'.[242] The Grand Prince's voevodas arrived at the city of Kazan' with all forces on the eighteenth day of the month of May, Thursday of the Fifth Week after Easter. They took the city of Kazan' on the ninth day of July and they took prisoner Khan Ali Khan,[243] his mother, his wife, and his two brothers; and, together with his sisters and with his princes, they brought them to Moscow. On the twentieth of July the Grand Prince received word that the city of Kazan' was taken by his voevodas and that the Khan was taken prisoner. This news was brought by Prince Fedor Khripun Riapolovskii. And Grand Prince Ivan Vasilievich of all Russia put Khan Mohammed Amin out of his hands to rule Kazan'.[244] The treacherous princes and *ulans*[245] received capital punishment, as well as the other conspirators. [In the meantime) Khan Ali Khan was sent under guard by the Grand Prince to Vologda, while the Grand Prince sent his mother, brothers, and sisters to Kargolom on the Beloozero, to be imprisoned there.

The same year the Grand Prince transferred from Novgorod the Great to Vladimir fifty families of the most outstanding merchants of Novgorod.

The same year on order of Grand Prince Ivan Vasilievich of all Russia Marco the Italian built a great palace on the estate of the Grand Prince, where before used to be the palace of the princesses.

The same year Marco the Italian completed building the Beklemyshev tower on the corner [of the Kremlin] down the Moscow River.

In the Year 6996 [1488]. On the twenty-seventh of May, Antonio the Italian laid the foundation of an artillery tower up the Moscow River where used to be the Sviblovskaia tower, and under it was built a secret underground passage. The same year on order of Grand Prince Ivan Vasilievich a new fortress was built in Kargolom on Beloozero, and it was ten *versts* distant from the old one.

242. Khan Mohammed Amin of Kazan' fled from Kazan', escaping his feudal lords, went to Moscow and asked Ivan III for aid. He was the son of the most senior wife of his father, Khan Ibrahim of Kazan'.

243. Khan Ali Khan was also the son of Khan Ibrahim, but by a "lesser," "junior" wife.

244. "Out of his hands": this means that Khan Mohammed Amin became the vassal of the Grand Prince of Moscow, ruling under his direction.

245. *Ulan*: a Turko-Mongol title of lower nobility.

The same year on the twelfth of August the Italian, Paolino **1489**
DiBosi [?], cast a big cannon.

The thirteenth of the same month after dinner in the ninth
hour of the day the Church of the Annunication at Boloto caught
fire, and from it [everything] burned down from the city to Kulishki,
almost to the [Church of] All Saints, and to the [Church of the]
Vestments [of Our Lady] in the Gardens [*Sady*] on the Neglinnaia
River, including forty-two churches.

The same year the Grand Prince sent Demetrius and Manuel,
sons of Ralo [Paleologue], to Rome and to Venice and to Milano.

In the year 1667 [1489]. The same year an ambassador named
Nicholas [von Poppel] came with an offer of [a treaty of] love and
friendship from the Roman Emperor Frederick,[246] and the Grand
Prince honored this ambassador and let him depart with love to
his sovereign.[247] And together with him the Grand Prince dispatched with love his own ambassador to Emperor Frederick—the
Greek, Iurii Trakhaniote.

The same winter the Grand Prince transferred from Novgorod
the Great many boyars, wealthy burghers, and leading merchants—
altogether, more than one thousand men. And he bestowed on
them [his good will] and gave them estates in the regions of Moscow,
Vladimir, Murom, Nizhnii Novgorod, Pereiaslavl', Iur'iev, Rostov,
Kostroma, and other cities. And he sent to Novgorod the Great
into their estates the better people of Moscow, the leading merchants, and the minor boyars. He also sent thither from other cities
of his Muscovite patrimony many other minor boyars and leading
merchants, bestowing on them [estates] in Great Novgorod.[248]

The same year on the sixteenth of May Bishop Gerasimus of
Kolomna passed away in the Monastery of St. Paphnutius. On the
twenty-eighth of the same month, Wednesday, at the eleventh hour

246. Frederick III Habsburg, Emperor of "the Holy Roman Empire
of the German Nation."

247. Nicholas von Poppel, a German knight, visited Russia first in
1486 and then as the ambassador of Emperor Frederick III in 1489. Frederick III offered Ivan III a king's crown but Ivan III declined it, considering
his title higher than a royal one.

248. In *Litsevoi svod* the deportation is mentioned of 7,000 *zhitii* persons. This information is contained only in the *Litsevoi svod* redaction of
this *Chronicle*. The eight other redactions which are quoted in *PSRL*, Vol.
XII, speak only of one thousand as having been deported. Perhaps this is
a confusion in the numbers cited by the chronicler.

1490   of the day, His Holiness Metropolitan Gerontius passed away and was buried in the Cathedral Church of the Annunication of the Most Pure, on its left side.

ABOUT VIATKA

On the eleventh of June of the same spring Grand Prince Ivan Vasilievich of all Russia sent his army against [the people of] Viatka because of their disloyalty. And there were Prince Daniil Vasilievich Shchenia, Grigorii Vasilievich Morozov, and other voevodas with large forces. They marched, captured cities, and brought the people of Viatka to pledge their fealty on the cross [to Ivan III]; and the Arskii people were brought to pledge their fealty.[249] The leading people of Viatka with their wives and children were forced to emigrate, as well as the Arskii princes, and then [the voevodas] returned home. The Grand Prince settled the rural people from the Viatka land in [the region of] Borovsk and Kremenets, and endowed them with lands; the Viatka merchants were settled in Dmitrov; and the Arskii princes were well treated by the Grand Prince, who let them return to their land, while the conspirators received capital punishment.

The same year on the ninth of August, the day the Holy Apostle Matthew is remembered, they consecrated the Church of the Annunication of the Most Pure Mother of God in the estate of the Grand Prince's palace.

On the twentieth of the same month when the holy prophet Samuel is remembered, the Chapel of St. Basil of Cesarea, within the Cathedral of the Annunication, was consecrated.

In the Year 6998 [1490]. The Hungarian King Matthias passed away. He had a treaty of concord, peace, and brotherhood with Grand Prince [Ivan III]. The Roman King Maximilian[250] wanted to bring the land of the Hungarian Kingdom under his rule, but the lords of Hungary and the entire land did not want him. Then Maximilian sent his forces against Belgrade in Hungary and oc-

---

249. "Arskii people": a small Finno-Ugric tribe in the region of Viatka which was ruled by the latter's princes. Viatka, itself, used to be a *de facto* independent Russian republic.

250. Maximilian, King of Germany (1486-1514), the son of Emperor Frederick III. Maximilian was Emperor of the Holy Roman Empire of the German Nation from 1493-1514. The treaty between him and Ivan III was concluded in 1491.

cupied it; but the lords of Hungary sent [their emissaries] to Vladi-   **1490**
slav, King of Bohemia, the son of King Kasimir of Poland; and
they [the lords] took him [Vladislav] from the Bohemian Kingdom
[of the Czechs] to the Kingdom of Hungary. The Roman King
Maximilian made a peace treaty with Vladislav: he gave up Belgrade to Vladislav, but Vienna and the entire Austrian land remained under Maximilian.

The same fall in December Prince Dimitrii Fedorovich Vorotynskii came with his own patrimony [from Lithuania] to Moscow
to serve Grand Prince Ivan Vasilievich, and gave up his service to
Lithuanian [and Polish] King Kasimir. The same year Prince Ivan
Mikhailovich Peremyshl'skii came to the Grand Prince, and with
him were Prince Ivan Belevskii with his brothers, Prince Andrei
and Prince Vasilii; and they came to serve [Ivan III] with their
patrimonies, and they relinquished their service to King Kasimir.

The same winter the brother of Grand Princess Sofia, by the
name of Andreas [Paleologue], came from Rome to Moscow. He
was the son of Thomas, Despot of Morea; and with him came the
Grand Prince's ambassadors, Princes Dmitrio and Manuel, the son
of Giovanni Ralo [Paleologue]. And they brought with them to the
Grand Prince the master physician, Leon the Jew, from Venice, as
well as architects, builders, gunmakers, and silversmiths.

ABOUT THE PASSING OF GRAND PRINCE IVAN IVANOVICH

The same winter on the seventh of the month of March at the
eighth hour of the night, from Saturday to Sunday, pious and
Christ-loving Grand Prince Ivan, the son of Grand Prince Ivan [III]
Vasilievich of all Russia, passed away. [He] was the eldest [son] of
Ivan III by his first [wife], Grand Princess Maria, daughter of Grand
Prince Boris Aleksandrovich of Tver'. He was buried in the [Cathe-
dral] Church of Archangel Michael of Moscow, where his forefathers are also buried. And altogether he lived for thirty-two years
and twenty days. And he was ill with *kamchuga* in the legs.[251]

When the master physician, Leon the Jew, saw him, he boasted,
telling Grand Prince Ivan Vasilievich, his father, "I will cure your
son, the Grand Prince, from this disease. And if I don't cure him,

251. *Kamchuga* was the medieval Russian name for various diseases
usually afflicting the legs: gout, infectious rash, and carbuncles. Most probably, in this case it was a carbuncle with subsequent blood poisoning.

1490 you will order me punished with capital punishment." Grand Prince Ivan Vasilievich accepted his speech as the truth and ordered him to treat his son, the Grand Prince. And the physician began to treat him and gave him various potions made of herbs to drink, and started burning his body with glass containers, pouring very hot water into them; and from this treatment he became worse and died. And Grand Prince Ivan Vasilievich ordered this master physician, Leon, arrested, and after forty days[252] of the death of his son, the Grand Prince, he ordered him executed and his head cut off. And they cut off his head on the twenty-second of April at the Bolvanovie.

On the ninth of July the Grand Prince's ambassador, Iurii Trakhaniote, the Greek, came from Rome; and together with him came the ambassador of the Roman King Maximilian, the son of Emperor Frederick, whose name was Giorgio Della Torre, bringing a treaty of concord, friendship, and brotherhood.[253]

In the same year on the fifth of August a son was born to Grand Prince Ivan Vasilievich, and he was named Andrei.

The same year on the nineteenth of August Grand Prince Ivan Vasilievich received with honor Giorgio Della Torre, ambassador of the Roman King Maximilian, and allowed him to return to his Sovereign. And together with him the Grand Prince sent to the Roman King Maximilian, son of [Emperor] Frederick [III], his ambassadors, Iurii Trakhaniote the Greek and his *diak*, Vasilii Kuleskin, to conclude a treaty of love and peace [with the King].

The same year Pietro Antonio the Italian completed building two gun towers, one at the Borovitskii Gate and the other at St. Constantine and St. Helen Gate. And he completed building a wall from the Sviblovskii gun tower to the Borovitskii Gate. [254]

252. In the Orthodox church the forty days after burial are a period of great mourning.

253. This Imperial ambassador, Giorgio Della Torre, who was also the German feudal prince of Turn and Taxis, was an outstanding diplomatic, political, and ecclesiastical person who later became the Bishop of Segovia. He wrote for Archbishop Genadius of Novgorod detailed instructions about the methods of the Inquisition: how to treat, punish, and execute heretics. According to these instructions the Novgorodian heretics of the sect of Judaizers were subsequently punished and executed, following very exactly even the processional rite of the Inquisition. This was the first instance of Western religious influence in Russia.

254. In *Obol.* only, not in *Ioasaf.*

In the Year 6999 [1491]. On the twelfth of September Zosima, **1491** Archimandrite of St. Simeon [Monastery], was elected Metropolitan, and on the twenty-sixth of September, Sunday, he was enthroned as Metropolitan of all Russia.

On the twenty-eighth of the same month Urus Bogatyr, [envoy of] Hussein, Sultan of Dzhagatai, came to the Grand Prince for [a treaty of] peace and friendship.[255]

The same fall, on the seventeenth of October, by order of Grand Prince Ivan [III] of all Russia, His Holiness Zosima, Metropolitan of all Russia, Archbishop Tikhon of Rostov, and Bishops Nifontus of Suzdal', Simeon of Riazan', Bassian of Tver', Prokhorus of Sarai, and Philotheus of Perm, with archimandrites, abbots, and the entire Sacred Council of the Russian Metropolia discussed in sessions of the Council [the cases] of monk Zakharius, Novgorodian archpriest Gabriel, priest Dionysius of [the Cathedral of] Archangel Michael, priest Maximus of St. John's Church, priest Basil of the [Cathedral of the] Intercession of Our Lady, deacon Macarius of [the Church of] St. Nicholas, deacon Gridia of [the Church of] Sts. Boris and Gleb, a certain Vasiuk, brother-in-law of priest Dionysios, and of the deacon Samukha of [the Church of] St. Nicholas. And Metropolitan Zosima, the bishops and the entire Sacred Council, having investigated their heretical teaching and having received the materials supplied by [Archbishop] Genadius [of Novgorod], which were sent to the [late] Metropolitan Gerontius, decided to excommunicate them from the holy church and to send them to be incarcerated.

THE MOSCOW COUNCIL AGAINST NOVGORODIAN HERETICS[256]

At that time in Great Novgorod there occurred, under the influence of a Jew, an evil and great confusion in the minds of many weak people. Obviously, the devil, himself, settled in their minds and, heeding his evil flattery, many obeyed him and became dissolute in their minds, deviating from the truth and following

255. Dzhagatai was a Turko-Mongol state in present Chinese Sinkiang and the eastern part of present Russian Central Asia. The name derives from that of the second son of Genghis Khan, who, after the division of his father's empire, received this portion of it.

256. Here is provided a more detailed text of the same Council as it is found in *Litsevoi svod*. The exact origin of this heretical sect is still not quite clear.

1491   the fables of evil people. There heretics spoke untruth about God, [spread] all manner of Judaic and astrological teaching, and taught the witchcraft of pagan people; and then they broke away from the grace and truth of the Gospel. And they did not believe in the Incarnation of Our Jesus Christ, the Son of Lord God from the Most Pure and Immaculate Maria. And they did not believe or venerate the holy icons and did not have any veneration for the [Eucharistic] Body and Blood of Christ; and they committed many other heresies and indecent deeds about which it is not even possible to write. The names of these dissolute [and arrested] persons were Zakharius the monk; archpriest Gabriel of [the Cathedral of] Holy Sophia [in Novgorod]; priest Dionysius of [the Church of] the Archangel [in Moscow]; priest Maximus of the Church of St. John; priest Basil of the Church of the Intercession of Our Lady; deacon Makarius of the Church of St. Nicholas; Gridia, *diak* of the Church of St. Nicholas; and others with them. And all of them kept their evil heresy in secrecy. Ivashka Maksimov and the other Ivashka, the son of archpriest Alexis, however, escaped [arrest]. But their evil design remained unhidden from Archbishop Genadius [of Novgorod] because this Archbishop was given wisdom by God. Thanks to his many worthy deeds he, as a clever fisherman with various nets, found out their evilminded deeds and their evil mysteries, and he learned in detail about all their God-rejected heresies; and he tried in every way to bring them to order. And seeing that their hearts were hard and their ways rebellious, and realizing that he could not bring them to order alone, he sent a message about them to Moscow, to His Holiness, his lord and his [hierarchical] father, Metropolitan Zosima of all Russia. Their rotten philosophizing came also to the ears of pious Grand Prince Ivan Vasilievich, Autocrat of all Russia, himself, on whose order a council about them was summoned in Moscow at that time.

And so in the same year 6999 [1491], on the seventeenth of October, by order of pious and Christ-loving Ivan Vasilievich, Sovereign of all Russia and Autocrat of other [lands] and defender of true Orthodoxy, there was a Council in the court of the Metropolitan, and at this Council were present Grand Prince Vasilii Ivanovich, who represented his father and Autocrat; His Holiness Metropolitan Zosima, Metropolitan of all Russia; and Tikhonus, Archbishop of Rostov; and Bishops Nephontus of Suzdal', Simeon of Riazan', Bassian of Tver', Prokhorus of Sarai, Philotheus of

Perm'; Abbot Athanasius of the Monastery of the Holy Trinity [and   **1491**
St. Sergius]; and the hermits and most virtuous elders, Paisius [Vel-
ichkovskii] and Nilus [of Sora]; and many archimandrites and abbots, archpriests and priests, deacons and elders, and all others of
the Sacred Council of the Russian Metropolia. And so they assembled to determine the truth and investigate these corrupters of the
Christian faith, shameful before God, the heretics of Novgorod;
Zakharius the monk, his comrades and accomplices, who wanted
to corrupt the pure and immaculate Orthodox faith which confesses
Our God, Jesus Christ, Glorified in the Trinity; and they wanted
to ruin the Christian flock of Orthodox Christianity which they
could not overcome and defeat but against which they were crushed
as on a stone, and were, themselves, smashed and defeated; and
their entire sophisticated wisdom was destroyed although they
seduced many simple people with their evil heresies. They were
brought to the Council and were asked concerning their heretical
crimes, but these accursed ones were first insidious and tried to
hide their lawlessness, denying that they belonged to a heresy. But
when they were exposed by irrefutable witnesses, then these accursed ones spilled their entire poison of their madness and so they
exposed themselves and their apostate deeds. And they began
speaking in a most unseemly way, saying of Jesus Christ, Son of
God, "How can God come to earth and be born from a Virgin like
a man? There is a difference: as a prophet, he is equal to Moses;
but he is not equal to God and Father." And they did not believe
either His Nativity from the Immaculate Virgin or in His Resurrection, and they did not worship Our Lord, Jesus Christ, Son of God,
as He was represented on the icon according to the image of man;
nor did they [venerate] the icons of the Most Pure [Theotkos] or
His holy saints. But they villified and abused [the icons], dese-
crating them, saying, "They have been made by the hand of man.
They have mouths but do not speak," and said other things: "Those
who created them and who put their hopes in them are similar to
them." And they celebrated the divine service in an unseemly way,
eating and drinking but not considering [it] as the Body of Christ,
but only simple bread, and the Blood of Christ as simple wine,
beer, or water. And they confessed many other unseemly heresies
against the rule of the Holy Apostles, the Holy Fathers; but they
adhered primarily to the Old Testament, celebrating Easter according to the custom of the Jews; they ate meat and drank milk on

1491 Wednesday and Friday; and they committed and spoke many other unseemly deeds and words which cannot even be written down. And they seduced many simple people with their evil heresies. And thereafter they entered a state of frenzy as if speechless; during the Council in the presence of the Grand Prince, the Metropolitan, archbishops and bishops, and before the entire Sacred Council of the Russian Metropolia, they denied their heresies and their evil deeds and their minds were in a state of frenzy. Grand Prince Ivan Vasilievich, Sovereign of all Russia and Autocrat of many other [lands], pious and Christ-loving, true pillar of Orthodoxy, whose attitude was like the second pious Emperor Constantine, together with his spiritual father, His Holiness Metropolitan Zosima of all Russia, and with the archbishops and bishops, and with the entire Sacred Council of the Russian Metropolitan, investigated these evil heresies according to the true documents of Archbishop Genadius which he sent to Metropolitan Gerontius, and on the basis of witnesses from Moscow made a decision about these heretics. The Novgorodian archpriest Gabriel, Zakharius the monk, priest Dionysius, and their aforementioned fellow-thinkers were excommunicated, cast out from the clergy, defrocked, and sent into imprisonment, some to prisons and some to monasteries.

And they [the members of the Council] confirmed their faith in the holy, immaculate Orthodox Christian faith, and glorified the Father, singing praises to the Son and venerating the Holy Spirit, confessing the Trinity of the Unity and the Unity of the Trinity with their hearts and with their lips, ever and ever. Amen.

The venerable Joseph, abbot of Volok-Lamskii, wrote epistles in which he exposed these God-fighting heretics of Novgorod, and other heresies, and this is a special book written for the affirmation of Orthodoxy.[257]

257. The decision of the Council of 1491 was a decisive condemnation of the so-called Heresy of the Judaizers. According to official sources and, especially, to the report of Archbishop Genadius of Novgorod and Abbot Joseph (Sanin) of the Volok-Lamskii Monastery—whose messages were collected in a book called *Prosvetitel'* (last edition, Kazan, 1896)—the initiator of the heresy was a Crimean or Kievan Jew named Skhariia (Zekharia), who went to Novgorod in 1470 and there converted a number of clergymen and lay people to his faith. Contemporary scholars believe that the movement did not adhere strictly to the Mosaic faith but was influenced by it, and also contained a number of humanistic and rationalistic features. In any case, they denied the divinity of Christ (as later did the Unitarian, or

The same fall, Thursday, the eighteenth of November, Abra-   **1491**
ham, abbot of [the Monastery of] Ugresh, was consecrated Bishop
of Kolomna by His Holiness, Metropolitan Zosima of all Russia.

The same spring in March Pietro Antonio the Italian laid the
foundation for two gun towers, one at the St. Flor Gate and the
other at the St. Nicholas Gate; and the foundation of the gun tower
of St. Nicholas was not laid on the old foundation. And he [began
to build] the wall to the Neglinnaia River.

ABOUT THE ORE

The same spring on the twenty-sixth day of March the Grand
Prince sent the Germans, Johann and Wiktor, to Pechora to look
for silver ore, and together with them were sent Andrei Petrov and
Vasilii Ivanov, son of Boltin.[258]

[WAR AMONG THE TATARS]

The same spring, in the month of May, Grand Prince Ivan
Vasilievich received news that the khans of the Horde, Seid Ahmet
and Shig Ahmet, were marching with their forces against the
Crimean Khan Mengli-Girei. In order to help the Crimean Khan
Mengli-Girei, the Grand Prince sent into the *pole* against the Horde
his voevodas, Prince Petr Nikitovich Obolenskii and Prince
Ivan Mikhailovich Repnia-Obolenskii, and with them many junior
boyars from his retinue; [he also sent] Satylgan, son of Khan
Merdulat, with his ulans and princes; and all the Cossacks, together

---

Anti-Trinitarian, teaching of Socinus, among others); they rejected the
Orthodox system of hierarchy, rites and Sacraments; and they did not
venerate icons. This sect did not endeavor to conduct open proselytizing
aimed at wide groups of the population, but, rather, formed small, secret,
societies while overtly adhering—especially, those clergymen who joined
them—to rituals and dogma of Orthodoxy. Some of them moved to Moscow, where they gained such influential supporters as Princess Elena of
Walachia (daughter-in-law of Ivan III and wife of Grand Prince Ivan
Ivanovich, son and co-ruler of Ivan III) and the powerful and brilliant
diplomat, Ivan Fedor Kuritsyn, with his brother, Volk Kuritsyn, as well as
several clergymen and other persons. They were able to influence even
Ivan III, who sympathized with their ideas concerning secularization of
church lands, and for decades he was reluctant to oppose them energeti-
cally. Apparently, also, Metropolitan Zosima, himself, sympathized with
the sect and was later forced to resign. See Kartashov, Vol. I, pp. 484–89.

258. This paragraph is from *Litsevoi svod.*

1491   with his voevodas.[259] And he also commanded the Khan of Kazan',
Mohammed Amin, to send his voevodas with all his forces, together
with the Prince [Satylgan] and the voevodas of the Grand Prince.
And he commanded [his brothers], Prince Andrei Vasilievich and
Prince Boris Vasilievich, to send their voevodas with their forces,
together with his own voevodas of the Grand Prince, but Prince
Andrei Vasilievich did not send either voevodas or troops. The
Grand Prince's voevodas met Prince Satylgan in the *polé*, as well as
Abash-Ulan and Burash, voevodas of the Khan of Kazan'. And
soon thereafter they were joined by Prince Boris' voevodas, and
they marched altogether against the Horde. The khans of the
Horde, hearing that the Grand Prince had sent large forces into
the *polé*, took fright and returned from Perekop while the Grand
Prince's forces went home without having fought.

The same spring, on order of Grand Prince Ivan Vasilievich,
Archimandrite Athanasius of [the Monastery of] St. Saviour laid
the foundation for a stone Church of the Transfiguration of Our
Lord Jesus Christ in the town of Novoe.

On the twenty-third of May, a Monday, the entire city of Vladimir burned with [its] suburbs. Inside the city even the church of
the Monastery of the Nativity of the Most Pure [Virgin] burned.
In it the relics of Grand Prince Aleksandr Iaroslavovich[260] also
burned. Altogether, nine churches in the city and thirteen in the
suburbs burned, and the Christian people of the city perished in
great misery.

The same year in June the entire city of Uglich burned, and
also [its] suburbs beyond the Volga burned; and there more than
five hundred households burned and fifteen churches.

The same year on the twenty-eighth of June the Grand Prince
let Stetsko, envoy of Stefan [Prince of Moldavia][261] go home, and
together with him the Grand Prince sent Skurata Zinovievich to
Stefan to Walachia, by way of Lithuania.[262]

The same year in the Simonovs' estate near the St. Nicholas
Gate the construction was completed of a stone Church of the
Presentation in the Temple of the Most Holy Mother of God.

259. *"Cossack"* at that time denoted a runaway or independent warrior,
usually from some Turkic tribe.
260. St. Alexander Nevskii.
261. In *Nik.*, Walachia.
262. Actually, Moldavia.

The same year the Italian architects, Marco and Pietro Antonio,   **1492**
completed construction on the Square [in Moscow] of the Grand
Prince's large palace. The same year construction of a stone fortress
in Great Novgorod was completed. And it was built on the old
foundation.

The same year Pietro Antonio the Italian completed construction of a gun tower on St. Frol.

The same year on the thirtieth day of August there came to
Moscow the Grand Prince's envoys to the Roman King Maximilian—
Iurii Trakhaniote the Greek and *diak* Vasilii Kuleskin—and together with them an ambassador named Giorgio Della Torre came
to Grand Prince Ivan Vasilievich from the Roman King Maximilian,
son of the Emperor Frederick.[263] And they brought from the King
a charter of agreement with a golden seal; and they gave him [the
King], also, a charter with the Grand Prince's golden seal. They let
the King pledge on this charter of agreement; and Maximilian's
envoy also let the Grand Prince give a pledge on this charter of
agreement.

In the Year 7000 [1492]. On the twentieth of September Grand
Prince Ivan Vasilievich of all Russia renounced his pledge given to
his brother, Prince Andrei Vasilievich [the elder], because of the
latter's treason. He betrayed [Ivan III] and, despite his pledge on
the cross, plotted together with his other brothers—Prince Iurii,
Prince Boris, and Prince Andrei the younger—against their senior
brother, Ivan [III] Vasilievich; he [Prince Andrei] had them pledge
on the cross that they would stand together against their senior
brother, the Grand Prince. And he sent his missives to Lithuania
to King Kasimir making alliance with the latter against the Grand
Prince. And together with his brother, Prince Boris, he had already
given up once[264] his [vassal obligation] to the Grand Prince; and
that time he sent his missive to Khan Ahmet of the Great Horde,
inviting him to march with his army into the Russian land against
the Grand Prince. And he did not send his voevodas and his forces
to the Grand Prince against the Khan of the Horde. In doing all
this, he betrayed the Grand Prince and broke his pledge on the cross.

Therefore the Grand Prince ordered him arrested and impris-

263. Giorgio Della Torre, King Maximilian's ambassador, sojourned
in Novgorod on his way to Moscow. See also footnote 253 in the year 1490.
264. In 1480.

1492   oned in the court of the Treasury in Moscow. That day he sent to Uglich Prince Vasilii Ivanovich, grandson of [Prince] Iurii, with many minor boyars, in order to arrest and imprison in Pereiaslavl' his [Andrei's] children, Prince Dmitrii and Prince Ivan. And so they did thus.

The same year in September, when [on the twenty-fifth of September] St. Sergius is remembered, the Grand Prince transferred the market from [the Monastery of] the Holy Trinity [and St. Sergius] to the town of Radonezh.

The same year Grand Prince Ivan Vasilievich sent [his officials] to the land of Tver' to survey their lands according to the Muscovite way. In Tver' the survey was conducted by Prince Fedor Olabysh; in Staritsa, by Boris Kutuzov; in Zubtsev and Opoka, by Dmitrii Peshkov; in Klin, by Petr Loban Zabolotskii; in Kholm and Novy Gorodok, by Andrei Karamyshev; and in Kashin, by Vasilii Karamyshev.

The same fall on the twentieth of October there came to Moscow Andrei Petrov and Vasilii Ivanov Boltin, whom the Grand Prince had sent with the Germans, Johann and Wiktor, to the Pechora land to seek out silver ore. They found silver and copper ore in the Grand Prince's patrimony, on the river Tsilma, not far—a half day's travel—from the Kozma River and seven days' travel from the Pechora River. And the very place where they found it is ten *versts* distant. From Moscow to that place it is three and a half thousand *versts* [*sic!?*]. And they found the ore on the eighth of August of the year 7000 [1492].[265]

The same year on the thirteenth of November, on the Simanov estate near the St. Nickolas Gate, the Church of the Presentation of the Most Holy Theotokos was consecrated.

The same month of November Prince Vasilii Romodanovskii came to the Grand Prince from the Crimea, and with him arrived the envoy of the Crimean Khan Mengli-Girei.

The same fall on the eighteenth of November Giorgio Della Torre came to Grand Prince Ivan Vasilievich of all Russia; he was the ambassador of the Roman King Maximilian, son of Emperor Frederick. And he let the Grand Prince pledge on this charter of agreement.

265. This was the first Russian ore to be found beyond the Volga River, not far from the Ural Mountains.

The same winter in February, on order of Grand Prince Ivan **1492**
Vasilievich, His Holiness Metropolitan Zosima and Archbishop
Genadius of Great Novgorod and Pskov turned over from the
Metropolia, and, from the archbishopric of Novgorod, their
churches in the city and suburbs of Vologda, to the Permian diocese
of Bishop Philotheus of Perm.

The same winter an envoy named Murat came to the Grand
Prince from Prince Alexander of the Iberian land.[266] In the same
month of February, Skurat Zinovievich came to the Grand Prince
from Walachia [Moldavia], and with him came Mushat, envoy of
Stefan, voevoda of Walachia [Moldavia].

The same spring in March the Grand Prince allowed the Crimean envoy to return home and, together with him, he sent Loban
Kolychev to the Crimea to Khan Mengli-Girei.

The same spring, Thursday, the fifth of April, the Grand Prince
left his old palace in the estate of Prince Ivan Iurievich, and moved
into the new one. The Grand Princess Sofia moved together with
him and with his children; his daughter-in-law, Grand Princess
Elena; and Prince Dmitrii, his grandson. And he ordered that the
old palace be torn apart and to begin building a new stone one.

On the sixth of April the Grand Prince let the envoy, Stefan
Mushat, return home to his sovereign, Stefan of Walachia [Mol-
davia]. Also, in April Grand Prince Ivan Vasilievich released Geor-
gio Della Torre, ambassador of the Roman King Maximilian, and
together with him Grand Prince Ivan Vasilievich sent Iruii
Trakhaniote the Greek, Mikhail Kliapik, and Ivan Volk Kuritsyn,
his own ambasaadors, to the Roman King Maximilian.

The same spring the Grand Prince sent his *diak*, Vasilii
Kuleshin, to build a wooden fortress in [the city of] Vladimir, according to the plan of Vasilii Mamyrev, and they built it in two
months. The same spring on order of Grand Prince Ivan Vasilievich
they laid the foundation for a square fortress on the German [Livo-
nian] border on the river Narva, on Devichii Hill, in the marshes,
and named it Ivangorod.

The same spring on the seventeenth of the month of May
Giovanni Salvatore the Italian, the tonsured chaplain of the White
monks of the Augustinian Order, gave up his religion and his

266. "Iberian" was the Russian name for Georgia in the Caucasus.
The Georgians were looking for Russian aid against the Turks and Persians,
and were prepared to accept Russian suzerainty.

1493   monastic vows and married, taking to wife [the daughter of] Aleksei Зсiнов. Аnd thе Grand Prince presented him with one village.

The same spring on the twenty-third of May Andrei Kasimir, the King of Poland and Grand Prince of Lithuania, passed away; his son, Alexander, ascended to the throne of the Grand Principality of Lithuania, and his [other] son, [Ian] Albrecht, ascended to the throne of the Kingdom of Poland. And his senior son, Vladislav, still during his [father's] life was invited to [rule] the Kingdom of Bohemia, and from the Kingdom of Bohemia he was invited to [rule] the Kingdom of Hungaria.[267]

The same summer on the tenth of the month of June, two hundred and twenty Tatar Cossacks from the Horde, led by Temesh, came to raid, and they sacked the district of Aleksin on the river Voshan; and thereafter they went home. They were pursued by the Grand Prince's troops, under Fedor Koltovskii and Goriain Sidorov. Altogether there were sixty and four [Russian] men, and they began to fight in the *polé* between Trudy and Bystrye Sosny. And in the Grand Prince's pursuing detachment forty people were killed, and sixty Tatars were [also] killed in this battle; and the remaining wounded Tatars died on their way, retreating to the Horde.

The same summer [in Novgorod] a wooden palace for the Grand Prince was built [in the Kremlin] on the Iaroslavl' estate behind [the Church of] the Archangel [Michael]. The same summer [in Moscow] they laid a foundation [for a stone wall] from the St. Frol gun tower to the St. Nicholas gun tower; and they laid a foundation for a new gun tower over the [river] Neglinnaia, with a secret tunnel. The same summer in the month of August Grand Prince Ivan Vasilievich sent his voevoda, Prince Fedor Telepnia Obolenskii, with a strong force, against the city of Mtsensk because of the latter's misdeeds; and they took the city of Mtsensk and campaigned in their land; and they captured their voevoda, Boris Semenov [grand] son of Aleksandr, and many others, and brought them to Moscow.

In the Year 7001 [1493]. In September the Grand Prince sent to the Crimea to Khan Mengli-Girei of the Crimea his envoy, Konstantin Zabolotskii; and he sent Ivan Andreevich Pleshcheev to Walachia.

267. Actually, Vladislav became the king of both kingdoms, of Bohemia and of Hungary.

The same fall on the sixth day of October *Pan* Stanislav **1493**
Glebovich came to Grand Prince Ivan Vasilievich from Prince Alex-
ander of Lithuania [to discuss] the border problem. The same fall
in November Iushka Ielizarov fled from Lithuania and joined the
service of the Grand Prince. The same year there came to the
Grand Prince [from Lithuania], to serve him, Prince Semion
Fedorovich Vorotynskii and his brother's son, Prince Ivan
Mikhailovich, with their patrimonies. And on the way to the Grand
Prince, Prince Semion occupied the Lithuanian cities of Serpeesk
and Mezechesk in the name of the Grand Prince.[268]

Thereafter to the cities of Serpeesk and Mezechesk there came
against them *Pan* Iurii Glebovich, voevoda of the city of Smolensk
of Grand Prince [Alexander] of Lithuania, and Prince Semion
Ivanovich Mozhaiskii.[269] They came with strong forces, and the
citizens were unable to resist them, and surrendered their cities.
Learning of this, Grand Prince Ivan Vasilievich sent against them
his sister's son, Prince Fedor Vasilievich of Riazan', and his own
voevodas, Prince Mikhail Ivanovich Kolyshko and Prince Aleksandr
Vasilievich Obolenskii; and with them [he sent] other voevodas with
strong forces, as well as Inka Izmailov, voevoda of Grand Prince
Ivan Vasilievich of Riazan', also with strong forces.

Learning of the Grand Prince's strong army moving against
them, *Pan* Iurii Glebovich, voevoda of Smolensk, and Prince Semion
Ivanovich Mozhaiskii left their many princes and *pany* in the fortresses of those cities to withstand the siege, while they, themselves,
took fright and fled to Smolensk. When the army of Grand Prince
Ivan Vasilievich arrived at the city of Mezechesk they [that is, the
Lithuanian commanders] took fright, could not withstand them,
and gave up their cities. In the city of Krevets [the voevodas of
Ivan III] captured the *okolnichii*[270] and many other princes and *pany*

268. All the towns and cities mentioned herewith—Vorotynsk, Serpeesk, Mezechesk, Mozhaisk, and other smaller places—are located south-
east and east of Kaluga and were populated by Russians and ruled by
Russian Orthodox princes claiming to be descendants of Prince Vladimir
of Kiev. In the early fourteenth century their lands were annexed by the
princes of Lithuania.

269. The title, *"Pan,"* designated an important noble magnate in
Lithuania and Poland.

270. *Okolnichii*: a rank of high official in the civil or military service
which was just under the rank of boyar. The okolnichii was usually a
member of the Boyar Duma.

1493 from Lithuania and Smolensk who were in the advance forces of Grand Prince Alexander [of Lithuania]. And they brought the *zemskii* people[271] and the *chernyi* people[272] to pledge to Grand Prince [Ivan III].

From thence the Grand Prince's army moved toward the city of Serpeesk, but they began fighting fiercely [with the city] and [the latter] did not want to surrender the fortress. The voevodas of Grand Prince [Ivan III] ordered their troops to besiege the city courageously with their artillery and harquebuses. They besieged the city, took it by force and inside the city captured Ivan Fedorov, the son of Pliuskov of Smolensk, and many other princes and *pany*, both Lithuanians and from Smolensk, from the retinue of Grand Prince Alexander of Lithuania. They sacked and burned the fortress and brought the *zemskii* people to pledge [their fealty to Ivan III]. Marching from thence, they took the fortress of Opakov, burned it and brought the *zemskii* and *chernyi* people to pledge [fealty to Ivan III].

And so they returned, bringing to Moscow the Lithuanians and people of Smolensk who were resisting the siege [in Serpeesk and Mezechesk], as well as other leading people of these cities; and the Grand Prince commanded that they be arrested and imprisoned in his own cities. At the same time Grand Prince Ivan Vasilievich sent his voevodas to campaign around the city of Viaz'ma; they were [under the command of] Prince Daniil Vasilievich Shcheniia. And they marched thither, captured the city of Viaz'ma, brought the local people to pledge [their fealty to Ivan III], and they took the princes and *pany* of Viaz'ma to Moscow. The Grand Prince granted them [service estates in the land of] Viaz'ma and ordered them to be in his service.

The same year Prince Mikhail Romanovich Mezetskii came [from Lithuania] into the service of the Grand Prince, and he brought [forcefully] with him his two brothers, Prince Semion and Prince Peter. The Grand Prince sent the latter under arrest to Iaroslavl', and granted Prince Mikhail his [Mikhail's] own patrimony, and commanded him to be in his service.

---

271. "*Zemskii*" people: free, but not noble and not obliged to render military service. They were largely urban middle class.

272. *Chernyi* people: taxable persons and sometimes lower-class urban commoners.

The same year on the eleventh of June there came from the **1493**
Crimea to serve Grand Prince [Ivan III] the Tatar Prince Abdul
Letif, son of Ibrahim, Khan of Kazan'. And he came together with
the Grand Prince's ambassador, Loban Kolychev.

The same winter Prokhorus, Bishop of Sarai,[273] gave up his
diocese and went from Krutitsa to the Monastery of Bogoiavlenié.[274]

The same winter on the thirty-first of January the Grand Prince
ordered the execution of Prince Ivan Lukomskii and the Polish
Catholic interpreter, Mathias, and they were burned in a cage on
the bank [of the Moscow River] below the bridge. And he also
ordered the corporal punishment of two brothers from Smolensk,
Bogdan and Olekhna Selevin. Bogdan died from the punishment,
while Olekhna was beheaded. This was done because they had been
sending their man, Volynets, with messages and intelligence to
Grand Prince Alexander of Lithuania. Prince Ivan Lukomskii was
sent from Lithuania to Grand Prince [Ivan III] by the Polish King
Kasimir under the pretext of joining the Grand Prince's service.
And he [King Kasimir] let him pledge on the cross that he would
either kill or poison Grand Prince [Ivan III]; and he sent his poison
with him, and this poison was found on him. Prince Ivan Lukomskii
then denounced Prince Fedor Belskii, saying that the latter wanted
to flee to Lithuania and abandon Grand Prince [Ivan III]. Therefore
the Grand Prince put Prince Fedor under arrest and sent him to
Galich to be imprisoned.

The same spring on Palm Sunday the entire city of Kostroma
was burned. The same spring on the sixteenth of April, on the day
of *Radunitsa*[275] the fortress of Moscow [Kremlin] burned inside and
there remained only the new palace of the Grand Prince behind
[the Monastery of the Miracles of] the Archangel [Michael]. And
in the Monastery of Miracles everything valuable burned.

273. At the beginning of the fifteenth century the Bishop of Sarai,
former capital of the Golden Horde, was transferred to Moscow and became the Metropolitan's suffragan bishop, with the title of "Bishop of
Sarai" (*Sarskii*) of the Don and Krutitsa, the small city near Moscow where
he officially resided.

274. *Bogoiavlenié*: Presentation of Our Lord of the Magi, Epiphany;
the holiday is celebrated on January 6.

275. *Radunitsa*: former East Slavic pagan holidays in honor of ancestors. After Christianization, Russians observed it with the Christian idea
of praying for their deceased parents and relatives. It was observed on the
first Sunday after Easter, or the subsequent Monday or Tuesday.

1493   The same spring on the third of May an envoy came from Konrad, Grand Prince of the Mazovian land, named Ivan.[276]

The same spring on the fourth of May elder Siluan, former abbott of [the Monastery of] Ugresh, was consecrated Bishop of Sarai, of the Don and Krutitsa, by His Holiness, Metropolitan Zosima.

The same summer in May the Grand Prince sent Manuel Angelos the Greek and Daniil Mamyrev to Venice and to Milan. The same month of May Grand Prince Ivan Vasilievich let Ivan, envoy of Mazovia, return to his land, and with him he sent his own envoys, Osanchiuk Zabolotskii and Tretiak Vasiliev, the son of Dalmat, to Konrad, Prince of Mazovia.

The same summer in June the envoy of Johann, King of Denmark, came to the Grand Prince from Denmark [*iz Nemets*] with an offer of peace and brotherhood[277]; the Grand Prince honored the envoy and let him return to his land. And together with him the Grand Prince sent his own envoys, Dimitrii Ralo the Greek and Dimitrii Zaitsev, to Johann, King of Denmark. The same summer Andrei Olekhnovich and Voitko Ianovich Klochko came from Lithuania, from Grand Prince Alexander.

The same summer on order of Grand Prince Ivan Vasilievich a log fortress was built in Velikie Luki on the foundation of the old one.

The same summer on order of Grand Prince Ivan Vasilievich the churches and estates beyond the Neglinnaia River were torn down so as to create an unoccupied area of 220 yards from the [Kremlin] walls to the next estates [for the purpose of defense]. The same summer on order of the Grand Prince a moat was dug from the Borovitskii gun tower to the Moscow River.

The same year the Tatar Cossacks from the Horde raided the Riazan' land. They took three towns and thereafter rapidly withdrew.

The same summer on the sixteenth of July, a Tuesday, at the

276. Mazovia: a region in northern Poland just south of the land of the German Teutonic Orders. Mazovians and Russians had common problems of defense against the encroachments of the German Orders of Teutonic and Livonian Knights.

277. "*Iz Nemets*": the Russians called people from Germany and from countries speaking Germanic tongues, "*Nemets.*" Thus, "*Nemets*" ("German") denoted also the people of Scandinavia.

eleventh hour, lightning and thunder struck the big domes of the **1493**
Cathedral Church of the Assumption of the Most Holy Mother of
God in Moscow and burned the wood under the iron [covering the
dome]. And the church's main altar gates were slightly burned,
and a cover on the ambo burned, and two wooden stands were
destroyed at the ambo. The fire on top of the church was quickly
extinguished and, by the grace of God, there was not much damage
done to the church. The same day the storm broke the cross on
top of the Church of the Annunciation of the Most Pure [Mother
of God] in [the city of] Vladimir.

[THE GREAT FIRE IN MOSCOW]

The same month on the twenty-eighth of July, a Sunday, at
the seventh hour of the day, a fire started from candles in the
Church of St. Nicholas on Pesok ["On the Sand"]. And at that time
a violent storm started up and the fire was carried by the wind to
the other side of the Moscow River, to [the Church of] All Saints,
and from thence to the stone Church of St. George beyond the
Neglinnaia [River]. At the same time a tempest began and the fire
began to burn in many places, and the whole suburb beyond the
Neglinnaia River from the Church of the Holy Ghost along the
Chertoroi [brook] up to the Church of Sts. Boris and Gleb on the
Arbat, and to Peter's suburb, burned; beyond the Moscow River,
everything burned from the Church of Holy Sophia to the Church
of St. Joachim and Anna. And from Zarechié the fire started inside
the fortified city [Kremlin] in the palace of the Grand Prince and
Grand Princess, and from thence in the barns and in the Podol[278]
it began to burn, as well as in the new palace of the Grand Prince
behind the [Cathedral of] Archangel [Michael], which burned entirely. And the estate of the Metropolitan burned entirely. And in
the Church of the Most Pure [Theotokos] the altar burned under
the German iron [roof]. And in the inner city all the [wooden] huts
burned because the people had not had time to build houses after
the [last] big fire. The Church of St. John the Precursor near the
Borovitskii Gate burned entirely and collapsed, and a priest there
burned; and the treasury of the Grand Princess [preserved in the
church's basement] burned entirely. The Borovitskii gun tower also
burned, as well as the roof of the fortress wall, and the new wooden

278. *Podol*: usually, a low section of the city near the river.

1494   wall at the St. Nicholas Gate. From the city the fire was carried to the market, and from thence to the suburb along the Moscow River, which burned up to the Church of the Immaculate Conception at the Vostryi section, and up to the old [Church of the Holy] Trinity. Stretenskaia Street burned up to the fields, and the stone Church of the Feast of Purification also burned. And there was great grief among the people. Over two hundred people burned, and an endless amount of goods also burned. And all this burned in one single afternoon, before night. The chronicle writer and old people say that there was not such a conflagration since Moscow was founded. At that time the Grand Prince remained in the peasant homes, in Podkopaev's place, near the Church of St. Nicholas on the Iauza River.

The same year Iurii Trakhaniote the Greek, Mikhailo Klopik, and Ivan Volk Kuritsyn, the Grand Prince's envoys, returned to Moscow from the Roman King Maximilian.

The same summer Metropolitan Zosima built three stone buildings with foundations on his estate.

In the Year 7002 [1494]. In September the city of Riazan' burned entirely. The same fall in October Ivan Andreevich Subota Pleshcheev came from Walachia [Moldavia]; and from the Crimea [came] Konstantin Zabolotskii; and they came by way of the *polé*. And in the *polé* they were robbed by Tatar Cossacks of the Horde.

The same fall on the sixth of November Prince Andrei Vasilievich the elder [brother of Ivan III] passed away; and he had remained in prison in the Treasury court of the Grand Prince in Moscow for two years and forty-seven days; and he was buried in the Church of Archangel Michael in Moscow at the northern door.

On Sunday, the tenth of the same month, the Grand Prince moved into his new palace in the [Kremlin] fortress to live there. After the fire he stayed next to the Podkopaev stables in the peasant's homes.

The sixteenth of the same month the Grand Prince let the Crimean envoy go home, sending with him to the Crimea, to Khan Mengli-Girei, his own envoy, Konstantin Malechkin.

The same winter on the seventeenth of January Lithuanian ambassadors came to Moscow to Grand Prince Ivan Vasilievich from Grand Prince Alexander Andreevich of Lithuania, with a treaty of peace and friendship. They were *Pan* Petr Ianovich, *Pan* Stanislav Ianovich, Voitko Klochko, and Fedka the scribe. And they concluded a treaty of peace with Grand Prince Ivan Vasilievich, **1494** and they wrote the treaty charters with the Grand Prince. And they gave up to the Grand Prince the cities of Viaz'ma, Serpeesk, Mezechesk, Vorotynsk, Odoev, and others, up to the Ugra River. And then the Lithuanian ambassadors spoke to the Grand Prince about the offer of Grand Prince Alexander Kasimirovich of Lithuania to marry [the Grand Prince's daughter]. Grand Prince Ivan Vasilievich agreed to their proposal and permitted his daughter, Elena, to become betrothed; and on the sixth of February, a Thursday, representing his sovereign Grand Prince Alexander of Lithuania, *Pan* Stanislav Ianovich, *Starosta*[279] of Samogitia, was betrothed to Elena. The [Grand Prince] highly honored those envoys and let them depart from Moscow on the twelfth of Feburary; and with them he released home those captured Lithuanians who had been taken in Serpeesk, Mezechesk, and Opakov and who remained as prisoners in various cities.

The same spring on the ninth of March the Grand Prince sent to Lithuania to his brother and son-in-law, Grand Prince Alexander Andreevich,[280] his ambassadors, Prince Vasilii Ivanovich Kosov and Prince Semion Ivanovich Riapolovskii, and *diak* Fedor Kuritsyn, to agree on the proposal of friendship and marriage. And they came to Wilno and let Grand Prince Alexander of Lithuania pledge on the treaty charter, and exchanged treaty charters between them [that is, between Grand Prince Ivan III and Grand Prince Alexander]. And in Wilno they received from Grand Prince Alexander Kasimirovich a charter with his seal, according to which he would permit the daughter of the Grand Prince [Ivan III] to keep the Greek law [that is, the Orthodox faith] and neither convert her nor force her into the Roman law; and that she should build a church in her court and retain priests of the Greek law. And so they returned with great honor and the Grand Prince's ambassadors came to Moscow on the twenty-fifth of May.

ABOUT ZOSIMA'S RELINQUISHMENT OF THE METROPOLIA

The same spring on the seventeenth of May Metropolitan Zosima resigned from his Metropolia [of all Russia], but not by his

---

279. *Starosta*: the mayor or governor or elder of a city administration.

280. Alexander's father had two names: Kasimir-Andrei; therefore he is sometimes mentioned as Kasimirovich, sometimes Andreevich.

1495   own will, but because he was drinking immoderately and did not look after the divine church; and he withdrew to a cell in the Simeon [Monastery] and from thence to the Monastery of the Holy Trinity and St. Sergius.[281]

The same month on the twenty-ninth of May Prince Boris Vasilievich passed away. His body was brought to Moscow and buried in the Church of Archangel Michael.

The same summer Manuel Angelos the Greek and Danilo Mamyrev, who had been sent by the Grand Prince to seek out master-artisans in Venice and Milan, returned to Moscow to the Grand Prince. They brought to Moscow Alevisio, a master of wall and palace building; Pietro, master of gunmaking; and other masters.

The same year there arrived in Moscow from Denmark Dmitrii Ralev[282] and Dmitrii Zaitsev, who had been sent by the Grand Prince to the Danish King Johann with a treaty of peace and brotherhood. During their mission they witnessed the King's pledge on the treaty charter and exchanged treaty charters; at the same time the Danish King's ambassador by the name of David came with them to Moscow, likewise concerning a treaty of peace and brotherhood.

[CONFLICT WITH THE KOLYVAN' GERMANS]

In the Year 7003 [1495]. The Grand Prince sent to his namestnik in Novgorod his *diaks*, Vasilii Zhuk and Daniil Mamyrov, in order to arrest in Novgorod the German merchants from the city of Kolyvan'.[283] And he ordered an inventory be made of their merchandise and that [merchants] be brought to Moscow because of their trespassing the treaty, for they had caused many offenses in Kolyvan' to the Grand Prince's merchants from Novgorod. They offended them and ordered that some of the Grand Prince's people be boiled in kettles; [and this they had done] without informing the Grand Prince and without any investigation. They also offended the Grand Prince's ambassadors who were traveling in the Grand Prince's service to Rome, to the Italian land, and to Germany. They also offended and harmed the Grand Prince's old merchants from

281. Another reason for the removal of Metropolitan Zosima was his passive attitude toward the heretical sect of Judaizers.

282. Also, Ralo or Rhalli.

283. Kolyvan': the main city in the Estonian S.S.R., or Reval—now named Tallin—at the time in Livonia.

Novgorod, and practiced piracy on the sea. For all this Grand Prince **1495** Ivan Vasilievich expressed his displeasure with them and ordered them to be imprisoned and their merchandise sent to Moscow; also, that their former business estates and their prayerhouse in Novgorod be confiscated.

The Germans, recognizing their guilt and misdeeds before the Grand Prince [Ivan III], sent their envoy to Grand Prince Alexander of Lithuania, the son-in-law of Grand Prince [Ivan III], and petitioned him [Alexander] to intercede with his father-in-law, the Grand Prince [Ivan III] because of the merchants' crimes and misdeeds, as well as with the purpose of releasing the German merchants. Receiving their petition, Grand Prince Alexander of Lithuania sent his envoy to Grand Prince Ivan Vasilievich, asking him to forgive the German merchants' crimes and misdeeds and release them for his own sake [that is, for the sake of the Grand Prince of Lithuania]. There came likewise an envoy from the Grand Master [of the Livonian Order], from the entire Livonian land, and from seventy German cities[284] to the Grand Prince to petition the latter to release the German merchants and agree to a conference on the land's problem on the island in the Narva River. Grand Prince Ivan Vasilievich of all Russia, in view of the intercession of his son-in-law, Grand Prince Alexander, and the petition of the Grand Master and seventy cities beyond the seas, and the entire Livonian land, was merciful and released the merchants from prison and sent them to their own land in April, 7004 [1496].[285]

In the Year 7003 [1495]. On the sixth of January, Tuesday, Prince Alexander Olshanskii Otoksta, *Pan* Ian Zaberezheskii, and *Pan* Iurii Zinovievich, the Lithuanian ambassadors of Grand Prince Alexander Andreevich-Kasimirovich,[286] came to Moscow to Grand Prince Ivan Vasilievich in order to get his daughter, Grand Princess Elena, who was to marry Grand Prince Alexander. The thirteenth of the same month, Tuesday, Grand Prince Ivan Vasilievich sent his daughter, Elena, to Grand Prince Alexander of Lithuania; and Simeon, abbot of the Monastery of the Holy Trinity, blessed Princess Elena in the Church of the Most Pure [Virgin Mary] because there

284. Here, certainly, is meant the German Hansa, the political and economic Union of German merchant cities.

285. Here, apparently, there is still some confusion between the September calendar year and the Ultra March calendar.

286. See the above footnote 280 for the year 1494.

1496   was no Metropolitan [in Russia] at that time. And together with her, he sent his ambassadors with their wives, namely, Prince Semion Ivanovich Riapolovskii, Mikahil Iakovlevich Rusalka, *diak* Vasilii Kuleshin, and many other princes and junior boyars of his court. They arrived in Wilno on the fifteenth of February, the week of the Prodigal Son, and first of all Grand Princess Elena went to the Church of the Most Pure Mother of God of our Greek law and there they celebrated a *Te Deum*, and from thence she went to the wedding. They were wed in the Church of St. Stanislav of the Roman law by the Bishop of Wilno, who celebrated in Latin, and in the presence of Thomas, the Grand Prince's priest, who was the only one [among the clergy present] of the Greek religion. Grand Prince Alexander honored the Grand Prince's ambassadors and the junior boyars of the latter's court, and let them return home with great honor. Grand Princess [Elena] kept with her in Wilno Prince Vasilii Romadanovskii, Prokopii Skurat, and Dmitrii Peshek. The Grand Prince of Lithuania [Alexander], however, without great delay sent them to Moscow and began to insist on her conversion to the Roman law. Grand Prince Ivan Vasilievich of all Russia sent to Lithuania to his son-in-law, Grand Prince Alexander, his envoys, Boris Vasilievich Kutuzov and *diak* Andrei Maika, asking him not to force Grand Princess Elena to give up the Greek law and to accept the Roman one.

ABOUT THE WAR WITH THE GERMANS [SWEDES]

In the Year 7004 [1496]. Grand Prince Ivan Vasilievich of all Russia sent his voevodas with an army from Moscow against the [Germans], against the Swedish land, toward the city of Viborg. They were Prince Daniilo Vasilievich Shchenia, Iakov Zakharievich, and Prince Vasilii Fedorovich Shuiskii with the levy of Pskov. The Grand Prince's voevodas, upon arriving there, campaigned in the Swedish land, burned it, captured [people] but did not take the city of Viborg; and on that occasion at the fortress of Viborg Ivan Andreevich Subota Pleshcheev was shot by a harquebus.

ABOUT THE CONSECRATION OF SIMEON TO BE METROPOLITAN

The same year on the sixth of September by the grace of God and with the assent of the sovereign and Grand Prince Ivan Vasilievich of all Russia, and on the advice of the holy fathers, archbishops, bishops, archimandrites, and the entire Sacred Council,

venerable Abbot Simeon of the Monastery of the Holy Trinity and **1496**
St. Sergius was elected and appointed to the holy metropolia of all
Russia and conducted into the palace of the Metropolitan. And he
was invested and consecrated as His Holiness, Metropolitan of all
Russia, on the twentieth of the same month of September, and at
his consecration were Archbishop Tikhon of Rostov, Bishops
Nephontus of Suzdal', Simeon of Riazan', Bassian of Tver',
Abraham of Kolomna, Siluanus of Sarai, and Philotheus of Perm'.
And Archbishop Genadius of Novgorod sent his charter, in which
he expressed his agreement with the Council concerning his
consecration.

When the divine service was over and the time arrived to en-
throne him in the see of the Metropolitan, the Grand Prince said,
"The Almighty and Life-Creating Holy Trinity Which has granted
us the entire Russian state grants you this holy and great see of the
archbishopric of the metropolia of entire Russia, through the appo-
sition of hands and consecration by the holy fathers, archbishops
and bishops of all our Russian state. Father, take this staff of the
Shepherd and ascend to the seat of senior bishop [of Russia] in the
Name of Our Lord Jesus Christ and his Most Pure Mother, and
pray God and His Most Pure Mother for us, your children, for all
the Orthodox world, and may Lord God give you health and life
for many years." And the *diaks* sang to His Holiness, "*Eis pola eti
Despota.*"[287] The Metropolitan answered, "Autocrat, lord and
sovereign![288] May the all-powerful and all-embracing hand of the
Almighty preserve your God-established tsardom; may your dominion be peaceful and last many years, and be victorious; and may
all your Christ-loving and obedient warriors be victors. And may
it be [at peace] with all other people forever and ever. Our pious
lord and autocrat, great Sovereign, abide in good health all the
days of your life; do good, and that for many years." And the *diaks*
sang the wish of many years' life to the Grand Prince.

287. "*Eis pola eti Despota*": Greek, "Many years (of life) to the lord
bishop!"

288. *Autocrat*, in Russian, *samoderzhets*: meant a ruler independent
from any foreign power and *not* an absolute autocratic monarch. This title
was assumed by Ivan III after he defeated the Golden Horde, liberated
Russia from the nearly two and a half century-old yoke of Turko-Mongols,
and became completely free of the Horde and any foreign power.

1496

The same fall boyar Fedor Laskar the Greek and his son, Dimitrii, came from Constantinople to serve the Grand Prince.

The same fall on the twentieth of October, Tuesday, Grand Prince Ivan Vasilievich journeyed from Moscow to his patrimony, Novgorod the Great, and together with him were his grandson, Prince Dimitrii, and his son, Prince Iurii; and in Moscow he left Grand Princess Sofia and his son, Vasilii, with the junior brothers. The Grand Prince arrived in his patrimony, Novgorod the Great, on Tuesday, the seventeenth of November. Genadius, Archbishop of this city, met the Grand Prince before the city with crosses and censers, as befitted his dominion; and with him were archimandrites, abbots, and priests of the entire Sacred Council of Great Novgorod. At that time in Novgorod the Grand Prince's namestniks were Prince Danilo Aleksandrovich Penko and Prince Semion Romanovich; and they also met the sovereign Grand Prince with the entire people of that city. And there was great joy in Novgorod the Great because of the arrival of the sovereign Grand Prince. And the Grand Prince attended a *Te Deum* and the liturgy in the [Cathedral of the] Divine Wisdom, Sophia, and he ate in [the palace of] Archbishop Genadius.

ABOUT THE WAR WITH THE GERMANS [THE SWEDES]

The same winter on the seventeenth of January the Grand Prince sent his voevodas from Novgorod into the Gam land, against the Germans—that is, against the Swedes. They were Prince Vasilii Ivanovich Kosoi and Andrei Fedorovich Cheliadnin. They advanced up to the fortress of Gam.[289] They devastated the Swedish land, burned, massacred, and captured a great many. And they defeated the [Swedish] advance troops and returned to Novgorod, to the Grand Prince, on the sixth of March; and everyone was in good health, and they brought a great many prisoners.

On the tenth of March of the same winter the Grand Prince went from Novgorod and came to Moscow on the twenty-fourth of March, a Thursday. It was an extremely cold winter. There were heavy freezes and much snow; and in spring in Moscow and everywhere there were great floods such as the people had not remembered for many years.

289. Gam: a fortress in the region located to the north of present Leningrad.

ABOUT THE KAIAN LAND [KARELIA]

The same spring the Grand Prince sent Prince Ivan Fedorovich and his brother, Prince Petr Ushatyi, into the Kaian land beyond ten rivers; and with him was the army, which was composed of the levies of Ustiug, Dvina, Onega, and Vag. And the names of the rivers in which they campaigned were Kem, Torma, Kolokol, Ovlui, Sigavaia, Snezhna, Gavka, Putash. And those who live on the Limenga River petitioned the Grand Prince and came to Moscow with his voevodas; and the Grand Prince honored them and let them go.

ABOUT KAZAN'

The same spring in May Grand Prince Ivan Vasilievich received information from Mohammed Amin, Khan of Kazan', that Mamuk, Khan of Shiban',[290] was marching against him with great forces and that he [the Khan] had been betrayed by the Kazan' Cossacks Kalimet, Urak, Sadyr, and Agish.[291] The Grand Prince sent to Kazan' to Khan Mohammed Amin to help him, his voevoda, Prince Semion Ivanovich Riapolovskii, with forces; and with him were many other junior boyars of his court. And from the cities of the Niz[292] he sent the junior boyars from Novgorod, Murom, Kostroma, and many other cities. The above-mentioned Kazan' lords,[293] having heard that the Grand Prince's voevodas were marching with strong forces under Prince Semion Ivanovich Riapolovskii, escaped from Kazan' to Khan Mamuk. And when Khan Mamuk learned of the strong forces of the Grand Prince's moving toward Kazan', he returned home. On the day of St. Simeon, because he no longer expected the arrival of Mamuk against Kazan', Khan Mohammed Amin of Kazan' let the Grand Prince's voevoda, Prince Semion

290. Shiban': a subdivision of the former Great, or Golden, Horde; Mamuk was Khan in the Central Urals and Western Siberia.

291. Cossacks, or *Kazaki*: a Tatar word for independent, or free, Tatars living outside an organized khanate or tribe; later, free frontiersmen. In the sixteenth century this word came to be applied to free or runaway Russian settlers of the prairie.

292. "Niz," or *Ponizovskaia zemlia*, denoted in this case the central Russian region between the Oka and Volga rivers.

293. Apparently, the chronicler speaks here of the treacherous Kazan' Tatar Cossacks, Kalimet, *et al.*

1497   Ivanovich Riapolovskii, with all his forces, go from Kazan' to Moscow, to their homes.

In the Year 7005 [1497]. Soon thereafter Khan Mamuk of Shiban', having learned that the Grand Prince's voevodas had left Kazan' and returned home with all their forces—[he had learned this because] there were traitors in Kazan' [who were] against Khan Mohammed Amın, who would have sent news from Kazan' to Mamuk—[Khan Mamuk] came forthwith with his army and with strong Nogai forces against Kazan';[294] and with him were the Kazan' lords-traitors; Khan Mohammed Amin of Kazan', fearing treason by his lords, himself fled from Kazan' with his wife and with the remaining princes, and came to Moscow to the Grand Prince in November, 7005 [1497]. The Grand Prince let him stay honorably in Moscow. In the meantime Khan Mamuk besieged the city with great forces and took Kazan' because he encountered no resistance. And he took with him those Kazan' lords Kalimet, Urak, Sadyr and Agish and their co-conspirators who had betrayed their ruler; and he robbed the merchants and all the people of this land. Shortly thereafter Khan Mamuk honored the lords of Kazan', released them, and together with them and with his army, came to the fortress of Arsk.[295] The lords of Arsk, however, did not surrender their fortress but fought strongly against them.

In the meantime the [treacherous] lords of Kazan' abandoned Mamuk and returned to the city of Kazan', fortified it and did not let Mamuk into the city. And they made him responsible for their treachery because he had captured the Tatar lords and robbed the merchants and others of this land. And those [treacherous] lords of Kazan' sent Barash Seid to Moscow to Grand Prince Ivan Vasilievich in order to petition for them and for their entire land, asking that the Grand Prince pardon them and forgive them their treason since they "betrayed their sovereign Khan Mohammed Amin, as well as the Grand Prince; and, please, be kind toward us; do not send us Khan Mohammed Amin of Kazan' because from him came much violence and much dishonor toward our wives;

294. Nogai: nomadic Tatars who lived then in the prairie between the Volga, Don and even Dnieper rivers. They received their name, "Nogai," from Khan Nogai (1230?-1300), who ruled in the southern Russian prairie. See *Nik.*, Vol. III, footnote 92, p. 69.

295. Arsk: a small Tatar-Finnic territory some thirty-five miles north of Kazan'.

and that is the reason why we betrayed him and abandoned him   **1497**
and went over to Mamuk." And Grand Prince Ivan Vasilievich
accepted their and their entire land's petition, put aside his dislike,
as well as pardoned the faults of the Kazan' lords, and showed
them his grace by not sending them Khan Mohammed Amin; and
he gave them for their ruler as Khan of Kazan' Prince Abdul Letif,
son of Ibrahim, junior brother of Khan Mohammed Amin. When
Khan Mamuk learned of the Grand Prince's graciousness toward
the lords of Kazan', he very soon left Kazan' and returned home,
but he died on the way.

In the [same] year 7005 [1497],[296] in April, Grand Prince Ivan
Vasilievich showed his favor to Prince Abdul Letif, son of Ibrahim,
and let him go from Moscow to Kazan' to be khan there in place
of his senior brother, Mohammed Amin; and together with him
he sent to Kazan' Prince Semion Danilovich Kholmskii and Prince
Fedor Ivanovich Palitskii. They arrived in Kazan' in the month of
May and enthroned Abdul Letif as Khan, and they had all the
Kazan' lords, *ulans*[297] and local lords of the land and other people
pledge to the Grand Prince, according to their faith. The same
spring the Grand Prince showed his favor to Mohammed Amin,
the former Khan of Kazan', and gave him the towns of Koshira,
Serpukhov, and Khatun, together with all the taxes, and let him
go from Moscow on the ninth of May. He did not, however, change
his ways and continued to abide in violence and greed.

ABOUT THE AMBASSADORS TO WALACHIA [MOLDAVIA]

In June, 7004 [1496],[298] Grand Prince Ivan Vasilievich sent his
envoys, Ivan Oshcherin and Luka Voloshanin, to voevoda Stefan
of Walachia [Moldavia]. They journeyed thither, accomplished
their mission and were released back; on their way, at Terebovl',
they were robbed by Iapancha Sultan, son of the Crimean Khan,
with his [Tatar] Cossacks. And they returned to voevoda Stefan,
who sent his envoy about these matters to the Crimean Khan

296. Most probably, the repetition of the same year 7005 (1497) results
from the use of the "March 1 New Year" and not the "September 1 New
Year" in the earlier chronicles and documents used by the writers of *Nik.*

297. *Ulan*: an aristocratic title among the Tatar-Mongols.

298. Once again, repetition of the same year results from the use of
the "March 1 New Year" and not the "September 1 New Year" in the
earlier chronicles and documents used by the writers of *Nik.*

1497 Mengli-Girei. The Khan ordered his lords and Cossacks to investigate and return whatsoever had been stolen. They investigated
but there was very little returned, and most disappeared. And they
came to Moscow in August, in the summer of 7005. And together
with them came Ivan Pitar, an envoy from Walachia. And the Grand
Prince allowed him to return on the third of September; and together with the Walachian envoy there came to the Grand Prince
the Abbot Paissios and three elder monks from the Holy
Mountain [that is, Mt. Athos] in order to ask for alms. And the
Grand Prince showed them his favor, gave money to them and to
the other Monastery of the Holy Mountain, and let them return
together with his envoy. He did this because in olden times this
Monastery of St. Panteleimon on the Holy Mountain was the creation of the former Grand Princes of Russia, beginning with great
Vladimir.[299]

ABOUT THE TAKING OF IVANGOROD BY THE SWEDES

On the nineteenth of August, a Friday, of the year 7004[300]
there came from beyond the sea, from Stockholm, from the Swedish
state of Prince Stenstur, into the Narva River near Ivangorod, seventy boats of thieving Swedes with cannons and harquebuses.[301]
And they set fire to the households of the city, shooting with fire,
because there was no resistance shown them. The daring voevoda
and namestnik of Ivangorod by the name of Prince Iurii Babich,
filled with fighting spirit and courage, did not resist the enemy or
arm the citizens but quickly took fright [!] and fled from the city.
So there was no voevoda in the city and but few people and few
military supplies in the fortress. Prince Ivan Briukho and Prince
Ivan Gundoz were sojourning with their people in the vicinity of
the city and saw that the city had been taken by the Swedes, but
they did not go to aid the city. The Swedes took the city, encountered
no resistance therein, and mercilessly sacked the goods and endless
amount of merchandise; and they massacred people, captured
others, and returned rapidly from the city to the sea.

299. St. Panteleimon's Monastery, which still exists as a Russian monastery on Mt. Athos, was established by Russian monks in the eleventh century.
300. Again, there is, apparently, some confusion over the calendar.
301. Sten Stur the Older, regent of Sweden ca. 1440–1503, liberated
the Swedes from Danish domination.

In the Year 7005 [1497].[302] In September the Grand Prince sent   **1497**
his envoy, Prince Ivan Zvenets, to the Crimea to Khan Mengli-Girei,
and he died there. And then he [Ivan III] sent his envoy, Mikhail
Andreevich Pleshcheev, to Constantinople to the Turkish Sultan
Bayazid, son of Sultan Mohammed, and together with him he let
a large number of merchants go from Moscow by way of the *pole*.
This Mikhail had never been [sent] before to the Turkish Sultan,
and this time Mikhail was sent for a treaty of friendship and peace.

The same fall on the eighteenth of September, a Sunday, the
stone Church of the Transfiguration of Lord God, Our Saviour,
Jesus Christ [in the Monastery of St. Saviour] in the Novoe was
consecrated by His Holiness Metropolitan Simeon of all Russia,
and at that time Athanasius Shchedryi was archimandrite there.

On the eighteenth of December, in the third week of the fast,
Protasius was consecrated Bishop of Riazan' by Metropolitan
Simeon.

[ABOUT THE WAR OF GRAND PRINCE ALEXANDER OF LITHUANIA AGAINST STEFAN, VOEVODA OF WALACHIA]

The same year the Polish King Albrecht, son of Kasimir, and
his brother, Grand Prince Alexander of Lithuania, started campaigning against Stefan, voevoda of Walachia [Moldavia]. When
Grand Prince Ivan Vasilievich learned that a war had begun against
Stefan, voevoda of Walachia, he quickly sent to his brother-in-law,
Grand Prince Alexander of Lithuania, his envoy, Loban Zabolotskii,
and *diak* Volk Kuritsyn, to encourage Grand Prince Alexander not
to break his agreement and not to wage war against voevoda Stefan,
the *svat*[303] of the Grand Prince.

Grand Prince Alexander [of Lithuania] committed a question-
able deed: he, himself, returned from the campaign but he sent
the Russian princes [from Lithuania] with an army to aid his
brother, Albrecht. The Polish King Albrecht invaded the Walachian land, started capturing, burning, massacring, and sacking.
He arrived at the fortress of Sochaev and his artillery destroyed

302. Again, repetitious chronology, which probably resulted either
from some poorly dated sources or from a mix-up in the March year with
the September year.

303. *Svat*: in this case, father-in-law of the late Grand Prince Ivan,
son of Ivan III.

1498   the walls. Voevoda Stefan, however, led him into a well-fortified place, defeated him, captured his artillery and his treasury, killed many of his *pany*, captured many others alive, and killed about forty thousand of his troops. The King, himself, barely escaped with a few people to the Russian princes [from Lithuania], who did not participate in this battle. And the King [of Poland] returned home in great shame.

The same summer in August Grand Princess Anna of Riazan', sister of Grand Prince Ivan Vasilievich, came to Moscow. The Grand Prince met her with great honor in the field [before the city] at Bolvanovié[304] together with his grandson, his children, his boyars, and, also, with Grand Princess Sofia and his daughter-in-law, Grand Princess Elena, and the boyars' wives. Grand Princess Anna remained in Moscow until Epiphany, after which the Grand Prince let her return home with great honor, with a large number of gifts; and she was accompanied by Prince Iurii and the boyars, up to Ugresh. The Grand Prince let her go because there was soon to be a wedding: the Grand Princess was giving her daughter in marriage to Prince Fedor Ivanovich Belskii, and the wedding took place in January in Riazan'.

[THE GRAND PRINCE'S SON, VASILII, FALLS OUT OF FAVOR AND
THE GRAND PRINCE APPOINTS HIS GRANDSON, DIMITRII,
TO BE HIS HEIR]

In the Year 7006 [1498]. In December, because of the devil's deeds, Grand Prince Ivan Vasilievich became angry with his son, Prince Vasilii, as well as with his own wife, Grand Princess Sofia [Vasilii's mother]. And because of his suspicion, he ordered the execution of the junior boyars Vladimir Elizarov, son of Gusev; Prince Ivan Paletskii-Khrulia; Poiarok, brother of Run; Shchavli Skriabin, son of Travin; *vvedennyi diak* Fedor Strumilov;[305] and Afanasii Iaropkin. And on the twenty-seventh of December they were executed on the ice and beheaded.

In the year 7006 [1498][306] Grand Prince Ivan Vasilievich of all

304. *Bolvanovié:* a suburb of Moscow.
305. *Vvedennyi diak*: a *diak* appointed to membership in the Boyar Duma.
306. In another MS of this same *Codex*, the so-called *Arkhivnyi II*, we find a more detailed report on the conflict between Ivan III and his son, Prince Vasilii. It is to be found in an appendix at the end of *PSRL*, XII, p. 263, and here we provide this important extended version.

Russia became wroth at his son, Prince Vasilii, and put him under   **1498**
arrest and surveillance by a police officer. He did so because the
latter [that is, Prince Vasilii] had learned from *diak* Fedor Strumilov
that his father, Ivan III, wanted [to deprive him of inheriting the
Muscovite throne] and grant the Grand Principality of Vladimir
and Moscow to his grandson, Dimitrii Ivanovich.[307] And then
Afanasii Ropchenok, a second precursor of Satan, organized a conspiracy in which *diak* Fedor Strumilov Poiarok, the brother of Run,
participated, and other junior boyars; some others even secretly
pledged on the cross that in case Prince Vasilii broke with his father,
they would seize the Grand Prince's treasury in Vologda and Beloozero and do away with [Prince Dimitrii], grandson [of Ivan III].
When Grand Prince Ivan Vasilievich learned of their evil scheme
and investigated it, he ordered the traitors' execution. Six of them
were executed on [the banks of the] Moscow River below the bridge.
Afanasii Ropchenok's arms and legs were cut off and then he was
beheaded; Poiarok, the brother of Run, had his arms cut off and
was beheaded; they and the other four—*diak* Fedor Strumilov,
Vladimir Elizarov, Prince Ivan Paletskii-Khrulia, and Shchavii
Skriabin, son of Travin—were beheaded on the twenty-seventh day
of December. And the other junior boyars were thrown into jail.
At the same time he [Ivan III] put his wife, Princess Sofia, out of
favor because some women who would visit her [brought her
poisonous] herbs; having investigated these evil women, the Grand
Prince ordered their execution, drowning them by night in the
Moscow River; and from that time he started living under greater
security for his safety from her.[308]

307. Dmitrii Ivanovich was the son of the late Prince Ivan Ivanovich,
who, himself, was a son and co-ruler of Ivan III. The late Prince Ivan the
junior was the son of Ivan III by his first wife, Maria, Princess of Tver'.
He had married Princess Elena of Walachia (Moldavia), and Dimitrii was
their son. Prince Vasilii was the son of Ivan III by his second wife, the
Byzantine Princess Sofia Paleologue.
308. End of the text from *Arkhivnyi II*. Russian sources provide rather
scant details of this conflict between Ivan III and his son, Prince Vasilii.
Apparently, the boyar entourage of Ivan disliked Sofia, considering that
after her arrival the Grand Prince became more autocratic and curtailed
discussion with them of state affairs. From the subsequent events in January, 1499, it can be seen that Prince Semion Ivanovich Riapolovskii and
Prince Ivan Iurievich Patrikeev with his son, Vasilii (later the well-known
monk and writer, Bassian), as well as the diplomat, *diak* Volk Kuritsyn,
intrigued against Prince Vasilii and Sofia, fearing that after the death of

1498   The same winter, on the fourth of February, a Sunday,[309] Grand Prince Ivan III blessed and invested his grandson, Dimitrii Ivanovich, to the Grand Principality of Vladimir, Moscow, and all Russia; and this investiture[310] was in the Church of [the Assumption of] the Most Pure [Mother of God] in Moscow.

Following a blessing by Simeon, Metropolitan of all Russia; by Archbishop Tikhon of Rostov; and by Bishops Nephont of Suzdal', Bassian of Tver', Protasius of Riazan', Abraham of Kolomna, Euthymius of Sarai, and by the entire Sacred Council, he was invested [and crowned] with the *barma* and hat of Monomakh.[311] And [then] his uncle, Prince Iurii Ivanovich, showered him thrice: before [the Cathedral of] the Assumption of the Most Pure [Theotokos], before [the Cathedral of] the Miracles of [Archangel] Michael, and before [the Cathedral of] the Annunciation. This happened in 7006, the sixth of February, Sunday of the week of the Publican and the Pharisees.

ABOUT THE INVESTITURE OF [IVAN III'S] GRANDSON TO THE GRAND PRINCIPALITY

In the middle of the church they prepared a large platform on which the bishops usually stand, and they placed three chairs in this place, for Grand Prince Ivan [III], for his grandson, Dimitrii, and for the Metropolitan. And when the appointed time arrived the Metropolitan, Archbishop, bishops, archimandrites, abbots, and entire Council donned sacred vestments and ordered that a pulpit be placed in the middle of the church, and Monomakh's hat and the *barma* were put on it. When the Grand Prince entered the church with his grandson, the Metropolitan and entire Sacred Council began celebrating a *Te Deum* in honor of the Most Pure Theotokos and holy Wonderworker Peter; and after the prayers,

---

Ivan III the regime would be even more autocratic. They preferred to have as ruler the infant Dimitrii and his mother, Elena of Walachia (Moldavia)—who, by the way, apparently was inclined toward the heresy of the Judaizers, as was *diak* Kuritsyn. Both the Riapolovskii and Patrikeev families were from Russian territories in Lithuania.

309. The *Ioasaf.* and *Obol.* resume here.

310. This was the first investiture in Russia or crowning of a "tsar."

311. *Barma*: a kind of coronation collar adorned with gems. It and the hat of Monomakh, the Grand Prince's inheritance, were considered to have been brought from Byzantium to Prince Vladimir Monomakh in the twelfth century. Actually, the hat was made in Sarai, capital of the Great Horde, in the fourteenth century.

the singing of *Dostoinno est'*,[312] the *Trisviatoe [Trisagion]*,[313] and the   **1498**
Troparia [chants], the Metropolitan and Grand Prince entered and
took their places on the platform, while the grandson took a place
on its upper step without ascending to the platform. And Grand
Prince Ivan said, "Our father, Metropolitan. By the will of God,
from the olden times of our forefathers to the present time, our
fathers, the Grand Princes, have always given the Grand Principality
to their first son. And so did I bless my first son, Ivan, to rule the
Grand Principality together with me. God willing, my son, Ivan,
did not remain alive. After him there remained his first son, Dimitrii; and now I bless him during my lifetime and for the future time
to be [together with me] Grand Prince of Vladimir, Moscow, and
Novgorod. And you, father, should bless him to be Grand Prince."
After the Grand Prince's speech, the Metropolitan ordered the
grandson to step onto the platform, and when he had done so, he
blessed him with the cross. And the invested one [Dimitrii] bowed
his head and the Metropolitan put his hand on his head and read
aloud the following prayer so that all could hear:

"Thou, Lord God, King of those who rule and Lord of those
who command; Thou, Thyself, through the prophet Saul, chose
Thy servant, David, and anointed him King of the people of Israel.
And now we entreat Thee to accept the prayer of us unworthy
ones and to look from Thy holy place upon Thy faithful servant,
Dimitrii; grant him to be raised to be Tsar' of Thy holy nation.
Strengthen him with the most pure blood of Thy Only Begotten
Son and commit me now to anoint him with the myrrh of joy.

"Endow him from above with power.

"Place on his head the crown from the stone of honor.

"Endow him with many days of life.

"Put in his right hand the scepter of Tsardom.

"Place him on the throne of justice.

"Protect him with all Thy might of the Holy Ghost.

"Strengthen his hand.

"Submit to him all barbarian nations.

"Put in his heart awe of Thee.

"Make him merciful toward those who obey.

"Preserve him in unblemished faith.

312. *Dostoinno est'*: a hymn in honor of the Virgin Mary.

313. *Trisviatoe*, or *Trisagion*: (Thrice:) Holy God, Holy Almighty, Holy
Immortal, have mercy upon us.

1498   "Disclose the rules of Thy conciliar church to this careful protector. Let him judge the people according to Thy justice, and let him save with his justice the sons of the poor and the weak.

"Let him be heir of Thy heavenly kingdom." [And then came] the exclamation [of the clergy]: "For Thine is the power and the kingdom and the glory of the Father, the Son and the Holy Ghost now and ever through ages and ages."[314]

After the prayer the Metropolitan ordered two archimandrites to bring him the *barma* from the pulpit. He took it, gave it to the Grand Prince, blessed the grandson with the cross, and the Grand Prince imposed the *barma* on the grandson. And the Metropolitan began reading this prayer quietly:

"God Almighty and King for ages and ages, this earthly man whom Thou hast made Tsar' has bowed his head to pray to Thee, Lord of all. Protect him under Thy shelter, protect his tsardom, let him do deeds pleasing to God. Let righteousness and peace shine on him throughout his days so that we may live peacefully in the tranquil piety and purity of his quiet reign!" [And then came] the exclamation, "Thou art the King of the world and Saviour of our souls, and we glorify Thee, Father, Son and Holy Ghost, now and ever unto the ages and ages."

After the "Amen" the Metropolitan ordered two archimandrites to bring him [Monomakh's] hat; he took it and gave it to the Grand Prince; and the Metropolitan blessed the [Grand Prince's] grandson with the cross, saying, "In the Name of the Father, the Son and the Holy Ghost." And the Grand Prince put the hat on his grandson and the Metropolitan blessed the grandson.

After the Litany, "Lord have mercy on us according to Thy great mercy," and, as is the custom, came the prayer to the Most Pure: "Most Holy Lady, Virgin, Mother of God, our Sovereign." After the prayer the Metropolitan and Grand Prince sat down in their places and the archdeacon, ascending the ambo, proclaimed

314. This prayer is found in most of the MSS of *The Nikonian Chronicle*. We find it, also, in the Byzantine and South Slavic text of the rites of coronation. Strangely enough, this prayer is not contained in the parchment, so-called *Synod Service Book* from the fifteenth century in which the coronation of Grand Prince Dimitrii Ivanovich is described. Barsov, E., *Drevne-russkie pamiatniki sviashchennogo venchaniia Tsarei na tsarstvo v sviazi s grecheskimi originalami*. Moscow, 1883, pp. 27 and 3.

loudly, "Long life!"[315] to Grand Prince Ivan and "Long life!" to **1498**
Grand Prince Dimitrii. The priests and deacons behind the altar
also sang, "Long life!" as is the custom.

After the "Long life!" the Metropolitan, Archbishop, bishops,
and entire Council arose, bowed and congratulated both Grand
Princes; and the Metropolitan said to Grand Prince Ivan, "By the
grace of God, rejoice and prosper, Orthodox Tsar' Ivan, Grand
Prince of all Russia and Sovereign, together with your grandson,
Grand Prince Dimitrii Ivanovich of all Russia, forever and ever!"
Thereupon the Metropolitan said to Grand Prince Dimitrii, "By
the grace of God, our lord and son, Grand Prince Dimitrii Ivanovich
of all Russia, together with your Sovereign and grandfather, Grand
Prince Ivan Vasilievich, Sovereign of all Russia, prosper forever
and ever!" Thereafter the Grand Prince's children bowed and congratulated both Grand Princes, and then the boyars did the same,
as well as all the other people.

THE METROPOLITAN'S SERMON

"Our lord and son, Grand Prince Dimitrii! By the will of God
your grandfather, the Grand Prince, has favored you and blessed
you to be Grand Prince; and you, lord and son, keep the awe of
God in your heart. Love truth, mercy, righteousness, and justice,
and be obedient to your lord and grandfather, the Grand Prince.
And care with all your heart for all Orthodox Christians. And we
bless you and pray God for your health—you, our sovereign and
son."

THE GRAND PRINCE'S SPEECH TO HIS GRANDSON

"Grandson Dimitrii! I have favored you and blessed you to be
Grand Prince. And you should keep the awe of God in your heart.
Love truth, mercy, and right justice, and care with all your heart
for all Orthodox Christians."

Thereafter the Metropolitan and Grand Princes descended
from their places, the Metropolitan read the final prayer, and then
began celebrating the liturgy. After the liturgy was celebrated the
Grand Prince went home, and Grand Prince Dimitrii, in the hat
and in the *barma*, went out through the doors of the Cathedral of
the Most Pure Mother of God; and here he was showered three

315. *"Mnogaia leta"*: "Many, many years!"

1499   times with gold and silver coins by Prince Iurii, son of the Grand
Prince. Thereafter the children of the Grand Prince [Ivan III] went
with him [Dimitrii], as well as all the boyars; and they also showered
him before the [Cathedral of the] Archangel and before the
[Cathedral of the] Annunciation with gold and silver coins.

The same winter in February Mikhailo Pleshcheev came to
Moscow from Constantinople.

[PRINCE DIMITRII FALLS INTO DISFAVOR]

In the Year 7007 [1499]. In the month of January the Grand
Prince ordered that his boyars be arrested: Prince Ivan Iurievich
[Patrikeev] with his children; and Prince Semion Ivanovich
Riapolovskii [his son-in-law]; and he ordered the execution of
Prince Semion Ivanovich Riapolovskii, and the latter was beheaded
on the fifth of February, a Tuesday, on the Moscow River below
the bridge. And Prince Ivan Iurievich [Patrikeev] was exonerated
from capital punishment and was sent to be a monk in the Monastery
of the Holy Trinity; and his son, Prince Vasilii Ivanovich Krivoi[316]
was sent to the Monastery of St. Cyril on Beloozero.[317]

The same summer in the month of March an envoy from
Mohammed Sultan, sovereign of Shemakha [in the Caucausus],
came to Moscow, to the Grand Prince. He was the son of Mohammed
Sultan, grandson of Shyrvan-Shah, and his name was Shah-Jebel-
Edin. And he was in charge of an embassy for a mission of peace.

In the same month of March the Grand Prince sent to the
Italian land beyond the sea for his own needs, an embassy [which
included] Dimitrii Ivanov, son of Ralev[318] the Greek; and Mitrofan

316. Krivoi: "Kosoi," in some other MSS.
317. Apparently, all of them were intriguing against Vasilii, Ivan III's
son, who a year earlier had lost the Grand Prince's favor and had been
arrested, while his nephew, Prince Dimitrii, was proclaimed co-ruler and
heir to the crown. Now the Grand Prince apparently became suspicious
of this intrigue and decided to return his favor to Prince Vasilii and punish
the culprits. The *Arkhivnyi II* MS of the same chronicle adds to the list of
those arrested another son of Prince Ivan Patrikeev, a certain Ivan Mynnin.
Vasilii Kosoi (or Krivoi). Later in the early sixteenth century he became
known under his monastic name, Bassian Patrikeev Kosoi. He was a
theological and political writer. The aforementioned *Arkhivnyi II* MS mentions that the intercession of Metropolitan Simeon and other bishops saved
Prince Patrikeev and his family from execution. Patrikeev was an influential
statesman and even head of the Boyar Duma.
318. Ralev: Ralo, Rhallis.

Fedorov, son of Karachar. And together with them he sent to **1499** Krakow to King Albrecht of Poland his ambassador, Mikhail Pogozhii, in order to ask the King to allow his embassy to pass through the Polish land. And this embassy journeyed from Krakow to Vladislas, King of Hungary, and from thence to Venice. The same month of March the Grand Prince sent Alesha Golokhvastov with his letters to Sultan Bayazid in Constantinople.

ABOUT GRAND PRINCE VASILII IVANOVICH

On the twenty-first of the same month of March, a Thursday, Grand Prince Ivan Vasilievich of all Russia honored his son, Prince Vasilii Ivanovich, naming him sovereign and Grand Prince, and gave him Novgorod the Great and Pskov as his Grand Principality.[319]

The same spring in the month of May the Grand Prince commanded that a foundation be laid for a [new] stone and brick palace, and under it were built cellars and an ice cellar. It was founded on the old estate near the Cathedral of the Annunciation and [then was also laid] a stone wall from this palace to the Borovitskii gun tower. And its builder was master Alevizio the Italian, from the city of Milan.

The same spring, on the first of June, the Grand Prince sent Vasilii Tretiak Dalmatov with carts[320] as his ambassador to Lithuania.

The same spring on the twelfth of June Euthymius, Bishop of Krutitsa, passed away. The same summer on the fourteenth of July, Sunday, Triphon, abbot of the Epiphany Monastery, was consecrated Bishop of Sarai and Krutitsa by Metropolitan Simeon of all Russia.

The same summer the Grand Prince sent his voevodas, Prince Semion Fedorovich Kurbskii, Prince Petr Fedorovich Ushatyi, and Vasilii Ivanovich, son of Brazhnik-Gavrilovich, with troops which included the levies of Ustiug, Dvina, Vychegda, and Viatka, against the land of the Ugra and Vogul.[321] They marched forward, occupied cities, conquered the land, captured their lords, and brought them

319. At the same time Grand Prince Ivan III's former heir, his grandson, Dimitrii—who the preceding year had been invested as Grand Prince of Moscow—fell into disfavor and lost his title and position as the heir and successor to Ivan III. See the year 1502 below.

320. Presumably, the carts were loaded with gifts.

321. Ugra, or Yugra, and Vogul: both tribes of the Finno-Ugric linguistic group in the northern Urals.

1500   to Moscow; and the other lords and people of this land were brought to pledge, according to their faith, their fealty to the Grand Prince. And the other princes, as well as many people of Ugra and Vogul, were killed. And they returned to Moscow, to the Grand Prince, in good health, in March of the year 7008 [1500].[322]

The same year, having received the blessing of Metropolitan Simeon, Grand Prince Ivan Vasilievich confiscated in Novgorod the Great the lands of the Archbishop and of the monasteries, and distributed them as estates to the junior boyars.[323]

The same year the Grand Prince was informed by Abdul Letif, Khan of Kazan', that Lord Agalak, brother of Mamuk, was marching against him, together with Lord Urak, one of the [minor] Kazan' lords. Hearing of this, the Grand Prince sent his voevodas to Kazan' to help him. They were Prince Fedor Ivanovich Belskii, Prince Semion Romanovich [Iaroslavskii], and Iurii Zakhar'ich with many men-at-arms. Hearing of the advance of the Grand Prince's voevodas with forces, Agalak and Urak ran home and the Grand Prince's voevodas returned to Moscow.

THE COSSACKS OF THE HORDE

In the Year 7008 [1500]. In the month of September [Tatar] Cossacks from the Horde and from Azov came to Kozelsk, and they occupied the town of Oleshnia in Kozel'sk [district]. Prince Ivan Peremyshl'skii and Princes Vasilii and Ivan Odoevskii, and the sons of Petrov Pleshcheev, caught up with them, defeated them, liberated the captured prisoners, captured some Tatars, and brought them to the Grand Prince in Moscow.

The same fall, in October, Prince Semion Romodanovskii came to the Grand Prince from the Crimea and with him came Salykhda-Alakoz, the Turkish envoy of Mohammed Shah-Zadeh, Sultan of Kaffa.[324] The Grand Prince rendered him great honor and on the sixth of March let him return to his sovereign, Mohammed Shah-Zadeh of Kaffa. Together with him the Grand Prince sent his envoy, Andrei Semionovich Lapenok. And he let them go on boats on the

322. It is unclear where the chronicler switched here from the year 7007 to the year 7008 (1500); probably, this is another instance of calendar confusion in the documents. The same dating is found in both *Ioasaf.* and *Obol.*

323. "Junior boyars": actually, the *"dvoriane,"* or service nobility.

324. Shah Zadeh was the son of Sultan Bayazid of Turkey and was only his governor, not Sultan of Kaffa.

river Mech to the river Don, and then on the Don to Azov.[325] And   **1500**
at the same time he [Ivan III] let Kasimir of the Crimea [?] go
home.[326] And together with Prince Semion [Romodanovskii] came
the Crimean envoy by the name of Azih-Alei, son of Azbaba.

The same winter in February a [Catholic] chaplain, Johann,
envoy of the Danish King Johann, came to Moscow.

In the same month of February there came from Constantinople Alesha Golokhvastov, who had been sent by the Grand
Prince with a charter to the Turkish Sultan Bayazid. The Sultan
rendered him honor and let him return to the Grand Prince.

The thirteenth of the same month of February, a Thursday,
Grand Prince Ivan Vasilievich gave away in marriage his daughter,
Feodosia, to Prince Vasilii Daniilovich Kholmskii, and they were
married by Metropolitan Simeon in the church of the Most Pure
[Virgin Mary].[327] The same spring on the second of April the Grand
Prince sent George Manuelovich the Greek and *diak* Tret'iak Dal-
matov as envoys to the Danish King Johann; and together with him
he let the [aforementioned] chaplain go. The seventeenth of the
same month of April the Grand Prince let the Crimean envoy, Azih
Alei, go, and together with him he sent Prince Ivan Semionovich
Kubinskii to the Crimean Khan Mengli-Girei; and he permitted a
large number of Muscovite merchants to go with them. They went
by way of the *polé* and were attacked by the Tatar Cossacks from
Azov under Uguz-Cherkass and Kara Bei, who robbed him in the
polé and captured some of the merchants, and killed others. And
some merchants with Prince Ivan [Kubinskii] and with the Crimean
envoy escaped on horseback on captured horses, and arrived in
the Crimea. And those junior boyars who accompanied them all
returned in good health to Moscow; [but] Prince Ivan Kubinskii
died in the Crimea.

The same spring the namestnik of Khotin by the name of
Fedor Isaev came to the Grand Prince.[328]

325. Azov at that time was a Turkish fortress at the mouth of the
Don River.

326. Kasimir of the Crimea, in some MSS Kizamir, Kazimer.

327. This Prince Kholmskii, son of the well-known army commander
and, himself, an outstanding military leader, was appointed to the head
of the Boyar Duma, thus succeeding Prince Patrikeev in this position.

328. Khotin: a city on the upper course of the Dniester River, in
northern Moldavia. Isaev was the "Walachian" envoy from the Moldavian
principality.

1500   The same spring on Friday, the twenty-ninth of May, at the third hour of the day, Ivan Vasilievich, Grand Prince of Riazan', passed away. And after him his son, Ivan, ruled [in Riazan'] for four and one-half years.

ABOUT THE LITHUANIAN CONFLICT

The same summer Grand Prince Ivan Vasilievich of all Russia was informed that his son-in-law, Prince Alexander of Lithuania, had begun forcing his [Ivan III's] daughter, [Alexander's wife] Grand Princess, to give up the Greek law and join the Roman law; [and he did this] despite his pledge on the cross and formal charter. Grand Prince Ivan Vasilievich of all Russia sent him his envoys, Prince Vasilii Romodanovskii and *diak* Vasilii Kulshin, that he should not force his daughter [Alexander's wife] the Grand Princess, to convert from the Greek law to the Roman law, and that he should permit her to remain in the Greek law according to the ratified charter. But Grand Prince Alexander of Lithuania told the Grand Prince's envoys that he refused not to force the latter's daughter to convert to the Roman law. Thereafter in the year 7008 [1500] Prince Semion Ivanovich Belskii[329] sent to Grand Prince Ivan Vasilievich petitioning him to accept him into his service [the Grand Prince's], together with his hereditary domains. He reported that the Greek law [that is, the Orthodox confession] there [in Lithuania] was in great difficulties, and he informed Ivan III that Grand Prince Alexander had sent to his Grand Princess the Bishop of Smolensk, Iosef, who had given up the Orthodox faith of the Greek law, as well as the Bishop of Wilno and monks of the St. Bernard Order, in order to persuade her that she should join the Roman law. And he did the same to the Russian princes and to the [Orthodox Russian] citizens of Wilno, and to all the Russians [in Lithuania] who were of the Greek law, and they were being forced to convert to the Roman law. He [Grand Prince Alexander] likewise promised to Bishop Josef the Metropolia of Kiev, but God sent illness and feebleness to him and he was appointed to the Metropolia being ill and weak; and he remained in this dignity only one year, then gave up this life.

Grand Prince Ivan Vasilievich of all Russia, taking this mis-

329. Prince Semion Ivanovich Belskii was a Russian Orthodox prince in Lithuania.

fortune into consideration, honored Prince Semion Ivanovich **1500**
[Belskii], accepted him with his domains, and approved his refusal
[to serve the Grand Prince of Lithuania]. And Grand Prince Semion
Ivanovich came to the Grand Prince on the twelfth of April, Palm
Sunday.

The same month of April Grand Prince Alexander [of
Lithuania] sent to Grand Prince Ivan [III] his envoys, *Pan* Stanislav
Kishka, namestnik of Smolensk, and Fed'ka Tolstoi the Scribe [to
negotiate] concerning Prince Semion Belskii, as well as about other
affairs. The Grand Prince answered the Lithuanian envoys that he
had accepted Prince Semion [Belskii] with his hereditary domains
in view of his difficult situation because he was under pressure to
accept the Roman law. And he [Ivan III] asked [Grand] Prince
Alexander through the latter's envoys, Stanislav and Fed'ka, not to
force his daughter, Elena, who was his own [Alexander's] Grand
Princess, to convert from the Greek law to the Roman law, and
that all Russians in [Alexander's] service should not be forced to
convert to the Roman law. And he asked [Alexander] to confirm
this by formal charter and a pledge on the cross. [And he added],
"If you continue to force them, then they [the Russians of Lithuania]
will come to us because of this pressure and we will accept them
with their hereditary domains, and we will stand behind them as
long as God helps us."

Thereafter, the same April Prince Semion Andreevich Mozhaiskii, grandson of Ivan, and Prince Vasilii Dmitrievich Shemiakin, grandson of Ivan,[330] sent to Grand Prince Ivan Vasilievich of
all Russia, petitioning him that since they were in great difficulties
over preservation of their Greek law, he, the Sovereign, should
show them his favor and accept them with their hereditary domains.
And they said that Grand Prince Alexander of Lithuania did not
adhere to the agreement in other matters, either. Grand Prince
Ivan Vasilievich of all Russia, in view of the difficulties encountered
by Prince Semion [Mozhaiskii] and Prince Vasilii [Shemiakin], accepted them into his service with their hereditary domains and sent
Ivan Teleshov with their refusal [to serve the Grand Prince of
Lithuania]. He sent Afanasii Shchenok Viazmitin to Grand Prince
Alexander with a declaration of war. And he sent his voevoda,

330. Prince Vasilii Shemiakin, in the reign of Vasilii II, had gone from
Muscovite Russia into Russian lands under Lithuanian rule.

1500   *boiarin* Iakov Zakharievich, and other voevodas with a great many
men-at-arms, to the Princes [Mozhaiskii and Shemiakin].

Iakov Zakharievich left Moscow on the third day of the month
of May, a Sunday, marched into the Lithuanian land, took the city
of Debriansk,[331] captured *Pan* Stanislav Bartashevich, voevoda and
namestnik of Debriansk, as well as the bishop of Debriansk, and
sent them to the Grand Prince in Moscow. From thence Iakov
Zakharievich marched to the [Russian] princes [in Lithuania] and
let them pledge on the cross that they would serve their sovereign
Grand Prince Ivan Vasilievich of all Russia, together with all their
hereditary domains. From thence Iakov Zakharievich marched with
[these] princes to the city of Putivl' and took it on St. Saviour's Day,
on the sixth of August. And he captured Prince Bogdan Glinskii,
together with his wife. The same spring the Grand Prince sent his
voevoda and *boiarin*, Iurii Zakharievich, with many people toward
the city of Dorogobuzh; and Iurii, marching forward, took
Dorogobuzh.

Learning of this, Grand Prince Alexander of Lithuania
gathered strong forces and sent against Iurii Zakharievich his voevodas, many *pany*, and *hetmans* with a great many people.[332] [In the
meantime] to help Iurii Zakharievich, Grand Prince Ivan Vasilievich
of all Russia sent his voevoda and boyar, Prince Daniil Vasilievich
Shchenia, with the troops of Tver'. The voevodas of Grand Prince
Ivan Vasilievich and the Lithuanian voevodas met on Tuesday, the
fourteenth of the month of July, at the Mitkovo Polé on the river
Vedrosh. This was the day when the memory of holy apostle Aquila
is observed. And there was a great battle between them and a bad
massacre. By the grace of God and His Most Pure Mother, the
voevodas of Grand Prince Ivan Vasilievich of all Russia defeated
the Lithuanian voevodas: they killed a great many soldiers of Grand
Prince Alexander, and others were captured alive, among them
the voevodas and *hetmans* and sons of the *pany*, including Prince
Konstantin Ostrozhskii; *Pan* Grigorii Ostiukovich; and the *marshalek*,[333] *Pan* Litavar, and many others. And they were sent to Moscow to the Grand Prince. The news about the battle was brought

331. Debriansk: apparently, the present city of Briansk.
332. *Hetman*: an army commander in Poland and Lithuania.
333. *Marshalek*: commander of the local militia of the nobility in
Lithuania and Poland.

to the Grand Prince in Moscow by Mikhail Andreev, son of **1501**
Pleshcheev, on Friday, the seventeenth of July, and he told the
Grand Prince about the health of his voevodas and that with God's
help they had defeated the Lithuanians. And there was great joy
in Moscow.

The same summer on the seventeenth of August, Monday, at
the eighth hour of the day, a conflagration started in Moscow at
Bobr, in the great suburb. And it burned along the Moscow River
and the Neglinnaia River, and it burned the cannon works and the
Monastery of the Nativity.

ABOUT THE NOGAIS

The same summer Murza Musa and Iamgurchei Murza, of the
Nogai Tatars, came with a great many armed men toward the city
of Kazan' [to fight] the Khan of Kazan', Abdul Letif, son of Ibrahim.
And they remained at the city for three weeks. At that time the
Grand Prince's voevodas in Kazan', who were with the Khan, were
Prince Mikhail Kurbskii and Prince Petr Loban-Riapolovskii, with
a few troops. The Khan of Kazan' ordered an *ostrog* be built near
the fortifications[334] and every day, sallying from the city, they fought
the Nogais. And through the intercession of God, all the Nogais
soon retreated home.

The same summer the Grand Prince's voevodas took the city
of Toropeesk [?, in Lithuania].

In the Year 7009 [1501]. In January an ambassador from Vladislav, King of Hungary, came to Moscow, and his name was Matthias.

The same winter in February an ambassador of the Polish King
Albrecht by the name of Olekhno Skaruta came to Moscow; and
Alexander, Grand Prince of Lithuania, also sent an envoy named
Stanislav Narbutov.

On the nineteenth of the same month of February pious Princess Feodosia, daughter of Grand Prince Ivan Vasilievich and wife
of Prince Vasilii Danilovich Kholmskii, passed away and was buried
in the Church of the Ascension in Moscow.

The same spring in April, on Wednesday of Easter, pious
Grand Princess Anna of Riazan', sister of Grand Prince Ivan Vasilievich, passed away in the sixth hour of the day.

---

334. *Ostrog*: in this case, a moving fortress composed of wagons arranged in a square formation to protect the soldiers of the sortie.

1502   The same spring in April Bishop Philotheus of Perm' gave up his bishopric and went to the Monastery of St. Cyril. On the twenty-third of April of the same year, for the sake of Christ, God cured a man with a crooked leg at the tomb of St. Maxim, Fool-in-Christ.

The same spring in Iur'iev[335] the Germans arrested the Grand Prince's merchants from Novgorod and Pskov, more than two hundred men. They sacked their goods and sent them to prison in various cities. The entire Livonian land[336] assembled and marched against the city of Pskov, patrimony of Grand Prince [Ivan III]. And they campaigned in the district of Pskov, and returned home.

The same summer on the eleventh of July, a Sunday, the Grand Prince's ambassadors, Prince Fedor Romadanovskii and Andrei Lapenok, as well as many merchants, were robbed in the *polé* and in the Poluzorovskii Wood by Tatar Cossacks from Azov under Oguz Cherkass and Karabai, and Andrei Lapenok died there.

The same summer in the month of August [the ambassadors] of Ivan [III], Iurii Staroi and Tretiak Dalmatov, came to Moscow from the Danish King [Johann], and together with them came the Danish king's ambassador, by the name of David.

The same year on order of Grand Prince Ivan Vasilievich, the old Church of the Miracles of Holy Archangel Michael in Moscow was torn down; it had been founded and completed by holy Metropolitan and Wonderworker Alexis in the year 6873 [1365]. And in the same place another foundation for a new church was laid by Archimandrite Theognost.

ABOUT MSTISLAVL'

In the Year 7010 [1502]. Grand Prince [Ivan III] sent his voevodas to campaign in the Lithuanian land; they were Prince Semion Ivanovich Mozhaiskii, Prince Vasilii Ivanovich Shemiakin, boyar Prince Aleksandr Ivanovich Rostovskii, boyar Semion Vorontsov, and Grigorii Fedorovich Davydov, and with them were a great many men-at-arms. On the fourth of November, Thursday, the voevodas arrived at the fortress of Mstislavl' and there they encountered Prince Mikhail Iziaslavskii, voevoda of Grand Prince Alexander of Lithuania and son-in-law of Prince Iurii Lugvenievich, and

335. Iur'iev: also, Dorpat or Tartu, in northeast Livonia, now the Estonian S.S.R.
336. Livonian land: German knights of the Livonian Order.

voevoda Ostafii Dashkov, with the retinue of [the Lithuanian] Grand   **1502**
Prince, who was in the advance detachment with professional
[mercenary] soldiers. And they [the Lithuanian forces], came out
of the fortress, and both armies met and by the mercy of God the
Muscovite armies of Grand Prince Ivan Vasilievich defeated [the
enemy] and massacred about seven thousand men of the Lithuanian
army; and others were taken prisoner and their banners were captured, while Prince Mikhail [Iziaslavskii] escaped into the city with
difficulty. The Grand Prince's princes and voevodas remained at
the city [awhile], devasted the land, and returned to Moscow with
a great many prisoners.

The same fall Abraham, Bishop of Kolomna, passed away.

The same fall in the year 7010 [1502], in the month of Sep-
tember, there came [to Moscow] with an offer of peace a certain
Alakaz, envoy of Shah Zadeh, the Sultan[337] of Kaffa, the son of
Sultan Bayazid [of Turkey]. In October of the same fall the Grand
Prince sent his [envoy] Fedor Mikhailov, son of Kiselev, to the
Crimea to Khan Mengli-Girei.

ABOUT THE GERMAN WAR [THE WAR WITH LIVONIA]

The same fall in October the Grand Prince sent his voevodas,
Prince Daniil Aleksandrovich Penka, Prince Daniil Vasilievich
Shchenia, and Prince Aleksandr Vasilievich Obolenskii, and other
voevodas with many troops to campaign against the German Livonian land because of [the latter's] misdeeds. [The Germans] had
campaigned in his patrimony of Pskov and had arrested his merchants in Iur'iev. The voevodas advanced and started campaigning
in the German land, and took prisoners, burned and massacred;
but, unexpectedly, on the twenty-fourth of November in the third
hour of the night they became engaged in a big battle. Secretly,
the Germans came from the other side with great forces, with
artillery and harquebuses, but by the mercy of God the Grand
Prince's voevodas defeated them. Some [Germans] were killed,
some were taken prisoner, and only a few of them escaped. At that
time Prince Aleksandr Vasilievich Obolenskii was killed in this battle. The voevodas campaigned near Kolyvan',[338] came out toward
Ivangorod, and devastated the German land.

337. Actually, the *governor* of Kaffa.
338. Kolyvan': also, Revel or Tallin.

1502   The same winter in December Prince Jabal and his brothers, Iamgurchei Murza and Prince Uiadam,[339] the envoys from Murza Musa of Nogai, came to Moscow to discuss peace.

In the same winter in December an envoy came to the Grand Prince from Shah Ahmet, the son of Ahmet, Khan of the Great Horde, about friendship and peace, and the name [of the envoy] was Prince Gazi-Eger.

ABOUT THE ARREST OF KHAN ABDUL LETIF

The same winter in January the Grand Prince sent Prince Vasilii Nozdrevaty and Ivan Teleshov to Kazan', and ordered them to arrest Abdul Letif, Khan of Kazan', because of his misdeeds. And they went, and did the following: they arrested the Khan and brought him to Moscow. The Grand Prince sent him to prison in Beloozero and appointed the former [Khan] Mohammed Amin, son of Ibrahim, to be Khan of Kazan'. And he gave him as wife a princess, the wife of [the late] Ali Khan, former Khan of Kazan'. And together with the Khan, the Grand Prince sent to Kazan' Prince Semion Borisovich Suzdal'skii and Prince Vasilii Nozdrevatyi.

The same winter in March, on Thursday of the fifth week of Lent, the Grand Prince sent back the envoy of Shah Ahmet Khan of the Great Horde, and together with him he sent to Khan Shah Ahmet his envoy, *iaselnichii* Davyd Likharev, to discuss peace.[340]

The same month of March the Grand Prince sent [his envoy] Aleksei Zabolotskii to the Crimea.

The same spring in April *Pan* Petrash Iepimakhovich came with professional [mercenary] soldiers[341] from Polotsk into the Pupovich district, and the Grand Prince's junior boyars killed many of these soldiers, and others they took prisoner.

The same winter on the ninth day of March the Germans attacked Ivangorod and they killed Loban Kolychev.

[ABOUT THE FALL FROM FAVOR OF DIMITRII, GRANDSON OF THE GRAND PRINCE]

The same spring on the eleventh of April, a Monday, Grand Prince Ivan [III] put his grandson, Grand Prince Dimitrii, as well as the latter's mother, Grand Princess Elena [Voloshanka], out of

339. Prince Uiadam: Iadam, in *Ioasaf*.
340. *Iaselnichii*: an aid to the stablemaster, an important court rank.
341. *Zholniery*: mercenaries.

favor; and beginning with that day he ordered that they not be **1502** mentioned in church prayers or in litanies, and that he not be called "Grand Prince"; and he put him under surveillance by police officials. The same spring on the fourteenth of April, a Thursday, when our blessed father, Pope Martin of Rome, is remembered, Grand Prince Ivan Vasilievich of all Russia restored his grace to his son, Vasilii, blessed him, and named him [as his co-ruler and] autocrat of the Grand Principalities of Vladimir, Moscow and all Russia; and he did this with the blessing of Simeon, Metropolitan of all Russia.[342]

The same spring on the first day of May, a Sunday, Abbot Nikon of St. Paul Hermitage was consecrated Bishop of Kolomna. On the fifth of the same month, a Thursday, Nikon, abbot of the Monastery of St. Dionysius in Glushitsy, was consecrated Bishop of Perm' by Simeon, Metropolitan of all Russia.

On the eighth of the same month of May the Grand Prince let Ali Hodja, envoy of [the ruler of] Kaffa, return home, and together with him he sent Alesha Golokhvastov to Shah Zadeh, Sultan of Kaffa.

The same month Ivan Mamonov came from the Crimea.

The same summer on the ninth of June, a Thursday, the Grand Prince went to his residence of Vorontsovo, and he sojourned there till the day when, in December, the memory of Wonderworker [Metropolitan] Peter is observed.

The same summer on the twenty-eighth of June, a Tuesday, Fedor Kiselev came from the Crimea. The same summer in June the Crimean Khan Mengli-Girei defeated Shah Ahmet, Khan of the Great Horde, and occupied the Great Horde. The same summer the Grand Prince's envoy, Davyd Likharev, came from the Horde. The same summer on the fourteenth of June, a Thursday, the Grand Prince sent his son, Prince Dimitrii, against the city of Smolensk in order to campaign in the Lithuanian land.[343]

The same summer the Germans [from Livonia] marched toward Pskov.

342. For earlier developments concerning Princes Vasilii and Dimitrii, see the years 1498 and 1499.

343. This Prince Dimitrii is not to be confused with Ivan III's grandson, Dimitrii, who, together with his mother, Elena, was probably already under house arrest.

1503   The same summer two Tatar lords came from Astrakhan to
serve the Grand Prince; they were Iusuf Sultan, son of Iakub Sultan;
and Shah Avliar Sultan, son of Bakhtiar Sultan. They were the
children of the brother of the late Khan Ahmet of the Great Horde.

In the Year 7011 [1503]. On the twenty-third of October, a
Sunday, Prince Dimitrii Ivanovich, son of the Grand Prince, returned to Moscow. He had campaigned in the Lithuanian land,
taken prisoners, but had not taken the city of Smolensk because it
was strongly fortified. The same winter in January Bishop Tikhon
of Rostov gave up his diocese because of poor health, and he went
to the Monastery of Saints Boris and Gleb on [the river?] Usia.

The same winter on the first of January, Sigismund, envoy of
the Hungarian King Vladislav, came to the Grand Prince, to
Moscow.

The same winter in March there came to Moscow the ambas-
sadors of Alexander, King of Poland, the son-in-law of the Grand
Prince.[344] They were *Pan* Petr Miszkowski, voevoda of Lanchit [?];
Pan Jan Buczacki, *starosta* of Mezhigozh and *podczaszii* [Keeper of
the Cup] of the Kingdom of Poland; Petr Drocinowski, *stolnik* of
Krakow; the secretary of the King and Canon of Poznan; and Prince
Stanislav Horecki. With [them] were the Lithuanian ambassadors,
Pan Stanislav Glebowicz, namestnik of Polotsk; Vojteh Janovichz,
namestnik of Koden'; and the scribe, Ivaszko Sopezicz. They concluded a truce for six years with Grand Prince Ivan Vasilievich of
all Russia, from the day of the Annunciation to the day of Annunciation; and they signed a treaty concerning the truce.[345]

The same spring on the seventh of April, a Friday, at the ninth
hour of the day, pious Grand Princess Sofia, wife of Grand Prince
Ivan Vasilievich, passed away; and she was buried in the city of
Moscow in the Church of the Ascension.

344. Alexander, Grand Prince of Lithuania, became King of Poland
after the death of his brother, the Polish King Jan Albrecht, in 1501.

345. The treaty of truce between Russia and Lithuania was signed
March 25, 1503. The truce was concluded for six years, and according to
the agreement Lithuania relinquished "for the period of truce"—athough,
as a matter of fact, this concession was permanent—the Russian-populated
lands on the upper Oka and the upper eastern bank of the Dnieper. This
newly-acquired territory included nineteen cities: among them, Chernigov,
Starodub, Gomel, Briansk, Putivl', Novgorod Severskii (the former appanage of Prince Igor, hero of the famous *Lay of Prince Igor*), and seventy
volosts (districts or counties).

The same spring on the seventh of May, a Sunday, the Grand   **1504**
Prince sent his ambassadors to Lithuania [and Poland] to his son-in-
law, King Alexander: they were his *okolnichii*, boyar Petr Mikhailovich Pleshcheev, Konstantin Grigorovich Zabolotskii, Mikhail
Kliapik, and *diak* Guba Moklokov; and they were to discuss a truce.
They returned to Moscow in September. The same year Archbishop
Genadius of Novgorod came to Moscow to participate in a [church]
council with Metropolitan Simeon of all Russia, and with the
bishops. And they decided that widowed priests and deacons should
not celebrate church services and should not participate in any
sacrament. And they also decided that no taxes should be levied
at the ordination of priests and deacons, and that no fees should
be assessed when they are appointed to parishes; and this [was
decided] according to the rules of the Holy Fathers. They [wrote
and] confirmed a charter about these matters, signed it, and affixed
their seals.

The same year Ali-iar, envoy of Khan Shah Ahmet, arrived,
and also Hodja, envoy of his brother, Hodja-Sultan; and with them
came Kem-Urus, envoys of Bogatyr Sultan.

The same year on the twenty-eighth of the month of July when
the memories of holy apostles Prokhor, Nikonor, Simeon, and Par-
men are observed, Grand Prince Ivan Vasilievich of all Russia became ill: Whom the Lord loves, He chastises!

In the Year 7012 [1504]. On the sixth of September the Church
of Holy and Great Archistrategos Michael[346] was consecrated in
Moscow in honor of his holy miracle which occurred in Khoni. It
was consecrated by His Holiness Simeon, Metropolitan of all Russia,
and Archbishop Genadius of Novgorod, and the bishops.

On the twentieth of the same month of September the Grand
Prince sent Ivan Oshcherin to the Crimea.

On the twenty-first of the same month of September, a Thursday, Grand Prince Ivan Vasilievich, together with his son, Grand
Prince Vasilii Ivanovich, and with the children, left Moscow and
spent that fall in the [Monastery of the] Lifegiving Trinity and St.
Sergius, and from thence he went to the cities of Pereiaslavl', Rostov,
and Iaroslavl'; and he returned to Moscow the same fall on Thursday, the ninth of November. The same fall Princess Uliana, [wife]

346. Archistrategos Michael, or Archangel Michael, is considered the
head of the heavenly host of angels.

1505   of Prince Boris Vasilievich [brother of Ivan III], passed away in Novgorod. Then, after her [death, her son] Prince Fedor Borisovich married; and his brother, Prince Ivan Borisovich, became ill during the wedding, died, and was buried in the Church of the Most Pure [Virgin Mary] in the Monastery of St. Joseph on the Volok.[347] The same year on the day of Ascension, on order of Grand Prince Ivan Vasilievich of all Russia, Archimandrite Mitrophanus of the Monastery of St. Andronikus, laid the foundation for a brick refectory. The same year railings were put along the streets of Moscow. The same year in June Archbishop Genadius of Great Novgorod and Pskov gave up his see because of his sickness, but he did this against his will. When he returned from Moscow to his see in Novgorod the Great he began to levy fees from the priests at their ordination, and even higher fees than before.[348] And he did this contrary to his promise, on the advice of his favorite *diak*, Mikhail Ivanov [Gostenkov], son of Aleksei, who was of the same mind as he. Having investigated this, the Grand Prince and the Metropolitan forced him to relinquish his see and come to Moscow, where he remained in the Monastery of the Miracles of Archangel Michael for two and a half years; and he died there.

The same year on order of Grand Prince Ivan Vasilievich, the old Church of Cosma and Damian in Moscow across from the Church of the Miracles of Archangel Michael was torn down, and the foundation for a new one was laid.

In the Year 7013 [1505]. In November the Grand Prince's several envoys returned to Moscow. They were Aleksei Zabolotskii, from the Crimea; Dimitrii Ralev [or Ralo] and Mitrofan Karacharov, who came from beyond the seas;[349] and they brought with them numerous masters, silversmiths, gunmakers, and builders. At the same time, Alesha Golokhvastov returned from Kaffa.

347. The Monastery of Joseph Sanin of Volok, who was the creator of the Josephite ideology and the Josephite movement in the Russian church.

348. Actually, Archbishop Genadius was unable to restrain the lay officials of his diocese, especially of his chief *diak*, Gostenkov. Probably, also, the heretics of Novgorod were instrumental in the removal of this staunch defender of Orthodoxy.

349. Primarily, Italy.

ABOUT THE EXECUTION OF HERETICS

The same winter Grand Prince Ivan Vasilievich and his son, Grand Prince Vasilii Ivanovich of all Russia, together with their [spiritual] father, Metropolitan Simeon of all Russia, and with the bishops and whole Sacred Council, investigated the heretics [of the sect of Judaizers] and ordered the execution of those evil ones by capital punishment.[350] And on December twenty-seventh they burned in cages *diak* Volk Kuritsyn,[351] Mitia Konoplev, and Ivaskha Maksimov; and they ordered that the tongue of Nekras Rukavov be cut out, and [thereafter] he was burned in Novgorod the Great. The same winter on their order, Archimandrite Cassian of the St. George Monastery [in Novgorod] was burned, together with his brother; and other numerous heretics they burned, and others were sent to prison, some to monasteries.

The same winter on the eighteenth of January, a Saturday, Grand Princess Elena of Walachia [Moldavia], who was the wife of the late Grand Prince Ivan Ivanovich [son of Ivan III], passed away.[352] And she was buried in Moscow in the Church of the Ascension.

The same spring on the twenty-first of May, on order of Grand Prince Ivan Vasilievich of all Russia, they tore down in Moscow, on the Square, the old Church of the Holy and Great Archangel Michael because of its dilapidation: it had been first built by pious and Christ-loving Grand Prince Ivan Daniilovich [Kalita] in the year 6841 [1333].[353] And on that same place they laid the foundation for a new Church of Holy Archangel Michael and removed the remains of the grand princes and of the apanage princes. At the

---

350. Being severely ill and feeling that he was close to death, Ivan III submitted to the insistent demands of Abbot Joseph of Volok, who, together with Archbishop Genadius of Novgorod, had demanded the suppression of the heresy.

351. *Diak* Volk Kuritsyn was the brother of the late all-powerful *diak*, Fedor Kuritsyn, who died in the late 1400s.

352. Grand Princess Elena of Walachia (Moldavia) had been under arrest because, apparently, she sympathized with the heretical movement of the Judaizers, as well as, probably, because of her intrigues against Grand Prince Vasilii.

353. Grand Prince Ivan Daniilovich Kalita was the actual founder of Muscovy and its power.

1506 same time they tore down another church, St. John Climacus under the Bells, which was built by Grand Prince Ivan Daniilovich in the year 6836 [1328]. And they laid the foundation for a new Church of St. John Climacus, but not on the former place.[354]

The same spring Khan Mohammed Amin of Kazan' sent to Grand Prince Ivan Vasilievich a message concerning some misdeeds of the city lord Saln Ufa; and the Grand Prince, according to his promise, sent him his envoy, Mikhail Kliapik, to tell the Khan that he should not abide such misdeeds. The same summer on the twenty-fourth of June, the day of the Nativity of St. John the Precursor, godless and malevolent Mohammed Amin, Khan of Kazan', who was [up to then] in alliance and under pledge with Grand Prince Ivan Vasilievich of all Russia, forgot his promise and trespassd his oath of fealty. He arrested Mikhail Kliapik, the Grand Prince's envoy in Kazan', as well as the Grand Prince's merchants; and some of them he massacred and others he robbed and sent to the Nogais [as slaves].

The same summer Ivan Oshcherin came to Moscow from the Crimea, and together with him came Alabata Ulan and Tetlain Berdei-Duvan.

In the Year 7014 [1506]. On the fourth of the month of September Grand Prince Ivan Vasilievich of all Russia wed his son, Grand Prince Vasilii Ivanovich, to Solomonia, the daughter of Iurii Konstantinovich Saburov. And the wedding of Grand Prince Vasilii Ivanovich and Grand Princess Solomonia was performed by His Holiness Simeon, Metropolitan of all Russia, in the Cathedral Church of the Dormition of the Most Holy Theotokos in the glorious city of Moscow.

The same month of September the impious Mohammed Amin of Kazan' waged war against the cities of Nizhnii Novgorod. He besieged that city for two days and stormed it but did not succeed in the least. The inhabitants of the city made sorties and killed many of his men, and on the third day he ran off from the city.

The same fall on the twenty-seventh of September, at the first hour of the night from Monday to Tuesday, pious and Christ-loving Grand Prince Ivan Vasilievich [III], Sovereign of all Russia, passed away. And he ruled the Grand Principality after his father, Grand

354. At the present time there remains only the belfry of this new Church of St. John Climacus, known as "Ivan the Great."

Prince Vasilii Vasilievich, for forty-three years and seven months; **1506** altogether, he lived sixty-six years and nine months. His body was buried in the new Church of Saint and Great Archangel Michael, which he founded during his life in the most famous and glorious city of Moscow. His forefathers have also been buried there.[355]

THE BEGINNING OF THE REIGN OF GRAND PRINCE VASILII IVANOVICH OF ALL RUSSIA[356]

The same fall Grand Prince Vasilii Ivanovich of all Russia examined the treaties of friendship and brotherhood between Khan Mengli-Gerei and his [late] father, Grand Prince Ivan Vasilievich of all Russia, wherein it was written that its validity extended to [the reigns of the] children of both of them. Having alike consulted his brothers and his boyars, he sent to the Crimea, to Khan Mengli-Gerei, his close advisor, Vasilii Naumov. He sent him on the seventh of December in order to tell the Khan about the demise of his father and to remind him of friendship and brotherhood, according to the ratified treaties.

ABOUT PETER, SON OF THE KHAN

The same fall the Khan's son, Kudaikul, son of Ibrahim, the [late] Khan of Kazan', approached His Holiness Simeon, Metropolitan of Russia, petitioning him to intervene with Grand Prince Vasilii Ivanovich of all Russia so that the Sovereign would command him, the Metropolitan, to baptize him [Kudaikul] into the Orthodox faith. After the Metropolitan's intervention Grand Prince Vasilii Ivanovich ordered the Khan's son to appear before his eyes, and then the latter petitioned [the Grand Prince], bowing with tears, to be permitted to be baptized. On the twenty-first of the month of December—a Sunday—by command of the Grand Prince, His Holiness Simeon, Metropolitan of Russia, instructed Archimandrite Athanasius of the Monastery of St. Saviour to baptize the Khan's son, Kudaikul, in the Name of the Father, Son and Holy Ghost, into the Orthodox church of the Greek law. He was baptized in the Moscow River near the secret tunnel to the Kremlin and he was named Peter in holy baptism. Grand Prince Vasilii Ivanovich, himself, Sovereign of all Russia, together with his junior brothers and with his boyars, attended this baptism.

355. End of Vol. xii of *PSRL*.
356. Beginning of Vol. xiii of *PSRL*.

1506

CONSECRATION OF BISHOPS SERAPION AND BASSIAN

The same winter on the fifteenth of January, Thursday, His Holiness Simeon, Metropolitan of all Russia, consecrated Serapion, Abbot of the Monastery of the Holy Trinity and St. Sergius, to be Archbishop of Great Novgorod. On the eighteenth of the same month, a Sunday, Simeon, Metropolitan of all Russia, consecrated Bassian, Archimandrite of the Monastery of St. Simeon, to be Archbishop of Rostov and Iaroslavl'.

THE WEDDING OF PRINCE PETER, THE KHAN'S SON

The same month, on the fifth of January, a Sunday, Grand Prince Vasilii Ivanovich of all Russia honored the recently baptized Khan's son, Peter, and wed him to his sister, Grand Princess Eudokia. Athanasius, Archimandrite of the Monastery of St. Saviour, performed the wedding of the Khan's son, Peter, and Grand Princess Eudokia in the Cathedral Church of the Holy Dormition [of the Virgin Mary] in the glorious city of Moscow.

The same winter on the fifteenth of February, Sunday, the envoys of the Polish King Alexander, *Pan* Iurii Glebovich, the scribe, Ivashko Sapezhich[357] and Ivan Fedorov Pliushkov came to Moscow to Grand Prince Vasilii.

[CAMPAIGN AGAINST KAZAN']

The same spring in the month of April Grand Prince Vasilii Ivanovich of all Russia sent his brother, Dimitrii Ivanovich, his voevoda, Prince Fedor Ivanovich Belskii, and some other of his voevodas by boats to wage war against Khan Mohammed Amin of Kazan'. At the same time he sent along the prairie route against Kazan' a cavalry army under his voevoda, Prince Aleksandr Vladimirovich Rostovskii, as well as other voevodas. On Friday, the twenty-second of the month of May, Prince Dimitrii Ivanovich, as well as the Grand Prince's voevodas, with their army reached Kazan' in the boats. They carelessly left their boats, and moved into the fields in the vicinity of the city, thus approaching the city on foot. The Tatars of the city marched against them, while other Tatars rode behind them, thus cutting them off from the boats. A battle ensued and because of our sins the Tatars defeated the voevodas and the junior boyars of the foot army who were in that field, and

357. Ivashko Sapezhich: apparently, the son of Prince Sapieha.

the others were captured; and many others were driven into Lake   **1506**
Pogan.

On the ninth of the month of June Prince Vasilii Glenin came with this news to Grand Prince Vasilii Ivanovich of all Russia, and the same day the latter sent his voevoda,, Prince Vasilii Daniilovich Kholmskii and other voevodas with another army against Kazan'. He also sent a missive to his brother, Prince Dimitrii Ivanovich, and his other voevodas, commanding their army to wait for Prince Vasilii Daniilovich and other of the Grand Prince's voevodas, and not to attack the city [of Kazan'] without them.

[In the meantime] Prince Aleksandr Vladimirovich and other voevodas marched with the cavalry army and came to Kazan' on the twenty-second of June. Not awaiting the army of Prince Vasilii Daniilovich [Kholmskii] and other commanders, and contrary to the order of the Grand Prince, they carelessly started to besiege the city of Kazan' on the twenty-fifth of the month of June. They did not succeed in the least against the fortifications of the city and were forced back by the Tatars. Then Prince Dimitrii Ivanovich with the voevodas of the Grand Prince marched from Kazan' back to Nizhnii Novgorod. Peter, the Khan's son, and the Grand Prince's voevoda, Fedor Mikhailovich Kiselev, also retreated toward Murom by way of the prairie.

Khan Mohammed Amin sent his troops to catch up with the Khan's son [Peter] and with Fedor [Kiselev], and they caught up with them forty *versts* before the Sura River. Thanks to God's grace, Peter, the Khan's son, and [voevoda] Fedor [Kiselev] defeated the Kazan' Tatars, however, and they captured the others, returning in good health with all their people.

ST. NICHOLAS' CHURCH

The same year on the twenty-first of June on command of Grand Prince Vasilii Ivanovich of all Russia, there was laid [in Moscow] a foundation for a brick Church of the Holy Great Wonderworker Nicholas, dedicated to the great holy Wonderworker Nicholas. They started building it in the same place where there used to be the old wooden Church of St. Nicholas of the Linen.[358] And it was built within nine weeks.

358. St. Nicholas of the Linen: probably, this was the church of the corporation of linen merchants.

1507

ABOUT THE CRIMEAN ENVOYS

The same year on the first of August the envoys of the Crimean Khan Mengli-Gerei came to Moscow to Grand Prince Vasilii Ivanovich of all Russia; their names were Murza Kazmir[359] and Mahmed Shah. They were accompanied by Vasilii Naumov. They brought a treaty charter of friendship and concord from Khan Mengli-Gerei to the Grand Prince; but these treaties were not those which the Grand Prince sought. Therefore Grand Prince Vasilii Ivanovich of all Russia instructed Murza Kazmir and his people to write a treaty agreement which would be in accordance with the charter of the treaty concluded by his father, Grand Prince Ivan. Kazmir and his people acquiesced and wrote the charter according to the Grand Prince's will, and he certified it with his round seal.

[ABOUT THE PASSING OF ALEXANDER, GRAND PRINCE OF LITHUANIA AND KING OF POLAND]

The same year in August Grand Prince Vasilii Ivanovich of all Russia received tidings that his brother-in-law, Alexander Andre-evich, King of Poland and Grand Prince of Lithuania, had passed away in Wilno. The Grand Prince sent Ivan Kobiak to visit his sister, Elena, [widow of the late King].

In the Year 7015 [1507]. On the first of October, a Thursday, the Church of the Holy Great Wonderworker Nicholas in the city of Moscow was consecrated by His Holiness Simeon, Metropolitan of all Russia; this happened during the first year of the reign of faithful and Christ-loving Grand Prince Vasilii Ivanovich of all Russia. Grand Prince Vasilii gave to the church an icon of the holy and great Wonderworker Nicholas of Gostun, which was adorned with gold, very valuable gems, and pearls. Many people were cured by it, and so it happens up to now to those who approach it with faith.

The same fall in the month of November the elders of the Monastery of St. Panteleimon at the Holy Mountain [of Athos] came to Grand Prince Vasilii Ivanovich of all Russia asking for financial assistance. They were Archdeacon Pachomius and Monk Jacob. The Grand Prince provided them with his succor and let them go home from Moscow on the ninth of May.

The same fall in December Grand Prince Vasilii Ivanovich of

359. Also spelled "Kazimir."

all Russia let the Crimean envoy, Murza Kazimir Kiat and his people,   **1507**
go home; with them he sent his own envoy to the Crimean Khan
Mengli-Girei, his *okolnichii*, boyar Konstantin Grigorevich Zabolotskii.

In the month of February of the same winter, during the week
of the Prodigal Son, IIis IIoliness Simeon, Metropolitan of all Russia, consecrated Metrophanus, Archimandrite of the Monastery of
St. Andronicus, to be Bishop of Kolomna.

The same winter on the twenty-first of March the envoys of
Sigismund, Grand Prince of Lithuania [and King of Poland], came
to Grand Prince Vasilii Ivanovich of all Russia in Moscow. They
were *Pan* Ian Nikolaevich and *Pan* Petr Ianov, the *Kukhmistr*,[360] and
Bogdan Sopieha, the scribe.

RELATIONS WITH KAZAN'

The same winter in the month of March Mohammed Amin,
Khan of Kazan', sent his envoy, Abdullah, to Grand Prince Vasilii
Ivanovich of all Russia with a charter and petition asking the Grand
Prince to be kind to him, to forgive him his trespasses, and to make
peace with him. On the twenty-fifth of March of the same month
Grand Prince Vasilii Ivanovich of all Russia released Abdullah, the
Khan's envoy, home, and with him he sent his own man, Aleksei
Luchin. He instructed the latter to say the following to the Khan:
"Release the Grand Prince's envoy, Mikhail Kliapik, and his comrades who were detained by the Khan." The Khan responded,
sending Aleksei back to the Grand Prince, and with him he sent
his *baksha*, Bozek,[361] with a charter and asked that the Grand Prince
agree to peace with him as of old and to abide in good friendship
as it used to be during the reign of his father, Grand Prince Ivan
Vasilievich of all Russia. "And I will send Mikhail Kliapik and his
comrades back to you as soon as possible, as well as those people
who, during the battle, were captured by us." Grand Prince Vasilii
Ivanovich of all Russia, after holding council with his brothers and
boyars, decided that for the sake of the Christians who had been
captured by Moslem hands, as well as for a Christian peace, to
forgive the Khan's trespasses and allow *baksha* Bozek to return

360. *Kukhmistr*: probably, from German "*Kochmeister*," head of the
kitchen and of supplies for the Lithuanian Grand Prince.
361. *Baksha*: According to Dal', this is a Tatar word for "elder."

1508 home. Together with him he sent his *diak*, Elka Sukov, to the Khan and commanded him to tell the Khan to release Mikhail [Kliapik], the Grand Prince's envoy, and that if he wanted peace he should send his own trusted man to this purpose. The same year Khan Mohammed Amin released Mikhail Kliapik, the Prince's envoy, as well as those people of the Grand Prince's whom he had caught and robbed in Kazan'. He sent them with Mikhail Kliapik and, together with them, he sent his envoy, Barash Seid, to Grand Prince Vasilii Ivanovich of all Russia. He ordered him to petition for peace, brotherhood, and friendship as it used to be under his father, Grand Prince Ivan Vasilievich of all Russia.

[RAID OF THE CRIMEAN TATARS]

The same year Grand Prince Vasilii Ivanovich of all Russia received tidings that a large number of Tatar men were marching in the prairie and were expected to attack the city of Belev on the frontier, as well as the land of Belev, of Odoevsk, and of Kozel'sk. For this reason the Grand Prince sent from Moscow to Belev his voevodas, Prince Ivan Kholmskii and Prince Ushatov. And he commanded Prince Vasilii Odoevskii, Prince Ivan Mikhailovich Vorotynskii, and Prince Ivan Strigin, the namestnik of Kozel'sk, to accompany his voevodas. The Grand Prince's voevodas were in Vorotynsk, where they received tidings that the Tatars had captured many people in the *ukraina*[362] and had retreated. Relying on God, the voevodas marched after them into the prairie. They caught up with them on the river Oka and, thanks to divine grace as well as to the health, mind, and luck of their Sovereign, Vasilii Ivanovich of all Russia, they killed many Tatars, captured many others alive, and took back all [Russian] captives; on Monday, the ninth of August, they chased them up to the small river of Rybnitsa. Those Tatars who had been caught during the battles said that the frontier [*ukraina*] had been raided by Crimean Tatars of Murza-Zam-Seid, son of Iankuvat, and his comrades. These tidings of the voevodas were brought to the Grand Prince on the fourteenth of August by Gridia Afanasiev.

In the Year 7016 [1508]. On the eighth of September Grand Prince Vasilii Ivanovich of all Russia let the Kazan' envoy, Barash Seid, go home, having concluded a treaty of peace, concord, brotherhood, and friendship with Khan Mohammed Amin [of

362. *Ukraina*: In this case, the word means "frontier."

Kazan']. And he also sent his envoys, boyar and *okolnichii* Ivan   **1508**
Grigoriev, son of Poplevin, and *diak* Aleksei Lukin, to the Khan of
Kazan'. On the fourteenth of the same month of March Grand
Prince Vasilii Ivanovich sent his voevodas, Prince Vasilii Daniilovich
Kholmskii and Iakov Zakhar'ich, to campaign in the Lithuanian
lands around the city of Mstislavl'.

ABOUT THE TRANSFER OF THE REMAINS OF THE GRAND PRINCES AND OF THE APPANAGE PRINCES TO THE [CATHEDRAL OF] ARCHANGEL MICHAEL

The same fall on the third of October[363] pious and Christ-loving
Grand Prince Vasilii Ivanovich of all Russia, on the advice of his
spiritual father, Simeon, Metropolitan of all Russia, instructed that
a place be prepared for the transfer of the remains of his
forefathers, the grand princes of all Russia. Metropolitan Simeon,
together with the entire Sacred Council, chanted the funeral hymns
and transferred to the southern side of the new Church of Holy
Archangel Michael [the remains of] Grand Prince Vasilii Vasilievich
and the latter's son, Grand Prince Ivan Vasilievich, from [the old
Church of] St. Simeon to the cathedral. On the other side of the
doors they placed the remains of Grand Prince Ivan Daniilovich
[Kalita], and of his senior son, Grand Prince Semion Ivanovich.
Beyond them were placed the remains of Grand Prince Ivan
Ivanovich, another son of Grand Prince Ivan Daniilovich and, to-
gether with him, the remains of Grand Prince Dimitrii Ivanovich
[Donskoi]. Beyond them they placed the remains of Grand Prince
Vasilii Dimitrievich, as well as of his great grandson, Grand Prince
Ivan Ivanovich. The remains of the appanage princes were placed
as follows: along the western wall in the corner were placed the
remains of Prince Andrei Ivanovich, third son of Grand Prince
Ivan Daniilovich, and together with him were placed the remains
of his son, Prince Vladimir Andreevich.[364] Beyond them were placed
the remains of Prince Georgii [Iurii] Dimitrievich, as well as the
remains of his two sons, Prince Vasilii Iurievich and Prince Dimitrii
Iurievich the lesser. Farther on were placed the remains of Prince
Andrei Dimitrievich, as well as of his brother, Prince Piotr Dimitrievich. Beyond them were placed the remains of Prince Ivan Vasilievich the senior, son of Grand Prince Vasilii Dimitrievich. Still

363. October 3 in *Ioasaf.*, October 7 in *Obol.*
364. Prince Vladimir Andreevich was the hero of the battle of
Kulikovo Polé on the Don River.

1508   farther were placed the remains of Prince Georgii Vasilievich and
his brothers, Prince Boris Vasilievich and Prince Andrei Vasilievich
the junior. Farther on were placed the remains of Prince Ivan Vladimirovich and Prince Iaroslav Vladimirovich. At the northern door,
to the right after entering the church, were placed the remains of
Prince Andrei Vasilievich the senior, and of Prince Vasilii Vladimirovich. On the other side of the altar were placed the remains
of Prince Vasilii Iaroslavovich.

The same winter in January there came from Kazan' to Moscow
Ivan Grigorovich Poplevin, who brought the charter of allegiance
from Khan Mohammed Amin addressed to Grand Prince Vasilii
Ivanovich of all Russia. According to these charters the Khan gave
an oath of friendship and brotherhood as it used to be under the
[Grand Prince's] father, Grand Prince Ivan Vasilievich of all Russia.
The Khan also released those of the Grand Prince's men who had
been captured by him during battle.

The same winter on the twenty-third of January His Holiness
Simeon, Metropolitan of all Russia, consecrated Dositheus Bishop
of Krutitsa.

The same winter on the eighth of March Bishop Neophont of
Suzdal' passed away and was buried in Suzdal'.

ABOUT GLINSKII

The same winter Prince Michael Lvovich Glinskii gave up his
service to King Sigismund [of Poland] and sent his men to petition
Grand Prince Vasilii Ivanovich of all Russia to accept him into his
service. Grand Prince Vasilii Ivanovich of all Russia granted him
his petition and accepted him into his service, together with his kin
and friends. The Grand Prince also sent him his *diak*, Guba Moklokov, to let him pledge on the cross that he, together with his kin,
would be faithful in his service to Grand Prince Vasilii Ivanovich
of all Russia and would wish him well. The Grand Prince also sent
him his voevoda, Prince Aleksandr Olenka, brother of Alabysh,
and with him the minor boyars, the Muromtsevs.[365]

365. Prince Mikhail Lvovich Glinskii was a powerful and wealthy Russian lord in Lithuania, who was also a well-known statesman and *condotiere*.
He grew up at the court of the German Emperor Maximilian, then served
Duke Albrecht of Saxony. Later serving as *condotiere* in Italy, he became
Catholic. When he returned to Lithuania at the end of the fifteenth century
he became the most powerful lord there and had considerable influence
on Grand Prince Alexander of Lithuania. He aimed at forming a separate

The same spring on the twenty-third of May Bishop Bassian **1508**
of Tver' passed away.

The same spring the Grand Prince commissioned Alovisio the
Italian to dig a moat around the fortress of Moscow, as well as
ponds, and to reinforce them with bricks and stones.

The same spring the Grand Prince commissioned Master Pietro
Francisco the Italian to start building a stone fortress in Nizhnii
Novgorod.

On the seventh of May of the same spring, during the second
week after Easter, Grand Prince Vasilii Ivanovich of all Russia,
together with his Grand Princess Solomonia, transferred his residence to the new brick palace, of which the foundation had been
laid by his father, Grand Prince Ivan Vasilievich, Sovereign of all
Russia, in the old place near the [Cathedral of the] Annunciation.

ABOUT THE CHURCH OF THE ANNUNCIATION

At the same time, pious Grand Prince Vasilii Ivanovich of all
Russia, inspired with great faith and the best intentions, prescribed
that the Church of the Holy Virgin Theotokos Mary, Who is above
the heights of the divine mountains, be embellished with gold in
honor of Her Venerable and Glorious Annunciation. He also commanded that all the icons in this church be embellished with silver,
gold, and pearls, as well as, especially, the *Deisus* icons, [of the
iconostasis],[366] the icons of the holidays, and of the prophets. He
also ordered that the cupola of this cathedral be recovered and
gilded with gold.

---

state out of the western Russian lands of Lithuania, and at becoming head
of this intended independent state. When Sigismund became King he
removed Glinskii from all the positions he occupied; but, together with
his brother, Glinskii started an insurrection against Sigismund, in which
he was defeated by the King. Thereafter he escaped to Muscovite Russia
and entered the service of Vasilii III. He continued his intrigue in Russia,
was jailed by Vasilii III and released only after the marriage of his niece,
Elena Glinskii, to Vasilii III in 1526. He again became quite influential
with the Grand Prince but participated in 1534 in the new conspiracy
against the Muscovite government, whereupon he was arrested once more
and died in prison shortly thereafter. Elena was the daughter of Prince
Michael's brother, Vasilii Glinskii. Her and the Grand Prince's first son
was Ivan IV. *SIE*, Vol. 4, p. 470.

366. The so-called icon of *Deisus* shows Jesus Christ on the throne
between the Virgin Mary and St. John the Baptist.

1509   The same spring on the fourteenth of May, a Sunday, there was a conflagration in the suburbs and market which started at the Panskii palace.

[THE LITHUANIAN CAMPAIGN]

The same spring, because of the misdeeds of the King [of Poland], Grand Prince Vasilii Ivanovich of all Russia sent his voevodas Iakov Zakhar'ich and others with a strong army to campaign in the Lithuanian land. The Grand Prince also commanded his voevoda, Prince Danilo Vasilievich, to march from Novgorod the Great with an army to campaign in the Lithuanian land. And the voevodas of Grand Prince Vasilii Ivanovich of all Russia started campaigning in the Lithuanian land, capturing people, burning, putting to the sword; and they went as far as Wilno. When King Sigismund learned of this he, himself, marched toward Orsha, toward the Grand Prince's voevodas, and from Orsha to Smolensk. Grand Prince Vasilii Ivanovich of all Russia commanded his voevodas to retreat toward Briansk, and he sent from Moscow toward Briansk another voevoda, Vasilii Danilovich Kholmskii, with an army to fight the King. King Sigismund then sent from Smolensk to Grand Prince Vasilii Ivanovich of all Russia a request for safe passage for his ambassador, and Grand Prince Vasilii Ivanovich of all Russia gave the King a safe passage for his ambassador.

The same year the *murzas*[367] of the Nogais sent envoys to Grand Prince Vasilii Ivanovich, Sovereign of all Russia, to petition him to allow the merchants of the Nogais to go to Moscow with horses and with all manner of goods.

ABOUT PEACE WITH LITHUANIA

In the Year 7017 [1509]. On the nineteenth of September, a Tuesday, the Lithuanian ambassadors of King Sigismund came to Grand Prince Vasilii Ivanovich of all Russia. They were *Pan* Stanislav Glebovich, voevoda of Polotsk; *Pan* Ivan Sopiezicz, who was marshall and secretary; marshall Voitekh Narbutowicz; and scribe Ivashko Bogdanov Sopiezicz—to negotiate peace, concord, and final agreement. And so Grand Prince Vasilii Ivanovich of all Russia concluded the treaty of peace and final understanding with King Sigismund: the Grand Prince received [old] Russian cities with their

367. *Murza:* tribal elder.

lands, which were his patrimony; and he [kept] the service princes, **1509** Prince Vasilii Ivanovich Shemiakin, Prince Vasilii Semionovich Starodubskii, as well as Princes Novosel'skii, Odoevskii, Vorotynskii, Belevskii, Trubetskoi, and Masalskii, with their hereditary lands. These final chapters were written according to the will of Grand Prince Vasilii Ivanovich of all Russia. Grand Prince Vasilii Ivanovich honored the King's ambassadors and let them return to the King on the tenth day of the month of October, and he commanded his voevodas to march from Briansk to Moscow and to disband the troops. The King also retreated from Smolensk back to Wilno. The Grand Prince ordered Prince Mikhail Glinskii to be in Moscow and he honored him, granting him for his sustenance the estate of Iaroslavets and the city of Borovsk.

TREATY WITH KHAN MENGLI-GIREI

The same month on the twelfth of October, a Thursday, Konstantin Grigorevich Zabolotskii came from the Crimea, bringing to Grand Prince Vasilii Ivanovich of all Russia a treaty with a pledge of peace from Khan Mengli-Girei, which the Grand Prince had sought and which was the same as that concluded [by the Khan] with his father, Grand Prince Ivan [III] Vasilievich of all Russia. Together with Konstantin there came from Khan Mengli-Girei to Grand Prince Vasilii Ivanovich of all Russia the Crimean envoy, Lord Mohammed Shah, the son of Mamysh; Tred Abdullah Avel Sheih Zadeh, son of Abdul Gair, who was the son of Shyv; and Kazem Bek Sheih Hodja, the son of Mohammed.

The same fall on the fifth of November, Sunday, the Church of St. John the Precursor near the Borovitskii Gate was consecrated. The same fall in Novgorod Prince Vasilii Danilovich Kholmskii was arrested and then died in prison.

The same month on the twenty-sixth of November, Sunday, Grand Prince Vasilii Ivanovich of all Russia sent his envoys to King Sigismund of Lithuania concerning the final agreement about peace and concord. They were: his boyar and *okolnichii*, Grigorii Fedorov, son of Davydovich, namestnik of Novgorod; his stable marshall, Ivan Andreevich Cheliadnin; his *okolnichii*, Mikhail Stefanovich Kliapik; and *diak* Nikita Guba Maklakov.

ABOUT KHAN ABDUL LETIF

The same winter in January Grand Prince Vasilii Ivanovich of

1509 all Russia released Abdul Letif, son of Ibrahim, Khan of Kazan',
pardoned his misdeeds, and honored him, giving him the city of
Iur'iev with all [estates]. And he assured him of his brotherhood
and concord. He did this because of the intercession of the Crimean
Khan Mengli-Girei and Khan Mengli-Girei's wife, whose name was
Nur Sultana and who was the mother of Khan Abdul Letif; and
the senior son of Mengli-Girei, by the name of Mohammed Girei,
became the guarantor [for Abdul Letif]. Mengli-Girei's ambassadors, Lord Mohammed Shah with his comrades, gave an oath
and Abdul Letif, also, gave an oath of allegiance that he would
serve Grand Prince Vasilii Ivanovich of all Russia and would wish
him well in all things.

THE PASSING OF GRAND PRINCE DMITRII IVANOVICH[368]

The same winter on the fourteenth of February pious Grand
Prince Dmitrii Ivanovich passed away in dire straits in prison, and
his body was buried in the Cathedral of Archangel Michael in
Moscow, in the vicinity of the body of his father, Grand Prince
Ivan Ivanovich.

JOSEPH OF VOLOK AND GRAND PRINCE VASILII[369]

The same [winter] Abbot Joseph of Volok and his brethren-
monks from the monastery petitioned Grand Prince Vasilii
Ivanovich of all Russia and complained that they endured misery
every day because of the attitude of Prince Boris Fedorovich,[370] and
they wept bitterly. They asked the Sovereign to show his mercy

368. Grand Prince Dmitrii Ivanovich (1483–1509), grandson of Ivan
III and son of the latter's son, Ivan, and Elena Voloshanka (daughter of
the Moldavian ["Walachian"] *Gospodar*, or ruler) was crowned Grand Prince
of Muscovy in 1498. In 1502, however, he was put under arrest by Ivan
III, who was influenced by the supporters of his senior son, Vasilii (later,
Vasilii III). See the entries under the years 1498 and 1502.

369.   Here, in *Ioasaf.*, pp. 155–56, we find information about Abbot
Joseph of Volok unavailable in any MSS of *Nik.*, including *Obol.* This
incident is of capital importance for understanding the political and
ecclesiastic power relationships in sixteenth-century Russia. The removal
of the St. Joseph Monastery in Volok-Lamskii from the diocese of Novgorod
and the subsequent expulsion of Archbishop Serapion from his see was a
resounding victory for the Josephites, supported by Grand Prince Vasilii.

370. Prince Boris Fedorovich was the appanage prince of Grand
Prince Vasilii Ivanovich and Volok was within his territory .

and take the monastery under his own jurisdiction, because other-   **1509**
wise the monastery would become altogether ruined. The Grand
Prince on several occasions contacted Prince Boris Fedorovich, asking him to abstain from such behavior and stop harrassing the
monastery. But Prince Boris Fedorovich took no heed and continued to cause the abbey still greater woe.

Observing the steady danger to this holy place, the Grand
Prince importuned his spiritual father, His Holiness Metropolitan
Simeon. Hearing of this matter, Metropolitan Simeon of all Russia
investigated and discussed it in council with many of his spiritual
children, archbishops, and bishops; and after having consulted the
divine and imperial rules, he gave a decision and beseeched and
blessed his spiritual son, Grand Prince Vasilii Ivanovich, to take
the monastery under his own jurisdiction, asking the Most Pure
Theotokos to take it under Her protection. After petitioning and
receiving the blessing [of the Sacred Council] Grand Prince Vasilii
Ivanovich took the monastery under his protection and supervision.

When Serapion, Archbishop of Novgorod the Great and
Pskov,[371] learned that Grand Prince Vasilii Ivanovich of all Russia
had taken over the monastery of [Abbot] Joseph, he disregarded
the divine and lay law—which points out that the Tsar's decision
not be judged or discussed[372]—expressed his disfavor toward Abbot
Joseph and excommunicated him. He also senselessly and disre-
spectfully opposed the Grand Prince in his speeches when His
Holiness Simeon, Metropolitan of all Russia, following the Grand
Prince's command, summoned this Archbishop Serapion to the
Sacred Council and asked him how he dared to trespass divine law
and holy rule, criticizing and resisting the Tsar's command and the
entire Council's blessing? By no means is he [the Archbishop of
Novgorod] not unaccountable in his writing.

His Holiness Metropolitan Simeon, together with the
archbishops and bishops, reexamined the divine rules and the cus-
tomary law and declared, "A bishop who is not inspired by the
divine rules and the law but who follows his own ire and lack of
strength, excommunicating from the sacred clergy—such a bishop
harms himself in his sacred post. And he who was unjustifiably
excommunicated and deprived of blessing is excused and blessed."

371. The Volok Monastery had belonged to the diocese of the Archbishop of Novgorod and Pskov.
372. "Tsar's," in this case, means the Grand Prince's decision.

1509   And so Metropolitan Simeon and the Council gave Joseph and his brethren their blessing and pardoned him. [Archbishop Serapion] however was ordered [to relinquish his see and] to reside in the Monastery of the Holy Trinity and St. Sergius. And he passed away on the seventeenth of March, 7024 [1516], on Palm Sunday.[373]

The same winter on the first day of the month of March, Thursday, the Grand Prince released the Crimean envoy, Lord Mohammed Shah, with his comrades, and together with them the Grand Prince sent to Khan Mengli-Girei of the Crimea his own envoy, Vasilii Grigorovich Poplevin.

The same winter on the first of March the envoys of Grand Prince Vasilii Ivanovich of all Russia returned from Lithuania. They were Grigorii Fedorovich, Ivan Andreevich, Mikhail Stefanovich, and *diak* Nikita Guba Maklakov. Sigismund, King of Poland and Grand Prince of Lithuania, gave an oath on the cross on the charter of the peace treaties with Grand Prince Vasilii Ivanovich of all Russia, which were sent to him, and he pledged that he would abide according to all that was written in this charter, and so it would be to the end of his life.

ABOUT THE GERMAN ENVOYS AND THE ARMISTICE

The same winter on the eighth of March, Thursday, there came to Grand Prince Vasilii Ivanovich of all Russia German envoys from the Grand Master of Livonia, from the Archbishop of Riga, from the Bishop of Iur'iev [Derpat], and from the entire Livonian land. They were Johann Gildorp, Chancellor Johann Oledensen, Johann Kauer, and Christian Suge, and they petitioned the Grand Prince on behalf of the Grand Master and the entire land of Livonia concerning an armistice. Grand Prince Vasilii Ivanovich of all Russia granted the armistice to the Grand Master of Livonia and the entire Livonian land, and he instructed the namestnik of Novgorod and the prince-namestnik of Pskov to conclude an armistice for fourteen years, beginning on the day of Annunciation [the twenty-fifth of March]. And he gave permission to his people to trade with them as it used to be of old. And they gave up the [alliance] with the Lithuanian King Albrecht.[374]

373. End of the text from *Ioasaf.*
374. Here should be Sigismund, King and Grand Prince of Lithuania, 1506–48. His brother, King and Grand Prince Albrecht of Lithuania, died in 1506.

The same year on the thirty-first of March the Lithuanian **1510** envoys came from King Sigismund to Grand Prince Vasilii Ivanovich of all Russia. They were: *Pan* Ian Nikolaevich, Voevodich of Wilno;[375] the King's marshall and master, *Pan* Voitekh; and the scribe, *Pan* Bogush Bogovitinov, to discuss "the *pany*,"[376] who had been taken prisoner in the battle of Vedrosha. Grand Prince Vasilii Ivanovich of all Russia granted them their petition and let [the prisoners] go.

The same year on command of Grand Prince Vasilii Ivanovich of all Russia a wooden fortress was built in Tula.

The same year on the twenty-first of August, Tuesday, Simeon, archimandrite of the Saint Andronicus Monastery, was consecrated Bishop of Suzdal' by His Holiness Simeon, Metropolitan of all Russia.

The same month on the twenty-fourth of August, Nilus, abbot of the Monastery of the Epiphany, was consecrated Bishop of Tver' by Simeon, Metropolitan of all Russia.

[ABOUT THE JOURNEY OF GRAND PRINCE VASILII TO NOVGOROD THE GREAT]

In the Year 7018 [1510]. On the twenty-third of the month of September, a Sunday, Grand Prince Vasilii Ivanovich of all Russia journeyed from Moscow to his hereditary land, Novgorod the Great. Together with him were his junior brother, Prince Andrei Ivanovich; the Khan's son, Peter; Metrophanes, lord Bishop of Kolomna; and Barlaam, Archimandrite of St. Simeon Monastery.

ABOUT THE ANNEXATION OF PSKOV

The same winter there came to Novgorod, to Grand Prince Vasilii Ivanovich of all Russia, many posadniks, merchants, and senior burghers of Pskov, representing the entire city of Pskov, complaining to their Sovereign about Prince Ivan Mikhailovich Obolenskii Repnia, the Grand Prince's namestnik.[377] Upon investigating the matter, Grand Prince Vasilii Ivanovich of all Russia decided that the people of Pskov were unjustified in complaining

375. "Voevodich" may be either the son of a voevoda or a voevoda's aid.

376. *"Pany"*: aristocrats, nobles, magnates.

377. Namestnik, and administrator, the personal representative of the Grand Prince or Prince.

1510 about his namestnik, that they did not respect him; and therefore he expressed his displeasure [*opala*] toward them.[378] Then he commanded that all the people from Pskov who were in Novgorod should be arrested, and he sent Tretiak Dalmatov to Pskov. He ordered him to tell the people of Pskov that he, the Sovereign, himself, wanted to rule Pskov, that he honors the Life-giving Trinity,[379] that he would, himself, govern and honor and that the *veché* bell should be removed.[380] Pskov accepted the Sovereign's will. Then Grand Prince Vasilii Ivanovich of all Russia journeyed from Novgorod the Great to his hereditary land of Pskov on the twentieth of January, a Sunday, and he arrived in Pskov on the twenty-fourth of January, Thursday. He venerated [the icons] and prayed in [the Cathedral] of Lifegiving Trinity and commanded that the people of his patrimony of Pskov should pledge him their fealty on the cross. The arrested men of Pskov were released and honored. He also commanded the leading burghers of Pskov to move to Moscow to reside there, and he sent the *veché* bell to Moscow. He left in Pskov two of his namestniks—Grigorii Fedorovich and Ivan Andreevich Cheliadnin. He took the necessary measures that all should proceed to the benefit of his rule and after the day of the Council he departed for Novgorod.[381] From Novgorod during the third week of Lent he went to Moscow, where he arrived during the fifth week of Lent, the seventeenth of March.

The same year in the month of July Vasilii Grigorovich Poplevin returned from [his mission to the] Crimea.

ABOUT THE KHAN'S WIFE, NUR SULTANA

The twenty-first of the same month of July, a Sunday, Nur Sultana, wife of the Crimean Khan Mengli-Girei, daughter of Temir, came to Moscow. Together with her came Seid Girei Sultan, [Khan] Mengli-Girei's son. Grand Prince Vasilii Ivanovich of all

378. *Opala*: an expression of displeasure leading to some sanction against the person or city out of favor.

379. The Cathedral of Pskov was dedicated to the Holy Trinity, which was considered the holy patron of that city.

380. The bell which sounded the *veché*, or town council, was the symbol of Pskov's autonomy. Its removal demonstrated the cancellation of this autonomy.

381. The day of the Council: now, usually called the Sunday of Orthodoxy, memorializes the Council of Constantinople, which restored veneration of the icons in A.D. 787.

Russia, together with the boyars, received her with honor. Khan   **1511**
Mengli-Girei's envoys also came to the Grand Prince. They were
Sheih Olla, Sheih Zadeh, and Lagim Berdi Duvan. The Khan's wife
came to visit her children, Khan Mohammad Amin of Kazan' and
Khan Abdul Letif, who was in the Grand Prince's service. The
Grand Prince let the Khan's wife go to Kazan' on the twentieth of
August, a Tuesday. The Khan's envoy, however, sojourned in Mos-
cow and the Grand Prince sent his embassy, under Ivan Kobiak,
to Khan Mohammed Amin.

The same year they completed construction of a brick Church
of the Nativity of the Most Holy Theotokos in the old St. Simeon
Monastery. The church was consecrated on the first of September,
a Sunday, by His Holiness Simeon, Metropolitan of Russia, in the
presence of Archimandrite Barlaam.

In the Year 7019 [1511]. On the eighth of the same month of
September, Grand Prince Vasilii Ivanovich of all Russia left Moscow
for Perciaslavl', and he left the Grand Princess [Solomonia] in his
place [in Moscow]. He visited Pereiaslavl' and thereafter Iur'iev,
Suzdal', Vladimir, and Rostov. The Grand Prince returned to Moscow on Thursday, the fifth of December.

The same fall in the month of November Grand Prince Vasilii
Ivanovich of all Russia sent Mikhail Iur'iev, son of Zakhar'ich, and
diak Vasilii Tretiak Dalmatov as envoys to Lithuania.

ABOUT PRINCE SEMION

The same winter in January Prince Semion Ivanovich attempted to escape to Lithuania from his brother, Grand Prince Vasilii
Ivanovich of all Russia. Learning of this, the Grand Prince sent his
men to him and commanded him to remain with his court, and he
wanted to express his *opala* to him. Because he was at fault, Prince
Semion Ivanovich accepted his guilt and petitioned his Sovereign,
the Grand Prince. Grand Prince Vasilii Ivanovich of all Russia, on
the intercession of Simeon, Metropolitan of all Russia, of his
brothers, and of his bishops, forgave him his fault but he commanded that his court, boyars, and minor boyars be replaced by
others.

The same winter in the month of March the envoys of the
Grand Prince returned from Lithuania. They were Mikhail Iur'iev,
grandson of Zakharii; and *diak* Vasilii Tretiak Dalmatov. On the
thirtieth of the month of March there came to Grand Prince Vasilii
Ivanovich of all Russia the envoys of the Lithuanian King Sigis-

1512   mund: *Pan* Stanislav Glebovicz; Voitko Kloszko; and State Secretary
Bogusz Bogovitinov. The Grand Prince let the Lithuanian envoys
return home the fourth of April.

On the twenty-sixth of the month of April, a Sunday, Simeon,
Metropolitan of all Russia, fell ill, and with the Grand Prince's
permission he sent for Serapion, former Archbishop of Novgorod
and Pskov, blessed him, asked him for forgiveness,[382] and let him
go back to the Monastery of the Holy Trinity and St. Sergius.
Simeon, Metropolitan of all Russia, passed away on the thirtieth of
April, at night from Tuesday to Wednesday, in the first hour of
the night; and his body was buried in the Cathedral of the Most
Pure Dormition of Our Lady in Moscow.

The same spring on the twenty-second of June, the Khan's
wife, Nur Sultana, returned from Kazan' to Moscow.

ABOUT THE INVESTITURE OF BARLAAM TO METROPOLITAN

The same year on the twenty-seventh day of the month of
June, a Sunday, Barlaam, Archimandrite of the Monastery of St.
Simeon, was conducted to the court of the Metropolitan and was
nominated Metropolitan of all Russia. He was invested Metropolitan
of all Russia on the third day of the month of August, a Sunday,
and at the ceremony there were present Archbishop Bassian of
Rostov; Bishop Simeon of Suzdal'; Bishop Protasius of Riazan';
Bishop Nilus of Tver'; Bishop Mitrophanes of Kolomna; and
Bishop Dositheus of Krutitsa. Bishop Nikon of Perm' sent his charter, in which he announced his agreement with this consecration.

ABOUT THE KHAN'S WIFE

In the Year 7020 [1512]. On Friday, the fifth of December,
Grand Prince Vasilii Ivanovich of all Russia let the Khan's wife,
Nur Sultana, wife of Khan Mengli-Girei, return from Moscow to
the Crimea; she was accompanied by Mengli-Girei's son, Seid Girei
Sultan. Together with her the Grand Prince sent to Khan Mengli-
Girei his envoy, *okolnichii* Mikhail Vasilievich Tuchkov. And he sent
Prince Mikhail Daniilovich Shcheniatev to accompany her up to
Putivl'.

ABOUT THE KHANS OF KAZAN'

The same winter there came to Grand Prince Vasilii Ivanovich

382. See the case of Joseph of Volok, year 1509.

of all Russia Shau Sein Seid, envoy of Khan Mohammed Amin of **1512**
Kazan', asking for firm peace and friendship. The Grand Prince
instructed his boyars to consider this with him, and so the Grand
Prince's boyars and Khan Mohammed Amin's envoy, Shau Sein
Seid, resolved that Khan Mohammed Amin and the Grand Prince
should abide in firm peace; and to confirm this, Shau Sein Seid
penned a charter. According to this charter, Shau Sein Seid in the
presence of the Grand Prince's boyars gave a pledge of allegiance
for Khan Mohammed Amin of Kazan', that before the envoy of
the Grand Prince and according to this charter the Khan would
pledge allegiance to the Grand Prince to the end of his life. The
Grand Prince sent Shau Sein Seid to the Khan with the charter
and, together with him he sent his own envoys, *okolnichii* Ivan
Grigorievich Morozov and his *diak*, Andrei Kharlamov. In Kazan'
Khan Mohammed Amin, in the presence of the Grand Prince's
envoys, gave his pledge of allegiance on this charter and attached
his seal to it; and he let Ivan [Morozov] go back to the Grand Prince.

The same winter in February Khan Mohammed Amin of
Kazan' sent Grand Prince Vasilii Ivanovich of all Russia his man,
Buzuk Baksha, and asked the Grand Prince to send him his trusted
man—specifically, Ivan Andreevich [Cheliadnin]. The Khan also
wrote the following to the Grand Prince: that in future, in case he
should make a wrong action, he should inform the Grand Prince
of it; and that he wants to abide in steadfast fealty to the Grand
Prince, and to have eternal peace, friendship, and concord with
him. Following the Khan's request, the Grand Prince sent to him
in Kazan' his boyar and stablemaster, Ivan Andreevich Cheliadnin,
and *diak* Elizar Sukov. They journeyed by horsecarts. Then Khan
Mohammed Amin confessed to Ivan Andreevich all his secret actions and again confirmed that he would abide in steadfast allegiance to the Grand Prince, as well as in eternal amity, friendship,
and concord. And so he let Ivan return to the Grand Prince. Together with him the Khan sent the Grand Prince his envoy, Shau
Sein Seid, and they both came to Moscow in the month of March.

ABOUT THE RAID BY THE CRIMEAN KHAN'S SONS
AGAINST THE FRONTIER LANDS [*UKRAINY*]

The same spring on the eighth of May the Grand Prince received tidings that the children of the Crimean Khan Mengli-Girei—
Ahmat Girei and Burnash Girei—stealthily and with a large number
of men had entered the Grand Prince's frontier land [*ukraina*] to-

1513   ward Belev, Odoev, Vorotynsk, and Oleksin.[383] Forthwith the Grand
Prince sent against them his voevoda and *boiarin*, Prince Daniil
Vasilievich Shchenia, and many other voevodas. The Tatars, hearing about the Grand Prince's voevodas, took fright and quickly
retreated.

At that time Grand Prince Vasilii Ivanovich of all Russia expressed his *opala*[384] against Khan Abdul Letif because of the latter's
misdeed, and he commanded that he be placed under house arrest;
and he took from him the town of Kashira.

The same year in the month of July, Mohammed, son of the
Crimean Khan, marched against Riazan'; but he learned that the
Grand Prince's voevodas had taken a position on the river Osetr.
They were Prince Aleksandr Vladimirovich Rostovskii and other
voevodas with a large army. In the meantime, on the Upa River,
voevodas Mikhail Ivanovich Bulgakov, Ivan Andreevich, and many
other voevodas with a large army, also took a position. And so,
hearing this, the Khan's son, Mohammed, did not enter the frontier
land and turned away from the *ukraina*. The Grand Prince's voevodas pursued him into the prairie as far as Sernava, but did not
catch up with him.

In the Year 7021 [1513]. In the month of October, Khan Mengli-
Girei's son, Burnash Girei, raided the Riazan' land with an army;
he took some fortifications and attacked the fortress [of Riazan'],
but did not succeed in taking it and retreated.

ABOUT THE KING'S TREASON

The same fall Grand Prince Vasilii Ivanovich of all Russia
received the tidings that the Polish King Sigismund had entered
into contact with the Moslems against the Christians, with the Crimean Khan Mengli-Girei. He suggested that he [the King] should
attack the Christians in the land of the Grand Prince and asked
the Khan to march with his army also against the Grand Prince.
Earlier, however, at the King's suggestion, Khan Mengli-Girei's
sons had raided the frontier lands [*ukrainy*] of the Grand Prince.
The King also began to perpetrate other misdeeds upon the Grand
Prince despite the peace treaty and his pledge on the cross. He

383. The chronicle uses the word, "*ukraina*," to denote the frontier
lands. These lands were not what is presently called "Ukraine," but, rather,
land along the upper Oka River.
384. *Opala*: See footnote 378.

ordered his *pany* of Wilno to arrest the sister of the late Grand   **1513**
Prince, Grand Princess Elena, dowager of King Alexander, and to
keep her under arrest in Bereshti, beyond Wilno. Because of this
hardship and, God knows, of other deeds, this Queen Elena passed
away. Because of these misdeeds toward his sister, this Queen Elena,
the Grand Prince on many occasions had sent his envoys and mes-
sengers to King Sigismund; but the King did nothing to correct
the misdeeds or even did not give an answer concerning the Queen
and Grand Princess Elena.

ABOUT GRAND PRINCE VASILII IVANOVICH'S FIRST CAMPAIGN AGAINST SMOLENSK

Grand Prince Vasilii Ivanovich of all Russia could not abide
the many misdeeds of King Sigismund, and informed him that he,
too, would renounce his pledge on the cross. The Grand Prince,
himself, together with his brothers, moved his army against the
King's land and departed from Moscow on the nineteenth of
December, a Sunday. In the month of January he marched into
the Lithuanian land, toward the city of Smolensk, caused much
sorrow and destruction there, occupied a considerable part of the
Lithuanian land, and then returned, arriving in Moscow the third
week of Lent.

The same winter the Grand Prince sent to Constantinople, to
the Turkish Sultan Selim Shah Handiker,[385] Mikhail, his envoy, the
son of Ivash, with a charter of concord.

The same winter in the month of February pious Grand Princess Evdokia, wife of Prince Peter, passed away on Tuesday of the
week of St. Theodore; and her body was buried in the Cathedral
of the Ascension of the city of Moscow.

The same spring in May pious Prince Fedor Borisovich Volotskii passed away; and his body was buried in the Monastery of
Joseph [of Volok].

THE GRAND PRINCE'S SECOND CAMPAIGN AGAINST SMOLENSK

The same year on the fourteenth of June, a Tuesday, Grand
Prince Vasilii Ivanovich of all Russia for the second time marched
against Smolensk. He marched first to Borovsk, and from Borovsk
he sent ahead against Smolensk his *boiarin* and voevoda, Prince

385. Sultan Selim Shah reigned 1512–20.

1514   Ivan Mikhailovich Obolenskii Repnia, and his *okolnichii*, Andrei
Vasilievich Zaburov, and many other of his voevodas, with a large
army. The voevoda and namestnik of Smolensk, *Pan* Iurii
Glebovicz, as well as the princes and boyars of Smolensk, and the
army commanders with troops, sallied from the city to fight the
voevodas of the Grand Prince on the fortifications. The Grand
Prince's voevodas chased off the voevoda and princes and *pany* of
Smolensk, killed many of their men, and captured several princes,
boyars, and soldiers, whom they brought to the Grand Prince in
Borovsk. Thereupon the Grand Prince's voevodas besieged the city
of Smolensk and campaigned in its land.

In the Year 7022 [1514]. On the eleventh of September the
Grand Prince marched from Borovsk to Smolensk, and the city of
Smolensk experienced great miseries because of the shooting of
the cannons and guns, which lasted many days. The city had strong
fortresses, which were built on the mountains and hills around the
city, and it was fortified with high walls. Occupying the entire land,
the Grand Prince returned to Moscow.

ABOUT THE EMPEROR'S AMBASSADORS

The same winter on the second of February there came to
Grand Prince Vasilii Ivanovich of Moscow, Sovereign of all Russia,
an embassy from the newly elected Emperor Maximilian and highest King of Rome. His name was Georg Snitzer Pommer [?]. This
adviser of His Imperial Majesty came concerning brotherhood and
friendship. Grand Prince Vasilii, by God's mercy Sovereign of all
Russia, concluded with the elected Emperor Maximilian and highest
King of Rome a treaty of amity, concord, and eternal agreement.
They wrote the treaty-charter and [the Grand Prince] attached his
golden seal to it. Having honored the Imperial ambassador, Georg,
he released him from Moscow on the seventh of March. Together
with him, the Grand Prince sent to Emperor Maximilian his own
ambassadors, by the name, Dmitrii Fedorov, Laskar the Greek, and
his *diak*, Elizar Sukov.

ABOUT THE DANISH AMBASSADOR

The same spring on the ninth of April the Grand Prince released David, the Danish King's ambassador, from Moscow. Together with him, the Grand Prince sent the Danish King Christian[386]

386. Christian II, King of Denmark, 1513–23.

his envoy, Ivan Mikulin, son of Iaryi, and his *diak*, Vasilii Belyi.   **1514**
The same summer on the fourteenth of August they returned to
Moscow, and the same David, ambassador of the Danish King Chris-
tian, arrived with them.

ABOUT THE [OTTOMAN] TURKISH AMBASSADOR

The same spring on the twenty-eighth of May there came to
Vasilii Ivanovich of all Russia in Moscow, from the Turkish Sultan
Selim Shah Handiker, from Constantinople, an envoy named
Kemal Bei, Lord of Mingun, to discuss friendship and concord.

ABOUT THE TAKING OF SMOLENSK

The same year on the eighth of June Grand Prince Vasilii
Ivanovich of all Russia for the third time marched from Moscow
against the city of Smolensk. Together with him were his brothers,
Prince Iurii Ivanvoich and Prince Semion Ivanovich. He left in
Moscow his other brother, Prince Andrei Ivanovich. He sent ahead
toward the city of Smolensk his voevodas, Prince Boris Ivanovich
Gorbatyi, Prince Mikhail Vasilievich Gorbatyi-Kiselka, and his boyar
and stablemaster, Ivan Andreevich, as well as many of his other
voevodas with a large army. These voevodas arrived and besieged
the city. At that time in the city of Smolensk there was the King's
voevoda, *Pan* Iurii Sologubovicz. In the month of July the Grand
Prince, himself, arrived with his brothers at the city of Smolensk
with large forces and with a large artillery detachment. The artillery
cannons and guns were placed around the city, and he ordered
that the city be bombed from all sides. He also ordered storming
to commence without interruption, and to bomb the city with fire
bombs. From the noise of these cannons and guns, from the cries
and shouts of the people and from the adversaries' firing of cannons, and the guns of the city's defenders, the earth trembled and
people could not see each other. The entire city was covered with
fire and smoke, which rose up ever higher. The people within the
city were seized by great fear and they began to cry and call out
from the city, asking the great Sovereign to be merciful, to still his
sword, to stop fighting, because they were willing to petition the
Sovereign [Vasilii III] and to surrender the city to him.

The Grand Prince quickly ordered that the fighting cease, and
Barsonuphius, Bishop of Smolensk, together with the princes and
boyars of Smolensk, with the burghers and with all the citizens,
came out from the city to petition the Grand Prince to be merciful

toward his patrimony and the land of his forefathers, to give up his distavor and wrath, to permit them to appear before his eyes, and they asked him to command them to serve him. The Grand Prince expressed his mercy toward his patrimony and the land of his forefathers. He told Barsonuphius, Bishop of Smolensk, the princes, boyars, burghers, and all the people of the city that he would lay aside his disfavor and wrath, and he commanded them to appear before his eyes and to be in his service.

And so, on the thirty-first day of July, the princes and boyars of Smolensk opened the city and themselves went to the tent of the Grand Prince to petition him, to appear before his eyes; and here they promised their loyalty to the Grand Prince, pledging on the cross. The Grand Prince honored them, gave them his word of pardon, invited them to table, and sent to the city of Smolensk his boyar and voevoda, Prince Danilo Vasilievich [Obolenskii] Shchenia, and other voevodas, with many troops. And he commanded them to bring to pledge on the cross the other men: the princes, boyars, burghers, and citizens of Smolensk, and to tell them the Sovereign's speech of pardon.

On the first of August, the day of the Elevation of the Venerable Cross, Grand Prince Vasilii Ivanovich of all Russia, together with his brothers and boyars, and with all his voevodas and people of other ranks, marched with great glory into the city of Smolensk. Barsonuphius, Bishop of Smolensk, with archimandrites, abbots and all the clergy, priests, and deacons, brought the wonderworking icon of the Most Chaste and Pure Theotokos, and with it many venerable crosses and very many other icons, and there were many choirs. They came out with princes and noble magnates, with the old and the young, with mothers, maidens, monks, nuns, and all the people of the city of Smolensk. There were young and old, men, women, and children, all with fair eyes and pure souls, who, with great love and great fervor, met the Grand Prince in the suburb outside the city.

The pious and great Sovereign, together with his brothers, all the boyars and voevodas, venerated the venerable and holy icons and received a blessing from Bishop Barsonuphius; then he marched behind the crosses to the Cathedral Church of the Most Pure Theotokos, consecrated to Her Honorable and Glorious Dormition. And there they began the church service of thanksgiving. After the church service of thanksgiving the protodeacon approached the ambo and in a loud voice started proclaiming to the **1514** Grand Prince the wishes for a long life. Then the Bishop, together with the sacred clergy and deacons, with both choirs, sang "Many Years" to the Grand Prince. The Bishop blessed the Grand Prince with the venerable and lifegiving cross and said, "Orthodox Tsar Vasilii, by the mercy of God, Grand Prince of all Russia, and Autocrat! Be the ruler of your patrimony and of the land of your forefathers, the city of Smolensk, for many, many years!" Thereafter the Grand Prince's brothers, as well as his boyars and voevodas, according to their rank, greeted the great Sovereign in his patrimony and land of his fathers, the city of Smolensk.

The princes, boyars, burghers, and all the citizens of Smolensk also presented their wishes to the Grand Prince. Thereafter they began to greet and embrace each other: the princes, boyars, and voevodas, and the Grand Prince's men. They rejoiced greatly and were happy in their great love, being brothers in the same faith. The women and children also rejoiced and greeted the victorious cross and pious Orthodox great Sovereign, thanking him for deliverance from the evil Latin heresy and from violence. They were happy, having their real shepherd and teacher, the Orthodox great Sovereign, and they embraced each other. And one could observe, thanks to the mercy of the Most Pure Theotokos and grace of the life-giving cross, that in the entire city of Smolensk there was vast and unspeakable joy and rejoicing on both sides.[387]

When it came time for the divine liturgy the great Sovereign attended the holy church service and then went with his brothers, boyars, and all his voevodas to his palace, and there sat down in his place. His brothers, boyars, and voevodas, as well as the princes and boyars of Smolensk, according to their rank, greeted him. The Grand Prince answered them with the wish for good health and commanded them to be seated. Thereupon the Grand Prince invited the princes, boyars, and burghers of Smolensk and told them his speech about organization and his favor. He appointed as voevoda and namestnik [to the city of Smolensk] his own boyar and voevoda, Prince Vasilii Vasilievich Shuiskii, and invited them all to his table. And they ate with the Grand Prince. Thereafter he began to present

387. The city of Smolensk and its principality was a part of the Western Russian lands seized by the Lithuanians and Poles after Mongol invasion and conquest.

1514   them sable coats, velour cloaks, and other precious clothes embroidered with gold, and many pearls, to each according to his dignity. He also gave presents to the lesser boyars, to the servicemen and burghers, to the commanders of soldiers and to the soldiers, according to their rank. He released the King's namestnik, *Pan* Iurii Sologubovich, to go to the King, and he ordered that he be accompanied as far as Orsha.

On the seventh of the same month of August the Grand Prince sent toward Mstislavl' against Prince Mikhail of Mstislavl' his *boiarin* and voevoda, Prince Mikhail Daniilovich Shcheniatev, as well as Prince Ivan Mikhailovich Vorotynskii, and his other voevodas, as well as princes and boyars from Smolensk, with a large army. Prince Mikhail learned of [this advance by] the Grand Prince's voevodas, met them, and petitioned the Grand Prince to take him into his service, together with his hereditary lands; and he pledged his fealty to the Grand Prince on the cross before the Grand Prince's voevodas, together with all his people; and he went to the Grand Prince with the latter's voevodas. The Grand Prince honorably accepted Prince Mikhail into his service and with him his patrimony, giving him rich vestments and money. And he did likewise to [Prince Mikhail's] boyars and junior boyars, and then sent him back to Mstislavl' to his patrimony. On the thirteenth of the same month the burghers and common people came from the cities of Krichev and Dubrovna, asking the Grand Prince to accept them into his service and to take the cities of Krichev and Dubrovna into his state. The Grand Prince granted their petition, accepted them into his service, and instructed that they be brought to pledge on the cross.

At the same time the Grand Prince sent his servant, Prince Mikhail Glinskii, with many people, to defend his patrimony, the city of Smolensk, and his other cities, from his enemy, Sigismund, King of Poland; and he also commanded that in the fields around Borisovo, Minsk, and Drutsk there be positioned the Grand Prince's voevodas and boyars, under voevoda Prince Mikhail Ivanovich Bulgakov and his brother, Prince Dmitrii Ivanovich Bulgakov, as well as his other voevodas, with men-at-arms.

ABOUT GLINSKII

Prince Mikhail Glinskii, forgetting God and his duties, broke his pledge on the cross which he had given the Grand Prince. He

betrayed him, entered into contact with the Polish King and with   **1515**
the lords of Poland and Lithuania, and attempted to turn them
against the people of the Grand Prince while he, himself, sought
to escape to the King. When the Grand Prince's voevodas, Prince
Mikhail Bulgakov and his comrades, learned of Glinskii's betrayal,
that he had established contact with the King and with the King's
lords, that he sought to turn them against the Grand Prince's men
and that he, himself, sought to escape, they arrested him and sent
him to the Grand Prince. And he [Vasilii III] sent to the Drutsk
region his boyar, Grigorii Fedorovich, and his boyar and master
of the stables, Ivan Andreevich, and his other voevodas, to be in
contact with Prince Mikhail [Bulgakov] and to guard the security
of the Grand Prince's land.

In the Year 7023 [1515]. On the tenth of September, a Sunday,
Grand Prince Vasilii Ivanovich of all Russia, having completed the
administrative affairs of his patrimony, the city of Smolensk [as
well as of other territories newly reannexed to Russia] and having
arranged the administrative affairs to his best advantage, left there
as voevoda and namestnik his boyar, Prince Vasilii Vasilievich Shuiskii, and a number of other voevodas with a large army in order to
protect the city of Smolensk. He, himself, left Smolensk for Moscow.
Then he commanded his voevodas, Prince Mikhail Bulgakov and
the other voevodas to march, also, with him to Moscow; but the
Grand Prince's voevodas remained in their places awaiting the
people who had been sent to the regions of Drutsk, Borisov, Minsk,
and the Dniepr River. At that time the Polish and Lithuanian commanders of King Sigismund, with whom the traitor, Prince Mikhail
Glinskii, was in contact, marched stealthily, and attacked the Grand
Prince's voevodas. The voevodas of the Grand Prince fought fiercely
with them and many men, voevodas, sons of *pany*, and princes,
both Polish and Lithuanian, were killed; however, the Grand
Prince's voevodas—Prince Mikhail Ivanovich Bulgakov; his brother,
Prince Dmitrii Bulgakov; Ivan Andreevich, and several other voevodas—were captured because of our sins by the Lithuanian troops.

ABOUT LORD BISHOP BARSONUPHIUS OF SMOLENSK

Bishop Barsonuphius of Smolensk, disregarding divine judgment and having betrayed his conscience, broke his oath and his
pledge on the cross. He betrayed the Sovereign and Grand Prince
[Vasilii III] and sent his nephew, Vaska Khodykin, to the King with

1515   a letter in which he wrote, "In the case you march to the city of
Smolensk or send your voevodas with many troops, you can easily
take the city." Learning of this treachery by the Bishop of Smolensk,
and of his breaking his pledge given to the Sovereign and Grand
Prince [Vasilii III], the princes and boyars of Smolensk, as well as
the burghers, made an investigation according to the pledge on
the cross, and informed the Grand Prince's boyars and the
namestnik of Smolensk [Prince Vasilii Vasilievich Shuiskii]. Having
learned from the princes and boyars of Smolensk, and from the
burghers, about their investigation of the treason by Bishop Barsonuphius, that the Bishop had invited the Latins to the patrimony
of the Orthodox Sovereign, Prince Vasilii Vasilievich [Shuiskii]
greatly praised them and sent Bishop Barsonuphius from Smolensk
to Moscow, to the Sovereign and Grand Prince.

[INTERVENTION BY PRINCE OSTROZHSKII]

Several days later, after the deportation of the Bishop, the
Lithuanian voevoda, Prince Konstantin Ostrozhskii, marched to
the city of Smolensk with other voevodas and large troops, and
sent many letters and messages to the city of Smolensk. On several
occasions he stormed the city; but, thanks to the help of God and
of the Most Pure Theotokos, the princes and boyars of Smolensk,
and all the burghers, together with the voevodas and the Grand
Prince's men, unanimously and vigorously resisted the Lithuanian
men, made several sallies from the city, and fought stoutly with
them. Godless Ostrozhskii, the betrayer of the Sovereign, did not
succeed at all at the city of Smolensk and retreated in great shame.
A large number of men from Moscow and Smolensk sallied from
the city and pursued his troops, killing many Lithuanian men and
capturing many sons of *pany* and *hetmans*.[388] So Prince Konstantin
fled, leaving his trains and carts with his treasury and supplies.

At that time Prince Mikhail Izheslavskii also betrayed his
Sovereign and Grand Prince, breaking his pledge on the cross; and
he abandoned the Orthodox great Sovereign; and, together with
the city of Mstislavl', he joined the Lithuanian King Sigismund.
The people of Krichev and Dubrova behaved the same way as those
who betrayed the Grand Prince, breaking their pledge on the cross,
and they rejoined the King.

388. *Hetmans*: commanders

The same fall on the first of December the Grand Prince's **1515** envoys returned to Moscow. They were Dmitrii Laskar and Elizar Sukhov, whom the Grand Prince had sent to the newly elected Emperor Maximilian and highest King of Rome. They were sent to conclude the treaty of friendship and eternal peace, and they brought with them to the Grand Prince the peace treaty with the Emperor. The Emperor had given a pledge on the cross in the presence of the Grand Prince's envoys that till the end of his life he would follow the treaty-charter in every respect. Together with them there came to Moscow, to Grand Prince Vasilii Ivanovich of all Russia, the envoy of the newly elected Emperor Maximilian and highest King of Rome, whose name was Doctor Jakob da Mavrez, to discuss friendship and concord.

ABOUT THE CONSECRATION OF THE BISHOP OF SMOLENSK

The same winter on the fifteenth of February, by the grace of the Holy Ghost, Joseph, Archimandrite of the Monastery of the Miracle of [Archangel] Michael, which is in Moscow, was elected Bishop of the city of Smolensk. [He was elected and consecrated by] His Holiness Barlaam, Metropolitan of all Russia, and the entire Sacred Council of the Russian Metropolia, according to the divine rules of the Holy Apostles and on instruction of Vasilii, by the grace of God Sovereign, Autocrat and Grand Prince of all Russia. And the Grand Prince let him go from Moscow to his patrimony, the city of Smolensk, on the fourth of March, a Sunday in Lent.

ABOUT THE ENVOYS

The same winter on the fifteenth of March Prince Vasilii Ivanovich of all Russia released home the envoy of the Turkish Sultan, Lord Kemal. Together with him the Grand Prince sent to Constantinople, to the Turkish Sultan Selim Shah, his own embassy. This was his own personal councillor, Vasilii Andreevich, the son of Korb. And the Grand Prince sent with alms Vasilii Kopylo Spiachev and Ivan Varavin to the Holy Mountain of Athos.

The same spring in April Grand Sovereign Vasilii Ivanovich of all Russia released home, back to his Sovereign, the imperial envoy, Doctor Jakob da Mavrez. Together with him the Grand Prince sent to his brother, the King of the Roman Empire, Maximilian, his own envoy, Alexis Grigorievich Zabolotskii, and *diak* Aleksei

1516   Malyi. And to the Danish King Christian the Grand Prince sent Ivan Mikulin, son of Iaryi, and the palace *diak*, Vasilii Belovo.

The same spring in April Grand Prince Vasilii Ivanovich of all Russia for the first time visited his patrimony in Volok Lamskii.[389] He journeyed thither for his own pleasure.

MENGLI-GIREI PASSED AWAY

The same spring in May the Grand Prince received tidings from the Crimea that Khan Mengli-Girei had passed away. After him his senior son, Mohammed Girei, became Khan of the Crimea.

The same year in August there came from the Crimea the Grand Prince's envoy, *okolnichii* Mikhail Vasilievich Tuchkov. Together with him, with confirmation of brotherhood and amity, there came to the Grand Prince Ianchura Duvan, envoy of the Crimean Khan Mohammed Girei, [also to announce the Khan's] brotherhood and amity.

The same year on the twenty-eighth of the month of August Bassian, Archbishop of Rostov, passed away in Dorogomilovo, and he was buried in Rostov.

In the Year 7024 [1516]. Simeon, Bishop of Suzdal', passed away on the twelfth of November and he was buried in Suzdal'.

The same winter in December Grand Prince Vasilii Ivanovich of all Russia released home the Crimean ambassador, Ianchura Duvan. Together with him the Grand Prince sent to the Crimea, to Khan Mohammed Girei, son of the late Mengli-Girei, his own envoy, his personal councillor, Ivan Grigorievich Mamonov, to confirm his friendship and brotherhood. But by God's will, Ivan Mamonov passed away in the Crimea.

The same winter in March the Grand Prince's envoy, Andrei Vasilievich Korobov, returned to Moscow from Constantinople, while Vasilii Kopyl left Constantinople for the Holy Mountain of Athos, with alms from Grand Prince Vasilii Ivanovich of all Russia. [The third envoy] Varavin remained in Constantinople to perform his duties [as envoy] of the Grand Prince.

The same spring on the sixteenth of March Serapion, former Archbishop of Great Novgorod and Pskov, passed away and he was buried in the Monastery of the Holy Trinity and St. Sergius.

The same year in the month of June the Grand Prince released

389. In Volok Lamskii was the monastery of Abbot Joseph.

home David the Old, ambassador of the Danish King Christian. Together with him the Grand Prince sent to the Danish King his *diak*, Nekras Kharlamov, and [with him] he sent his treaty of peace to the King.

The same year in June there came to Grand Prince Vasilii Ivanovich an envoy of the Kazan' Khan Mohammed Amin, a certain Shau Sein Seid, [and with him] the local lord Shaisup and the *baksha* Boziuk. Saying that Khan Mohammed Amin was ill, they most humbly petitioned the Grand Prince to permit [the Khan's] brother, Abdul Letif, to be Khan in Kazan'. [And they asked the Grand Prince] to give up his disfavor and wrath toward him [Abdul Letif] and release him from detainment. [And they added that] Mohammed Amin and the entire Kazan' land would accept the Grand Prince's conditions, whatsoever he wanted, because without the Grand Prince's assent there was no way to have a khan in Kazan'.

And this Shau Sein Seid wrote with his own hand a statement concerning the manner of treaty of allegiance which the Khan and the land of Kazan' would give [to the Grand Prince].

And so the Grand Prince released home the Khan's envoy, Shau Sein Seid, with this treaty. Together with him Grand Prince Vasilii Ivanovich of all Russia sent to Khan Mohammed Amin of Kazan' his *okolnichii*, Mikhail Vasilievich Tuchkov; his master of arms, Nikita Ivanovich Karpov; and his *diak*, Ivan Teleshev.

Khan Mohammed Amin and the entire land of Kazan' gave a pledge on this treaty of their allegiance to the Grand Prince, in the presence of the Grand Prince's envoys. Thereafter the Khan released the Grand Prince's envoys, to go home. Together with them the Khan sent the Grand Prince his envoy, Shau Sein Seid, with a humble petition on behalf of his brother [Abdul Letif]. For the sake of Khan Mohammed Amin, the Grand Prince honored his brother, Abdul Letif, released him from detainment, gave up his disfavor and wrath toward him, and granted him the city of Kashira in his own land.

In the Year 7025 [1517]. On the tenth of February, a Tuesday, by the will of God, His Holiness Barlaam, Metropolitan of all Russia, consecrated Genadius, former Archimandrite of the Nativity of the Holy Theotokos, to be Bishop of Suzdal'. [He did this] on advice of the Sacred Council of bishops and in agreement with the instruction of pious Grand Prince Vasilii, Sovereign of all Russia by the grace of God.

1517   On the twelfth of the same month of February, Thursday, Sergius, Archimandrite of the Monastery of St. Andronicus, was consecrated Bishop of Riazan' by His Holiness Barlaam, Metropolitan of all Russia.

ABOUT THE GROSSMEISTER OF PRUSSIA

The same winter in March there came to the Grand Sovereign Vasilii from Albrecht, Grossmeister of the German Order of Prussia, an envoy whose name was Theodore Shönberg [?]. He asked Grand Prince Vasilii to abide in friendship with him [the Grand Master], to stand together with him against his enemy, the King of Poland, to be in alliance with him, and to protect him against the King.[390] Grand Sovereign Vasilii honored him and let this Theodore, envoy of the Grossmeister, return home. Together with him the Grand Prince sent to Albrecht, Grossmeister of Prussia, his own personal councillor, Dimitrii Zagriashskii. Together with him he sent a sealed epistle that he, Grand Sovereign Vasilii, by the grace of God, Tsar' and Sovereign of all Russia, agrees to abide in alliance with Albrecht, Grossmeister of Prussia. The Grossmeister was asked to pledge on the cross in the presence of Dimitrii that he would act in accordance with the Grand Sovereign's epistle; and to promise to act accordingly to the end of his life.

ABOUT THE EMPEROR'S ENVOY

The same spring the knight, Sigismund von Herberstein, envoy of his [Vasilii's] "brother," Maximilian, the elected Emperor and highest King of Rome, came asking and praying the Grand Sovereign Vasilii that for the sake of the Emperor he allow the Polish King Sigismund to send him envoys and to make peace, so that there be no more war between them [Russia and Poland] and no Christian blood shed. He also asked for a letter of safe conduct for the King's envoys. Through his boyars, Grand Prince Vasilii answered Herberstein, Maximilian's envoy, "For the sake of my brother, the elected Emperor Maximilian, we are willing to abide in peace with the Polish King Sigismund, and to do so in a manner that befits us." He also instructed that a safe conduct letter be given for the King's envoys. The Emperor's envoys, the knight Sigismund von Herberstein, sent these safe conduct letters to the King through

390. The text in *Nik.* is repetitious.

his nephew, Johann.[391] The same year [however] the Polish King   **1517**
Sigismund sent to the Crimea his *Pan*, Albrecht Martinov, with a
very considerable treasury for the Moslem rulers, the sons of [the
late] Khan Mengli-Girei. And he suggested that they march against
the Christians and raid the frontier *[ukraina]* of Grand Sovereign
Vasilii.

THE CRIMEAN RAID

The same year in August, on the advice of King Sigismund,
the Crimean Tatars began to raid [Russia]. They were Tokuzan
Murza, son of Lord Shirin Agish; Kudash Murza Bekterev, son of
Shirin; Uidem Murza Mangit, brother-in-law of the Khan's son,
Alp; and, together with them, twenty thousand raiders. They raided
the Grand Prince's *ukraina* near the cities of Tula and Bezputa, [392]
and started campaigning there. The Grand Prince's voevodas,
Prince Vasilii Semionovich Odoevskii, Prince Ivan Mikhailovich
Vorotynskii, and other voevodas sent ahead of their troops against
the Tatars some junior boyars with a few men and, particularly,
Ivan Tutykhin and the Princes Volkonskii. And he [Vasilii III]
commanded them to attack the Tatars from all sides so that they
not be able to advance. The voevodas, themselves, marched behind
them against the Tatars. The aforementioned Ivan Tutykhin and
his comrades arrived and began to attack the Tatars on all sides,
not permitting them to campaign; and they killed many of their
people. Learning of the arrival of the Grand Prince's voevodas, the
Tatars rapidly retreated. Ahead of them, many [Russian] footmen
from the *ukraina* [frontier] proceeded forward through the forest.
They made abatis, did not let the Tatars raid, and killed many of
them. When the advance cavalry of the voevodas arrived, they
attacked the Tatars and fought them at the fords and roads, while
the frontier footmen fought them in the forest. With God's help,
many Tatars were killed. Many other Tatars drowned in the river,
and yet others were captured alive. Such was God's help for this

391. The intercession of Emperor Maximilian (1493–1516) on behalf
of the Polish King was most probably prompted by the rapid advance of
the Ottoman Turks into central Europe. The Emperor thought that an
alliance between the German empire, Poland and Russia would stop the
advance of the Ottoman Turks.

392. In some other MSS, instead of "Bezputa," "*bez puti*"—"avoiding
roads." In *Ioasaf.*, "Bezputa."

1518   victory over the Tatars. As we have heard from reliable sources, and even from the same Tatars who later came from the Crimea, out of twenty thousand [Tatars] only a few returned to the Crimea, and even those lost their horses and were naked and barefoot.

WAR WITH POLAND

In the Year 7026 [1518]. In September the Polish King Sigismund, having an evil thought in mind, sent his envoys to Grand Sovereign Vasilii according to the [latter's] safe conduct letter. They were marshall and governor of Mogilev, *Pan* Jan Szczit, and marshall and state secretary Bogusz. In the meantime, King Sigismund, himself, marched against Polotsk with his Polish and Lithuanian troops, and from thence he sent his voevoda, the supreme *Hetman*, Prince Konstantin Ostrozhskii, and all his other *hetmans*, and the voevodas of Poland and Lithuania; and with them were a large number of mercenaries whom he had succeeded in obtaining. [He sent them] with a strong detachment of artillery cannons and guns against the frontier of the Grand Prince, against the Pskovian city of Opochka. Hearing of this, the great Sovereign's voevoda, Prince Aleksandr Vladimirovich Rostovskii, and many other voevodas who were positioned in Velikie Luki, informed Sovereign Grand Prince Vasilii. They also sent against the King's voevodas their own voevodas of light troops: Prince Fedor Vasilievich Obolenskii Lopata, Ivan Vasilievich Liatskoi, and other voevodas, as well as junior boyars with small numbers of troops, and ordered them to support the town of Opochka and to attack the Lithuanian army from all sides.

The voevodas, themselves, marched with a larger army against the King's voevodas. The Grand Prince ordered Prince Vasilii Vasilievich Shuiskii to march with numerous men from Viazma and, together with many other voevodas, to advance against the King's voevodas. The King's army, which was in great strength, besieged the town of Opochka, started to shell it with artillery cannons and guns, and stormed it from all sides. Vasilii Mikhailovich Saltykov, the voevoda and namestnik of Opochka, with God's help fought strongly with the city people against the King's army. During the attacks against the city, he slew a great many people of the King's army with artillery cannons, guns, and large stones, and organized ambush. In this way the Velikaia River was filled with corpses all

around the city, and human blood flowed like river streams. They **1518**
killed the commanding Polish voevoda, Sokol, and seized his
banner.

Sovereign Grand Prince Vasilii's voevodas, who were in the
vanguard—Prince Fedor Vasilievich Obolenskii, Ivan Vasilievich
Liatskoi,[393] and other voevodas—marched against the Lithuanian
army, attacked it from three sides, and killed many men in the
Lithuanian regiments. At that time Ivan Vasilievich Liatskoi received tidings that a large number of Polish men were marching
to the aid of the King's army. And so Ivan Vasilievich Liatskoi with
his comrades went forward against them and fought them. With
God's help, he killed many Polish voevodas and four thousand of
their men. They also captured several voevodas: Cherkas Khreptov;
his brother, Misuria; and Ivan Zelepugin. And they also captured
many other men alive; they captured artillery cannons and guns,
and sent them to their Russian commanding voevodas.

God's enemy and the Sovereign's betrayer, the supreme King's
Hetman, Konstantin Ostrozhskii, together with all the King's *hetmans*
and voevodas, realizing that there had not been a victory but
[rather] the defeat of their army, and having received tidings concerning the Grand Sovereign Vasilii's great voevodas, abandoned
all their military trains and arms, which were directed toward the
destruction of the city of Opochka and retreated in great shame.
The advance men of Grand Sovereign Vasilii's voevodas pursued
them, killed many men of the Lithuanian army, and took all their
weaponry. All this evil was the result of the thought of King Sigismund, who, because of his mischief, sent his envoys to Grand
Sovereign Vasilii and, at the same time, sent his army to fight on
the frontiers *[ukrainy]* of Grand Sovereign Vasilii, as we mentioned
before. He relied upon the vast strength of his army; but he did
not succeed in his vanity, and Merciful God, through His mercy
and right judgment, did as He wanted. He—[the King]—forgot
what was written: "One who digs a pit will, himself, fall into the
pit which he has dug."

Grand Sovereign Vasilii [III] in no way harmed the envoys of
King Sigismund—his marshall, Jan Szczit, and his marshall and
state secretary Bogusz. He did so for the sake of his brother, the

393. "Liadskii," in *Ioasaf.*, "Liatskii" in *Obol.* Also, "Liatsko."

1518   Emperor; he commanded that they not be accepted as envoys but that they be quartered in Dorogomilovo and be given sufficient supplies.

When the Sovereign's godless traitor, *Hetman* Ostrozhskii,[394] returned in shame from Opochka, Grand Sovereign Vasilii commanded King Sigismund's envoys—Jan Szczit and Bogusz—to be admitted, listened to their speeches, and released them on the fifteenth of November, without responding to their sovereign King Sigismund.

The same fall on the eighteenth of November Grand Sovereign Vasilii let Sigismund von Herberstein return to his sovereign, Emperor Maximilian. With him the Grand Prince sent to his brother, the elected Emperor and highest King of Rome, Maximilian, his own envoy, *diak* Vladimir Semionov, son of Plemiannikov.

The same autumn in November Prince Vasilii Ivanovich Shemiatich sent his good man, Mikhail Ianov, to Grand Prince Vasilii Ivanovich, Sovereign of all Russia, with tidings that the Crimean Tatars were raiding the frontier, their patrimony, around [the city of] Putivl'. Prince Vasilii [Shemiatich], relying on God's mercy and the fortune of his sovereign Grand Prince, marched against them, caught up with them beyond the Sula River, killed many Tatars, captured others, and sent some prisoners to the Grand Prince for interrogation.

ABDUL LETIF DIED

The same fall on the nineteenth of November Khan Abdul Letif of Kazan' died.

ABOUT METROPOLITAN GREGORY
AND THE ELDER MONKS OF THE HOLY MOUNTAINS

The same spring on the first of March, Thursday of the third week of Lent, Vasilii Kopyl and Ivan Varavin returned to Moscow from Constantinople. Together with them there came to the Grand Sovereign Vasilii Ivanovich of all Russia, from Constantinople, from the Oecumenical Patriarch Theopempt, an envoy, Metropolitan

394. The chronicle writer calls Konstantin Ostrozhskii a "traitor" because, although this leading aristocrat was neither a Catholic Pole nor Lithuanian, but an Orthodox Russian from the Russian-populated territories of Lithuania, he nonetheless supported the Polish Catholic King against Russian Orthodox rule.

Gregory the Greek, who was from the city of Zhikhna [?] of the   **1518**
region of Constantinople. Together with him, some elder monks
from the Holy Mountain of Athos arrived to see the Grand
Sovereign and head of the Russian church, Metropolitan Barlaam
of all Russia. [The monks] came to petition the great Sovereign to
aid them with alms because of their poverty. From the Monastery
of the Annunciation of the Most Pure Theotokos in Vartoped there
were three elder-monks: Maxim the Greek,[395] priest-monk Neo-
phitus the Greek, and Laurentius the Bulgarian. From the Russian
Monastery of the Holy and Great Martyr, Panteleimon, also came
Abbot Sabba. One year earlier than these elder-monks, the monk-
priest Isaiah the Serb came from the Monastery of the Holy Forty
Martyrs in Xeropotama. Together with Metropolitan Gregory,
there [also] came the Patriarch's deacon, Dionysius the Greek.
Grand Prince Vasilii, Sovereign of all Russia, gave a very honorable
audience to Metropolitan Gregory and to the elder-monks of the
Holy Mountain of Athos. He told them to reside in the Monastery
of the Venerable and Glorious Miracles of Holy Archangel Michael.
He commanded that they be fed and supplied with all necessities
from his—the Sovereign's own—table. The head of the Russian
church, Metropolitan Barlaam of all Russia, also showed his great
love and honor toward Metropolitan Gregory of Zhikhna [?]. He
also showed his great love and honor toward the elder-monks of
the Holy Mountain. He often invited them and discussed religious
problems with them.

The same year on the twenty-sixth of June, Saturday, at the
twelfth hour of the day, pious Prince Semion Ivanovich, brother
of Grand Prince Vasilii, passed away. And his body was buried in
the Cathedral of Archangel Michael in Moscow, where his forefathers are all buried. He was placed between the graves of Prince

395. Maxim the Greek, lay name, Maxim Trivolis (about 1470–1556),
was well known as a writer and theologian. He spent many years in Italy
completing his studies in the famous Dominican monastery of Savonarola
and was befriended by many Italian humanists. He returned to Greece
(which had been conquered by the Turks) and again became Orthodox,
living as a monk on Mt. Athos. Upon coming to Russia, he became a leading
translator of ecclesiastic books from Greek to Russian, became involved in
the controversy between the supporters and opponents of the monastic
estates, and was confined to a monastery. He greatly influenced many
sixteenth- and seventeenth-century Russian writers. Kartashov I, p. 467;
Zenkovsky, p. 60.

1518   Ivan Vasilievich the senior, son of Grand Prince Vasilii Dimitrievich, and his own uncle, Prince Georgii [Iurii] Vasillevich. He was
buried on Sunday and Grand Prince Vasilii, together with Grand
Princess Solomonia, attended the funeral and accompanied his body
with many tears. The service was celebrated by Barlaam, Metropolitan of all Russia, with bishops, archimandrites and abbots, and with
the entire Holy Council. Metropolitan Gregory, who came from
the Patriarch, and the abbots and elders of the Holy Mountain of
Athos also attended the burial.

The same year in June Metrophaneus, Bishop of Kolomna,
gave up his See because of his poor health.

ABOUT THE RAINS

The same year during St. Peter's Fast and after the day of St.
Peter there was a great amount of rain, and the water in the rivers
was higher than in spring. This was a manifestation of Our God's
chastisement, to lead us to our salvation, and because of our sins.
Grand Prince Vasilii Ivanovich of all Russia asked his spiritual
father, Metropolitan Barlaam of all Russia, to pray to Lord God,
Our Saviour Jesus Christ, His Most Pure Mother, the Holy Theotokos Maria, and all the holy and great Russian wonderworkers,
and to celebrate the church service, asking the mercy of God for
good order on this earth, for the warmth of the sun and for good
weather. He, the Metropolitan, celebrated the church service with
bishops, archimandrites and abbots, and with the entire Holy Council; and he appealed to all Orthodox Christians to observe fasting
and to pray with sincere repentance and tears. Thereafter,
thanks to the Lord's mercy and the intercession of His Most Pure
Theotokos, as well as thanks to the intercession of the holy Russian
wonderworkers, the dark skies with their storms were scattered,
the light came and at dawn the sun appeared with its warmth. The
supreme Sovereign, together with the head of the Russian church,
rendered his gratitude to Christ-God, to His Most Pure Mother,
and to all the holy Russian wonderworkers.

ABOUT THE HOLY ICONS

The same year His Holiness Barlaam, Metropolitan of all Russia, having taken counsel with his Sovereign and [spiritual] son,
pious Grand Prince Vasilii Ivanovich of all Russia, sent to the city
of Vladimir to instruct the clergy of Vladimir to bring to the glorious

city of Moscow the old holy icons, and to repair and renovate those
which had deteriorated over many years. At the same time pious
and Christ-loving Grand Prince Vasilii received a blessing from his
spiritual father, Metropolitan Barlaam, and went to the Monastery
of the Lifegiving Trinity and Holy Wonderworker, venerable Sergius, to pray and to receive a blessing because he wanted to campaign for his cause against his enemy, Sigismund, King of Poland.
He instructed his spiritual father, Metropolitan Barlaam, to meet
the holy icon from Vladimir in the most honorable way, with crosses,
with the entire Holy Council, and with crowds of people. When
the holy icons drew near the glorious city of Moscow on Friday,
the second of July, the holiday of the Deposition of the Vestments
of the Most Pure Theotokos, this news reached the Metropolitan.
Then His Holiness Barlaam of all Russia, together with bishops,
archimandrites, abbots, and with the entire Sacred Council, went
forward [in procession] to meet the holy icons in the most dignified
way, with crosses, the singing of psalms, and with the thanksgiving
service. Also, the population of the glorious city of Moscow, the
tremendous number of them—princes, boyars, great merchants,
old and young, mothers, maidens, monks, nuns, men, women, and
children—with great joy met the holy icons in the fields outside the
suburbs. The Metropolitan, himself, as well as the Sacred Council,
met the holy icons from Vladimir in the vicinity of the Monastery
of the Purification. There was an extremely beautiful icon of Our
Almighty Lord God and Saviour, Jesus Christ, which was painted
in Byzantium, as well as an icon of the Holy and Most Honorable
Queen and Virgin, Theotokos Maria, Mother of Christ, Our King
and Lord. Having sung the chants and celebrated the church service, the [procession] went into the city, the holy icons were placed
in the Cathedral Church of the Most Pure Theotokos, and everyone
praised and thanked Our Lord Christ and His Most Pure Mother.
At that time the sovereign [Grand Prince] Vasilii, himself, came to
the city of Moscow from the Monastery of the Lifegiving Trinity,
and he went to the Cathdral Church of the Most Pure Theotokos
and approached the holy icons of the Saviour and His Most Pure
Mother which had been brought from the city of Vladimir. He
prayed at length with deep faith and venerated the icons of Our
Almighty Lord God, Christ, and His Most Pure Mother; with great
joy he venerated these and other holy icons, making the sign of
the cross. He attended the thanksgiving service and divine liturgy

1519   and then he told his [spiritual] father, Metropolitan Barlaam, to renovate the holy icons which had deteriorated over so many years.

His Holiness Barlaam, Metropolitan of all Russia, instructed that the holy icons be renovated and adorned in his palace. Because of his great faith he, himself, on many occasions worked with his own hands, renovating the holy icons, and very soon the holy icons were restored and appeared better than before. They were adorned with silver and gold and were given new frames and new veils.[396]

The same year on the twenty-seventh of July there came to Moscow the Grand Sovereign's *diak*, named Vladimir Semionov, son of Plemiannikov, who had been sent by the Grand Prince to his brother, Emperor Maximilian. Together with him there came to Moscow, to the Grand Sovereign Vasilii, the envoys of his brother, Maximilian, the elected Emperor and highest King of Rome. The names of the envoys were Francisco da Colla and Antonio di Comit [*sic*]: they were the Emperor's councillors. The Grand Prince received them, and thereupon let them return home.

In the Year 7027 [1519]. In January Emperor Maximilian passed away. In the same year, 7027, in the month of November, Grand Prince Vasilii Ivanovich of all Russia sent his envoy, Prince Iurii Pronskii, to the Crimea, to Khan Mohammed Girei.

The same year in the month of August the elder-monk Clement the Greek came to Grand Prince Vasilii Ivanovich, Sovereign of all Russia, in Moscow. He came from the Mount of Sinai, where the Prophet Moses received the Law from God. He came to obtain financial support, and the Grand Prince honored him, gave [what he asked], and let him go home.

The same year in the month of August, on order of pious Grand Prince Vasilii Ivanovich of all Russia, an old church in the Monastery of the Ascension within the city of Moscow was disassembled because of its deterioration over time, and there was laid the foundation for a new one, which was [also] dedicated to the Ascension of Our Lord God and Saviour Jesus Christ.

In the same year 7027 on the twelfth of the month of September, a Sunday, His Holiness Barlaam, Metropolitan of all Russia, consecrated beyond the river Neglinka a church dedicated to Holy Wonderworker Leontius of Rostov.

---

396. *Veil*: in Russian, *pelena,* an embroidered replica of the icon, covering the icon so as to protect it from the elements, especially from the smoke of candles.

The same month on the fourteenth of September, on the day of the Elevation of the Venerable Cross, Grand Prince Vasilii Ivanovich of all Russia went from Moscow to Volokolamsk to hunt there, and he returned to Moscow on the day of Saint Demetrius.

The same fall on the twenty-first of November, a Sunday, His Holiness Metropolitan Barlaam of all Russia consecrated a church dedicated to the Presentation of the Holy Theotokos in the Temple. This church is located on the street of Candlemas in Moscow.

The same month on the twenty-eighth of November, a Sunday, in the city of Moscow in the Monastery of the Venerable Miracles of Holy Archangel Michael in the vicinity of the grave of Holy Wonderworker Alexis, and thanks to his prayers, God glorified His saint, demonstrating His mercy, and miraculously cured a paralyzed man by the name of Vasilii, who was unable to move either his arms or his legs. And so he became sound, and God demonstrated this miracle for the sake of His servant, Metropolitan Alexis. And this happened in the days of our pious and Christ-loving Grand Prince Vasilii Ivanovich, Sovereign of all Russia, and of His Holiness Barlaam, Metropolitan of all Russia, when Jonas was archimandrite of this most saintly monastery.

The same winter on the twelfth day of the month of February when the memory of our Holy Father and Wonderworker Alexis, Metropolitan of all Russia, is celebrated, a certain Helen, wife of Ivan Shiraev, was cured, thanks to the prayers of the Most Pure Queen, the Virgin Theotokos. This happened in the newly-built Church of Her Honorable Presentation in the Temple, which is located behind the market and which was erected thanks to God's mercy, by Vasilii, Sovereign of all Russia. Lord God demonstrated thus His mercy, during the church service to His Most Pure Mother. Helen had a crooked arm and could not move her leg; but she became healthy in the first hour of the day.

The very same day before the liturgy a poor blind pilgrim by the name of Ivan was cured at the grave of Holy Wonderworker Alexis, late Metropolitan of all Russia. And this happened, thanks to God's mercy and the holy prayers of St. Alexis. [This blind pilgrim] was given the ability to see, and his eyes became well. Pious Grand Prince Vasilii Ivanovich, who, together with his spiritual father, Metropolitan Barlaam, witnessed this miracle, thanked and glorified God, His Most Pure Mother, and the holy Metropolitan, Wonderworker Alexis.

The same year on the twenty-first of February, a Thursday, a

1519   certain Afanasii was miraculously cured, thanks to God's mercy, at the grave of Holy Wonderworker Alexis, Metropolitan of all Russia.

KHAN SHEIH ALI

In the Year 7027 [1519]. On the twenty-ninth of the month of December, there came to Grand Prince Vasilii Ivanovich of all Russia an envoy from Kazan' by the name of Kul Derbish, with a missive from the *seids, ulans,* lords, *karachis, icheks, murzas, mullahs, molns, shah-zadehs*[397] and from all the people of Kazan'. In their missives to the Grand Sovereign they wrote that, by the will of God, Khan Mohammed Amin of Kazan' had passed away, and they petitioned the Grand Prince, "This land of Kazan' belongs to God and to you, our sovereign Grand Prince. We are the servants of God and of you, our Sovereign. Oh, Sovereign! Please think about our land and be merciful to the land of Kazan', and we petition you to care for us and consider what we should do in the future."

On the sixth day of January Grand Prince Vasilii Ivanovich of all Russia sent to Kazan' his envoy, the palace master in Tver', Mikhail Iur'iev, son of Zakhar'ich, and his *diak,* Ivan Teleshev. He granted his good will to the leading *seids, ulans,* lords, *karachis, murzas, mullahs, molns, shah-zadehs,* and to all the people of Kazan', and told them that he, the Grand Sovereign, would care for them and protect them, and that he would give Kazan' a new khan, a certain khan's grandson, Sheih Ali [also, Sheih Galei].[398]

Learning of the Grand Prince's good will, that he gave them as Khan of Kazan' the Khan's grandson, Sheih Ali, they sent with Mikhail Iurievich Abi Bazi, Karach-bulat, Lord Shirin, Lord Shaisup, and Baksha Bazuk as the envoys of the leading *seids, ulans,* lords, *karachis,* and all the men of the land of Kazan', to petition the Grand Sovereign Vasilii of Moscow. Then they petitioned the Grand Prince that the sovereign Grand Prince bear good will toward all those aforementioned, and that he give them the Khan's grandson, Sheih Ali, the son of Sheih Avlear, as ruler and Khan of Kazan'.

397. *Seids, ulans,* lords, *karachis, icheks, murzas, molns, shah-zadehs* are Tatar titles. *Mullahs* are Moslem clergymen.
398. Sheih Ali, or Shi-Galei, in *Nik.,* was a Tatar lord (*tsarevich*) from Kasimov, a Tatar principality founded in the 1440s on Russian territory on the Oka River in the present Riazan' *oblast'* by an expatriate Tatar Lord Kasim, who accepted Russian (Muscovite) suzerainty. *SIE,* Vol. 6, p. 782, and Vol. 7, p. 86.

Grand Prince Vasilii, Sovereign of all Russia by the grace of **1519** God, expressed his good will toward them all, and on the first day of the month of March agreed to appoint Sheih Galei as Khan of Kazan'. He agreed with him that they both should abide in friendship and concord as it used to be under Khan Mohammed Amin. The Grand Prince commanded to write such a treaty of allegiance as would befit both the Grand Sovereign and Khan Sheih Galei. Khan Sheih Galei also gave a charter of agreement to the Grand Prince and Sovereign that in Kazan' he would care for the Grand Prince's interests, would not fail to stand for him, and that he, with the entire Kazan' land, would be faithful to him throughout his lifetime. Sheih Galei gave a pledge to the Grand Sovereign on this charter, and made it in writing.

Besides this treaty of allegiance, the nobles of Kazan' gave another written pledge that during Khan Sheih Galei's rule in Kazan' they would care for the Grand Prince's interests and would be faithful, together with the entire land of Kazan', to the Grand Sovereign throughout their lifetimes. They also confirmed that they and their children would never try to receive a khan without the agreement of the Grand Sovereign, and they gave the Grand Sovereign a special pledge in the name of the *seids*, the lords, and all the people of the Kazan' land.

On the eighth of the month of March Grand Prince Vasilii sent back to Kazan' Khan Sheih Galei and the nobles of Kazan'. Together with them he sent to Kazan' Prince Dmitrii Ivanovich Belskii, Mikhail Iurievich, who was the master of the palace in Tver', and his *diak*, Ivan Teliashev, in order to invest the Khan to the Khanate of Kazan'. They went to Kazan' and on order of the Grand Prince invested Sheih Galei as Khan of Kazan' in April. They also brought the *seids, ulans,* lords, *caliphs, murzas, molns,* and the *shah-zadehs,* and all the men of the land to pledge their allegiance to the Sovereign and Grand Prince throughout their lifetimes.

[VASILII III'S PILGRIMAGE]

The same spring in the month of May the Grand Prince departed from the city of Moscow and journeyed to the Monastery of Wonderworker St. Nicholas in Ugresh. From thence he went to Ostrov, sojourning there till the eve of St. Peter's Day. He returned to Moscow and passed the entire summer till autumn in Vorontsovo.

ABOUT THE MIRACLES OF HOLY WONDERWORKER ALEXIS

The same year on the thirteenth of the month of June a certain maiden, Anna, was brought from a village, the daughter of a Christian family, who had had paralyzed legs for seven years and who, because of this ailment, had been bedridden for seven years. When she was brought to the Wonderworker's grave, in which repose the relics of His Holiness St. Alexis, she was cured by this saint's prayers, became sound, and walked away by herself.

The same year on the third of the month of July, a Sunday, there was brought to the Wonderworker's grave an old man by the name of Semion, from Zlobin's estate of Bulatnikov, who could not see and who was gravely ill. He venerated the relics of His Holiness Alexis the Wonderworker, with faith, and after a church service for his health he became cured.

On the eighth day of the same month of July they brought a blind woman named Solomonia to the grave of holy Alexis the Wonderworker, and after a church service on behalf of her health she was brought to the Wonderworker's grave, in which repose the relics of His Holiness Alexis; and thanks to his prayers, her eyes were cured. The very same day St. Alexis the Wonderworker cured a blind maiden by the name of Anna, and she recovered her sight in her only preserved eye, the left one, and she saw everything very well. Numerous people who approached with faith were cured, and some cases were known, others remained unknown; but they are all known to God. Jonas, Archimandrite of this church, informed His Holiness Metropolitan Barlaam and Great Sovereign and Autocrat Vasilii about these miracles. When pious and Christ-loving Grand Prince Vasilii Ivanovich and his spiritual father, His Holiness Barlaam, Metropolitan of all Russia, as well as the bishops, archimandrites, abbots, and the entire Holy Council heard about it, the entire clergy, singing psalms, with candles and censers, came to the Cathedral of Holy Archangel Michael, to the grave where the holy body of His Holiness and Wonderworker Alexis was buried. They chanted hymns and rendered great praise to Almighty God and to His servant and Wonderworker, Alexis. The people of Moscow came in great numbers to see the most wonderful miracles of Holy and great Wonderworker Alexis. Pious and Christ-loving Grand Prince Vasilii Ivanovich also came thither: seeing these miracles, he knelt and venerated the holy, divine relics of His Holiness,

Wonderworker St. Alexis. He greatly rejoiced and, sighing from **1519** the depths of his heart, he said, "I praise and glorify Thee, My God, and I praise and glorify Thy Most Pure Mother and Thy servant and wonderworker, Alexis. Thanks to the grace of Thy Holy Spirit, Thou gavest new power to his relics to provide these miracles. And Thou granted me, Thy servant, during my years, to behold such miracles to the glory of my state. And Thou gavest to our city of Moscow another blessed source which performs such wonderful miracles." They most piously celebrated a church service, thanking God and His servant, Holy Wonderworker Alexis.

ABOUT APAK MURZA

In the Year 7028 [1519]. In March there came to Moscow, to Grand Prince Vasilii Ivanovich of all Russia, an envoy from the Crimean Khan Mohammed Girei, son of Khan Mengli-Girei. This important envoy, by the name of Apak Murza, and his father-in-law, by the name of Mohammed Pasha, son of Khali, brought the Grand Prince a treaty confirmed by Moslem oath, and this treaty was that which the Grand Prince had requested. Apak Murza told the Grand Prince that Khan Mohammed Girei had decided to abide in staunch amity and brotherhood with the Grand Prince, and it would be just as the Grand Prince instructed his envoy. Khan Mohammed Girei did all according to this treaty, and decided that he, himself, his son, Kalga Bogatyr, his brothers, and other members of his family, together with the *seids*, *ulans*, and lords, would be together with the Grand Prince against all their common foes.

In accordance with this treaty, the Grand Prince asked Khan Mohammed Girei to send [to campaign] into Lithuanian and Polish lands his son, Kalga Bogatyr, and other members of the Khan's family. [And the Grand Prince] added, "And I, myself, from my side, will send thence my own voevodas." At the request of Grand Prince Vasilii Ivanovich, his brother, Khan Mohammed Girei of the Crimea, sent into the Lithuanian and Polish lands his son, the great Kalga Bogatyr, and other lords, together with his brothers and his children, as well as a vast host with a large number of his men. And so Kalga Bogatyr, son of the Khan, marched into the Polish land and campaigned there as far as the city of Krakow. Then Konstantin Ostrozhskii gathered the Polish people and the people of Podolia and Volynia and marched against the Khan's son; but the Khan's son, [Kalga] Bogatyr, killed many Polish voevodas, *pany*

1519 and men, and captured many others, so that Ostrozhskii, himself, escaped only with difficulty. In this battle the Khan's son killed Prince Vasilii Chetvertinskii; Prince Alexander Boriamskii; the princes Vasilii, Alexander, and Lev Koretskii; the *hetman* of Krakow, son of Ferlei; *Pan* Stanislav, lord mayor of Kamenets; his brother, Ian Skarutskii; and many other Polish men. The others they captured and took with them [to the Crimea]. He campaigned and captured people in the Polish land because of his friendship with Grand Prince Vasilii Ivanovich of all Russia, and he returned to the Crimea with a large number of captives.

The same year Grand Prince Vasilii Ivanovich of all Russia sent an army against his enemy, Sigismund, the Lithuanian [Grand Prince and Polish] King, under the command of the Khan's son, Avdovlet, son of Akhturt of Sheban'. [With them he sent] his boyar and voevoda, Prince Vasilii Vasilievich Shuiskii, namestnik of the city of Vladimir, and several other voevodas: Prince Ivan Mikhailovich Vorotynskii; Prince Fedor Vasilievich Obolenskii-Lopata; Prince Vasilii Andreevich Mikulinskii; his *okolnichii* and voevoda, Andrei Vasilievich Saburov; Andrei Nikitich Buturlin; and Iurii Ivanovich Zamiatnin.

And from the Novgorodian and Pskovian frontier [*ukraina*] Grand Prince [Vasilii] also sent against [Sigismund] the Lithuanian [Grand Prince and Polish] King his voevodas, Prince Mikhail Vasilievich Gorbatyi, namestnik of Pskov; Prince Danilo Bakhteiar; Prince Ivan Vasilievich Obolenskii-Kasha; Ivan Vasilievich Kolychev; Dimitrii Grigorievich Buturlin; and his other voevodas, with a large army. The Grand Prince also commanded the following voevodas to march from Starodub-Severskii: a namestnik and voevoda, Prince Semion Fedorovich Kurbskii; Prince Ivan Fedorovich Obolenskii; Petr Fedorovich Okhliabinin; and his other voevodas, also with a large army. And so the Grand Prince's voevodas marched from Smolensk to Orsha, and from Orsha to Mogilev and Minsk. From Minsk they went straight to Wilno and to Krev, located thirty miles from Wilno, capturing the entire land. Then the Lithuanian commanders [also] got together; they were Nikolai Nikolaev, voevoda of Wilno; Albert Martynov, voevoda of Troki; Iuri Nikolaev Radziwill, voevoda of Grodno; Ian Nikolaev, son of [the aforementioned] Radziwill; *starosta* of Zhmud' [Zhemotia]; Prince Mikhail Izheslavskii; and many other Lithuanian *pany* with numerous men-at-arms.

The Grand Prince's voevodas asked for divine help, advanced

straight against them, killed many of the [Lithuanian] advance men,   **1520**
defeated Prince Vasilii Polubenskii-Vorotynskii, the King's noble
Chizh, and killed many other men-at-arms. They captured an important noble of the King by the name of Rai, as well as several
other nobles of the King, and took the train of Iurii Nikulai, the
voevoda of Grodno.

The Grand Prince's voevodas wanted to fight the great *pany*
of the King but the Lithuanian *pany* and voevodas retreated from
the Grand Prince's voevodas and hid their troops in the fortresses.
The Grand Prince's voevodas arrived at these fortresses but they
encountered too narrow a terrain for battle and therefore did not
follow them because of these fortresses and narrow battlefields.

They campaigned and captured the following Lithuanian
places: Lozhesk, Minsk, Krasnoe Selo, Molodechna, Markovo,
Lebedevo, Krev, Oshmono, Medniki, Miadelo, Korensko, Berezo-
vichi, Viazin [Viazma (?)], Radoshkovichi, and Borisovo. They also
occupied many places as far as Wilno, and on both sides of Wilno,
and even beyond Wilno. After campaigning and occupying Lithuanian lands, the Grand Prince's voevodas returned with all their
troops and, thanks to God, they all returned in good health, having
taken an endless number of prisoners of war.

In the Year 7028 [1520]. On the eighth of the month of September Grand Prince Vasilii Ivanovich of all Russia honored the
Crimean envoys, the Tatar Lord Apak, and Mohammed Pasha,
and let them return to their ruler. Together with them the Grand
Prince sent to the Crimea, to his brother, Khan Muhammed Girei,
his own envoy, Fedor Klimentiev, to confirm his friendship and
concord.

On the eleventh of the month of September the Grand Prince
released home Metropolitan Gregory, who had come to the Grand
Sovereign from Theopempt, the Oecumenical Patriarch of Constantinople, in order to secure financial support. He also sent home
Sabba, the monk-elder of the Holy Mountain [of Athos], who was
abbot of the Russian Monastery of the Great Martyr Panteleimon,
as well as Isaiah, who came from the Monastery of the Forty Martyrs
of Xeropatama. Grand Sovereign Vasilii, Sovereign by the grace
of God, sent to the Patriarch and the Holy Mountain very sizable
financial support, and he also gave money, horses, and clothing to
Metropolitan Gregory and to the elders of the Holy Mountain,
supplying them with all necessities.

1520

ABOUT THE ICON OF THE CITY OF VLADIMIR

On the fifteenth day of the same month of September, a Thursday, pious and Christ-loving Vasilii, by the grace of God, Sovereign of all Russia, following the counsel of his spiritual father, Barlaam, Metropolitan of all Russia, permitted the return to the glorious city of Vladimir of the holy icons which were mentioned before and about which it was explained that they had been brought from Vladimir to the most honored city of Moscow for the purpose of restoration and adornment. Over many years they had deteriorated, and they were restored and beautifully embellished with silver and gold. These holy icons were accompanied by His Holiness Barlaam, Metropolitan of all Russia, as well as by bishops, archimandrites, abbots, and the entire Sacred Council, and they all chanted psalms and celebrated a church service. They were followed by pious Grand Sovereign Vasilii Ivanovich of all Russia, together with his princes and boyars and the entire population of the glorious city of Moscow—men, women and children: a great number of them accompanied the holy icons beyond the suburbs with great joy and prayers. A new church was built, dedicated to the Venerable and Glorious Purification of Our Most Pure Lady Theotokos. Arriving there, Metropolitan Barlaam, with the bishops and the entire church Council, consecrated the newly-built church, celebrated a thanksgiving service and divine liturgy, and let the holy icons be taken to the city of Vladimir. He sent Ignatius, Archimandrite of the Monastery of St. Andronicus, to accompany them to the city of Vladimir. Pious Grand Prince Vasilii, together with his spiritual father Barlaam, with the Bishop and archimandrites, as well as with his princes and boyars, celebrated this day fairly and joyously, and offered a great banquet. Praising God and His Most Pure Mother, he distributed alms to the priests and poor throughout the entire city. Since that time this holiday has been celebrated in honor of the Most Pure Theotokos, on the fifteenth day of September.

The same winter on the ninth of February, a Thursday, John, Archimandrite of the Simeon Monastery, was consecrated by Barlaam, Metropolitan of all Russia, to be Archbishop of Rostov and Iaroslavl'.

On the fourteenth of the same month, a Thursday, Tikhon, abbot of the Monastery in Ugresh, was consecrated Bishop of Kolomna by Barlaam, Metropolitan of all Russia. On the sixteenth of the same month of February, Thursday, Metropolitan Barlaam **1520** consecrated Pimen, abbot of the Solovki Monastery, to be Bishop of Vologda and Perm'.

The same winter in the month of March the Grand Prince sent his man, Boris Golokhvastov, to the Turkish Sultan Selim Shah, son of Sultan Bayazid, to present him wishes for good health and to see him. He let him go by way of the Don River, on which he went to Azov. From Azov he went by sea to Kaffa, and thence from Kaffa he went to Constantinople by the Black Sea. From Constantinople he journeyed by the land route to the field of Iadren,[399] and from the field of Iadren he went to meet the Sultan in Demotitsa. The Sultan asked Boris to sojourn with him, rendered him great honor, and provided him with goodly supplies. From thence he let him go home by the river Danube, through the Serbian land. He journeyed by the river Danube as far as Kelia, and from Kelia to Belgrade. From Belgrade he journeyed to Takovo, and to the great river Dniestr. He continued his route toward the Dniepr, and then toward Perekop;[400] and from Perekop he journeyed to the Crimean Khan Mohammed. The Khan let him go home, following [the Grand Prince's envoy] Prince Iurii Pronskii, and Boris caught up with Prince Iurii in Putivl', coming to Moscow with the Prince on the eighth of January.

The same year an envoy came to the Grand Prince in Moscow from the Pope of Rome. His name was Paul, and he brought a message.

The same year they built a stone fortress in Tula. It was named as before, with the name of the town of Tula; and it is located on a river also named Tula.

The same winter Metropolitan Barlaam consecrated John to be Archbishop of Rostov.

On the sixteenth of the same month he consecrated Pimen to be Bishop of Vologda.

*

* *

399. Iadren: Iadran, the Serbian name for the Adriatic Sea.

400. Perekop: a narrow isthmus connecting the Crimea with the continent.